# How to Manage Training
**THIRD EDITION**

A Guide to Design and Delivery for High Performance

CAROLYN NILSON

AMACOM

**American Management Association**

New York • Atlanta • Brussels • Buenos Aires • Chicago • London • Mexico City
San Francisco • Shanghai • Tokyo • Toronto • Washington, D.C.

*Special discounts on bulk quantities of AMACOM books are available to corporations, professional associations, and other organizations. For details, contact Special Sales Department, AMACOM, a division of American Management Association, 1601 Broadway, New York, NY 10019.*
*Tel.: 212-903-8316. Fax: 212-903-8083.*
*Web site: www.amacombooks.org*

*This publication is designed to provide accurate and authoritative information in regard to the subject matter covered. It is sold with the understanding that the publisher is not engaged in rendering legal, accounting, or other professional service. If legal advice or other expert assistance is required, the services of a competent professional person should be sought.*

*Although this publication is subject to copyright, permission is granted free of charge to use and print pages from the enclosed CD-ROM. Only the original purchaser may make copies. Under no circumstances is permission granted to sell or distribute on a commercial basis material reproduced from this publication.*

*Library of Congress Cataloging-in-Publication Data*

Nilson, Carolyn D.
    How to manage training : a guide to design and delivery for high performance / Carolyn Nilson.—3rd ed.
      p. cm.
    Includes bibliographical references and index.
    ISBN 0-8144-0779-X
    1. Employees—Training of.  I. Title.

HF5549.5.T7 N526   2003
658.31'24—dc21

                                              2002153095

© *2003 Carolyn Nilson.*
*All rights reserved.*
*Printed in the United States of America.*

*This publication may not be reproduced,*
*stored in a retrieval system,*
*or transmitted in whole or in part,*
*in any form or by any means, electronic,*
*mechanical, photocopying, recording, or otherwise,*
*without the prior written permission of AMACOM,*
*a division of American Management Association,*
*1601 Broadway, New York, NY 10019.*

*Printing number*

*10  9  8  7  6  5  4  3  2  1*

*To my wise, caring,
and very patient husband
Noel W. Nilson*

# Contents

| | |
|---|---|
| List of Figures | vii |
| List of Training Management Checklists | ix |
| List of Training Management Forms | xiii |
| Preface to the Third Edition | xvii |
| Chapter 1 How to Lead Learning Organizations | 1 |
| Chapter 2 How to Make the Most of E-Learning | 27 |
| Chapter 3 How to Run the Training Operation | 45 |
| Chapter 4 How to Manage Outsiders | 85 |
| Chapter 5 How to Manage Training for Teams | 108 |
| Chapter 6 How to Manage Coaching and Mentoring | 131 |
| Chapter 7 How to Train for Innovation | 154 |
| Chapter 8 How to Support Learners on Their Own | 190 |
| Chapter 9 How to Assess Training Needs | 211 |
| Chapter 10 How to Design and Write Training | 241 |
| Chapter 11 How to Implement and Deliver Training | 312 |
| Chapter 12 How to Evaluate Training | 346 |
| Appendix: Models for Individual and Organizational Learning | 385 |
| Bibliography | 413 |
| Index | 419 |
| About the Author | 425 |

# List of Figures

| | | |
|---|---|---|
| Figure 3.1. | ISD instructional system design. | 80 |
| Figure 3.2. | ASTD human performance improvement process model. | 81 |
| Figure 3.3. | Performance technology model. | 81 |
| Figure 3.4. | Budget format. | 82 |
| Figure 3.5. | Task By Objective Worksheet. | 82 |
| Figure 10.1. | Elements of problem solving. | 304 |
| Figure 10.2. | Cognitive skills. | 305 |
| Figure 10.3. | Psychomotor skills. | 305 |
| Figure 10.4. | Human needs. | 306 |
| Figure 10.5. | Stages of concern. | 306 |
| Figure 10.6. | Left brain, right brain. | 307 |
| Figure 10.7. | Memory. | 307 |
| Figure 10.8. | Conditions of learning. | 308 |
| Figure 10.9. | Frames of mind. | 308 |
| Figure 10.10. | The five disciplines. | 309 |
| Figure 10.11. | 8-step program for creating change. | 310 |
| Figure 10.12. | Performance technology model. | 311 |
| Figure 11.1. | Instructional delivery model. | 341 |
| Figure 12.1. | Kirkpatrick's 4 levels of evaluation. | 380 |

# List of Training Management Checklists

**Chapter 1  How to Lead Learning Organizations**     1
- 1.1   Strategies for Everyone     11
- 1.2   Checklist of "... ing Words" for Managers     12
- 1.3   Tough Questions for Leaders     13
- 1.4   Concrete Actions for Developing Learning Organizations     15
- 1.5   Evidence of a Learning Organization in Progress     16

**Chapter 2  How to Make the Most of E-Learning**     27
- 2.1   The Training Manager's Checklist for E-Learners' Successful Transition from the Classroom to E-Learning     32
- 2.2   Tips for Easing the Growing Pains     33
- 2.3   Primary Characteristics of Learning Objects     34
- 2.4   Working with a Learning Content Management System (LCMS)     35
- 2.5   The Training Manager's Readiness Checklist for E-Learning     36

**Chapter 3  How to Run the Training Operation**     45
- 3.1   Guidelines for Building in Quality     53
- 3.2   Business Plan Data Checklist     55
- 3.3   Budget Input Information     56
- 3.4   Rationale for Hiring Instructional Designers     57
- 3.5   Rationale for Hiring Training Specialists     58
- 3.6   Training Staff Design     59
- 3.7   Considerations in Setting Up Training Files     60
- 3.8   Training Facilities and Equipment Checklist     61
- 3.9   Training Scheduling Checklist     62
- 3.10   Establishing the Visibility of Training     64
- 3.11   Ethics Checklist     66

**Chapter 4  How to Manage Outsiders**     85
- 4.1   Consultant/Vendor Contract Details     90
- 4.2   The Basics of a Value-Added Outsider Proposal     91
- 4.3   Ten Strategic Reasons for Outsourcing     92
- 4.4   Potential Cost Benefits of Hiring Outsiders     93
- 4.5   Project Management Checklist     94
- 4.6   Characteristics of a Good E-Learning Supplier     95
- 4.7   Protection of Intellectual Property     96

# List of Training Management Checklists

| | | |
|---|---|---|
| **Chapter 5** | **How to Manage Training Teams** | **108** |
| 5.1 | Success Factors for Individual Learning Within the Team | 112 |
| 5.2 | The Care and Feeding of Team Members | 114 |
| 5.3 | How Fewer People Can Do More Work | 116 |
| 5.4 | Checklist for Behavioral Feedback | 118 |
| 5.5 | Team Performance Checklist | 120 |
| **Chapter 6** | **How to Manage Coaching and Mentoring** | **131** |
| 6.1 | Roles of Coaches | 135 |
| 6.2 | Mentoring to Overcome Women's Barriers to Advancement | 136 |
| 6.3 | Cautions about Coaching | 137 |
| 6.4 | Management Support Checklist | 138 |
| 6.5 | Feedback and Evaluation from the Coach or Mentor | 139 |
| **Chapter 7** | **How to Train for Innovation** | **154** |
| 7.1 | Trustbusters: Where to Look for Obstacles to Building Trust | 163 |
| 7.2 | Empowerment Slogans that Need to Be Turned into Action | 166 |
| 7.3 | The Empowering Manager's Guide to Good Behavior | 167 |
| 7.4 | A Top Twelve List of Don'ts for Empowering Managers | 168 |
| 7.5 | Employability Skills | 170 |
| 7.6 | Fifteen Ways to Learn on the Job from Work Itself | 172 |
| 7.7 | Fundamentals of High Performance | 175 |
| 7.8 | Organizational Indicators of Innovation | 177 |
| **Chapter 8** | **How to Support Learners on Their Own** | **190** |
| 8.1 | Checklist for Learning to Learn Skills | 195 |
| 8.2 | Baldrige Information and Analysis Self-Assessment Tool | 196 |
| 8.3 | Setting Yourself Up for Learning, or, How to Use Information | 197 |
| 8.4 | Active Processes for Moving Beyond Data | 198 |
| 8.5 | Individual Learning Designs Anchored in ISD | 199 |
| 8.6 | Checklist of Learning Benefits of "On Your Own" | 200 |
| **Chapter 9** | **How to Assess Training Needs** | **211** |
| 9.1 | General Guidelines for Success | 215 |
| 9.2 | Staff Self-Assessment Readiness Check | 217 |
| 9.3 | Where to Look for Companywide Contacts | 218 |
| 9.4 | Drivers of Change ("Triggers") | 219 |
| 9.5 | Help in Finding Performance Discrepancies | 221 |
| 9.6 | Guidelines for Investigation Methodology | 222 |
| 9.7 | Job Analysis Checklist | 223 |
| 9.8 | Task Analysis Checklist | 224 |
| 9.9 | Defining Needs Assessment Results | 225 |
| 9.10 | Cost-Benefit Analysis | 226 |
| 9.11 | Rationale for the Training Proposal | 228 |
| **Chapter 10** | **How to Design and Write Training** | **241** |
| 10.1 | Designing Training for Customers | 247 |
| 10.2 | Setting Training Expectations | 248 |

# List of Training Management Checklists

| | | |
|---|---|---|
| 10.3 | Designing Training for Adult Learners | 250 |
| 10.4 | Overcoming Constraints on Transfer | 251 |
| 10.5 | Fostering Learning to Learn | 252 |
| 10.6 | Dealing with Learning Styles | 254 |
| 10.7 | Building Learning Taxonomies | 256 |
| 10.8 | Categorizing Types of Transferable Skills | 257 |
| 10.9 | Focusing on Results | 259 |
| 10.10 | Continuous Enabling through Organization Development | 260 |
| 10.11 | Policy Development Guidelines | 261 |
| 10.12 | What to Look for in a Vendor's Proposal | 262 |
| 10.13 | When and How to Promote (Not Just Design and Deliver) Training | 263 |
| 10.14 | Catalog Design Checklist | 264 |
| 10.15 | Writing Competencies for Course Authors | 265 |
| 10.16 | Elements of a Course | 266 |
| 10.17 | Authoring System Checklist for Instructional Design Software | 267 |
| 10.18 | Trainee Manual Development Checklist | 268 |
| 10.19 | Instructor Manual Development Checklist | 269 |
| 10.20 | Writing Checklist for Computer-Based and Interactive Video Training | 270 |

### Chapter 11  How to Implement and Deliver Training  312

| | | |
|---|---|---|
| 11.1 | Topics in a Train-the-Trainer Course | 317 |
| 11.2 | Vendor Instructor Evaluation Checklist | 319 |
| 11.3 | Quality Checklist for Instructional Support Media | 320 |
| 11.4 | When to Use a Job Aid Instead of Training | 321 |
| 11.5 | When to Choose the Big-Ticket Items—Computer-Based Training (CBT) and Interactive Videodisc (IVD) | 322 |
| 11.6 | Checklist for EPSS Use | 324 |
| 11.7 | What to Expect from Training via the Internet | 325 |
| 11.8 | Checklist for Setting Up a Training Intranet | 326 |
| 11.9 | Checklist for Setting Up One-to-One Instruction | 328 |
| 11.10 | Preparation Checklist for Classroom Training | 329 |
| 11.11 | Distance Training Checklist | 330 |
| 11.12 | Checklist of Items You Might Forget When Planning a Conference | 331 |

### Chapter 12  How to Evaluate Training  346

| | | |
|---|---|---|
| 12.1 | Overall Program Evaluation | 350 |
| 12.2 | Training Project Evaluation | 351 |
| 12.3 | Evaluation Documentation | 352 |
| 12.4 | Evaluating Training Staff | 353 |
| 12.5 | Evaluating Team Learning | 354 |
| 12.6 | Evaluation of Training Materials | 355 |
| 12.7 | Doing a Dry Run/Field Test of a Course | 356 |
| 12.8 | Course Evaluation for Trainees | 357 |
| 12.9 | Course Evaluation for Instructors | 358 |
| 12.10 | Formative Evaluation Checklist | 359 |
| 12.11 | Evaluation of Tests | 360 |

# List of Training Management Forms

**Chapter 1　How to Lead Learning Organizations**　　　1
  1.1　Personal Learning Needs and Wants　　　18
  1.2　Action/Reflection Learning　　　19
  1.3　Empowered Listening　　　20
  1.4　The Basic Math of Problem Solving　　　21
  1.5　Skills Bank Online　　　22

**Chapter 2　How to Make the Most of E-Learning**　　　27
  2.1　Planning Critical Paths and Milestones for E-Learning Development Projects　　　38
  2.2　Matrix of Blended Content and Process　　　39
  2.3　Team Assignments for E-Learning Development　　　40
  2.4　Development Standards Matrix　　　41

**Chapter 3　How to Run the Training Operation**　　　45
  3.1　Business Plan Format　　　68
  3.2　Budget Planner　　　71
  3.3　Curriculum Chart　　　72
  3.4　Training Organization Chart　　　73
  3.5　Job Description Form　　　74
  3.6　Course Registration Form　　　75
  3.7　Course Registration Confirmation　　　76
  3.8　Equipment Deployment Form　　　77
  3.9　Facilities Layout　　　78

**Chapter 4　How to Manage Outsiders**　　　85
  4.1　Vendor/Consultant Overview Analysis Matrix　　　98
  4.2　Vendor/Consultant Contract Format　　　99
  4.3　Project Status Report Form　　　101
  4.4　Project Notebook Format　　　102
  4.5　Matrix for Identifying Intellectual Property in Courses　　　103

**Chapter 5　How to Manage Training for Teams**　　　108
  5.1　Basics of Personality Type　　　123
  5.2　Language Baggage　　　124
  5.3　Process Improvement　　　125
  5.4　"Capture the Flag"　　　126
  5.5　Influence Linkages and Support Networks　　　127

## xiv List of Training Management Forms

| Chapter 6 | How to Manage Coaching and Mentoring | 131 |
|---|---|---|
| 6.1 | Reasons for Coaching and Mentoring | 141 |
| 6.2 | Matching Mentor and Protégé | 142 |
| 6.3 | Coaching Skills | 143 |
| 6.4 | Cross-Training Planning Form | 145 |
| 6.5 | Success Factors Needs Analysis | 146 |
| 6.6 | An Individual Learning Plan | 148 |

| Chapter 7 | How to Train for Innovation | 154 |
|---|---|---|
| 7.1 | Skills Matrix: What I Need and Where to Get It | 179 |
| 7.2 | Online Who's Who Skills Directory | 180 |
| 7.3 | "The Way I See It . . ." Journal | 181 |
| 7.4 | Process Quality Self- and Organizational Assessment | 182 |
| 7.5 | Wanted: Creative Workers—Am I One of Them? | 183 |
| 7.6 | Change Management Matrix: Trainer into Performance Consultant | 184 |

| Chapter 8 | How to Support Learners on Their Own | 190 |
|---|---|---|
| 8.1 | Individual Learning Plan | 202 |
| 8.2 | Self-Evaluation for Needs Assessment | 203 |
| 8.3 | Resources that Enable Performance | 205 |
| 8.4 | Where to Look for Learning Opportunities | 206 |
| 8.5 | Using 360-Degree Feedback for Individual Learners | 207 |

| Chapter 9 | How to Assess Training Needs | 211 |
|---|---|---|
| 9.1 | Self-Assessment Skills Inventory | 230 |
| 9.2 | Self-Assessment Group Discussion Guide | 231 |
| 9.3 | Key Contact Chart | 232 |
| 9.4 | Performance Discrepancy Form | 233 |
| 9.5 | Guide to Closed and Open Questions | 234 |
| 9.6 | People-Data-Things Job Analysis | 235 |
| 9.7 | Task List by Job Responsibility | 236 |
| 9.8 | Cost-Benefit Summary | 237 |

| Chapter 10 | How to Design and Write Training | 241 |
|---|---|---|
| 10.1 | Customer Contact Sheet | 273 |
| 10.2 | Components of Training Design | 274 |
| 10.3 | Creating Objectives that Push Performance | 275 |
| 10.4 | Components of Classroom Training Delivery | 276 |
| 10.5 | Employee's Training Opportunity Profile | 278 |
| 10.6 | Training Problem Analysis Worksheet | 279 |
| 10.7 | Organizational Support Time Line | 281 |
| 10.8 | Survival Skills Hierarchy | 282 |
| 10.9 | Training Transfer Follow-Up Questionnaire | 283 |
| 10.10 | Follow-Up Feedback Form | 284 |
| 10.11 | The Structure of the Policy | 285 |
| 10.12 | Catalog Entry Format | 286 |
| 10.13 | Public Relations Article Structure | 287 |
| 10.14 | The Learner Objective | 288 |
| 10.15 | Lesson Plan | 289 |

|  |  |  |
|---|---|---|
| 10.16 | Classroom Trainee Manual | 290 |
| 10.17 | Self-Study Trainee Workbook | 292 |
| 10.18 | Instructor Manual | 298 |

### Chapter 11   How to Implement and Deliver Training — 312

|  |  |  |
|---|---|---|
| 11.1 | The Master Schedule | 333 |
| 11.2 | One-to-One Training Decision Factors Chart | 334 |
| 11.3 | Classroom Training Decision Factors Chart | 335 |
| 11.4 | Delivery Components in CBT Lessons | 336 |
| 11.5 | Dry-Run Trainee Feedback Form for Classroom Training | 337 |
| 11.6 | Dry-Run Trainee Feedback Form for Self-Study | 338 |
| 11.7 | Performance Review for Classroom Instructor | 339 |

### Chapter 12   How to Evaluate Training — 346

|  |  |  |
|---|---|---|
| 12.1 | Authorization to Begin Evaluation | 362 |
| 12.2 | Training Program Standards | 363 |
| 12.3 | Project Monitoring Form (Formative Evaluation) | 364 |
| 12.4 | Program by Objectives Evaluation Report (Summative Evaluation) | 365 |
| 12.5 | Departmental Self-Study Problem Analysis Chart | 366 |
| 12.6 | Training Staff Evaluation Form | 368 |
| 12.7 | Criteria for Evaluating Training Materials | 370 |
| 12.8 | Field Testing | 372 |
| 12.9 | Course Evaluation Form (Trainee) | 374 |
| 12.10 | Course Evaluation Form (Instructor) | 376 |
| 12.11 | Evaluation of Tests | 377 |
| 12.12 | Skill Observation Form | 378 |

# Preface to the Third Edition

## Tools for All Training Managers and Learning Professionals

*How to Manage Training* has been crafted from the elegantly simple notion that all training managers are not created equal. It is perhaps the first book to recognize the reality, perhaps unique to the training field, that business managers come from widely diverse backgrounds and are jumping onto the training management learning curve at various points. Therefore, this book provides help, in a disciplined way, not only in a variety of management content areas but also for a variety of managers.

With corporate layoffs, downsizings, and bankruptcies of recent years, outsourcing of critical work, and changes in benefits across corporate America, there are more and more independent consultants and consulting companies providing training services of all sorts. ASTD, the American Society for Training and Development, based in Alexandria, Virginia, estimates that about 20 percent of the design and delivery work in American corporations is done by consultants and contract staff. The number of consultants in training, learning, performance, and human resources management has increased steadily every year since 1995, and these professionals will find *How to Manage Training* to be of enormous help. In addition, training directors and human resources directors, who are in positions with executive responsibility, will find this succinct "how to" approach, particularly the checklists that tend to expand thinking, very helpful. Executives will quickly see the scope of the various aspects of training and be aided in decision making about the broad range of their responsibilities. The key references mentioned in Chapter 10 and the full Appendix with summaries of the best thinking in the field provide especially useful information for people whose job it is to "think big picture" and to structure and staff the training operation. Managers of training and trainers, no matter what their titles, will find in this book all the tools they need for any learning challenge. Flatter organizations, empowered employees, and teams today often create trainers where none have been before. This third edition, in its entirety, is custom-made for you. It is, above all, a tool for training managers as well as all others who are in charge of designing, delivering training, and facilitating learning.

In this book, I focus on training management issues relevant to changes we can expect as we move through the first decade of the new millenium and on the tools you'll need to forge a viable training operation. The features of the book include:

- More than 200 checklists and forms, figures, and charts
- Succinct analysis of critical issues
- Sections of detailed additional related information
- Chapter-by-chapter discussions on how to be effective, even in tough times when budgets are tight and resources are limited
- An Appendix containing an in-depth review of literature in the essential field of workplace learning
- An extensive Training Management Bibliography

The Appendix is a book within a book, included to provide the training manager with a focused discussion of the essential elements of learning design, educational psychology, and organizational development that together create an environment for transfer of training from training manual and presentation mode to the employee's job and the company's bottom line. The Appendix is a model-driven guide to individual and organizational learning.

*How to Manage Training* was written to give doers, facilitators, and decision makers in training organizations clear guidance and immediately usable ideas and techniques for accomplishing successful and cost-effective training in our fast-changing, human resources–dependent business environment. It is an immediately useful tool for anyone who is already a training manager and provides insights into the field of training management for those on the path to becoming training managers.

This book was written for trainers who have titles such as:

Vice-president of training and development
Human resources director
Learning consultant
Chief knowledge officer
Knowledge engineer
Learning officer
Learning strategist
Personnel director
Training director
Training manager
Training and development manager
Manager of human resources development
Training administrator
Training supervisor

### Preface to the Third Edition

Training coordinator
In-service education manager
Corporate trainer
Safety training manager
Quality assurance manager
Facilitator
Training specialist
Employee involvement manager
Continuing education manager
Apprentice coordinator
Instructor
Instructional designer
Instructional analyst
Evaluation specialist
Coach
Mentor
Training writer
Course author
Technical writer/editor
Subject matter expert
Instructional technologist

## What This Book Will Do for You

In *How to Manage Training,* I provide the tools you'll need to run your training operation and describe in concrete ways the actions you'll need to take to make training work for your trainees and for your bottom line. Specific advice for getting through tough times of personnel shortage, tight budgets, limited spaces, and fleeting time, as well as the good times of adequate staff and intact budgets, is included.

*How to Manage Training* contains "how to's"—practical, proven techniques to enable you to train your workforce effectively within the realities of a rapidly changing business environment. In it, I have tried to go right to the heart of training administration, design, and delivery in easy-to-understand language and easy-to-use, results-oriented working forms and dispense with the tangential and the superfluous.

This book is meant for the manager on the move who needs to choose quickly and use efficiently the right management tools. A wide variety of checklists and forms is presented so that training managers with varying experience levels can pick and choose exactly what they need.

Good training is a powerful aid to good business, and good training managers need to know what makes training work and how to run it effectively. Reading this book will help you understand what makes training cost-effective and guide you in performing training tasks quickly and with style. I suggest ways to use training as a vehicle for organizational development and to ensure training's influence and future as a critical business function.

Above all, *How to Manage Training* gives you the confidence to plan and to implement good training, secure in your application of a wide range of specialized management skills for making learning happen, for running your training operation, for developing your training staff, and for serving your training customers.

## How to Use This Book

*How to Manage Training* is presented in chapters further subdivided into four consistent sections throughout this book. These four sections are:

   Section 1: Key Management Issues
   Section 2: Checklists
   Section 3: Forms
   Section 4: More Information

You can use this book by reading all of the Key Management Issues sections (Section 1 of each chapter), by extracting all of the Checklists sections (Section 2 of each chapter), by using only the Forms (Section 3 of each chapter), or by referring only to the More Information text (Section 4 of each chapter). How you proceed depends on how informed and experienced you are as you begin reading the book. Each chapter features a discussion of compromises you can live with if you have limited resources and of enhancements you can make to your program if you have adequate staff and budget.

The book is unique in its structure, because it's presented both horizontally and vertically—in effect, a training management how-to-matrix. *How to Manage Traning* can be read and used in either a sequential and linear fashion or by focusing on only a topic or management tool of particular interest. For example, you might want to gather all of the checklists together for use at a planning workshop, or you might want to distribute all of the forms at team meetings. You'll find these in the same place in each chapter throughout the book.

The book's format is itself a model for learning, presenting first the big picture, then checklists for idea generation, then forms and tools for direct aid, and, finally, details of additional information on each chapter topic.

You are encouraged to add your own company information to the checklists and forms found throughout the book to reflect your special corporate interests—your company logo, your own letterhead—and to adapt the forms and checklists as necessary, for example, by adding more space for computation or writing, inserting additional items in lists, or tacking on additional rows and columns on charts. You can personalize the management tools presented here by substituting your own culture-sensitive words such as *learner* versus *trainee, checkpoint* versus *milestone, vision* versus *goal, standard* versus *objective, teacher* versus *instructor,* and *adviser* versus *advisor.* You are also expected to add identifying data, such as date, name, job title, telephone number, and department, to the forms and checklists. *How to Manage Training* is written to engage you in the kind of management that you specifically need.

## Changes in the Field Since the Second Edition

*How to Manage Training,* Third Edition, is an updated version of the 1998 second edition of the work, edited throughout to include new concepts, terminology, and training practices. This new edition features thirty new checklists, twenty new forms, fifty new references in the Bibliography, and six new features in the Appendix. The third edition includes substantial additions to four chapters, important modifications to four chapters, four entirely new chapters, and a refocusing throughout the book toward training that contributes to high performance, the bottom line, and continuous learning.

Specific new text and tools are included on how to lead learning organizations, make the most of e-learning, train for innovation and employability, run the training operation, and manage training for teams. Updates are included on designs and documentation to facilitate learning as well as on tools and practices for making training accountable as a viable business function. The Third Edition includes more focus on the individual learner. We also provide a CD-ROM containing all checklists, forms, figures, and charts.

A chapter-by-chapter synopsis follows:

Chapter 1, "How to Lead Learning Organizations," emphasizes the training manager as learning facilitator, enabler, and designer of learning experiences of all kinds that are delivered in many places—on the job, at computers, in classrooms. There is also a focus on the need for training managers to adopt a systems perspective, constantly monitoring the results of training in terms of business—not only learning—impact.

Chapter 2, "How to Make the Most of E-Learning," focuses on the issue of making decisions about e-learning to maximize its use in your particular company. Ideas in "blended training," the potential of 24/7 around the globe learning, interactivity and collaboration, and content standards are all here for your investigation. We present this chapter in the context of growing pains of the field and give you some concrete help in choosing wisely.

Chapter 3, "How to Run the Training Operation," contains all-important information about the "make or buy" decision, that is, whether, when, and how to hire outsiders. It also contains important cost-saving worksheets and checklists and a new section on legal and government involvement in training.

Chapter 4, "How To Manage Outsiders," is driven by the recent rise and demise of dot-com enterprises with consequent availability of outsiders for hire as consultants, training designers, and instructors. We help you identify the factors that might lead you to outsource some of your training operation and give you guidance on the kinds of paperwork you'll need to manage projects, protect your company's intellectual property, and stay within employment law.

Chapter 5, "How to Manage Training for Teams," is devoted exclusively to the special training challenges of teams. It specifically covers how to meet the learning needs of individual team members as well as of the team as a whole, and how the working of people in teams is different from other kinds of work efforts.

Chapter 6, "How to Manage Coaching and Mentoring," brings you up to date on the ever-growing field of coaching and mentoring. We explore some new understandings about the benefits and the pitfalls of coaching, and provide some details about specific forms of coaching and mentoring such as for promotion of diversity, advancement of women, and executive development. This chapter contains a wealth of forms and checklists to guide the training manager in facilitating and developing these most important avenues for learning.

Chapter 7, "How to Train for Innovation," discusses the twin issues of the retention of competent employees and the longevity of the training operation. Linkage with "significant others" outside the training operation and career flexibility are two important concepts here. This chapter shows how to make empowerment win-win for everyone—the individual as well as the company, and how this can foster innovation.

Chapter 8, "How to Support Learners on Their Own," helps you recognize the power of self-directed, on-demand, just-in-time learning that occurs in workplaces that demonstrate that they value it. Numerous sources, including ASTD, have identified the phenomenon of learners learning on their own as one of three major new trends in training. In this chapter we give you specific guidance in how to encourage learners on their own, and how to create a culture of support for the variety of learners in today's organizations.

Chapter 9, "How to Assess Training Needs," Chapter 10, "How to Design and Write Training," Chapter 11, "How to Implement and Deliver Training," and Chapter 12, "How to Evaluate Training," are the heart of the training manager's systematic approach to creating the training that serves individual learners.

The field is presented in a systems orientation from the training manager's point of view, including how to assess training needs, design and write training, deliver training, and evaluate training. Today's managers of the learning enterprise are both challenged and given the tools to rethink assumptions about training, learning, and performance in order to lead organizations of learners in today's less hierarchical and more empowered workplaces. *How to Manage Training*, Third Edition, recognizes the pull between optimal learning design and strategies for simply staying in business and the tug of serving the learning needs of the team as well as those of the individual learner on that team. This book provides tools and support for meeting these and other current training management challenges.

Improving performance is the bottom line—your personal performance and the performance of your trainees, whether in a classroom or at a PC. Whether you are a consultant, manager or supervisor, team leader, or a trainer of any sort, this book is your number-one source for time-saving, high-quality, proven successful tools for managing training and supporting workplace learning.

# How to Lead Learning Organizations

American business is already beginning to experience the dramatic changes that have been evident since the year 2000—changes in the structure of business organizations, in the view of change itself, and in the makeup of the employee workforce.

**KEY MANAGEMENT ISSUES**

■ *Changes in the Structure of Business Organizations.* Throughout the business community, organizations are becoming both smaller and flatter, with fewer clear lines of command. We are getting used to having major decisions made by those below the top ranks—midlevel managers who now have power over critical budgets and personnel resources. We are seeing customer-driven development of all sorts, from R&D operations to product design. We are becoming comfortable with coalition problem solving, with the influence of networks, and with a political kind of business culture that values group effort through work teams, ad hoc task forces, and advisory groups. We are seeing executive and upper-management levels disappear. In training management especially, we are finding a wide diversity of managerial titles and job responsibilities, more management coalitions and advisors, more teams, and front-line decision making.

We are seeing an affirmation of the value of a company's human resources, enunciated in less rigid ways. We are experiencing a renewed interest in the people who make a business work; we seem no longer to be focused primarily on filling slots in prescribed and defined organization structures, in chains of command, and in narrowly defined job requirements. The psychological effects of the terrorist attacks on September 11, 2001 are manifest in a greater consciousness of people and human concerns in the workplace. We are beginning to view learning, the most human effort of all, as a strategic work process.

■ *A Different View of Change Itself.* The knowledge explosion of recent years, fueled by advances in telecommunications and computers, has speeded up the rate of change. More information, more channels through which it can flow, and easier access to it are helping to create "experts" around every corner—not just in the executive suite or high-powered laboratory. Change can and does originate in unexpected places; it is no longer an evolutionary process that grows out of a slow-simmering event or the result of a directive cast down from the top. Change seems to be discontinuous and random; it demands both an informed and more immediate response and more flexible responders. Training can play a critical role in helping persons at work manage career and organizational change.

■ ***Changes in the Makeup of the Employee Workforce.*** Expert systems, simulations, smart machines, miniaturization, and the organizing power of computers have and will be removing people from jobs, especially as the twenty-first century progresses. The individuals who are responsible for electronic "nonmechanical" machines need to know things of a more sophisticated nature: how systems and machines interrelate, how to troubleshoot problems with various logic systems, or how to set correct and efficient parameters for computations and report generation. Training workers today is a different matter than it was a generation ago, and workers' environments for interface with the tools of business are also very different.

Today's workforce looks different from the way it did even during the early 1990s. More younger professional women with families are at work; there are more women at all levels; there are more minorities and foreign-born workers from entry level to boardroom; there are more part-time workers and consultants, more older workers, and more workers on the payroll who work at home and are linked electronically with the office. The changing human profile of the workforce requires training that is designed and delivered in ways that spark the imaginations and unleash the potentials of this new employee pool. Outsourced work brings with it new responsibilities for development of human resources.

■ ***Questions for Training Management.*** These changes raise important questions for trainers: "How can we manage a company's knowledge and skills base so that employees develop with change?" and "What methodologies for training management will keep a company's human resources tuned and ready to move the business forward?"

In this book, I suggest answers to these questions by providing guidelines that recognize the need for flexibility as well as structure. These guidelines are based on a methodology that recognizes training as a system of inputs, outputs, and feedback based on nurtured operational relationships and program objectives tied to business goals. Training management is much more than coordinating vendor-delivered courses and watching the department's bottom line.

■ ***Management Assumptions.*** This chapter highlights some major themes that recur throughout the book, and it proceeds from certain assumptions about management and about training managers. These assumptions are as follows:

1. Management believes that its human resources are what makes the company strong.
2. Management currently commits a dollar amount to training that is equivalent to at least 2 percent of its payroll budget.
3. Management supports training in other visible ways, such as by providing training facilities, training staff (professional and administrative), training materials and production capability, conference support, and online services.
4. Management pays attention to "process" quality assurance.
5. Management carries out procedures that flow from policy.
6. Training managers value equally the potential contribution of each trainee.
7. Training managers behave as if they believe in flexibility, especially during needs analysis and course delivery.
8. Training managers view training as a strategic business tool.
9. Training managers have a broad view of the benefits of human resources development and see training as one of the critical empowerment tools.
10. Training managers see themselves as continuous facilitators of learning.

In this book, I also assume that training managers have widely varying backgrounds and responsibilities and that training management occurs on various levels. Some training managers know what to do and how to do it; a reminder of the dimensions of key training issues is enough to prod them into action. Other training managers need a checklist or "to do" list to use as a planning tool to get things rolling; others prefer to go right to the forms for direct use in moving the program forward; still others want to go through each chapter, page by page, from key issues through ancillary information to get the big picture before addressing the details of implementation.

Many managers prefer to understand issues first and then engage in idea generation, brainstorming, and choosing options. They organize a specific response to a problem and then review other relevant information that might have a bearing on the problem. This book is meant to be a practical guide during these various stages of thought and action.

## A PERSPECTIVE ON TRAINING MANAGEMENT

■ *Adopting a Systems Orientation.* As training departments change their structure and become both smaller in numbers of employees and flatter in terms of hierarchy, it is more important that the core employees have a systems orientation to the work of the training organization. That is, when fewer employees have more responsibility and flexibility in carrying out that responsibility, it's important to always be sure that the group as a whole is working toward the same ends and through similar means. It's very tempting to measure the wrong things—numbers of trainees, numbers of classes, numbers of videos, how employee A is doing compared to employee B with these numbers, etc.—rather than the outcomes and results of training. Training managers must lead the way out of the isolated accumulation of details *about* training to the realization of changed performance as a result of learning.

One way to begin this leadership process is to adopt a systems orientation to your thinking. The foundation of this kind of thinking is the simple systems model of inputs, processes, and outputs, with continuous evaluation and feedback; this is a different way of thinking from the old-style linear thinking that often featured doing your job according to prescribed procedures and the best way you could, getting signoffs that your work was acceptable, and then going on to the next task. Systems thinking requires lateral thinking—its structure is more like a web than like a straight line; it requires that the thinker be flexible and on the lookout for inputs from numerous sources. It requires that the thinker be innovative in devising new and improved processes for work; it means that self-assessments and the assessments of others be an automatic part of all persons' work, and that evaluations are used to make mid-process correction if necessary.

Learning is this kind of systemic process. Building a learning organization requires leaders who think this way too and who consciously build bridges and networks within the company, especially to leverage the positive effects of learning.

■ **Running the Training Operation.** Cost-effectiveness in human resources development—and not just cost—is the major criterion for training management success. More sophisticated, more informed, and also more specifically needy employees are demanding effective training that helps them to do better work. They will no longer accept the generalized vendor-developed course presented by a well-meaning but off-target outsider.

*Training Magazine*'s 1996 Industry Report estimates that training managers go outside their corporations for $13 billion worth of training services and products, or 22 percent of all corporate training and development.* This 22 percent certainly indicates that outsiders are a significant part of training program design and delivery, and it also sends a signal that managers inside corporations should be taking a good hard look at how this 22 percent is integrated into the corporate culture, goals, and business plans of the companies they serve. ASTD's (The American Society for Training and Development) 2002 *State of the Industry Report* confirms this percentage and indicates an upward trend to 29 percent currently.† *Training Magazine*'s 2001 Industry Report reports that companies are spending $57 billion to train workers, up 5 percent from 2000. The number

---

* *Training Magazine*, October 1996, p. 42.
† ASTD report, *State of the Industry Report 2002*.

of corporate universities has increased phenomenally from its start in 1990 with 400 such institutions to 2,200 in year 2002. *Training Magazine's* executive editor, Tammy Galvin, was quoted in a *Yahoo! News* Reuters Technology brief as saying that companies are "beginning to place a premium on human capital," and that "issues such as time-to-market and time-to-knowledge are in the forefront of companies' launch of a new product."* These are learning-intensive and learning-dependent measures—signs of new thinking in how to lead and manage learning organizations and of the strategic importance of human resources issues.

The numbers are staggering, especially because they indicate that huge amounts of money are being spent on training. Yet, according to ASTD, only about 16 percent of all employees receive training. More than 27 million American adults—most of whom are employees—are functionally illiterate, and U.S. businesses spend about $25 billion annually and growing for remedial programs in reading, writing, math, English as a Second Language (ESL), and basic problem-solving skills.† In recent years, corporate spending on ESL programs has continuously increased by 15–20% per year, according to the Training Industry Reports, 1996 and 2001, cited above. Stricter federal legislation in 2001 supporting the Department of Labor in occupational safety, against sexual harassment, and for diversity has increased a company's requirements for training. (See the Web site of the Society for Human Resource Management, shrm.org, and Chapter 3 of this book for more information on legislation.) ASTD also estimates that more than 80 percent of Fortune 500 and other large companies view training as important in meeting business goals. Yet fewer than half of these companies integrate training and development into their strategic planning processes. New legislation could change this.

Taken together, these numbers seem to indicate that both the current standards for and the current practices that constitute good training management are not at all clear. In addition, there seems to be a need for more equitable distribution of training services by training managers to employees—and a better accounting for these services—for the sake of good business.

Unquestionably, changes in the organization of business are leading us toward planning that assigns human resources functions a prominent place in corporate policy and in operational goal statements. Businesses are changing rapidly because of mergers, downsizing, and a genuine desire to be more collaborative. Organizationally, business looks different today from how it did in the 1960s, 1970s, 1980s, and 1990s—the lifetime of most of the training managers of today. As we have progressed through the decades, the service sector of the economy has continued to grow, driving the search for quality in processes such as customer service, sales and marketing, communications, personnel administration, and training itself. Training managers must be able to articulate a place for training as

---

* *Yahoo! News*, "Firms Augment Training with Online Courses" by Sherwood Ross, May 4, 2002, p. 1.
†ASTD report, *Training America: Learning to Work for the 21st Century*, 1989.

a contributor to process quality—and the best place to start is with the business planning process.

In your training operations, remember to keep design and delivery methods flexible so that both the people in your organization and your budget can respond quickly and effectively. Combine writing your own courses, facilitating one-to-one learning experiences, buying vendor courses, and creating training projects—apprenticeships, mentoring, conferences, field trips—always within the context of an identified corporate business strategy. Run your training operation as if everything that you do matters to the composite of individual employees who define your business. Link training to stated corporate directions, not to the most visible or most vocal potential client. Your actions should be driven by cost-effectiveness and a clear business goal, not by a desire to save the most or spend the least money on a particular course.

Tools for addressing the current issues in running the training operation are discussed in Chapter 3.

■ *Assessing Training Needs.* One of the biggest mistakes a training manager can make is to get carried away by the enthusiasm of a fellow manager who says, "I need you to develop a course for my people" or by the CEO who declares, "We need more training around here at every level." In the rush of excitement created by being asked, and in a desire to please an important customer, many a training manager has thrown training at a problem that wasn't a training problem at all.

This unfortunate scenario happens, of course, when training is run as an "ad hocracy" of unplanned responses, unconnected to more carefully developed and articulated business planning. It happens when there is no formal, objective analysis of needs—no needs assessment phase of the training system. It is "penny-wise and pound-foolish"—in other words, probably not cost-effective—to validate the need for training by listening to only one person's opinion about training, no matter how important that one person is.

A better course of action is to stick to a system that requires multiple inputs—in this case, inputs on why someone needs to learn, exactly who that learner will be, exactly what needs to be learned, and how often this learning will need to be taught to other workers. Generally, the opinion of one person is not sufficient to verify these kinds of learning needs.

Keep in mind, too, that organizational, technological, political, and demographic changes can and do occur outside the planning process. And training that you devise to deal with change should receive verification from multiple input sources. Take the time before beginning your development efforts to clarify what the training problem really is.

Don't be surprised, if, during your needs assessment activities, you find out that the problem isn't a training problem at all and that it can be solved more effectively by information, person-to-person communication, job redesign, incentives, or some other human resources intervention. Save training solutions for good, solid, verified training problems. You'll find focused help on Needs Assessment in Chapter 9—you might

# How to Lead Learning Organizations

find the process being called a "performance analysis," so be prepared for some flexible thinking.

■ ***Designing and Writing Training.*** The ultimate goal of most training is to improve work. This long-range goal is reached through shorter-range objectives tied to specific business policy and planning statements. Such specific training must be designed for maximum transfer to work—the processes, ideas, and skills that are learned in the training environment must be put to work quickly and effectively on the job.

This kind of training focuses on the subject itself, on the tasks inherent in mastering the subject, on the ways in which adult learners behave, and on the individual learner at work. It is learning designed to respond to a specific learning deficit or identified gap in a business situation and is structured in written language to communicate clearly its objectives for learning. It is training offered equitably to varied constituencies.

This kind of training incorporates built-in follow-through evaluations that are based on the reality of the trainee's working environment back on the job. It is "tight" training in the sense that it is driven by cost-effectiveness, not only by effectiveness. Training designed for transfer typically saves time, because, in the design process, the "nice to knows" have been eliminated. This kind of training can respond to a company's unique organizational structures and to the unique learning needs of its diverse employees; it is built on objectives for learning that flow from business objectives and is designed for the purpose of transfer to work, not for entertainment, for show, for reward, or for diversion. These principles are applied also to individual learners on their own (see Chapter 8) and to e-learners (see Chapter 2).

Tools for getting it down on paper—for designing and writing training, and for creating good training documentation—are presented in Chapter 10.

■ ***Implementing and Delivering Training.*** One secret of maintaining a flexible training organization is providing variety in the way training is delivered. A useful way to think about training delivery is in terms of the degree of activity or passivity demonstrated by the learner. Look for ways to implement training that engage the learner in active learning—in setting up and solving work problems, in initiating interactions with peers in small groups or one-on-one dialogue, in making choices about what should be learned next, in doing self-evaluations, in doing demonstrations and presentations, in generating hypotheses, and in experimenting. Pay particular attention to implementation systems for e-learning.

Consider all your options before falling back on the old standby of classroom training using slides or "overheads." Choose a method of delivery that enhances the skill being taught; for example, work in teams during training if the knowledge being acquired will be used in work teams back on the job. Always move from theory to practice, from "book learning" to real time.

Consider computer-based, video-based, and performance support delivery options in which the learner controls the pace of delivery and the choice of topics. Remember that if your workforce is culturally diverse, classroom training could be an embarrassing waste of time. If lessons are geared to an "average" American adult and expressed in typical American English, your training might go right over the heads in your class. One-to-one on-the-job training, coaching, or mentoring assignments might be a more cost-effective delivery method. Self-paced online learning is an option. And don't forget the value of a good book.

The point is that you should try to be very open-minded when choosing an appropriate training delivery method. Revise your train-the-trainer course to reflect the many choices that you have, and don't be afraid to ask potential trainees for their ideas on how they learn best before you determine how the training will be delivered.

Tools to help you with training delivery are discussed in Chapter 11.

■ ***Evaluating Training.*** Perhaps the most relevant concept today concerning training is the notion that its evaluation should be ongoing in order both to mirror and to capture the fast-moving changes in the organization and in the employee resource base. If you wait until the end of a course for evaluation, you will have allowed yourself to miss critical opportunities along the needs assessment-design-development-delivery path for in-process evaluation and improvement.

The process known as "formative evaluation" holds out a promise of quality assurance and consonance with today's more rapid rate of change. Formative evaluation techniques focus on critical value decision making during training development, making evaluation an ongoing and useful process. Formative evaluation applies with equal relevance to evaluation of programs, projects, courses, and training materials. The critical step, then, of closing the improvement loop through feedback almost always follows formative evaluation. "Three hundred sixty–degree" evaluation can be used effectively in evaluating training.

Evaluation that relies on the "smiles test" at the end of training is simply too-little-too-late for the changing character of the current business scene.

Evaluation tools are the topic of Chapter 12.

■ ***Guaranteeing Training's Longevity.*** Training flourishes in companies to the extent that training managers take positive and bold action to secure its place as an active, not reactive, business partner. On the other hand, training remains on the periphery of business if training managers assume that others will establish training's worth just because it's usually considered a "good thing" for people and for business.

Training managers must do what seems to be the obvious—write a statement of purpose that flows from an overall organizational and corporate vision, mission, or goal. If your company doesn't have a mission or goal statement, push senior management to write one. Work with senior management to make training's reason for being a visible outgrowth of the greater corporate vision. Don't assume that training is seen as integral to that vision—be persistent until you get it down in black and white.

Training managers must tie training needs to supervisors' annual performance review documentation. Get training written into a personal database system, so that you are linked to career development of individuals through their supervisors or other peer review rating systems. Secure a budget structure that allocates money to training based on a rational and predictable process and formula. Get management support for training at all levels through public statements and in business plans, project plans, and strategic plans.

Training managers must see themselves and their staffs as keepers of the keys to building learning organizations. The molds for empowered employees are often set in training sessions—trainers of all stripes must seize the opportunity to create organizations of learners, to shape the supports for learning, to stir up every employee's motivation to learn, and to manage the knowledge resources of a company. Training managers first and foremost must be proactive strategic thinkers. The opportunities for training managers in today's knowledge-intensive economy are enormous—and so are the responsibilities.

Planned, integrated training cannot continue to reach only 16 percent of the American workforce if it is to be a viable business function. Training has great potential to help American corporations meet the challenges of this new century because it has a lot going for it now—huge investments of money, a place somewhere on almost everyone's organization chart, rich and varied delivery options, and enthusiastic and committed supporters across the spectrum of American corporate organizations.

What training needs is focus, discipline, strategic thinking, vision, and leadership. This book can help you achieve them.

# Chapter 1 Checklists
## For Leading Learning Organizations

The following group of checklists provides focus to your thinking about what you need to do as a leader of a learning organization. The important concepts are that individuals come first: What and how, where, and when they learn is what builds a learning organization. Some would say that indeed the sum is greater than its parts—that is, individuals who are well-tuned learners can in fact mold and continue to mold the organizations in which they work into truly world-class competitors, greater in the kind of wisdom, power, and performance capability than the individuals in them. Our knowledge-intensive, global economy demands learning organizations and requires special kinds of leaders.

**LIST OF CHECKLISTS FOR LEADING LEARNING ORGANIZATIONS**

- **1.1** Strategies for Everyone
- **1.2** Checklist of " . . . ing Words" for Managers
- **1.3** Tough Questions for Leaders
- **1.4** Concrete Actions for Developing Learning Organizations
- **1.5** Evidence of a Learning Organization in Progress

# Learning Organization Checklist 1.1

## Strategies for Everyone

\_\_\_\_\_ 1. Tolerate questions. Cultivate the art of asking helpful questions. It's often the quality of questions rather than answers that leads you to deeper understanding.

\_\_\_\_\_ 2. Think of knowledge as strategy. Work hard to experiment with ideas and make discoveries, share what you know, hang around and observe high performers. Try for more and better ideas; keep a journal of them and reread it in a disciplined way—for example, every Wednesday after lunch.

\_\_\_\_\_ 3. Learn to deal or negotiate with ideas: make it a point daily to play with ideas. Prioritize, categorize, correlate, recognize bias, separate fact from fiction, defend an opinion, add to, delete from, compare, contrast.

\_\_\_\_\_ 4. Enjoy surprises. It's okay to make a mistake as long as you learn something from it.

\_\_\_\_\_ 5. Redefine your work as a resource for learning. Inherent in every task, job, and work process is the kernel of insight. Learn to look at your work as something to learn from; approach your work as if you were learning to do it for the first time. Pay attention to what's great about it and to what can be improved. Think in terms of learning before doing your work, while doing your work, and after doing your work. Practice action and reflection.

\_\_\_\_\_ 6. Be responsible. Your work is your work, not your "company's" work. Be responsible for making it the best you can make it. If changes are needed to increase the value of your work, make the changes. The value of your work as intellectual capital is your responsibility.

\_\_\_\_\_ 7. Teach someone else; ask someone else to teach you.

# Learning Organization Checklist 1.2

## Checklist of "...ing Words" for Managers

People who study learning organizations often talk about "process"—that is, the interweaving of the way things are happening and the way people interact with each other as work progresses. One way to teach yourself to "think process" is to use the "...ing" form of words instead of verbs, which tend to stop the action: "planning" instead of "plan," for example. You'll be amazed at how this simple word trick can train your thinking in the direction of "process."

_____ 1. *Visioning* instead of vision.

_____ 2. *Changing* instead of change.

_____ 3. *Communicating* instead of communicate.

_____ 4. *Leading* instead of leadership.

_____ 5. *Understanding* instead of understand.

_____ 6. *Doing* instead of do.

_____ 7. *Motivating* instead of motivation.

_____ 8. *Supporting* instead of support.

_____ 9. *Listening* instead of listen.

_____ 10. *Modifying* instead of modify.

_____ 11. *Revising* instead of revise.

_____ 12. *Simplifying* instead of simplify.

_____ 13. *Analyzing* instead of analyze.

_____ 14. *Differentiating* instead of differentiate.

_____ 15. *Finding* instead of find.

_____ 16. *Accessing* instead of access.

_____ 17. *Interpreting* instead of interpret.

_____ 18. *Searching* instead of search.

_____ 19. *Verifying* instead of verify.

_____ 20. *Evaluating* instead of evaluate.

# Learning Organization Checklist 1.3
## Tough Questions for Leaders

Leadership these days is getting a lot of press. It's clear that workers in today's flatter, less hierarchical, more empowered workplaces need leaders who are cast in a different mold from those of yesterday, who "looked out for number one," "walked silently and carried a big stick," or came to work to "kick butt." Leadership today, especially leadership of learning organizations, is clearly in transition from the authoritarian models to models of egalitarianism. During such times of transition, leaders are pushed to think hard about some tough questions that will frame their behaviors in their new worlds. These are some of them:

_____ 1. How can I be comfortable facilitating team and group learning? What self-disciplines do I need to develop in order to be patient and truly caring about each person's growth as it impacts the growth of the team?

_____ 2. How can I reward (money and recognition) employees who make outstanding contributions? How can I preserve what's best of the company's historical salary and grade successes, yet move the company forward through employees who do truly outstanding learning work? How much and how often should rewards be given?

_____ 3. How can I demonstrate my encouragement of "generative conversation" among employees? How can I show them that talking on the job with each other is a good thing that often leads to breakthroughs? How can I teach them the value of dialogue and active listening, positive evaluation, and feedback?

_____ 4. How can I take steps to encourage dissent, questioning, and feedback during meetings in front of peers and supervisors? How can I prevent dissent from occurring behind backs and closed doors?

_____ 5. What alliances within my company do I need to make in order to help push the integration of learnings? Should I have an action plan to accomplish these alliances? How proactive can I be? Where should I start? Have I accurately identified the stakeholders within the company? Do I use levers?

_____ 6. Do I know how people learn in this company? Are supports in place to help them?

_____ 7. What evidence is there that this company values learning? Can this become more overt? What can I do to help demonstrate the value of learning?

_____ 8. Do employees at both ends of the longevity range get the message equally? That is, do senior employees as well as new employees know that they are expected to learn at work—from each other, by themselves, and from the work that they do?

_____ 9. Do I know deep down in my heart that leadership means having followers? Do I conduct myself in such a way that followers happen? Do I earn my authority, not grab it?

_____ 10. Do I have enough guts to invest in human capital to make it grow? What kind of money and other resources (staff, hardware, buildings, etc.) can I get, and when should they be invested? What kinds of studies do I need in order to demonstrate a probable payoff?

# Learning Organization Checklist 1.4

## Concrete Actions for Developing Learning Organizations

_____ 1. Take time to do things. Talk with and listen to colleagues.

_____ 2. Ask for help. The Lone Ranger died a long time ago.

_____ 3. Tell people more than they need to know. Communicate widely and openly about the direction the business is going in, the values espoused by top managers and the board, the successes and the failures. Involve everyone in information about the company. Trust people to take what information they need and to perhaps find something exciting in information for which they don't immediately see a need.

_____ 4. Encourage individuals to state a personal vision for their work.

_____ 5. Encourage individuals to develop a learning plan, with topics or skills they'd like to learn and when and where they could learn them. Review these regularly and assist individuals in learning what they have identified as their learning challenges.

_____ 6. Promote, reward, and recognize excellence in learning. Look for all kinds of learning, not just that which happens in classrooms. Enlist team leaders, supervisors, shift leaders, and others to help you identify excellence in learning.

_____ 7. Set up forums for ideas. Quantity of ideas leads to quality of ideas. Do this on a regular basis; record the sessions either on paper or on tape.

_____ 8. Allow people the time to learn on the job from each other. Encourage teaching, coaching, and mentoring.

# Learning Organization Checklist 1.5

## Evidence of a Learning Organization in Progress

Use this checklist as a guideline for your leading "by walking around." As you talk with people and observe them at their jobs, see if you can find these telling signs that learning can be happening.

\_\_\_\_\_ 1. The company subsidizes subscriptions to learning and training journals and pays for national conference attendance.

\_\_\_\_\_ 2. The company provides easy access to library, databases, and the Internet for all employees.

\_\_\_\_\_ 3. Best practices are rewarded.

\_\_\_\_\_ 4. Nobody shoots messengers.

\_\_\_\_\_ 5. On-the-job training, coaching, and mentoring happen at all levels.

\_\_\_\_\_ 6. Cross-training and cross-functional teamwork are apparent.

\_\_\_\_\_ 7. Ideas are welcomed, not censored or ignored.

\_\_\_\_\_ 8. Employees can be seen in "communities of practice" solving problems.

\_\_\_\_\_ 9. "Bag More Than a Lunch" programs are available for continuous learning.

\_\_\_\_\_ 10. E-Learning opportunities motivate self-directed learners on the job and on company time.

# Chapter 1 Forms
## For Leading Learning Organizations

Forms listed here can help you help your employees organize their thinking toward becoming organizational learners. These forms can act as a job aid or crutch as people become more self-responsible, communicative, and innovative.

**LIST OF FORMS FOR LEADING LEARNING ORGANIZATIONS**

- **1.1** Personal Learning Needs and Wants
- **1.2** Action/Reflection Learning
- **1.3** Empowered Listening
- **1.4** The Basic Math of Problem Solving
- **1.5** Skills Bank Online

**How to Manage Training**

**Learning Organization Form 1.1**
**PERSONAL LEARNING NEEDS AND WANTS**

### How To Use This Form
1. This is for each employee to complete either on his or her own, or with guidance from colleagues, supervisors, or trainers. It is for an individual's personal record, not to be used as part of a performance review or salary review.
2. Review this chart periodically with the employee, either individually or as part of a team meeting, for example, once each quarter (March, June, Sept., Dec.).

Employee's name _____ Date _____

Job title or brief job description _____
_____

### My Learning Needs

| Description of training | Where to get it | When it should be done |
|---|---|---|
| 1 | | |
| 2 | | |
| 3 | | |
| 4 | | |
| 5 | | |
| 6 | | |
| 7 | | |
| 8 | | |

### My Learning Wants

| Description of training | Where to get it | When it should be done |
|---|---|---|
| 1 | | |
| 2 | | |
| 3 | | |
| 4 | | |
| 5 | | |
| 6 | | |
| 7 | | |
| 8 | | |

# How to Lead Learning Organizations

**Learning Organization Form 1.2**
**ACTION/REFLECTION LEARNING**

### How To Use This Form
1. This chart is a brief reminder, a stimulus to reflective thinking, which can be used by any employee on a regular basis as a self-teaching tool as you build your own capacity for reflection. Keep it at hand in a desk drawer or posted on a wall nearby.
2. Action is the American worker's first response to almost any situation: "make it go, give the correct answer, repeat after me, do as I say, keep all the balls in the air. . . ." It's hard work to learn reflective thinking. As an adjunct to action, reflection is a winning complement. Action/reflection learning is a system of thinking that features the best of one very good way to build a learning organization.

### *"DON'T JUST DO SOMETHING, STAND THERE!"*
*Blanchard, Carlos, and Randolph,* Empowerment Takes More Than a Minute, *San Francisco: Berrett-Koehler, 1996, p. 66.*

### Practice Guide for Reflective Thinking

|  | Notes on when and how I did this |
|---|---|
| 1. Questioning "What if? . . ." |  |
| 2. Generating options |  |
| 3. Formulating hypotheses |  |
| 4. Testing hypotheses |  |
| 5. Seeking consensus |  |

## How to Manage Training

**Learning Organization Form 1.3**
**EMPOWERED LISTENING**

### How To Use This Form
1. Simply use this form whenever you ask an employee's opinion. Put it on a clipboard or make copies and bind them together in a pad. The heading of this form will always be a reminder to practice active listening.
2. Like other skills, the skill of empowered listening requires practice. This form can help you practice.

-------------------------------------------------- *cut here* --------------------------------------------------

### LISTENER'S NOTE PAD

**EMPOWERED LISTENING REQUIRES THAT YOU:**
1. Receive the message, not initiate it.
2. Accept what you hear without passing judgment on it. (Listen, don't talk.)
3. "Say more" is your appropriate response if you need clarification.
4. The word underlined above is "you." Adopt the mind-set that the person to whom you are listening has the most important things to say, not yourself.
5. Go away full of what you've heard; save acting upon it for another time.

# How to Lead Learning Organizations

**Learning Organization Form 1.4**
**THE BASIC MATH OF PROBLEM SOLVING**

### How To Use This Form
1. Use this as a job aid or handout at a team meeting at which problems must be solved.
2. Basic math concepts and functions are listed down the side of the page. Often these functions can be applied to problem statements, with astonishing results. Foster learning through analogy.

Problem statement: _____

_____

|  | Notes |
|---|---|
| Add |  |
| Subtract |  |
| Multiply |  |
| Divide |  |
| Substitute |  |
| Reverse |  |
| Raise to the power of |  |
| Truncate |  |

**Learning Organization Form 1.5**
**SKILLS BANK ONLINE**

> **How To Use This Form**
> 1. Use this as a template for creating an employee skills bank online. Distribute this to each employee and set a date by which information should be entered into the system.
> 2. Update this once every quarter, as part of an overall "how're we doing?" periodic review.

Name _____   Business Telephone _____

e-mail _____

Date joined the company _____   Present job _____

Information I'd like to have:                          Skills I'd like to learn:

Job-related skills I can teach someone:

Hobbies, crafts, sports, leisure activities I can share with someone:

# Chapter 1
# More Information on How To Lead Learning Organizations

## Why We Should Pay Attention to Cognitive Psychology

For many decades, training has been associated largely with behavioral psychology. Job and task analysis, measurable behavioral objectives, time and motion studies—all were the hallmarks of training in our industrial economy. When training managers thought about the totality of training, this behavioral model of design came to mind.

It's no secret, however, that things are different today. First, we are in a postindustrial economy, and a global one to boot. Factories, R&D labs, workers, markets, and consumers are worldwide. Information is the organizer, not industrial production. An information-driven economy requires a different perspective on training. Cognitive psychology and the potential in the concept of "learning" are this perspective.

This shift in orientation from behaviorism to cognitivism is primarily characterized by a shift in thinking from "*in*struction" to "*con*struction." Cognitivism requires that we think always in terms of "moving toward" or "moving through"—that is, of "process" or something always in flux. "Inquiry," "involvement," "reflection," "reconstruction," "evaluation," "alignment," "integration," "relationship," and "network" are all favorite terms to the cognitive psychologist. To be sure, the idea of training to a task is still relevant; the task, however, now must be framed in terms of constructionism—that is, what I need to do in order to begin building my learning. A knowledge economy, after all, builds its strength according to the depth and breadth of involvement and the innovative quality of its individual and group members. It depends on the ability of persons to frame the issues in, proactively seek, and cost-effectively use information. It is a different economy from the one that turned out pieces of things and objects to view, hold, smell, or otherwise possess in a sensory way. Growth in the information economy depends more strongly on the personal, individual initiative that is driven by action and reflection, evaluation, and speedy use of feedback than it is on the certification of mastered tasks and acceptable product count. Four excellent books on the nature of constructing knowledge are:

> *In the Age of the Smart Machine: The Future of Work and Power* by Shoshana Zuboff, Basic Books Inc., 1988
> *Things That Make Us Smart: Defending Human Attributes in the Age of the Machine* by Donald Norman, Addison-Wesley Publishing Company, 1993

*The Knowledge-Creating Company* by Ikujior Nonaka and Hirotaka Takeuchi, Oxford University Press, 1995

*Thinking for a Change: Discovering the Power to Create, Communicate, and Lead* by Michael J. Gelb, Harmony Books, 1995

*Training Complex Cognitive Skills* by Jeroen J. G. van Merrienboer, Educated Technology Publications, 1997

## The Indisputable Value of Diversity

R. Roosevelt Thomas, Jr., makes the point in his very important book, *Beyond Race and Gender* (AMACOM, 1991), that within the last decade our approach to diversity in the workplace has changed from one of "assimilation" to one of "valuing diversity" and its extension, "managing diversity." By valuing he does not mean some soupy, vague "respect everyone" sort of platitude, but rather a business person's perspective on finances, customer service, quality, innovation, and a host of other rewards that can be realized because of a well-developed diverse workforce.

It used to be that persons who were obviously different from the majority of workers were simply expected to "fit in"—that is, to be assimilated into the mainstream white male workforce. Thomas makes the astute observation that those instructed to fit in were generally stifled from ever being able to be themselves, to contribute what they perceived as their strengths, or to be free to generate innovative ideas from their own special intellectual and cultural experiences. Roosevelt Thomas's entire book is a guide to not only valuing diversity of all stripes, not just racial and ethnic, but also to managing the workplace in order to release the creative and productive potential of a rich human network of talent, motivations, skills, ideas, and competencies. One of the great resources of a learning organization is a diverse workforce. Training managers, particularly, are often called upon to facilitate the release of this potential. Getting rid of an "assimilation mentality" is your first step toward success. Another book by R. Roosevelt Thomas, Jr., is also worth reading: *Redefining Diversity* (AMACOM, 1996).

## "The Fifth Discipline"

Peter Senge in 1990 started what has come to be a quiet revolution in the way managers think about the purpose of organizations. In his bestselling book *The Fifth Discipline: The Art & Practice of the Learning Organization* (Doubleday/Currency, 1990), Senge popularized two very important ideas: (1) that of "the learning organization" and (2) the idea of "systems thinking," or as Senge names it, "the fifth discipline."

Corporate America has embraced the learning organization as a goal as well as a process, and throughout the decade we've seen numerous examples of companies and nonprofits that have tried various approaches to becoming learning organizations. Professor Victoria Marsick of Columbia University, and ASTD itself, has done considerable work since 1991 in finding and tracking the progress of companies and organizations who call themselves learning organizations. ASTD's work in this regard is summarized below. Peter Senge is known throughout the world for his celebration of the workplace as a learning place.

What is not so enthusiastically embraced or practiced is Senge's idea of "the fifth discipline," or systems thinking. In his book, he makes impassioned pleas for us to see the world as a whole. He even says that "it should come as no surprise that the unhealthiness of our world today is in direct proportion to our inability to see it as a whole" (p. 68). He argues for systems thinking as a discipline for seeing wholes, interrelationships rather than things, patterns rather than snapshots. He makes the convincing argument that systems thinking is needed more now than ever before because our world is so complex, and all around us is evidence of systems breakdowns. Senge's focus on wholes is often translated into such slogans as "think globally, act locally," or "see the forest as well as the trees," or "bring the whole into the parts."

Trainers should resonate with Senge's thinking, but too often we have not taken the initiative to learn what the big picture is. Trainers have often been accused of getting mired in the small stuff. Building a learning organization won't happen because it seems like an obvious "Motherhood and apple pie" kind of thing; it takes perspective, vision, hard work, and persistence. Senge started it all; now it's up to us to keep it going.

## ASTD's Benchmarking Forum

Since 1991, the American Society for Training and Development (ASTD) has been systematically tracking fifty companies on a variety of "best practices" in an attempt to codify what behaviors lead to changes that foster learning and improve performance. *ASTD's Guide to Learning Organization Assessment Instruments,* published in 1996, describes specific methods, many of which have come out of the experience base of companies in the Benchmarking Forum, for assessing learning organizations. Instruments focus on the individual, the team or group, and the organization. Check the ASTD Web site at astd.org or by phone at 703-683-8100.

### If You Have Limited Budget and Staff . . .

For about $150, you can purchase the books referenced in the above paragraphs and begin to fill your mind and spirit with new ideas. For no money at all, you can use these books as action guides, and with a little bit of prudent risk taking and a lot of faith, you can start to make changes. For the price of a telephone call or e-mail connection, you can talk with people at ASTD in Alexandria, Virginia, who can help you become part of a network of persons at your particular level of change-making.

## If You Have Adequate Budget and Staff . . .

If you have the time and staff resources to experiment with new organizational arrangements, you might consider freeing up your resident in-house instructor staff to meet one-to-one with supervisors and managers to help them understand and set learning goals for the individuals and groups within their organizations.

Another idea is to formalize a coaching or mentoring program of "training the trainers," whereby your instructional staff pairs up with team leaders, managers, or supervisors to continuously help them become teachers and learners.

Another possibility is for you, the training manager, to personally interview each person in your training organization regardless of job assignment or level in order to find out exactly what each needs to do his or her job to peak performance. Then make it your mission to go find the resources they said they needed—budget, hardware, software, personnel, skills, contacts, furniture, space—whatever it takes. Listen to their language; don't impose what you think they need. Act as a facilitator and provide support. Be an advocate for the individuals in your own organization as they become more competent. And . . . expect them to go and do the same throughout the company.

# 2

# How to Make the Most of E-Learning

E-learning is here to stay in some form. Business literature is often full of stories of learning successes and cost savings because of e-learning; it is sometimes also full of stories and commentaries about failures and problems. In this chapter, we try to present e-learning in perspective as it is going through evolutions in hardware, systems, and content. Our focus here is to help the training manager make the most of what we've learned about e-learning.

**KEY MANAGEMENT ISSUES**

- ***Blended Training.*** Training managers are faced with the classic dilemma of building on the best of educational psychology and learning theory, yet taking advantage of all that's new and truly helpful in enabling computer hardware, software, and systems. The current call is to find a "blend" of the old and the new—high touch and high tech together. But how?

Answers might be found in studying the differences between instruction, generally defined as trainer-designed and -delivered, and learning, generally defined as a process inside an individual that enables one to work better, faster, and especially smarter. There are some kinds of things that people need to know that clearly benefit from instructional design and instructional management. Many of these things are informational in nature—announcements, descriptions of products, information about training opportunities, reports of competitors' work, information about new employees, scenarios and case studies, scholarly papers and conference information—and they can very usefully become part of e-learning. Information-based materials can provide background information, be a library-type repository for just-in-time referral by learners, and provide motivation to look further and to keep learning. These kinds of things are designed and managed by an instructional system, a key part of an e-learning endeavor.

Instructional design of courses and learning activities definitely have a role in e-learning too, but designers are cautioned not to create psychologically restrictive online learning experiences that quickly bore the e-learner or waste time. And, of course, there must be a balance between information and instruction so that one supports the other for learning. A good lesson to be reminded of is that of the classic technology versus psychology lesson of PowerPoint misuse. Just because the bells and whistles are there, doesn't mean they are appropriate or even useful for learning.

There is a great deal of business press being devoted to new models for learning, based on what we know of the educational psychology of the past and the promise of advances in computers and systems. This dialogue generally is known as the "blended training" dialogue. It refers to preserving the classroom as a site for person-to-person live interaction and stimulation for problem-solving that is seen as one of the classroom's strengths. Blending, therefore, can encompass a variety of learning approaches: informational online self-study, video or CD–based online viewing and reaction, synchronous and asynchronous discussions, lectures, reading, workbooks, training games, coaching, mentoring, workshops, and conferences. The savvy training manager will begin to see his or her job as designing, developing, and managing the blend.

■ ***Collaboration: Extending Resources and Opportunities.*** Under the banner of "collaboration," training managers are challenged to become more important voices for extending the resources of the business and creating opportunities for the business through learning. E-learning has opened the eyes of senior management to the possibilities for greater influence, especially in the 24/7 anytime-anywhere potential for online learners to get together. Asynchronous designs have collapsed time zones across the globe; laptop access has enabled learners to sign into courses or log on to information no matter where they are. Scalability is an especially attractive feature. Online collaboration across companies, stakeholders, divisions, and among individuals means more influence and opportunity. Training managers have a new opportunity to help drive the business rather than just react to it.

Beyond this influence function, the training manager also must pay attention to staffing e-learning design and delivery with competent persons. It's a good idea to examine the skills such staff needs—such as designing for motivation, maximizing online socialization of learners, facilitating information exchange between e-learners, and building and verifying acquisition of knowledge. Those staff who function as e-trainers or e-facilitators need to know how to encourage, support, and give feedback to e-learners. Collaboration for building a learning environment online is a new responsibility of the training manager.

■ ***Content.*** The main complaint about e-learning content is that it is often shallow. In the rush to get e-learning products to market, new companies often focus mostly on hardware and software, minimizing content issues or worse, trying to sell clearly inferior content with their new systems. Many such companies are no longer in business. Old companies too fall into the trap, and simply key into some format or course template from the old courses they had hanging around for years. Obviously this doesn't work either. Academics, too, do not escape, and often are accused of simply putting their lectures onto a web page and calling it e-learning. Learners then rebel, and a cry goes out for content experts and instructional designers.

Obviously content for learning online is a mix of information, instructor-designed material, and on-the-spot kinds of aha! experiences that come from intense independent study or from interaction and collaboration with other e-learners. Two major trends are contributing to the growth and depth of e-learning content: 1) the integration of performance support into job functions so that learning can hardly be avoided when one is doing the job, and 2) the creation of learning objects and learning content management systems to manage them. The goal is to embed knowledge into the tasks of a job and to provide both the content and the process for learning what you need to know when you want to know it.

The work in developing learning objects has been promoted heavily by the Department of Defense and its Advanced Distributed Learning (ADL) initiative. Before the learning object can be developed, ADL reasoned, standards for its content and the processes for effective use of content had to be in place. In the creation of these standards, ADL collaborated with the White House Office of Science and Technology, the Institute of Electrical and Electronics Engineers (IEEE), the Information Management Society (IMS), and the Aviation Industry Computer-Based Training Committee (AICC) to devise the framework for the content standard that has become known as SCORM, the Sharable Content Object Reference Model. Refer to the ADL Web site—adlnet.org—and the Appendix of this book for more information.

■ ***Growing Pains.*** When version one of SCORM was made public in January 2000, the word for "content" was "courseware." Over the months, it became apparent that content was the real issue, and the word was changed. This vocabulary lesson speaks of a deeper concern over how to make content reusable by a variety of learners. The clash with learning styles, what a learner brings in terms of experience in that content, the appropriateness of the content design to the e-learning format, choices in delivery mode—all these and more were issues uncovered by the collaboration spawned by the ADL and the user feedback from companies that used SCORM standards.

Other content issues that training managers have to contend with are those associated with cleaning out the old courses. A major problem is that it is often quite apparent that major parts of the old course are much better delivered as online information, as support to the classroom learner. Redesign of existing courses is a challenge and is part of the growing pains of making the most of e-learning.

Other growing pains include the integration of existing knowledge management systems for archiving, scheduling, reporting, and learner evaluation with learning content management systems. These new systems devote attention to such processes as pretesting, creation and use of course design templates, storing, accessing, and sharing learning objects, and customizing content for individual e-learners.

Research on how learners learn online is rather thin. E-learners complain that they are expected to spend personal time learning, whereas previously, they could attend a classroom on company time. Training managers complain that e-learners seldom complete courses they begin. E-learners complain that online courses are boring and a waste of time, and that they encourage playing around—doing e-mail, lurking in chat rooms, forwarding parts of courses to friends or to their own files. They also complain that they can't make their systems work and that navigation is slow or troublesome. Training managers complain about high costs and hidden costs, vendor hype, lack of system compatibilities, and lack of bandwidth to do everything they want to do. Both e-learners and training managers complain that it's hard to know whether e-learning experiences transfer to improvements in the business.

Cost savings, performance improvements, productivity increases, and increased reach and access to learning opportunities are all promises of e-learning. Some companies are reporting successes; many others are still struggling.

# Chapter 2 Checklists
## To Make the Most of E-Learning

The following checklists will help you to think about training in a new way—a "blended" way. The focus is not on stand-up training and overheads but rather on customized learning experiences for all of the stakeholders in the training department. This includes employees, customers, suppliers, and perhaps even politicians and community leaders of importance to the company. With e-learning, much more is possible for less time and money when it is blended appropriately with face-to-face learning experiences in classrooms and workshops and when you remember that technology is only a tool. Making the most of e-learning means defining the best of many training delivery systems and using e-learning when and where it simply is the best way for people to learn.

**LIST OF CHECKLISTS TO MAKE THE MOST OF E-LEARNING**

- **2.1** The Training Manager's Checklist for E-Learners' Successful Transition from the Classroom to E-Learning
- **2.2** Tips for Easing the Growing Pains
- **2.3** Primary Characteristics of Learning Objects
- **2.4** Working with a Learning Content Management System (LCMS)
- **2.5** The Training Manager's Readiness Checklist for E-Learning

# E-Learning Checklist 2.1
## The Training Manager's Checklist for E-Learners' Successful Transition from the Classroom to E-Learning

The most important thing when introducing e-learning is to focus on learners' needs. The following points are guidelines to help you, the training manager, help learners make a successful transition to e-learning. Classroom biases and habits will remain, so be sure to take learners from where they are, acknowledging their grounding in the classroom.

_____ 1. Make sure the learner knows how much time is typically required for an online course. Be realistic from the very beginning.

_____ 2. Be sure the learner knows how to use the hardware. If necessary, provide a coach, help line, or classroom or online training before the e-learner begins the course.

_____ 3. If there are technology options, be sure the learner understands how each works and what to expect of each in terms of the learning process.

_____ 4. Promote and advertise e-learning. Tell success stories. Encourage experimentation and learning from mistakes.

_____ 5. Help e-learners get out of a course if it is not right for them, without embarrassment or performance repercussions.

_____ 6. Encourage just-in-time learning; let e-learners know that e-learning time is company time and is not meant to impinge on personal time.

_____ 7. Focus on the business reasons for e-learning.

_____ 8. Be sure that e-learners know how to enter and exit an e-learning experience and account for what they've learned.

# E-Learning Checklist 2.2
## Tips for Easing the Growing Pains

Here are some tips for managers as you deal with the changes in systems focus as you introduce e-learning.

_____ 1. Remember that technology is a tool. Guard against overzealous sales pitches. Buy what you need for learning, and be sure to have the salesperson demonstrate all features of the technology so that you can make an informed decision.

_____ 2. Identify your business need for e-learning and focus relentlessly on it.

_____ 3. Tell your stakeholders about your venture into e-learning; keep them continuously informed. Be sure that internal departments, key individuals, and external collaborators are all aware of what you're doing. Send reports and newsletters, and have online information that they can access to become part of the e-learning experience.

_____ 4. Be aware that you are instituting cultural change with the introduction of e-learning and the expectation that employees will want to learn that way. A major internal marketing effort is necessary. Develop a formal plan, with timelines and evaluation points, to accomplish marketing to your learners.

_____ 5. Do some research on online learning. Current studies suggest that e-learners prefer spending only about an hour to an hour and a half online at one sitting. If learning objects are used, these are generally short—about fifteen minutes each, to be used alone as just-in-time learning or to be put together in sequences appropriate for particular learners.

_____ 6. Think of all workplace learning as a competitive advantage. Structure e-learning for product, process, and price advantage to the company.

# E-Learning Checklist 2.3
## Primary Characteristics of Learning Objects

The Appendix to this book includes information about SCORM standards and their development. The "c" in SCORM stands for content. Whether you use these content development and deployment standards or some other standards, or create your own, there are some primary characteristics of a learning object that you need to adopt. A learning object:

_____ 1. Contains one learning objective for the learner.

_____ 2. Is self-contained within its own structure.

_____ 3. Introduces or describes itself to the learner.

_____ 4. Is easily accessible and easily navigable.

_____ 5. Is reusable and shareable within and between courses.

_____ 6. Is modularized and consistent in format with other corporate learning objects, but varied in levels of learning that are built in.

_____ 7. Is designed with high levels of cognitive motivation to avoid becoming boring.

_____ 8. Is part of a management system for tracking and evaluating each learner's progress.

# E-Learning Checklist 2.4
## Working with a Learning Content Management System (LCMS)

The term "knowledge management system" has been around for a few years, and now we are seeing a subset of that idea with "learning management system." This typically refers to the administrative functions around and outside a course such as scheduling, cataloging, tracking, archiving, reporting, testing, and connecting e-learners to e-learning experiences. The Learning Content Management System (LCMS) is a system to manage what happens inside a course. The following list contains some typical features of an LCMS. Use this checklist to check your LCMS. A Learning Content Management System:

_____ 1. Is set up to accommodate many users, including designers and learners.

_____ 2. Provides templates for course design that are sophisticated enough for your use.

_____ 3. Provides formats for instructors to insert their individuality.

_____ 4. Stores and moves learning objects according to learner needs.

_____ 5. Provides precourse learning materials—research studies, case studies, articles, book references, pretests and self assessments, company reports, competitor information, etc.

_____ 6. Provides software for content conversion and system compatibility in order to speed up development efforts.

_____ 7. Tracks learner behavior online in order to isolate difficult questions and pinpoint problem content and offers help to solve the learning problems.

_____ 8. Uses clear and consistent standards in the design and development of all e-learning experiences.

# E-Learning Checklist 2.5
## The Training Manager's Readiness Checklist for E-Learning

E-learning is sometimes entered into in order to save money. As with most training, that's the wrong place to start. Cost savings are a result of the right kind of learning experiences, and those savings often take years to become obvious. This checklist can help you identify the management issues in determining your readiness to begin an e-learning effort.

_____ 1. You have determined a percentage goal and time line for e-learning; for example, you want 10 percent of your courses to be e-learning courses for years one and two; 20 percent thereafter.

_____ 2. You have researched the global implications and needs for e-learning in your company. You understand what the cultural and technical issues are and have plans to deal with them.

_____ 3. You have a plan for hiring design and development staff and vendors. You have checklists for the competencies you seek. You have a plan for interviewing personnel so that they can demonstrate their competencies.

_____ 4. Vendor and development timelines seem realistic and meet your needs.

_____ 5. You realize that e-learning courses have a short shelf life—some say one year, some say two years. You have inventoried your courses to see the extent of your conversion and transition problems.

_____ 6. There is a sufficiently high level of interest in e-learning. If you build it, they will come. It seems to be worth the effort. You've calculated the risk.

# Chapter 2 Forms
## To Make the Most of E-Learning

The forms listed here can help you do some of the critical planning and management tasks to make the most of e-learning.

**LIST OF FORMS TO MAKE THE MOST OF E-LEARNING**

- **2.1** Planning Critical Paths and Milestones for E-Learning Development Projects
- **2.2** Matrix of Blended Content and Process
- **2.3** Team Assignments for E-Learning Development
- **2.4** Development Standards Matrix

## How to Manage Training

**E-Learning Form 2.1**
**PLANNING CRITICAL PATHS AND MILESTONES FOR E-LEARNING DEVELOPMENT PROJECTS**

### How to Use This Form

1. There are thirteen items listed here to suggest the dimensions of planning an e-learning development project. Use additional sheets to add more items.
2. Prioritize the items and give each a target date by which it should be accomplished.

| Priority 1–13 | Target date | |
|---|---|---|
| | | 1. Learn the principles of web design for learning. Find and study examples. |
| | | 2. Learn about the options in and effects of navigational design on e-learning. |
| | | 3. Learn about the options in and effects of instructional design on e-learning. |
| | | 4. Find and hire vendors and additional staff if needed. |
| | | 5. Identify your resource requirements. |
| | | 6. Define staff and vendor responsibilities. |
| | | 7. Design technical hardware, software, and system specifications. |
| | | 8. Define file-naming and other system and content conventions. |
| | | 9. Define what content information will be information-based only. Define what kinds of repositories and archives you want. |
| | | 10. Define what content will be interactive. Identify options. |
| | | 11. Develop content. |
| | | 12. Develop periodic (formative) assessments and final evaluations (summative) for each e-learning experience. |
| | | 13. Pilot-test your work with real e-learners. Revise as indicated. |

**E-Learning Form 2.2**
**MATRIX OF BLENDED CONTENT AND PROCESS**

### How to Use This Form
1. The list below focuses on typical elements of course content and various processes of development and delivery. Add other elements that apply specifically to you. This matrix will help you see the possibilities in blended training.
2. Put a check mark in the cell where you intend to place each element.

Course title: _____

|  | *Web* | *Internet* | *Classroom* | *Other* | *(Notes)* |
|---|---|---|---|---|---|
| Reference materials |  |  |  |  |  |
| Support persons |  |  |  |  |  |
| Pretests |  |  |  |  |  |
| Post-tests |  |  |  |  |  |
| Workbooks/worksheets |  |  |  |  |  |
| Extra credit work |  |  |  |  |  |
| Chat groups |  |  |  |  |  |
| Team meetings |  |  |  |  |  |
| Audio/video |  |  |  |  |  |
| Follow-up to training |  |  |  |  |  |

**E-Learning Form 2.3**
**TEAM ASSIGNMENTS FOR E-LEARNING DEVELOPMENT**

> **How to Use This Form**
> 1. This is a "who" form. Enter development team members' names and emails across the top. Add extra sheets if needed.
> 2. Put a check mark in the cell of the team member(s) responsible for each element of e-learning development.

Course title: _____

|  | Team members' names and emails ||||| 
|---|---|---|---|---|---|
| Name/email |  |  |  |  |  |
| 1. Securing licenses |  |  |  |  |  |
| 2. Putting in place an administrative LMS |  |  |  |  |  |
| 3. Creating content |  |  |  |  |  |
| 4. Producing graphics |  |  |  |  |  |
| 5. Producing audio, including streaming audio |  |  |  |  |  |
| 6. Producing video, including streaming video |  |  |  |  |  |
| 7. Developing interactive online lessons |  |  |  |  |  |
| 8. Instructing/delivering the course |  |  |  |  |  |
| 9. Hosting the course |  |  |  |  |  |

# How to Make the Most of E-Learning

**E-Learning Form 2.4**
**DEVELOPMENT STANDARDS MATRIX**

### How to Use This Form
1. Use this matrix as a monitoring or assessment aid as you develop your catalog of e-courses. Add more titles and characteristics as needed.
2. Make notations in each course cell as appropriate.

| Desirable characteristics of e-courses | Course titles | | | | |
|---|---|---|---|---|---|
| 1. Standards-based | | | | | |
| 2. Learning-centered | | | | | |
| 3. Individually customizable | | | | | |
| 4. Online evaluation | | | | | |
| 5. Collaborative authoring capability | | | | | |
| 6. Collaborative learner opportunities | | | | | |
| 7. Easily accessible content | | | | | |
| 8. Reusable learning objects | | | | | |
| 9. Variety of content | | | | | |
| 10. Nontrivial content | | | | | |
| 11. Widely scalable | | | | | |
| 12. Easily navigable | | | | | |

# Chapter 2
## More Information on How To Make the Most of E-Learning

### Research the Costs

There is no doubt that e-learning is expensive to initiate. As a project, it is one that requires a great deal of up-front investigation and an analysis of needs throughout the company. The savings from e-learning come later—sometimes many years later. The wise training manager will ask a lot of questions from a lot of sources before beginning an e-learning initiative.

ASTD is one source of information at its conferences, on its Web site (astd.org), and in its publications. The July 2002 issue of ASTD's *T+D* magazine lists some e-learning costs on page thirty-one. One of the cautions is to do the math; that is, pay attention to the multiplication and division. Costs are quoted in a wide variety of ways: per student user, per year, per 1,000 users, per author, per course, per content hour per person, per month per user, per add-on service, etc. These are some of the prices quoted in the ASTD article:

| | |
|---|---|
| Off-the-shelf courses | $50 to $1,500 per user |
| Authoring tools | $2,000 to $8,000 per user |
| Training for 1,000 persons or less | $200,000 to $400,000 |
| LCMS for 1,000 persons or less | $100 to $150 per user |
| Maintenance | 15 percent to 20 percent of total cost |

Other good sources of current information are:

masie.com
brandon-hall.com
adlnet.org
imsglobal.org

### Know How You Feel about E-Learning Interactivity and What You Can Do

The major criticisms leveled at e-learning by learners often focus on the triviality of what's online. Learners complain that too often lecture notes are simply copied into an online system, and that this is no learning experience. Learners seem to want face-to-face live interaction with other learners to acknowledge and verify their own learning and to learn how to solve problems. Learners and managers complain, too, that online learning encourages diversion, and that the interactions of classmates seem to help maintain focus. Furthermore, a company's information technology infrastructure is frequently inadequate for the kinds of interactivity that e-learners and instructional designers want, and the I.T. department and the training department often don't talk to each other.

Therefore, the best advice is to listen to instructional designers who work from learner evaluation reports. Know how your workforce responds to various kinds of interactivity: classrooms, dialogue groups, workshops, chat rooms, assignments that require online team work, relationships with customers and suppliers, etc. Know the pluses and minuses of synchronous and asynchronous learning systems. Talk to your I.T. folks: Get to know how they operate. Know the technology capabilities of your company before you begin contacting vendors or developing your own e-courses. Begin where you are, so that you have reasonable chances for success. Know how far you can go with the infrastructure you have, and know how much "blending" you want to do—e-learning and classroom, clicks and bricks, high tech and high touch.

## If You Have Limited Budget and Staff . . .

Focus on information first; go into instruction slowly. Get high-level support for even the most basic e-learning venture. Show how information sharing will be part of your eventual total e-learning project. Create archives and file sharing, and be sure that everyone knows how to access them. Offer coaches and peer-to-peer tutoring throughout the company so that everyone knows what's online and how to get it when they need it. Offer company information to customers and suppliers through e-mail or tie-ins with your company's intranet. Publicize success stories and numbers of users, and promote your information services as a foundation for e-learning.

Go to one national or international conference per year; take along one colleague. Cover as many features of the conference as possible for general information; or, get the conference program ahead of time and deliberately choose only those speeches and workshops on which you want to focus. Attend only those sessions, but attend them together so that you can dialogue intensively about them after the conference. Here are some conferences where you'll find stimulation for e-learning:

- The American Society for Training & Development (ASTD) International Conference and Expo (generally held in June)
- The MASIE Center and partners' E-Learning Festival in Dublin, Ireland (generally held in July) and the MASIE Center and partners' TechLearn (generally held in October)
- The International Society for Performance Improvement (ISPI) Annual Conference and Expo (generally held in April)
- VNU Business Media's Online Learning Conference and Expo (generally held in September)

Browse the Web for information about authoring systems, but make no commitments until you see what's out there and know what your second steps should be. Here's one place to look: college.com. Consider diving into instructional design and course development only after you have an overwhelming proportion of your workforce who have successfully navigated your existing systems and accessed and used the information you put there. Let success drive success.

### If You Have Adequate Budget and Staff . . .

Call in the experts. Contact leaders from the companies you read about in the business press, leaders of whatever title who have had successes with in-depth and large-scale e-learning. Knowledgeable persons can be found in these companies: Cisco Systems, Motorola, IBM, and Ernst & Young, among others. Visit them; talk with e-learners at various levels in the companies. Think about how what they've done can be adapted by your company.

Be prepared to interview a multitude of vendors, many of whom will sound alike and use all of the hot terminology of the e-learning field. Insist on demonstrations of their capabilities and references from other companies that have bought their systems and products. Be ready to discuss tough topics such as standards for quality in course design and user learning experience. Be ready to get heavily involved in learning system architecture; know what you want in terms of instructional design and process. If you require 24/7 around-the-globe e-learning opportunities, be sure that a vendor-developer has had experience dealing with cultural issues. Ask for proof. Take your time and compare the resources out there. Know that companies come and go these days, and that e-learning is still very much in an early evolutionary stage.

Here are a few vendors you might start with:

> click2learn.com
> globalknowledgenetwork.com
> digitalthink.com
> achieveglobal.com
> elementK.com
> docent.com
> mentergy.com
> knowledgequest.com
> learn2.com
> trainersoft.com
> netg.com
> thinq.com
> facilitate.com
> groove.com
> icohere.com
> sitescape.com

# 3

# How to Run the Training Operation

In this chapter, structured aids are provided to help you manage the training operation—the people, the files, and the planning and systems that support your training efforts. Whether you are a new manager, a seasoned manager new to training, or a career manager looking for new ideas, you'll find help here.

## KEY MANAGEMENT ISSUES

■ *Cost Center or Profit Center.* A key issue facing most training managers is whether to position the training operation within the corporation as a cost center or a profit center. Training is generally positioned as a cost center to which other operations of the business contribute funding in the form of tuition or cost per course per trainee and sometimes in the form of a funding floor determined by a formula based on head count or a percentage of the department budget. Training can, however, be positioned, as a profit center. It may be organized as a set of projects, each with a target margin figure, or structured as a minicompany within the larger corporation, with its own profit and loss statement and other standard financial controls.

Especially if you are a manager just setting up a training operation, consider this issue of cost center versus profit center carefully. It's easier to set up as a cost center, but that means that in the big picture, your operation will be seen as an expense to the corporation and you will always need to justify what you do. On the other hand, if you contribute direct profit to the company as a profit center, you will be seen as a valued function with direct and positive bottom line impact. To do this, however, training managers must become involved with systems and processes throughout the company—customer service and product development, planning and control processes, recruitment and retention, and support systems like marketing, research and development, and financial systems. Simply put, you have to get out of the training department to responsibly run the training operation.

■ ***Make or Buy.*** The fundamental course development issue facing most managers is whether to "make" the training yourself from scratch in your own shop or to "buy" it from a vendor or consultant. This issue has great implications for your budget and staffing decisions. Among the things you'll need to consider are these: Do you need to hire instructional designers? Do you need to hire instructors? Does your staff need project management expertise? What will be your staff's relationship with subject matter experts? What's a fair price to pay for a vendor-developed delivered course? How can you assure quality in course development and delivery? What percentage of your budget should be paid to outsiders, that is, to nonemployees? Can your training budget afford the benefits paid to employees? How much expertise do you desire to have under your own umbrella? How much do you prefer to have housed elsewhere, to be transferred in to you only when you need it? Is it more cost-effective to make instruction or to buy it? Should you outsource any of it; and exactly what will be lost or gained if you do? Chapter 4 deals with these questions in greater detail.

■ ***Quality.*** How to manage quality in the training operation is a critical issue, especially if you choose to rely heavily on courses designed and delivered by vendors and consultants. It is easier to develop quality design standards and to control their use when your staff includes instructional designers and writers as full-time employees. In addition, you must resolve larger quality issues that influence whether training is viewed as an employment opportunity or as a requirement of employment tied to performance reviews and pay considerations. Producing quality products such as manuals, job aids, videos, and slides is one kind of challenge; another challenge is producing quality processes in training that are creative, focused, and on schedule and instructional processes that feature facilitative, well-informed, and excellent teachers. It's important, too, that you have procedures in place to ensure quality in the work of "telecommuters" and part-time employees working from their homes.

■ ***Ethics.*** A good place to start in running an ethical operation is to determine what your operational values are and to articulate them. If you find that they are not what you think they should be, take steps to change them. Check the incentives you actually are providing for doing good work, and bounce them off the values-driven behaviors that you see. Remember that ethics and law are very different from each other; never assume that if you are following the law you are also being ethical. In the wake of year 2002's ethical scandals in corporate America resulting in fraud and gross mismanagement in Enron, WorldCom, Arthur Andersen, Adelphia, ImClone, Tyco, and others, and the revelations this same year of persistent sex abuse scandals in the upper echelons of the Catholic Church in America, managers of all sorts should have a wake-up call to pay attention to alignment of vision, values, and behavior. Training managers can help significantly in assessing corporate needs regarding ethics because of your human resources development perspective.

- ***Technology.*** Training managers are constantly faced with decisions that deal with technology. How much of your operations should be computerized? Where is human involvement still absolutely essential? Will you have enough students over time to make it worthwhile to buy or to make your own videodisc courses? Which courses are right for electronic delivery devices? How much print support and human involvement are needed even with electronic delivery systems? Do you have programmers and hardware specialists available if systems or machines fail? Do you have either the mainframe dedication you need or the numbers of PCs you require for effective training? Do you have adequate telephone lines and bandwidth? Do you have instructional designers or learning specialists who can advise you adequately, so that you don't have to rely only on information from a supplier's account rep? What is your relationship to your company's management information system manager? Who manages Internet or corporate intranet usage for training? Do you know enough about e-learning? Simulation? The virtual workplace?

- ***The Law and Government Initiatives.*** Training managers must be aware of current federal legislation affecting the workplace. How you run your classrooms, how you provide equal access to opportunities through training, how you give financial incentives for education and training, whom you hire and at what wage, how you reach out to the community in which your company is located, and how you treat the employees who work for you are all important issues that are more and more defined by legislation. These are some initiatives you need to be familiar with:

  - *Post–September 11 Updates to Title VII*—After the terrorist attacks on September 11, 2001, the Equal Employment Opportunity Commission (EEOC) issued a statement updating enforcement of the Civil Rights Act of 1964. In this November action by the EEOC, employers are prohibited from discrimination against individuals of Arab, Muslim, Middle-Eastern, South Asian, or Sikh descent. One of the key and complex provisions of the new statement is a "duty to accommodate" provision, which applies to accommodation based on religious beliefs. Such accommodations typically include dress code modification, time and spaces for prayer breaks, and dietary considerations. A related issue addressed in the November directive is the issue of sexual harassment based on religious or cultural practices. Regarding this issue, the new directive places responsibility on the employer for training, counseling, and disciplining the aggriever, in spite of 9/11–related nationality. Title VII is clear and strong in its protection of workers against these kinds of discriminations and abuses. Training has a new and expanded role in compliance. Fact sheets from the EEOC that provide practical guidance on compliance are available on the EEOC Web site at eeoc.gov. More information can be found at the Society for Human Resource Management (SHRM), particularly in its peri-

odic publications, *Mosaics* and *Legal Report*. See the SHRM Web site, shrm.org.
- *Tougher Law on Sexual Harassment*—In the year 2000, annual claims for sexual harassment skyrocketed to 16,000, 10,000 more than 1990s' 6,000 claims. The Civil Rights Act of 1991 and Supreme Court decisions in the 1990s have imposed tougher requirements on employers to try to stem this trend. Among these are "steps to prevent and correct promptly" sexually harassing behavior. Training is a practice seen by the courts as both preventive and corrective. Attorneys writing in SHRM's *Legal Report*, July–August 2002, state that "a carefully crafted, effectively executed, methodically measured, and frequently fine-tuned employment practices *training* program is a powerful component of a strategic Human Resources Development (HRD) plan. . . ." They state that the human and financial costs of neglect are serious, and that the benefits are foundational to long-term success of a company.*
- *No Child Left Behind Act*—The George W. Bush administration has been known for its accountability emphasis in corporate and public life. Amidst what is often reported as a plague of underachieving and failing schools and children who can't read, write, or do basic math, Congress passed new legislation in 2002 to improve accountability by school districts for their students' learning. In cities, especially, educational standards and learning opportunities are seen as too low; the new legislation is intended to correct this. For example, in New York City, a basic education is defined as one that "will prepare students to vote, to hold low-level jobs, and to serve on a jury."† Courts and business groups are questioning whether this is enough to encourage workplace learning and enhance productivity. The Conference Board in New York City, for example, has an annual Business and Education Conference where collaboration between business and the public schools is discussed. Contact the Conference Board's Customer Service number (212-339-0345) for information about this conference and for conference reports that could be useful to you. Critics of "No Child Left Behind" say that enforcement will be difficult, and that funding incentives are slim, although funding for assessment and testing in basic literacy and math skills is expected for 2003. Watch for training managers to get involved in this dialogue.
- *Family and Medical Leave Act, FMLA* (1993)—Provides up to twelve weeks of unpaid job-protected leave to eligible employees to allow them to care for ill immediate family members. Of interest to train-

---

*W. Kirk Turner and Christopher S. Trutchley, PHR, "Employment Law and Practices Training: No Longer the Exception—It's the Rule" in *Legal Report*, Society for Human Resource Management (SHRM), July–August 2002, p. 1.

†Robert F. Worth and Anemona Hartocollis, "Johnny Can Read, but Well Enough to Vote? Courts Grapple with How Much Knowledge Students Need as Citizens" in *The New York Times*, June 30, 2002, p. 21.

ing managers is the "protected" language, meaning that opportunities such as specialized training must be offered equally to an employee on "family leave" as to an employee on the job. Write to the U.S. Department of Labor, Employment Standards Administration, Wage and Hour Division, Washington, D.C. 20210 for more information. A change is anticipated for the near future to include small businesses of 25 employees. If this change will affect your company, you'll need to develop information and training programs to be in compliance with the law. See the Department of Labor's Web site, dol.gov.

- *Federal Minimum Wage*—As of September 1, 1997, the minimum wage is $5.15 per hour. Rules for child labor and overtime pay are also included in the legislation. Request a copy from the U.S. Department of Labor at the above address or by phoning 1-866-487-9243. State laws often have a minimum wage higher than the federal $5.15, in which case the higher wage applies. For state laws, see this Web site: dol.gov/dol/toprequested.htm. To speak to someone about wage and compliance issues, phone the toll-free call center at 1-866-4USA-DOL.
- *Equal Employment Opportunity*—In addition to legislation (1964) preventing discrimination based on race, color, religion, sex, and national origin, newer legislation protects wage equity between men and women and protects employees age 40 and over (1967) from discrimination in "hiring, promotion, discharge, compensation, terms, conditions, and privileges of employment." A 1974 law provides that "affirmative action" be taken to "employ and advance in employment" Vietnam era veterans and other specially qualified disabled veterans.
- *Americans with Disabilities Act (ADA)*—The 1990 Americans with Disabilities Act protects those with disabilities against all forms of employment discrimination, and provides that the employer must make "reasonable accommodation" to allow that disabled employee to be productive to his or her full capacity. Training rooms, computer desks, conferences, field trips, and visual and media aids all become affected by the "reasonable accommodation" provision. Recent court decisions regarding the ADA have generally favored employers in accommodation questions. As with sexual harassment prevention, in accommodation for employees with disabilities, the courts are viewing that upholding the law depends upon information and training. As of court actions in 2002, employers who prove that these measures are in place and working equitably are generally favored against accommodation claims. This is a trend to watch, particularly because it places so great a burden on training as a solution to the perceived problem of lack of accommodation. Clarification of these EEOC laws is available from the U.S. Equal Employment Opportunity Commission (EEOC), 1901 L Street, N.W., Washington, D.C. 20507, 800-669-4000.

- *Occupational Safety and Health Act of 1970*—Protects employees and employers alike from "recognized hazards" in the workplace. OSHA inspectors are required by law to give both an employer and an employee representative the opportunity to be present during an inspection. Employees are required to comply with safe procedures on the job. Stiff fines are assessed for violations. More information is available from OSHA's 24-hour hotline, 1-800-321-OSHA, or through regional offices listed in the telephone book.
- *Polygraph (lie detector) Testing*—Federal law prohibits most private employers from using polygraph testing for pre-employment screening or during the course of employment. This kind of testing (mental and physical) is an issue to watch in the years ahead. Psychological testing and drug testing are two hot topics in many places; invasion of privacy is often at issue here. In terms of training applications, training managers must be careful to use testing and evaluations for only demonstrably job-related performance measurement. More information on polygraph and other testing of employees is available from the U.S. Department of Labor at the above address.

In addition to these specific pieces of legislation, there are current legislative debates going on that will affect how you manage the training operation. These are some of the issues in flux:

- *Employer-provided education assistance*—The debate centers on tax breaks offered to employers for paying tuition and other education expenses for employees. As of now, there is a cap of $5,250 per employee for undergraduate education. Graduate education is no longer covered. Watch for this debate to continue as American politicians debate the nation's "educational preparedness" issue in the coming years.
- *Government jobs programs*—Consolidation of federal jobs programs is an item probably destined to stay mired in partisan politics. Democrats want separate funding for programs for "the disadvantaged" and for "school-to-work" programs; Republicans want block grants to the states. Meanwhile, numerous reports decrying the lack of effectivenss of many job programs seem to keep coming from various sources. Watch for this debate to continue.
- *Welfare reform*—The landmark welfare reform legislation enacted in America is known as the Personal Responsibility and Work Opportunity Reconciliation Act of 1996. The new term "workfare" has come into our vocabulary in 1996, with the first attempt in many years at welfare reform. Many states have experienced success with new models encouraging welfare recipients back into the workforce. Trainers can be expected to play a significant role in workfare programs; this is a debate worth following. New models out of state offices can be expected to proliferate over the next several years.

Watch for provisions to maintain block grants to states at current levels through 2007, thus diminishing their clout; look for legislative restrictions on number of months allocated to training; and pay attention to the current administrative suggestion that a "70-40" rule apply. That is, states would be penalized unless 70 percent of families receiving welfare were working or in certain work-related activities for at least 40 hours a week. Critics of current proposed reauthorization reforms say that states' roles would shift from helping people to find jobs to the more bureaucratic tasks of counting, tracking, and verifying numbers and hours to satisfy the 70-40 directive.*

For more information on legislation of specific interest to trainers, contact: the American Society for Training & Development (ASTD)'s Policy and Public Affairs Division at 703-683-8152 or the Society for Human Resource Management (SHRM) at 703-548-1305.

---

*Mark Greenberg, "Bush's Blunder," in *The American Prospect,* Summer 2002, pp. A2–A5.

# Chapter 3 Checklists

## To Focus Your Attention on Various Aspects of Running the Training Operation

This section contains a variety of checklists to help you manage the training operation. If you are a seasoned manager, you'll find these checklists useful to jog your memory about the details involved in specific operational functions. If you're new to training management, you'll find them a valuable aid to planning and executing the fine points of these operational responsibilities.

A group of forms follows this checklist section. Use them after you review the checklists to get into specific tasks of operations management.

**LIST OF OPERATIONS CHECKLISTS**

- **3.1** Guidelines for Building in Quality
- **3.2** Business Plan Data Checklist
- **3.3** Budget Input Information
- **3.4** Rationale for Hiring Instructional Designers
- **3.5** Rationale for Hiring Training Specialists
- **3.6** Training Staff Design
- **3.7** Considerations in Setting Up Training Files
- **3.8** Training Facilities and Equipment Checklist
- **3.9** Training Scheduling Checklist
- **3.10** Establishing the Visibility of Training
- **3.11** Ethics Checklist

# Operations Checklist 3.1

## Guidelines for Building in Quality

This checklist will be especially useful as you embark on development of new courses or major revision of existing courses. In all training development work, whether with vendors and consultants or with your own staff, be sure to place your efforts in the larger context of current and future business needs.

These items will help you focus on ideas for building in quality as you manage course development and training project implementation.

_____ 1. Tie training goals to corporate goals.

_____ 2. Know your customers' expectations regarding quality.

_____ 3. Be sure all persons working on a training project know the scope and the standards of the project.

_____ 4. Have a bias for action early in the project. Don't spend too much time planning and organizing. Trust your gut after exploring sources and options.

_____ 5. Identify constraints and the effects of each constraint.

_____ 6. Predict the results of risks.

_____ 7. Spend a lot of time identifying your target audience. Check with at least three sources.

_____ 8. Think of each course as a project.

_____ 9. During course development, define problems early and correct problems early.

_____ 10. Count bugs—monitor your own work and strive for fewer errors. Think of errors as your friends.

_____ 11. Get peers involved as reviewers. Use peers to verify and check your perceptions and approaches. Encourage broad ownership of developed courses among your staff.

_____ 12. Communicate process information.

_____ 13. Ask for and immediately use feedback.

_____ 14. Document process information, not just end results, during development.

_____ 15. Define objectives for learners.

_____ 16. Manage and evaluate projects against learner objectives.

_____ 17. Work for transfer of learned skills.

**54    How to Manage Training**

_____ **18.** Break design and development work into projects. Hold a design review of each product as it is completed in draft form. This applies to vendor-developed projects as well as projects developed by your own staff.

_____ **19.** Quantify results whenever possible. Find ways to report successes in terms of numbers.

_____ **20.** Use "before" and "after" measurements. Measure changes.

_____ **21.** Show visible support to others who are working to improve quality.

_____ **22.** Don't give up.

# Operations Checklist 3.2

## Business Plan Data Checklist

This is a checklist of items to research as input data for your business plan. Use it to make sure you cover all bases before creating your plan. Items to research are:

_____ 1. At least six specific ways in which training contributes to corporate growth and profit—backed up with numbers and dollar figures. Specify results.

_____ 2. Corporate values, beliefs, mission, and quality statements. Relate these to training goals and operations.

_____ 3. Clearly defined, specific needs that are addressed by training.

_____ 4. An identifiable market, including potential client lists, for your training products and services.

_____ 5. Dollar figures for projected costs and profit.

_____ 6. Evidence (data, statistics) that you are an excellent manager of training and can carry out the plan you propose.

_____ 7. Data about your competition and reasons why your plan will succeed and theirs won't.

_____ 8. Controls—tasks, time lines, reporting relationships, responsible persons.

_____ 9. Correct titles and locations of persons to whom the business plan will be distributed.

# Operations Checklist 3.3
## Budget Input Information

Use this checklist to help you arrive at essential numbers regarding training costs and benefits.

\_\_\_\_\_ 1. Assign dollar figures to the cost of each problem that will be addressed by training.

\_\_\_\_\_ 2. Figure out how much the training solution will save the corporation. Compare and contrast if necessary.

\_\_\_\_\_ 3. Define in dollars how much the corporation saved in the past by implementing previous successful training programs.

\_\_\_\_\_ 4. Figure out costs of line items (e.g., course design, instruction, hardware, production of materials, online services, promotion and marketing, support, supplies, equipment).

\_\_\_\_\_ 5. Compute course design costs according to this guideline: forty person-days of design and development for each day of class for classroom training. CBT and videodisc course development takes a great deal longer.

\_\_\_\_\_ 6. Compute course delivery costs separately for new courses and for existing courses according to this guideline: for a new course, three person-days preparation for each day of class (including a field test or dry run of the course) per instructor; and, for an existing course, one person-day preparation for each day of class.

\_\_\_\_\_ 7. A rule of thumb for classroom training is to double the development and delivery costs to present the "opportunity lost" costs of having trainees leave their regular jobs to attend class. This figure includes salary and benefits and work not done by the trainee because of attendance at the class.

# Operations Checklist 3.4
## Rationale for Hiring Instructional Designers

Use this checklist as you examine your operational needs and wants regarding the design and development of training. If most of the items listed below mirror your needs and wants, then you probably want to hire in-house instructional designers. Instructional designers often come with doctorate degrees (Ed.D. or Ph.D.) in adult learning, educational psychology, training design, or evaluation, or from universities with master's degree programs in adult education, corporate human resources development, or instructional design.

_____ 1. Your corporation has a strong and well-articulated sense of identity, beliefs, and purpose.

_____ 2. You determine that training can best enhance this sense of identity by being developed in-house, with clear tie-in to the corporate value system.

_____ 3. You are distressed by the quality issues surrounding vendors—how to find good ones, how to guarantee their work, how to be sure that they can talk your language and understand your company quickly without wasting time and money.

_____ 4. You have a commitment to setting quality development standards and developing a monitoring system to ensure that development is done according to these standards.

_____ 5. Your corporation has a very special product or service, such as a strong research and development component, a product or service targeted to a niche market, a unique organizational structure, or clients who require training in using your products.

_____ 6. You believe in the value of instructional systems design, including needs analysis up front and evaluation during the development cycle.

_____ 7. You have gotten over the sensitivities associated with giving and receiving feedback. You are adept at or are committed to becoming adept at using evaluation feedback to improve training.

_____ 8. You want to create your own courses and place them within a curriculum structure that is hierarchical and that makes sense.

_____ 9. You are committed to being a development organization instead of simply a coordinating or administering organization.

_____ 10. You can find instructional designers who are adequately prepared and who fit within your corporate culture.

## Operations Checklist 3.5
### Rationale for Hiring Training Specialists

Use this checklist to determine whether you should hire training specialists as part of your in-house support staff.

\_\_\_\_\_ 1. Your operation is large enough that you can't do all of the work yourself.

\_\_\_\_\_ 2. You're not sure whether you need instructional designers and instructors as full-time employees.

\_\_\_\_\_ 3. You can find competent human resources development practitioners, either company employees or others who have had college preparation in training, organization development, technical writing, adult education, or related fields.

\_\_\_\_\_ 4. You can devise a full-time position for each training specialist you think you need. Duties might include developing vendor contracts; handling registration of employees for courses; organizing training materials such as slides and video libraries; writing the course catalog and promoting training through internal mail, electronic means, in-house TV broadcasts, and newsletters; doing evaluation-form analysis and feeding back the results to instructors; handling maintenance contracts for training equipment; scheduling classroom and conference facilities; and browsing the World Wide Web for training opportunities online.

# Operations Checklist 3.6
## Training Staff Design

This checklist is especially useful for the manager who is new to training or for the training manager who is charged with setting up a new training department. It is a list of points you should consider as you set up your training staff. Use this list to focus your thoughts as you structure your organization.

_____ 1. What is the function of your training organization?

_____ 2. What are the job titles of both professional and nonprofessional staff members that you want to have in your organization?

_____ 3. What are their level designations and salary ranges?

_____ 4. To whom does each staff member report? Is the span of control acceptable according to corporate practices?

_____ 5. How will you deal with the need for new courses? Will you "make" them or "buy" them? Who will do the writing or decide which courses to buy?

_____ 6. Who is responsible for maintaining courses?

_____ 7. What is the procedure for getting help with graphics and word processing?

_____ 8. Do you want tech writers and production support staff within the training department? Or is it more cost-effective to purchase these services through a chargeback arrangement with another internal department or through an outside vendor?

_____ 9. What computerized systems do you need, and who will manage them?

_____ 10. Who is the arbiter of writing style for course manuals?

_____ 11. Do you want instructors as part of your employee staff? Would it be better to rotate them in from other content specialty areas of the business or to hire vendor instructors?

_____ 12. What kinds of evaluation documents will you need and who will be in charge of getting evaluation information, organizing it, and communicating it to the right people?

_____ 13. What kinds of training will your training staff need?

# Operations Checklist 3.7
## Considerations in Setting Up Training Files

A good filing system helps you in four important ways: It keeps straight all the bits and pieces of the complexity of training; it helps you achieve consistency in all communications about courses and operations; it ties in directly to your corporate accounting system; and it helps you budget line items accurately.

In order to ensure thoroughness, it is a good idea to use a three-digit numbering system, using the tens place for major categories (e.g., 110 = Company Orientation Courses) and the ones place for subcategories of the tens designation (e.g., 111 = Benefits Seminar; 112 = Company Clubs and Social Events). Use this checklist to avoid overlooking any major file that has program, budget, and accounting possibilities. Add other categories as your needs dictate. Sample categories include:

_____ 1. Generic Courses and Seminars (e.g., orientation, quality, how to use your PC, good writing, making presentations)

_____ 2. Management Training

_____ 3. Sales Training

_____ 4. Technical Training

_____ 5. Computer Training

_____ 6. Staff Salaries and Benefits

_____ 7. Instructional Materials

_____ 8. Purchased Services

_____ 9. Training Equipment

_____ 10. Facilities

_____ 11. Contingent Employees

# Operations Checklist 3.8
## Training Facilities and Equipment Checklist

This checklist deals with both facilities and equipment because these are the tangible, visible symbols of the viability of the training operation. Facilities and equipment are part public relations and part operations. They provide that important first impression to visitors—your trainees who come to you to learn. Use this checklist as you review your facilities and equipment with the trainee's impression in mind, and make sure that:

\_\_\_\_\_ 1. Training spaces and equipment are clean of fingerprints, coffee stains, crumbs, and scrap papers from previous users.

\_\_\_\_\_ 2. All equipment works.

\_\_\_\_\_ 3. Facilities are environmentally comfortable—temperature is easily adjustable, lighting is good and adjustable, restrooms are nearby, light food and drinks are available, etc.

\_\_\_\_\_ 4. A staff member is available to troubleshoot facilities and equipment problems while trainees are present. Instructors have this person's phone number.

\_\_\_\_\_ 5. If you are using a classroom format, small-group "breakout" spaces are available near larger classrooms.

\_\_\_\_\_ 6. Sturdy chairs with supportive backs and arms are available for trainees during training.

\_\_\_\_\_ 7. Adequate writing space (enough to spread an open $8^{1}/_{2}$- by 11-inch binder plus a note pad) is available, especially alongside computer terminals or PCs.

\_\_\_\_\_ 8. Sightlines from each trainee's desk to all equipment, such as screens, video monitors, white boards, and flip charts are clear.

\_\_\_\_\_ 9. A copy machine is available for trainees and instructors to use during training sessions.

\_\_\_\_\_ 10. Comfortable chairs are available for trainees to rest, reflect, and converse during breaks and after class.

\_\_\_\_\_ 11. Public telephones are nearby.

\_\_\_\_\_ 12. A coat closet or coat rack is nearby and securable during times when trainees are at lunch or out of the area.

\_\_\_\_\_ 13. A facilities floor plan is available for those who want it.

\_\_\_\_\_ 14. Tours of the general corporate facilities are available for those who want to look around after training.

\_\_\_\_\_ 15. Equipment manuals, procedure job aids, and safety information are very visible and easy for trainees to use.

\_\_\_\_\_ 16. Current employment laws and corporate diversity and ethics policies are prominently posted.

# Operations Checklist 3.9
## Training Scheduling Checklist

Generally, a registrar maintains the training schedule; in big training operations, several registrars may be needed to handle large volumes of paperwork or electronic mail associated with running numerous courses and many classrooms at once.

The checklist below contains reminders about the various types of schedules common to training operations. In a small training operation, you, the manager, may have to prepare and maintain the schedule. If you do, here are some guidelines to follow for scheduling classroom training:

**MASTER SCHEDULE**

_____ 1. Each course is coded so that it can be traced to a specific curriculum or program of courses and to an account line item for budgeting.

_____ 2. Each course has a number that corresponds to the catalog numbering system.

_____ 3. Each course has a specified number of meeting days listed on the schedule.

_____ 4. A three-month master schedule is posted for all to see and is updated as necessary. It is part of your employee electronic database available as current employee information.

_____ 5. Course locations, cities, buildings, and classroom numbers are clearly coded on the schedule.

_____ 6. Your name or that of a training contact person is listed on the schedule in case further information is needed.

**MONTHLY SCHEDULE**

_____ 7. A breakdown of each month by day is available at the end of the previous month.

_____ 8. Instructor information is added to each monthly schedule.

**WEEKLY COURSE SCHEDULE**

_____ 9. The instructor completes the weekly schedule and gives it to the registrar for information at least one week prior to class, in case registered trainees need information about topics in the course prior to their arrival for training.

_____ 10. The hours of training, e.g., 9 A.M. to 5 P.M, are clearly spelled out on the weekly schedule.

_____ 11. Break times and lunch times are indicated on the weekly schedule.

_____ 12. Topics for each day are listed in appropriate time slots.

_____ 13. The weekly schedule contains the instructor's name and telephone number, the dates of training, and the room location and number.

**DAILY COURSE AGENDA**

_____ 14. The instructor prepares a daily course agenda for each day of class and forwards a copy to the registrar for file.

_____ 15. The daily course agenda assigns logical learning topics to half-hour or hour time periods. Lunch and break times are included.

_____ 16. A new daily agenda is available for each trainee.

_____ 17. The daily course agenda is posted on the training room door.

## Operations Checklist 3.10
### Establishing the Visibility of Training

For too long, training has functioned in corporations as a support service loosely connected to the "real" functions of the business. It has been easy for trainers to adopt a "receiving end" mentality, always cheerfully giving training to people who said they wanted it, and to ignore the internal communications aspect of training, because training has seldom had to promote itself in its traditional ancillary role.

But the all-important phenomenon of transfer is enhanced when training is clearly related to business purposes. What better way to promote training than to establish training's visibility through the business planning process?

This checklist will help you act more like an initiator of action and manager of training that is tied to corporate goals.

\_\_\_\_\_ 1. You have involved your manager peers throughout the company in your training department's mission and goal statements, incorporating their input in those statements if possible.

\_\_\_\_\_ 2. You have communicated your training business planning documents to your superiors in the company, so that higher management knows that training means business.

\_\_\_\_\_ 3. You have dovetailed your goals and plans with one or more larger corporate goal or plan.

\_\_\_\_\_ 4. You have widely disseminated information about courses, programs, self-study materials, conferences, and other development opportunities to all employees.

\_\_\_\_\_ 5. You have promoted training at all levels in the company through a variety of media, including electronic bulletin boards, electronic mail, videotape, television, flyers, catalogs, memos, and newsletters.

\_\_\_\_\_ 6. You have a planned, organized, managed training information/marketing function reporting to you.

\_\_\_\_\_ 7. You have refined your formats for promoting training by seeking design ideas from graphics specialists, technical writers, and marketing specialists, and you have sought and incorporated feedback on your marketing efforts from users of your training services.

\_\_\_\_\_ 8. You think organizationally; that is, you promote training solutions to identified problems of entire organizations, not just of individual persons.

## How to Run the Training Operation  65

_____ 9. You promote training as a system, requiring commitment of resources at the input side and at the output side. You promote the idea that analysis, evaluation, and feedback are critical parts of the training system.

_____ 10. You offer a variety of training seminars, on-the-job training, classroom courses, computer-based training, off-site courses, and videodisc opportunities in order to spark the imagination of all kinds of employees.

_____ 11. You entice employees at all levels by the interesting and relevant training that you have in store for them. You're not afraid to be a little bit salesy and have fun.

# Operations Checklist 3.11
## Ethics Checklist

Use this checklist as you survey the practices in your company. Responses to these items can become a needs analysis document to help you fix what's wrong. Engage in this exercise from the point of view of training development and learning.

_____ 1. Is this company responsible to its employees and their communities?

_____ 2. Is responsibility to shareholders the only obvious value in this company?

_____ 3. Does the company do work that expresses its values and upholds its traditions?

_____ 4. Does arrogance interfere with good work or compassion?

_____ 5. Does cynicism undermine creative risk-taking?

_____ 6. Does aggressiveness get in the way of assertiveness?

_____ 7. Are the company's core values deeply ingrained and defining the culture?

_____ 8. Are the company's future-focused aspirational values realistic?

_____ 9. Can employees act in good faith to report problems?

_____ 10. Will problems be taken seriously by management?

_____ 11. Will problems be investigated fairly by objective reviewers without penalty to the employee who reports them?

_____ 12. Is there a process in place to handle breaches of faith and to uncover truth?

_____ 13. Are reports of problems handled discreetly and in confidence?

_____ 14. Do employees have the incentive to go to any supervisor or manager, not just their own, with ethical problems that need solving?

# Chapter 3 Forms
## To Help You Run the Training Operation

The operations forms on the following pages provide a structure as you manage critical operations of your organization and provide you with tools for planning and accountability.

**LIST OF OPERATIONS FORMS**

- **3.1** Business Plan Format
- **3.2** Budget Planner
- **3.3** Curriculum Chart
- **3.4** Training Organization Chart
- **3.5** Job Description Form
- **3.6** Course Registration Form
- **3.7** Course Registration Confirmation
- **3.8** Equipment Deployment Form
- **3.9** Facilities Layout

**Operations Form 3.1**
**BUSINESS PLAN FORMAT**

### How to Use This Form
1. This is a sample format for a 20-page business plan for training. For large or complex operations requiring more business analysis and controls, expand sections D and E accordingly.
2. Remember that this plan is based on competitive analysis. Each section, A to F, should make it obvious to the reader that implementing this plan will increase the company's competitive position in the training field.

| | |
|---|---|
| A. EXECUTIVE SUMMARY | 1–2 pages |
| B. REASONS FOR THE PLAN | 2–4 pages |
| C. OPERATIONAL PLAN (issues, dates) | 1–2 pages |
| D. BUSINESS ANALYSIS | 4–6 pages |
| E. CONTROLS (measures, persons) | 2–3 pages |
| F. RESOURCE REQUIREMENTS | 2–3 pages |

The following two pages contain a sample layout of the business plan.

This form originally appeared in *Training Program Workbook & Kit*, by Carolyn Nilson, copyright 1989. It is reprinted by permission of the publisher, Prentice-Hall, Inc., Englewood Cliffs, N.J.

*(continues)*

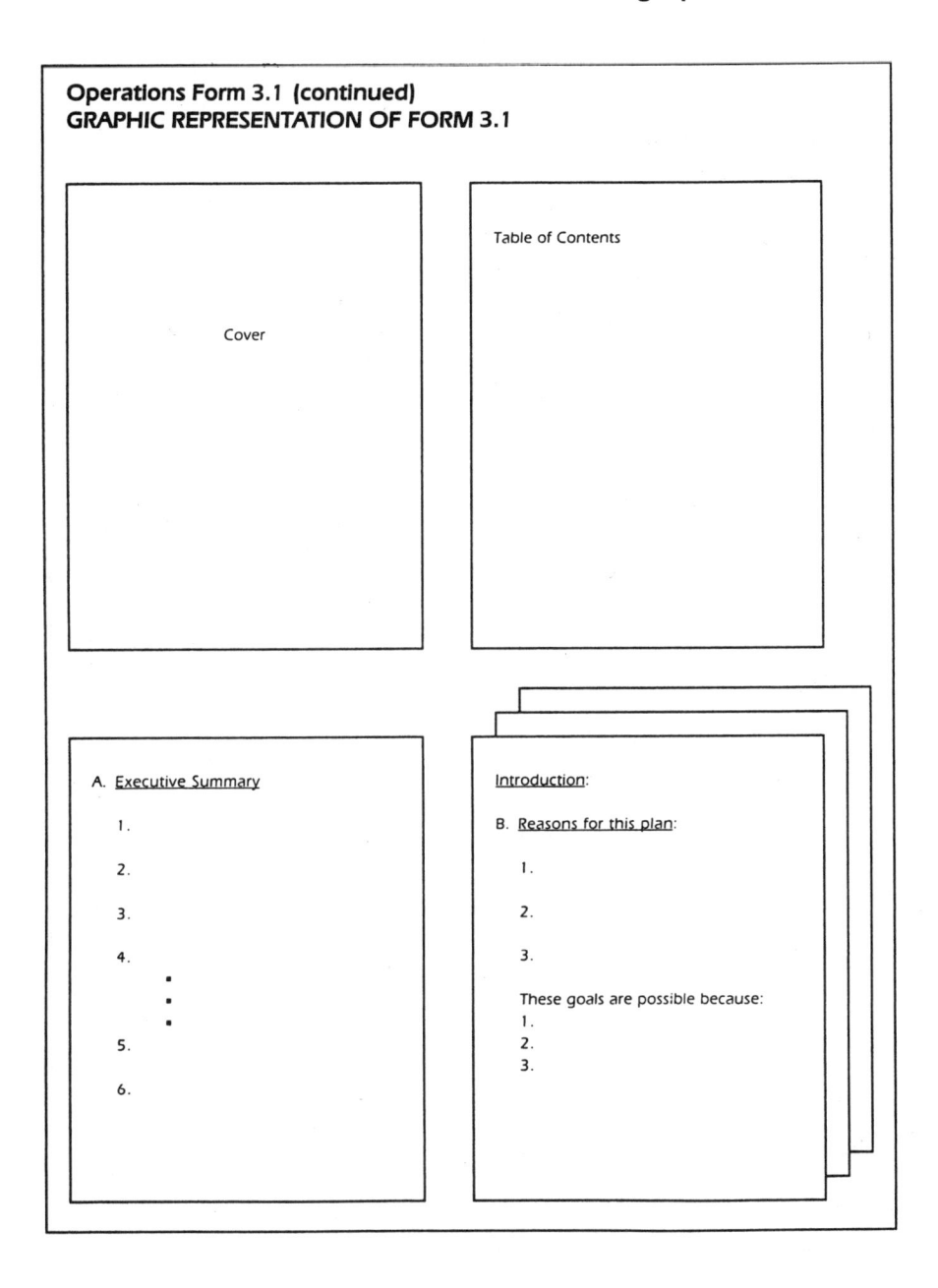

# How to Run the Training Operation

**Operations Form 3.1 (continued)**
**GRAPHIC REPRESENTATION OF FORM 3.1**

Cover

Table of Contents

A. Executive Summary
1.
2.
3.
4.
   - 
   - 
   - 
5.
6.

Introduction:

B. Reasons for this plan:
1.
2.
3.

These goals are possible because:
1.
2.
3.

## 70  How to Manage Training

**GRAPHIC REPRESENTATION OF FORM 3.1**

C. <u>Operational Plan</u>

|  | -15 | -30 | -15 | -30 | -15 | -30 | -15 | -30 |
|---|---|---|---|---|---|---|---|---|
| Decision 1 ... | | | | | | | | |
| Decision 2 ... | | | | | | | | |
| Decision 3 ... | | | | | | | | |
| Decision 4 ... | | | | | | | | |
| Decision 5 ... | | | | | | | | |

D. <u>Business Analysis</u>

- 
- 
- 
- 
- 
- 

E. <u>Controls</u>

| event | date | person responsible |
|---|---|---|
| | | |
| | | |
| | | |
| | | |
| | | |
| | | |
| | | |
| | | |
| | | |
| | | |
| | | |
| | | |
| | | |

F. <u>Resources Required</u>

- 
- 
- 
- 
-

# How to Run the Training Operation 71

**Operations Form 3.2**
**BUDGET PLANNER**

### How to Use This Form
1. Check with your accountant to determine the logical groupings of budget categories according to the latest tax regulations. Design your budget accordingly—make it easy for an accountant to comprehend.
2. Add other accounts to each section, as appropriate.

| FY 200__ | Projected Annual Total |
|---|---|
| Salaries | $ |
| Benefits | $ |
| Overhead | $ |
| Training Equipment | $ |
| Facilities | $ |
| Hardware | $ |
| Software | $ |
| Training Materials | $ |
| Office Supplies | $ |
| Marketing | $ |
| Consulting Services | $ |
| Contingent Worker Services | $ |
| **TOTAL TRAINING BUDGET** | $ |

**Operations Form** 3.3
**CURRICULUM CHART**

### How to Use This Form

1. This chart can help you see the hierarchical relationship between courses. Adapt it as required to reflect your range of courses. This chart is an example; yours will probably be different.
2. Each box represents one course. Arrange your courses to optimize learning by considering:
    - complexity of concepts to be learned
    - complexity of skills to be learned
    - complexity of course materials (e.g. reading level, breadth of application, conceptual or skill dependence on former or future courses)
3. Start with the basic course.
4. Design a curriculum for each major type of training: management, sales, financial, data processing.

Basic-level courses

Mid-level courses

High-level courses

# How to Run the Training Operation 73

**Operations Form** 3.4
**TRAINING ORGANIZATION CHART**

### How to Use This Form
1. This organization chart depicts the levels of jobs typically found in a mid-size training operation; it is included here as a starting point for your own job design.
2. A large training organization will probably have more managers, each with curriculum area specialties (e.g., training in quality techniques, training for basic skills development, management training, sales training, technical training, clerical training). Instructional designers, media specialists, registrar, and clerical staff may be shared by several managers.

```
                          manager

vendor                              instructional        subject
contract         instructors         designers       matter experts
coordinator

editors        graphic artists     multi-media         registrar
                                    specialists

word processing     production
operators/          and packaging                    clerical staff
computer            staff
specialists
```

**Operations Form 3.5**
**JOB DESCRIPTION FORM**

---

**How to Use This Form**

1. The main purpose of this form is to set and describe an individual training job for compensation considerations. Fill out the "level/employee code" and "pay range" lines last.
2. Be sure that biased or discriminatory language is eliminated. Have a trusted colleague review the completed form to ensure that it is not biased regarding equal pay, race, religion, ethnic background, gender, age, handicapping condition, or any other consideration of equal employment opportunity.
3. Differentiate this job from other training jobs in the critical areas of know-how, problem-solving requirements, and range of accountability.

---

Job title: _____ Level/employee code: _____

Reports to (position): _____ Pay range: _____

Major responsibilities:

- Any duty taking up 5 percent or more of one's time
- Quantitative and qualitative results expected
- How much and what kind of efforts are required
- Required supervisory duties and span of control
- Unusual or extraordinary working conditions

Background desired

- Skill requirements
- Education
- Certifications, memberships
- Years of experience
- Personal qualifications

# How to Run the Training Operation

**Operations Form 3.6**
**COURSE REGISTRATION FORM**

### How to Use This Form

1. Send the form to each potential trainee as soon as you receive the first inquiry from that person.
2. Generate this form and the list of potential trainees on your computer so that you can easily follow up any of the information categories on the form.
3. Especially note the "Approval" box. This is particularly helpful in training cost center operations where supervisor buy-in to training is essential and in companies in which charge-back accounting is practiced for internal services such as training.
4. Include a number of blank forms in your course catalog and in employee information racks around the company.

---

**COURSE REGISTRATION FORM**
(Please print or type all information.)

Course Number and Title: _____
Course Dates and Location: _____
Have the prerequisites for this course been met?  ___YES  ___NO

Name: _____  Job Title: _____
Employee Number: _____  Telephone: _____
Work Location: _____  Room Number: _____
Department Name: _____  e-mail: _____
Account Number To Which Training Should Be Billed: _____

**APPROVAL**
I approve this employee's taking this course, and understand that the account number specified above will be charged for this course.

Supervisor's Name: _____  Telephone: _____
Supervisor's Work Location: _____
Company's Name: _____
Supervisor's Signature: _____

Mail this completed form to:

REGISTRAR
Company Name          telephone (XXX) XXX-XXXX
Street Address
City, State, Zip

This course is accessible to handicapped persons. If you require special services, please indicate the kind of service you need:

---

This form originally appeared in *Training Program Workbook & Kit*, by Carolyn Nilson, copyright 1989. It is reprinted by permission of the publisher, Prentice-Hall, Inc., Englewood Cliffs, N.J.

**Operations Form 3.7**
**COURSE REGISTRATION CONFIRMATION**

### How to Use This Form
1. Send this form to the trainee as soon as you receive the course registration form with the supervisor's signed approval.
2. Print it on colored paper, so that it serves as a visual memory jogger to busy employees.
3. Attach a master schedule covering at least 3 months to this form to promote interest in other training.

---

COURSE REGISTRATION CONFIRMATION

Name of registered trainee: _____

Telephone: _____

- - - - - - - - - - - - - - - - - - - - - - - - - - - - - - -

___ Course is Cancelled     Course is Rescheduled for _____

- - - - - - - - - - - - - - - - - - - - - - - - - - - - - - -

You are registered in the following course:

Course Number and Title: _____
Course Dates: _____
Daily Time: _____
Course Location: _____

Please retain this registration notice. It is the only notice you will receive.

If you have questions, please contact the REGISTRAR at (XXX) XXX-XXXX; e-mail XX@XX.com.

If you cannot attend this course, please notify the Registrar at least 15 days before the course is due to begin or the full tuition fee will be charged.

Trainee substitutions are permissible provided the substitute trainee has met course prerequisites.

Thank you for your interest in the Training Center courses. Attached is a three-month master schedule for your future training needs.

---

This form originally appeared in *Training Program Workbook & Kit*, by Carolyn Nilson, copyright 1989. It is reprinted by permission of the publisher, Prentice-Hall, Inc., Englewood Cliffs, N.J.

# How to Run the Training Operation

**Operations Form 3.8**
**EQUIPMENT DEPLOYMENT FORM**

### How to Use This Form
1. Use this form to plan the circulation of your training equipment. A three-month time period is suggested.
2. Use this information to schedule equipment maintenance during slack times of circulation and to project when the budget might need to expand for the purchase of additional items.

THREE-MONTH PLANNER

Course title: _____

Expected dates this course will be delivered: _____
_____

Target number of students per course: _____

| Item of Equipment | Course Location | Needed When A.M.  P.M. | Total Required of This Item |
|---|---|---|---|
|  |  |  |  |
|  |  |  |  |
|  |  |  |  |
|  |  |  |  |
|  |  |  |  |

**Operations Form 3.9**
**FACILITIES LAYOUT**

### How to Use This Form
1. This layout contains all of the basic elements of a training center.
2. As you plan your facilities, include these:

- classroom (for twenty trainees), with at least five PCs
- seminar or breakout room(s) for small groups
- self-study carrels with VCR and small monitor
- lab space
- lounge with telephones, vending machines, a copy machine, and a PC for trainee use
- library of videos, books, journals, manuals
- reception area fully staffed during training
- comfortable chairs with arms throughout
- rectangular tables that can be moved to accommodate U-shaped, square, or theater-style seating.

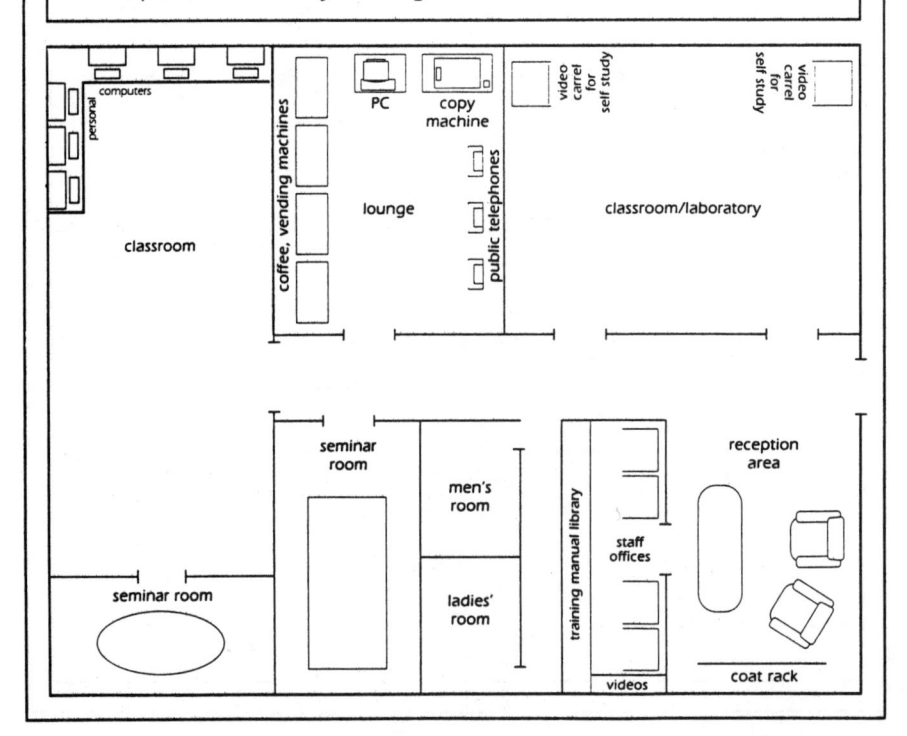

# Chapter 3
# More Information on How to Run the Training Operation

## More on Writing the Training Business Plan

### When to Write a Training Business Plan
Write your plan annually, or even more often, because training has so much potential for contributing to corporate income. It is a business function that is rich in client contact and that has a positive impact on the lives of many people in a company. In addition, the market for training can be very fluid, changing to reflect new ideas in corporate commitments, values, systems, products, legislation, and economic realities, driving growth and change in training operations.

Because the training business plan is market-driven, it is appropriate to write one whenever the training market seems open to a change. This market orientation separates it from an annual plan that follows the calendar year or fiscal year. Don't write a business plan to bring in the new year just because the calendar reminds you that the old year is done.

The training business plan is a market-driven planning and funding document. It is a document of hope, backed up by solid data reinforcing training's potential, operational capabilities, and financial requirements. It should be written whenever the economics of the training market and your operational "smarts" drive it.

### How to Analyze Business Factors
Look at business factors in two essential categories—those outside the company and those within the company. In the Business Analysis section of your plan (Form 3.1, Section D), spell out with clear prose and accurate details the impact of these factors.

Among those factors to consider are these:

| Largely External | Largely Internal |
| --- | --- |
| Competitors' current activity | Corporate financial resources |
| Market segmentation | Profits |
| Availability of market channels | Probable gross margin |
| Stated needs of target customers | Strength of the training organization |
| Probable volume of sales | Projected stages of growth for the new venture |

## Overview of Training and Performance Systems

### Instructional System Design

For several decades, professional training managers have been guided by a management and development methodology known as Instructional System Design (ISD). Since the huge training challenge of defense production training of the mid-1940s, instructional designers, instructors, and especially training managers have measured their training operational results by standards set under the systems approach to training. Countless books, graduate school programs, seminars, and corporate training empires have been built on the solid foundation of ISD.

In a nutshell, the systems approach practitioners refuse to see training as an isolated event; instead, they view it as a set of inputs, outputs, and feedback focused on the needs of the learner for new information and skills. This approach to training management is more popular today than ever before. Figure 3.1 shows the essential components.

**Figure 3.1. ISD instructional system design.**

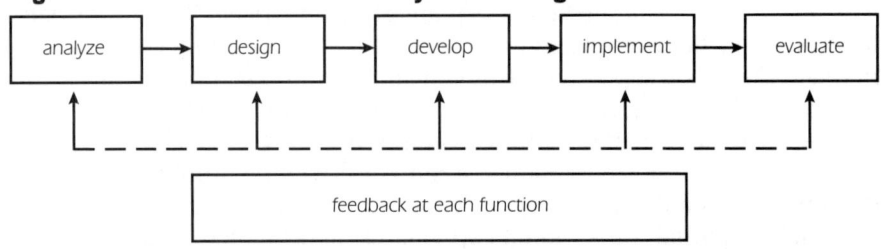

analyze → design → develop → implement → evaluate

feedback at each function

### Performance Technology

The focus and techniques of performance technology are the performance itself—the demonstration of on-the-job knowledge and skills. The key question to be answered is, "Is this competent performance?"

To answer this question, the training manager identifies the obstacles to performance and takes steps to remove them. Often, the training manager discovers that the best solutions are not training solutions; the training manager then becomes a messenger who informs colleagues that other, nontraining problems are adversely affecting performance. These nontraining factors may include outdated motivation or rewards, cliques or company politics, poorly made chairs or bad lighting, unclear communications, impossible procedures, badly timed responses, broken equipment, problems at home, or a host of other factors that can't be solved by all the training in the world.

Performance technologists recognize that training should be saved for those specific situations in which a documented skill or knowledge deficiency can be solved by training targeted at that deficiency. Performance technologists spend a lot of time asking the tough questions, examining the people themselves and the organization in which those people perform their work. When training is the solution of choice, the training manager who holds a performance technologist point of view will, in all likelihood, following the instructional system design methodology to build the appropriate training (see Figures 3.2 and 3.3). ASTD's 1996 Human Performance Improvement Process Model is quite similiar to the ISD model (Figure 3.1) above.

**Figure 3.2. ASTD human performance improvement process model.**

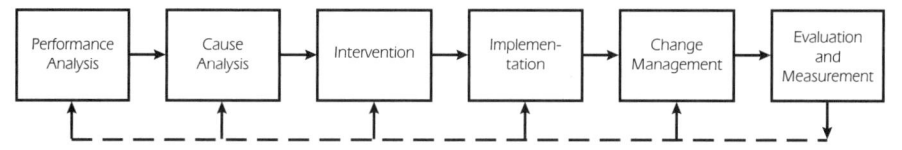

Performance Analysis → Cause Analysis → Intervention → Implementation → Change Management → Evaluation and Measurement

*Source:* Reprinted from William J. Rothwell, *ASTD Models for Human Performance Improvement* (Alexandria, VA: ASTD). Copyright 1996, the American Society for Training and Development. Reprinted with permission. All rights reserved.

**Figure 3.3. Performance technology model (Gilbert).**

|  | Information | Instrumentation | Motivation |
|---|---|---|---|
| Environment | I. Data<br>• Objectives<br>• Directions<br>• Expectations<br>• Feedback | II. Resources<br>• Tools and equipment<br>• Time, money, people<br>• Rules and procedures<br>• Work environment<br>• Organization structure | III. Consequences<br>• Incentives<br>• Penalties/ punishment<br>• Social rewards<br>• Recognition |
| People | IV. Knowledge and Skills<br>• Prerequisites<br>• Technical K&S<br>• Managerial K&S<br>• Knowledge of company and industry<br>• Political K&S | V. Capacity<br>• Physical<br>• Emotional<br>• Intellectual | VI. Motives and Needs<br>• Motivation<br>• Reasons for working<br>• Rewards and preferences<br>• Hierarchy of needs<br>• Career goals |

*Source:* Reprinted, with permission, from *Performance & Instruction*, Volume 27, Number 4, copyright © National Society for Performance and Instruction, 1988.

## Three-Phase Cost Assignment Based on ISD

This budgeting system estimates costs of each line of your training operation in three phases: the development cost phase, the implementation cost phase, and the maintenance cost phase. Training managers sometimes neglect the maintenance costs of processes such as writing a course or marketing a course and often have trouble assigning costs to the development phase of training operations. Three-phase cost assignment can be especially helpful if you are new to training management or if you've had trouble developing a realistic budget. Your budget form should look something like Figure 3.4.

**Figure 3.4. Budget format.**

| Line Item | Development Cost | Implementaion Cost | Maintenance Cost |
|---|---|---|---|
|  |  |  |  |
|  |  |  |  |
|  |  |  |  |

## Task By Objective Accounting

The Task By Objective method of accounting and budgeting is particularly suited to training because of training's focus on learning objectives, program objectives, and personal development objectives.

Task By Objective accounting is a way of planning for expenditures and encumbrances against account totals identified with a specific objective. Because part of the fiscal documentation process involves listing the tasks or cost items associated with accomplishing each specified objective, each Task By Objective budget worksheet contains many different account numbers.

What you learn from this method of budgeting is that you have expended or intend to expend a certain amount of dollars on a specific objective and that after this amount is accounted for, you will have $_____ left in that account.

This kind of planning worksheet for recording current expenditures against objectives can be a valuable input document when you do annual budget projections.

The Task By Objective Worksheet might look like Figure 3.5.

**Figure 3.5. Task By Objective Worksheet.**

Objective: _____

| Task | Account Number | Date | Amount | Account Balance |
|---|---|---|---|---|
|  |  |  |  |  |
|  |  |  |  |  |
|  |  |  |  |  |

## If You Have Limited Budget and Staff . . .

Consider writing a training business plan as soon as you have a good idea for developing your training operation in a new direction—for example, when you want to create an instructional design department, when you want to offer consulting services, when you want to hire e-learning specialists, when you want to add a computer lab and training curriculum.

If you are currently on a tight budget and have very little help or staff, use the opportunity of writing a business plan to build your training operation. A word of caution: Do your homework before putting fingers to keyboard or pen to paper, and support your expansion idea with a strong market analysis foundation. Use the training business plan to validate your growth potential through careful study of the training market.

The first ironclad rule is never to skip a phase of the Instructional System Design methodology if you have chosen training as the solution of choice to your performance problem.

What you can do, however, to save time and money, is to shorten or compress the products of each phase of ISD. For example:

- Use the telephone or e-mail instead of face-to-face meetings to interview key people who can help you identify training needs. If you do this, be sure to use a structured interview schedule so that your questioning is consistent and responses can be analyzed with at least some sense of reliability.
- Tighten the design of a course, making it two days instead of three days.
- Take the instructor to the trainees, not the other way around. It's cheaper to pay one person's travel costs than those of a whole classroom of students.
- Deliver parts of your course via video at trainees' job locations, saving on instructor time and trainee "lost opportunity" time.
- Use wall charts, templates, and job aids instead of trainee manuals.
- Find errors early and conduct design review at many points along the way if you write your own courses. Errors cost much less if you find and fix them early in the development process.
- Give your instructors high-quality clerical help. Don't waste their salaries and energy on tasks they probably don't do very well; save your instructors for the thing that they do well—instruction.
- Create a one- or two-page course evaluation feedback form that can be used in every course; structure it so that responses can easily be tabulated by an evaluation clerk, using PC software for making charts and graphs.

## If You Have Adequate Budget and Staff . . .

Look for opportunities to maximize the talents of your staff and the capacity of your equipment and facilities. In good times around the training department, it is often easy to forget about the special expertise or interests of your instructors or instructional designers. It's easy to get in a rut, having the same people teach the same courses and work on the same kinds of projects, and to use your equipment and facilities in the same way over and over again.

Review the personnel documents filed by your staff at the time they were hired, and study their recent training records to see how you might create opportunities for increased individual contributions to your operation. Look for those hidden talents. Introduce change if you can see a payoff in terms of interest, motivation, expertise, career development, and profit. A large staff provides you with many opportunities for creative programming. A well-managed suggestion box can often yield outstanding ideas for growth. Design and implement a corporate ethics program.

Never assume that your adequate budget and staff will last forever. As you write your training business plan, base the development of training operations on a thorough market analysis, including an incisive analysis of competition. Pay special attention to the analysis of your own internal corporate competition, and make it clear to your reader that training, and not some other department, deserves the lion's share of the budget. And remember, too, that it won't continue to happen without some assertive planning on your part.

- Involve your potential trainees (customers) in your needs assessment deliberations; conduct focused small-group meetings for dialogue and consensus regarding training needs.
- Hire instructional designers, some with e-learning design experience.
- Develop a network of in-process or formative evaluation procedures that are used throughout the design and development phases of ISD.
- Train your own subject matter experts to be instructors; this takes some time but results in more credible instructors.
- Employ a manager or coordinator to be in charge of each phase in ISD—a needs assessment manager, a design manager, a development manager, an implementation manager, and an evaluation manager.
- Be sure that all these managers talk to each other.
- Get yourself a fiscal manager.

# 4

# How to Manage Outsiders

The recent dot-com rise and demise has left a field of vendors and consultants with some very good products and services to sell. In times of economic uncertainty, many talented people choose to work independently of corporate structures, and many training managers can find suitable workers without putting them on the payroll. Escalating healthcare costs to corporations have made managers shy away from adding to the benefits burden of the company, and managers can find in vendors and consultants the kind of focused workers they need.

Experimentation and success in e-learning systems and content have created a whole new dimension to the training and learning function of a company. Academics and professional associations are continuing apace to do research studies on the benefits and pitfalls of e-learning and are discovering some new understandings about how people learn. As with any training, the needs of learners provide the motivation for creating any infrastructure and content for learning. Outside vendors and consultants are also working hard in this area, but, of course, let the buyer beware.

This chapter addresses some of the issues and practices in managing outsiders, especially outsiders with training and learning systems expertise.

## KEY MANAGEMENT ISSUES

Some of the key management issues and practices you should consider when working with training and learning consultants include:

- ***Identifying Company Factors Leading to Outsourcing.*** This issue is often presented as the classic "make or buy" decision. In making this decision, a formal analysis should be done in order to identify factors leading to outsourcing—or leading to developing training from within the company. The first and most important factor involves careful analysis of your employees' needs for new information or skills, and how to transfer knowledge to their work for the benefit of the company. Discovering what people need to learn should comprise the first factor in your deciding to "make" or to "buy." Off-the-shelf, vendor-developed, or consultant-facilitated training programs are among your choices in the "buy" category. But if you don't know the road you're on, the old saying goes, you probably won't get there.

Some training programs are full of proprietary information or the intellectual property of your company and should be developed from within. If you don't have instructional design staff, you might want to consider hiring some in order to protect the competitive advantages your company has built up over the years. A thorough analysis of your various learning opportunities and their impact on the company's competitive position should precede any consideration of outsourcing training in all of its phases—analysis, design, development, delivery, evaluation, and systems support.

Another factor to consider before embarking on a program to hire outsiders is the age and relevance of your current training programs. If you have had only classroom training, you might want to review all of your current courses to be sure they contain only content and processes that still matter to the company. In the age of so many options for learners—interactive e-learning, e-learning alone, video, audio, just-in-time learning, performance support systems, workshops, conferences, and classrooms—the typical trainee has been conditioned to want training fast and on company time. Be sure that your catalog of training programs is relevant.

Some courses and programs are standard fare for most companies and can easily be provided by a vendor or consultant. These might include programs addressing communications skills, negotiation skills, leadership development, and information technology skills, among others. Buying such courses "off the shelf" can save you money and can preserve your staff-building budget. Hiring vendors for e-learning design and development to work with your staff can be a way to assign this area to a "variable cost" budget category that can be more readily adjusted than the "fixed cost" of creating e-learning from within. Outsourcing is not only about finding content; it is also about making good business decisions. But first, it is about meeting the learning needs of your workforce.

■ *The Paperwork of Hiring Vendors: RFPs and Beyond.* The Request for Proposal (RFP) is the document you prepare to give to potential vendors and consultants to show them what it is that you need from them. It is not a contract; it is a statement of need and a description of your company. It is sent in the same form to as many potential suppliers as you want to respond to you with their proposals. Be sure to pay attention to fairness in the solicitation process.

The RFP typically contains company "boilerplate," descriptive information about the company size, organization, technology infrastructure, markets, products, services, mission statement, and statement of future directions. It also contains specific features and functions of what you want in terms of learning outcomes and programs to accomplish them. It contains an accountability outline involving monitoring, periodic evaluations, your desired development and delivery schedules, and a statement of nondiscrimination and nondisclosure.

The RFP also contains specific instructions about how a vendor or consultant should submit the proposal to you. Give guidelines about the criteria you will use to judge proposals, whether or not you want interviews and demonstrations, and the format in which you want their costs itemized. Be as specific as possible, especially in the costs category, so that you can fairly compare proposals when they come in. Consider that possibly you will want only part of a particular proposal; keep all options open and carry out a fair process of rejection. Remember the EEOC.

Keep your executive management informed of your actions; they should know with whom you are dealing. They might also have opinions or information you don't have about supplier reliability and quality. Don't do this RFP process alone; get executive input, intelligence, and support. Ask your purchasing department to review your RFPs; ask your information technology department to check it for being up-to-date.

Be sure to inform those who have submitted proposals to you of your timeline for reviewing them and for making the final decision about whom to hire. Treat all submissions with the same respect; you might need the ones you reject next time around.

■ ***Managing Outsiders Once They're on Your Team.*** Once you have chosen the vendors and issued contracts, and they report on the job, you'll have specific kinds of tasks and outcomes to manage that will probably differ substantially from those done by your own staff. It's important to let your vendors or consultants know what you expect of them in terms of products and services, how they should behave while on your company premises, how their work will be promoted within the company, and how they will be evaluated. It's a good idea to assign one staff member to be in charge of each contract and the people who are sent with it to work with you. A multidepartment in-process review committee is also important, with a major responsibility in providing feedback to the outsider in order to improve the work that's done. Adopt a project management approach for greater accountability.

■ ***Being a Good Client.*** Being clear about what you want is an important first step in being a good client. Being realistic about the stress your department or company is in is also an important consideration. You need to have a good idea of the balance between change management and successful completion of the separate parts of a contract. Don't expect the impossible or more than your contract specifies. Know yourself is the first requirement in being a good client.

Remember that suppliers serve the best clients with the best value because it costs them less aggravation, time, and money to provide products and services. Vendors and consultants want to do a good job for you, and they need your cooperation. This means being honest, communicating throughout the organization, encouraging good working relationships between supplier staff and your own employees, and using your management skills and insider understanding to keep the project moving along on target. Don't abandon your outsiders; give them helpful periodic feedback; help them work to both their and your advantage. Appreciate and facilitate their ability to contribute to the important mission of your new training and learning goals. Allow them visibility and be generous with compliments for jobs well done.

# Chapter 4 Checklists

## To Manage Outsiders

The following checklists help you with the specifics of managing consultants and vendors who are contracted to work with your staff in developing various training projects and programs. Outsourcing is a useful practice in today's world of reduced staffs, increasing benefits' costs, and a proliferation of persons working independently. Managing those who are on contract in conjunction with those who are on payroll is a challenge; these checklists will help.

**LIST OF CHECKLISTS TO MANAGE OUTSIDERS**

- **4.1** Consultant/Vendor Contract Details
- **4.2** The Basics of a Value-Added Outsider Proposal
- **4.3** Ten Strategic Reasons for Outsourcing
- **4.4** Potential Cost Benefits of Hiring Outsiders
- **4.5** Project Management Checklist
- **4.6** Characteristics of a Good E-Learning Supplier
- **4.7** Protection of Intellectual Property

# Managing Outsiders Checklist 4.1
## Consultant/Vendor Contract Details

Use this checklist to be sure you've included important contract details that will help to ensure a clear working relationship.

_____ 1. Several brief sentences describing the project

_____ 2. Succinct description of the consultant/vendor's role: i.e., writing, teaching, coaching, evaluating, etc.

_____ 3. Specific hours the consultant/vendor is expected to work

_____ 4. Consultant/vendor rate (per hour, per day, per contract, per product, etc.)

_____ 5. Overtime and contract overrun restrictions and rates

_____ 6. Travel, lodging, and expense considerations

_____ 7. Provisions for office space, telephone, secretarial help, duplication, and computers and computer support (or none of these)

_____ 8. A single contact person on your staff for the consultant/vendor

_____ 9. Start and end dates for this contract

_____ 10. Billing procedures and copies of forms to be used

_____ 11. Protection of intellectual property statement and nondisclosure provision

_____ 12. A statement concerning acceptability and quality of work performed

_____ 13. Space for contract acceptance signatures, including space for dates and for the titles of the consultant/vendor, yourself, and/or the person authorized to sign contracts and checks

# Managing Outsiders Checklist 4.2
## The Basics of a Value-Added Outsider Proposal

This is a checklist to help you look behind the obvious data in a supplier's proposal. Data about schedules, costs, and content come in many ways. Here are some items to indicate an added value to the proposal data that you've requested. This checklist can help you choose the best among the proposals submitted to you.

\_\_\_\_\_ 1. Evidence of experienced instructional design; deep and varied designs for learning

\_\_\_\_\_ 2. Evidence of quality standards having been used

\_\_\_\_\_ 3. Engaging delivery, without unnecessary "bells and whistles"

\_\_\_\_\_ 4. Only the content you specified in your RFP

\_\_\_\_\_ 5. Provision for independent learning, either online or offline

\_\_\_\_\_ 6. Monitoring of learning; formative evaluation of learners

\_\_\_\_\_ 7. Evaluation and evaluation reports at the end of learning (summative evaluation)

\_\_\_\_\_ 8. Internet and intranet access to e-learning courses and information

\_\_\_\_\_ 9. Cost structure that is advantageous to you and reasonable for the supplier

\_\_\_\_\_ 10. Clear, descriptive language that refrains from judgmental opinion or bias

\_\_\_\_\_ 11. Provision for feedback, reflection on results, and follow-up for learners

# Managing Outsiders Checklist 4.3
## Ten Strategic Reasons for Outsourcing

It is easy to get carried away with a beautiful sales pitch, especially in these days of so many pitches from which to choose. Like the pharmaceuticals salesperson bursting in on doctors and patients and handing out samples, the training supplier seems to be everywhere. Sometimes this is a good thing. The trick for the training manager is to keep thinking strategically and to buy with strategy-based consumerism. This checklist gives you ten typical strategic motivations for outsourcing. It can spark your imagination to add more.

_____ 1. Competency superior to that of your staff

_____ 2. Obvious potential for increased use of needed training

_____ 3. The vendor's brand is a leader in the industry, to your benefit.

_____ 4. Changes in state or federal laws

_____ 5. An internal need to develop capacity

_____ 6. An internal need to facilitate collaboration among staff and between departments

_____ 7. A time crunch

_____ 8. A personnel hiring freeze

_____ 9. Mitigation of business risk

_____ 10. Asset transfer from salary to expense

# Managing Outsiders Checklist 4.4
## Potential Cost Benefits of Hiring Outsiders

The list below contains potential cost benefits of hiring outsiders. Add more items as appropriate to your company. Review the list before writing your Request for Proposal (RFP).

_____ 1. A temporary work overload for your staff makes hiring outsiders reasonable because their work can be terminated as soon as it is delivered, without having to put another person on the payroll.

_____ 2. You are a one-person training department with a sizable development mission. It makes sense to hire outsiders to get started in accomplishing your goals, until you see exactly what kinds of staffing and salary expenses to expect.

_____ 3. Leasing technical capacity and development experts to go along with training sometimes makes more sense than buying your own machines.

_____ 4. There is an economy of scale in going with an outsider.

_____ 5. You can find a partner outside the company with high visibility, a good brand name, and marketing already in place.

_____ 6. The outsider can work better and faster than your own staff.

# Managing Outsiders Checklist 4.5
## Project Management Checklist

This checklist is organized around the four essential elements of project management: content, cost, schedule, and control. The more defined and finely tuned each of the four elements is, the better the project as a whole will be and the greater its chance of profit. Use this checklist to manage all critical parts of each essential element of your vendor or consultant's project.

_____ 1. Objectives

_____ 2. Scope

_____ 3. Staff                                  **Elements of Content**

_____ 4. Tasks

_____ 5. Products/services

---

_____ 6. Salary (person-days)

_____ 7. Materials

_____ 8. Leased machine or computer
          costs                                 **Elements of Cost**

_____ 9. Purchased services

_____ 10. Operations overhead

---

_____ 11. Milestones

_____ 12. Tasks by person-days; total
          person days                           **Elements of Schedule**

_____ 13. Lapse-time to complete each task; total lapse-time

---

_____ 14. Roles and responsibilities

_____ 15. Relationships among project staff, tasks, and time

_____ 16. Communications, correspondence, documentation, reports to client

_____ 17. In-process evaluation reviews         **Elements of Control**

_____ 18. End-of-project evaluation report

# Managing Outsiders Checklist 4.6
## Characteristics of a Good E-Learning Supplier

These are some of the characteristics to look for in an e-learning supplier. You'll probably think of more, and that's good. In a field of high-powered salespersons and glitzy systems capabilities, it's a good idea to work from a checklist of this sort as you evaluate sales materials, interview vendors and consultants, and review proposals.

_____ 1. Has your interests foremost when it comes to e-learning strategy, both short-term and long-term

_____ 2. Will work with you and your information technology group on system installation

_____ 3. Provides monitoring and evaluation capabilities for the system itself as well as for learners

_____ 4. Offers training in their hardware and software at your site

_____ 5. Shows you how to set up administrative functions

_____ 6. Contains adequate archival functions

_____ 7. Contains relevant and nontrivial content options

_____ 8. Provides support for in-house content developers

_____ 9. Provides for integration of your own in-house work with their work

_____ 10. Provides online or hotline support for e-learners

# Managing Outsiders Checklist 4.7
## Protection of Intellectual Property

Use this checklist to analyze your department's training courses and programs for intellectual property content. When hiring outsiders, there is always a caution about access through training to competitive and proprietary information. (See the "More Information" section at the end of this chapter.)

Course title: _____

_____ 1. Information in this course does not/should not belong in the public domain.

_____ 2. Information in this course is focused on our company's competitive advantage.

_____ 3. Delivering this course in another company would hurt our sales or reputation.

_____ 4. Systems and processes described in this course are unique to us and one reason for our success.

_____ 5. Objectives, task lists, and competency development guidelines in this course describe our competitive products and market edge.

_____ 6. This course contains information about one or more of our patented products.

_____ 7. This course contains one or more of our trade secrets.

_____ 8. Databases and other electronic files associated with this course contain information that should not be shared with outsiders.

# Chapter 4 Forms

## To Manage Outsiders

The forms listed here focus on some of the important details in actually managing the outsiders you hire. Several "project management" forms are included here because work contracted out is generally defined as a project. Of course, internal analysis, design, development, delivery, and evaluation efforts can also be defined as projects. In that case, these project management forms will also be useful for in-house projects.

**LIST OF FORMS TO MANAGE OUTSIDERS**

    **4.1**  Vendor/Consultant Overview Analysis Matrix

    **4.2**  Vendor/Consultant Contract Format

    **4.3**  Project Status Report Form

    **4.4**  Project Notebook Format

    **4.5**  Matrix for Identifying Intellectual Property in Course

**Managing Outsiders Form 4.1**
**VENDOR/CONSULTANT OVERVIEW ANALYSIS MATRIX**

### How to Use This Form
1. Make a list of all the vendors/consultants you are considering hiring down the left side of the form.
2. Rate each on a scale of 1 to 10 in each of the three areas of technology capability, content quality and quantity, and services.
3. Add extra pages for notes and narrative comments.

1 = low; 10 = high

| Vendor/consultant's name | Technology capability | Content quality and quantity | Services |
|---|---|---|---|
| | | | |
| | | | |
| | | | |
| | | | |
| | | | |
| | | | |
| | | | |
| | | | |
| | | | |
| | | | |
| | | | |
| | | | |
| | | | |
| | | | |
| | | | |
| | | | |

## How to Manage Outsiders

**Managing Outsiders Form 4.2**
**VENDOR/CONSULTANT CONTRACT FORMAT**

### How to Use This Form
1. Refer to this contract template as you write your contract with outside vendors or consultants.
2. Be careful to describe the project completely and to define the vendor/consultant's role(s).

| |
|---|
| Today's date |
| Vendor/consultant's name, address, telephone number, and e-mail. |
| Simple statement authorizing the services of the vendor/consultant, by name, to your organization, by name |
| Project description (several sentences) |
| Consultant's role(s) (Use action words whose impact you can measure.) |
| Duration of engagement (start date, end date, and major milestone due dates for interim reports or products) |
| Rate of pay (per day, per hour, or total contract) (State any restrictions such as overtime or project extensions.) |

**How to Manage Training**

| |
|---|
| Agreements regarding travel, lodging, mileage, office space, secretarial support, and computer support |
| Your project manager (Name a staff member as the official contact with the outsider. Make it clear that all communications between vendor/consultant and you go through this person.) |
| Nondisclosure statement (Get the legal wording from your attorney.) |
| Statement regarding acceptable quality of services |
| Billing procedures and formats (Spell this out clearly; attach forms if required.) |
| Dated signatures (lines for yours and vendor/consultant's)<br><br>_____     _____<br><br>_____     _____ |

# How to Manage Outsiders

**Managing Outsiders Form 4.3**
**PROJECT STATUS REPORT FORM**

### How to Use This Form
1. Use this form on a periodic basis to document project work. One- or two-week intervals are suggested.
2. This is a useful form for a vendor/consultant to use to keep you informed. Attach a stack of these forms to your vendor/consultant contract so that your outsider knows what to expect.

Project name _____  Date of report _____

Period covered by this report _____

Accomplishments during this period:

- 
- 
- 
- 
- 
- 
- 
- 

Still pending/to be accomplished during the next period:

- 
- 
- 
- 
- 
- 

Concerns/obstacles/modifications:

- 
- 
- 
- 

Vendor/consultant signature and date: _____

**How to Manage Training**

**Operations Form 4.4**
**PROJECT NOTEBOOK FORMAT**

### How to Use This Form
1. Use this form to design your project documentation notebook.
2. Keep track of the work in progress weekly according to these four areas of project management: content, cost, schedule, and control.
3. Use either handwritten or computer-generated input data.
4. Use this notebook either to document the management of internal training projects or with your vendor/consultant as required.

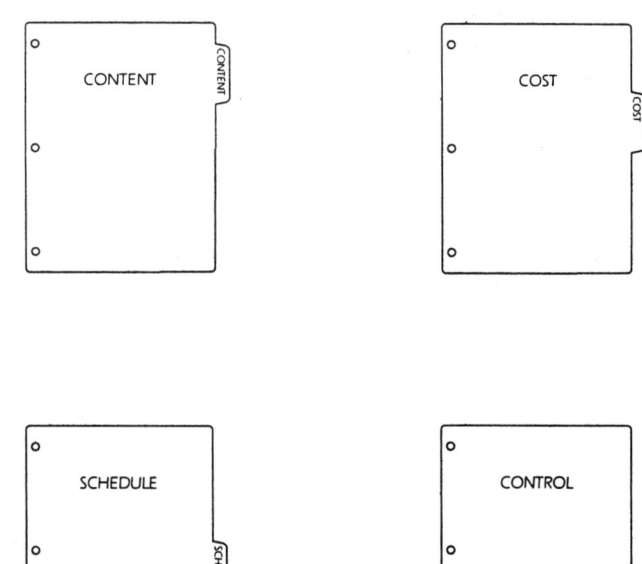

CONTENT

COST

SCHEDULE

CONTROL

# How to Manage Outsiders

**Managing Outsiders Form 4.5**
**MATRIX FOR IDENTIFYING INTELLECTUAL PROPERTY IN COURSES**

### How to Use This Form
1. This quick reference form will help you spot the courses in which your intellectual property resides. It can help you make better decisions about outside involvement with your courses. List courses down the left side of the page.
2. Place a check mark in the appropriate cell opposite each course indicating the kinds of intellectual property each course contains.

| Courses | Patent | Trademark | Copyright | Trade secret |
|---------|--------|-----------|-----------|--------------|
|         |        |           |           |              |
|         |        |           |           |              |
|         |        |           |           |              |
|         |        |           |           |              |
|         |        |           |           |              |
|         |        |           |           |              |
|         |        |           |           |              |
|         |        |           |           |              |
|         |        |           |           |              |
|         |        |           |           |              |
|         |        |           |           |              |
|         |        |           |           |              |
|         |        |           |           |              |
|         |        |           |           |              |
|         |        |           |           |              |
|         |        |           |           |              |
|         |        |           |           |              |
|         |        |           |           |              |
|         |        |           |           |              |

# Chapter 4
## More Information on How to Manage Outsiders

### More About Being an Irresponsible Contractor

It's very easy when you are the contractor calling the shots to neglect both the common courtesy elements and the contractual and legal elements of a good working relationship. These considerations all begin when you issue your Request for Proposal (RFP). They continue after you have hired your chosen outsider. This is a list of some common complaints of vendors and consultants, a list that describes an irresponsible contractor.

- ***You're misinformed.*** You haven't kept up to date with what competing vendors in the field have to offer.

- ***You're a snoop.*** You never did intend to sign a contract—just "went fishing" for information about how a vendor or consultant does things.

- ***You waste time.*** The RPF was issued for legal reasons only; that is, EEOC guidelines require that certain vendors/consultants be issued RFPs, even if the decision has already been made about whom to hire.

- ***You sneak in extra work.*** You add on small projects beyond what the contract called for, decreasing the amount of pay for work the vendor/consultant earns.

- ***You don't give timely and useful feedback.*** Outsider projects progress well because of a collaborative relationship built on honest and useful feedback. Often the feedback process to the vendor/consultant is carried out poorly.

- ***You don't give access to the needed people or information.*** You haven't done complete reviews of existing products and services, or provided contact information to key files and people.

### More About Intellectual Property

A company's intellectual property falls into four main categories of law: patent law, trademark law, copyright law, and trade secret law. Violations of the first three categories are punishable as federal crimes; trade secrets generally are handled by state courts.

The training department, by its forward-looking mission to educate the company's workforce, often contains a wealth of intellectual property in its courses. If you are heavily using outsiders to work with you, be sure that they have access to only what you want them to access, and that they sign nondisclosure statements to protect the company's intellectual property.

Copyright protection is generally the most important category for training managers. The Copyright Act enacted by Congress in 1976 is the standard by which most print materials are governed. New legislation more focused on web and Internet-based information was enacted in 1998. For more information on copyright, see these sources:

- Fishman, Attorney Stephen. *The Copyright Handbook*, 4th edition. Berkeley, CA: Nolo Press, 1997.
- loc.gov/copyright
- Lee, Robert E. *A Copyright Guide for Authors.* Stamford, CT: Kent Press, 1995.
- U.S. Copyright Act, PL 94-553, October 19, 1976
- U.S. Copyright Office: Library of Congress, Washington, DC 20558; (202) 707-9100
- U.S. Digital Millennium Copyright Act of 1998
- Vaidhyanathan, Siva. *Copyrights and Copywrongs.* New York: New York University Press, 2001.

## Important Details of Copyright Law for the Training Manager

Copyright legislation was enacted to balance the rights of ownership of the author with the privileges of public education and research. Since the 1990s, newer copyright legislation and interpretations have extended the author side of the balance. This has happened largely in response to digital technology, which makes pirating very easy and is designed to speed copying and distribution. The music industry especially has been thrown into turmoil over pirating and distribution of copyrighted songs; creators of software programs that can be easily copied are also complaining. The cry is for fairer definitions of "public good." Questions arise about who should be included in the fair use of information: Should databases, freelance writers, emerging musicians, and experimental artists of all sorts be considered in the same category as students, teachers, readers, and users of libraries? Copyright law for the digital age is complicated and still under development. Those affected by it, such as training managers, need to be involved in serious dialogue about the future of copyright protection and the public good and about its use to encourage innovation.

## What Does Copyright Protect?

Simply stated, copyright protects the way words are expressed by an author. It does not protect the author's ideas or facts used in writing. In addition, many kinds of other creative expression can be covered by copyright protection, including:

- Literary works
- Sound recordings
- Computer software
- Dance choreography
- Dramatic works
- Graphic designs
- Audiovisual productions
- Musical arrangements
- Architectural plans

Copyright protects any such work in all media and for all derivative uses as soon as it is created. Many of these items are parts of training courses and programs. As training manager, you'll need to be sure that copyrights are in place and that any outsiders you hire are aware that your materials are protected.

## Fair Use

Fair use policy causes many authors great grief. Especially in training departments who are in the education business, the limits of "fair use" are sometimes fuzzy. They become even fuzzier when consultants or vendors are modifying copyrighted materials, hard copy, or digital copy. Recent interpretation of the law has resulted in criminal prosecution of persons who broke encrypted code or walked off with software programs. Fair use allows criticism of a work such as a book review, commentary about a work, news reporting about a work, making multiple copies of a work for classroom teaching, use of the work in scholarship or research (PL 94-553, section 107, 1976). Fair use would not allow a consultant to make multiple copies of your training materials to use in a classroom with other companies, that is, for his or her commercial purposes. Fair use would allow, with attribution to your company, use of a very limited string of words to illustrate a point or describe what your company does. Courts have consistently ruled according to a "percentage of total words" guideline and on a case-by-case basis. Fair use policy can be a training manager's nightmare. Get a good library of references on the subject and order copies of the current federal legislation. Start with the references cited above. Engage your legal counsel.

### If You Have Limited Budget and Staff . . .

Focus on hiring one vendor or consultant, not a group of many. Carefully define the product or service you need, and define the work as a "project." Be sure to follow the guidelines in the checklists and forms earlier in this chapter. Focus on a collaborative working relationship with frequent feedback sessions.

## If You Have Adequate Budget and Staff . . .
Do your homework regarding who's out there providing what kinds of products and services. Check the bios and references of potential providers. Interview several. Focus on your vision and plans for the future of training and learning in your company. Think about global implications and the communities of practice either on shop floors or on networks throughout the world. Think about how people learn and about how training and learning experiences should be designed and delivered in the future. Hire outsiders carefully so that they complement your company's learning and training needs. Construct a management system that is solid and fair to all concerned. Involve more than the training department in hiring and evaluative decisions. Be sure you know what you want; don't spend more money than you have to spend to get what you want.

# 5

# How to Manage Training for Teams

By all accounts, teams are here to stay. Today's operative words are "cross-functional" teams. Collaboration with sales, marketing, operations, and especially with information systems organizations is on the rise and expected to grow—actually to double—in the coming years.* Issues for trainers and for team leaders and facilitators center on several key ideas: making the most of individual learning, designing and implementing learning experiences specifically for team learning, and taking a fresh look at performance standards for teams.

## KEY MANAGEMENT ISSUES

■ *Up With People.* Realities of today's workplace include the facts that the workforce is more diverse in many ways and that organizations contain fewer people than they did a few years ago. New jobs are being created, to be sure, but new bureaucracies and hierarchies are not. Horizontal is in; vertical is out.

One of the problems is that most people working today are familiar with vertical organizations, where numerous signoffs on work, levels of reporting relationships, and "please the boss" and "cover your tail" are still norms. Most of us have learned to deal and to survive in those kinds of companies. Companies where teams have worked well continue to flood the business press, however, and their successes entice other companies to convert to team structures. What's hard is the transition because, with a team structure, those old familiar ways of working simply don't fit.

Successful teams have a "people first" point of view: it's not always the quickest route to the bottom line that drives them. Managers make strategic errors during transition times if they continue to think in terms of the boxes on the organization chart, chains of command, and "keep

---

*ASTD Technical and Skills Training *Issues and Trends Report,* fall 1996, p. 2.

your head down, your mouth shut, and your nose to the grindstone." In a team structure, people simply are not sorted the same way as they were before.

The structural challenges of a team-based organization are typically felt in the training arena early in the development of teams. Most often, the team will consist of persons at different power levels, pay scales, years of experience, job function, education levels, and so forth. The training audience in the old days was far more homogeneous—more likely to be made up of similar persons, most often a classroom of people. Today's training for teams is aimed at a heterogeneous audience, a collection of individuals whose differences and diversity provide the fuel to ignite team work. Training managers especially need to quickly adopt a new mind-set regarding for whom the training is designed and delivered.

The easiest way to reorient your thinking is to think first of the group, the team, as a collection of individuals. Don't think of your learners as a "class." Think about how to maximize the diversity of the members. Think up with people, not down to the bottom line—more like an anthropologist than an accountant.

■ *New Designs for Learning.* One of the most important things for those responsible for designing the learning experiences and contexts of team-based learners to do is to learn to be guided by a mission, a business reason, not by a narrow "training objective." Team learning designers must first think broadly, not narrowly. At the same time, business goals—and often not directly related to profit, sales, and production quotas—must drive training design for teams. Business goals for teams are often stated in terms of quality, service, innovation, and improved processes. It is tempting when designing team training to think first of some "feel good" psychological goals; you'll have more lasting success with team training if you don't yield to this temptation.

Critics of teams and observers of the failures of teams cite failure of leaders and facilitators to set the proper strategic direction and failure of training to transfer as two of the most obvious reasons why teams fail.*

■ *Defining the Real Work of Teams.* One of the trickiest things to define is the performance standards for teams—that is, for the team as a whole as well as for the individuals in it. The measurement gurus among us immediately want to turn everything into numbers, and that's not a bad idea if the measurement designer can exhibit some flexibility and think with a hefty dose of common sense at the same time.

Teams have different work from the work that traditional measurers, needs analysts, and evaluation specialists are used to measuring. Teams make decisions differently, solve problems differently, communicate differently, have different commitments, and collaborate differently from persons in more hierarchical groups. Performance measures for teams must reflect these differences. Training to these new performance mea-

*Steven B. Rayner, *Team Traps,* New York: John Wiley & Sons, Inc., 1996.

sures is where training managers and designers can begin to work on the transfer issue. Defining the real work of teams is the first step. Managers and team leaders can create a climate of development that features stretching assignments in which team members are encouraged to network with, to coach, and to learn from each other.

■ ***Distributed and Virtual Teams.*** Managing training for teams who are distributed throughout the country or world and who work together by means of computers is a challenge, to say the least. Numerous studies, particularly ones from the Institute for Research on Learning (IRL), Palo Alto, California, suggest that team members need "face time" to learn best and to solve the problems on which the team is working. Among other things, IRL researchers found that social organization, physical space, and the normal rhythms of work in time had great impact on the ability of workers to learn. See irl.org. A typical team's commitment to specific goals and outputs is affected by how the team learns and how the individuals within it learn.

Distributed and virtual teams do not have these advantages and need particular kinds of training in order to fulfill their objectives and deliver their deliverables. Training managers need to have an understanding of the complex relationships among people and tasks, including recognition of the barriers erected by technology as well as the benefits of technology. A recent *Info-Line* publication of ASTD suggests some ideas for team building in a virtual environment.* Among ASTD's points are those that pertain to adhering to schedules and commitments that seem easier to ignore online, taking the time for constructive online feedback between team members and team leader, readily and willingly sharing knowledge resources, and acknowledging and addressing conflict. Training distributed and virtual teams must focus on skills that facilitate accomplishment of these points, build trust, and clarify procedures. Many companies have found that gathering distributed or virtual team members together at a conference or workshop where there is plenty of social interaction and "face time" is also a good idea.

---

*Tara L. Guilot, *Info-Line: Team Building in a Virtual Environment,* ASTD product number 250205. Order by phoning ASTD at 703-683-8100.

# Chapter 5 Checklists
## To Manage Training for Teams

**LIST OF TEAM TRAINING CHECKLISTS**

- **5.1** Success Factors for Individual Learning Within the Team
- **5.2** The Care and Feeding of Team Members
- **5.3** How Fewer People Can Do More Work
- **5.4** Checklist for Behavioral Feedback
- **5.5** Team Performance Checklist

# Team Training Checklist 5.1
## Success Factors for Individual Learning Within the Team

Use this checklist as a reminder to think first of the individual learner. The learning context for teams is a collection of individuals, not a class.

**CLEAR ROLE DEFINITION AND ACCEPTANCE**

\_\_\_\_\_ 1. Has a clear role been defined for this person?

\_\_\_\_\_ 2. Have you involved this person in the definition of the role?

\_\_\_\_\_ 3. Does this person understand this role? If not, what will you do to clarify his or her understanding of it?

\_\_\_\_\_ 4. Does this person accept this role?

**COMPETENCY AND COMPETENCY DEVELOPMENT**

\_\_\_\_\_ 5. Have you engaged in dialogue with this person regarding his or her competencies as he or she applies to the work of the team? Do you know this person's strengths and weaknesses? Does this person concur about strengths and weaknesses?

\_\_\_\_\_ 6. What specific steps can/will you take, together, to help this person acquire needed missing competencies for the work of the team, and enhance those he or she already has?

\_\_\_\_\_ 7. Have you considered competencies in at least these three areas:
—*Intellectual skills*, cognitive competencies, information-based knowledge
—*Motor skills*, "know-how," eye-hand coordination skills, demonstration and presentation skills, ability to observe ergonomic and safe work procedures
—*Emotional skills*, controlling temper, having patience, dealing with bias and gender, avoiding burnout, behaving ethically, being assertive, taking initiative

**PERSONAL PREFERENCES**

\_\_\_\_\_ 8. Have you discussed "psychological type" and "behavioral style" preferences with this person? Does this person know her- or himself well enough to be able to identify a personal preferred type or style?

_____ 9. Can you use specific examples of his or her work to illustrate your perception of this person's preferred way of approaching work?

_____ 10. Have you taken specific steps to encourage this person to recognize and value the personal preferences of other team members?

_____ 11. Do you show by your actions and by the rewards you give that you equally value persons for who they are and for the unique contributions they can make because of their personal preferences?

_____ 12. What specific steps will you take to value diversity and use it as a strategic tool?

**INDIVIDUAL NEED FOR AFFILIATION**

_____ 13. Have you adjusted your thinking about the expenditure of time in order to accommodate dialogue, brainstorming, exploration of fringes, peer training, guided self-study, just-in-time training, reflection, and other extemporaneous ways in which individuals learn from each other?

_____ 14. Have you intentionally set up opportunities—places and times—for the individuals on teams to focus on knotty problems and complex tasks?

_____ 15. What motivations have you devised to encourage collaboration?

# Team Training Checklist 5.2
## The Care and Feeding of Team Members

This checklist will give you some ideas about the motivations and rewards that are appropriate for teams. They are aimed at individuals first, then at the team.

_____ 1. Persons at work want to do a good job. Tell them when and where they do good work, not just during training. Don't wait for performance review; give applause on the spot.

_____ 2. Most people like to learn. Reinforce the informal learning activities that go on all around you; encourage managers and team leaders to make time for and value one-on-one peer teaching and learning within the team. Try to get away from the mind-set that "accuses" clumps of people trying to figure out a solution as wasting time—that clump might just be on the verge of a real breakthrough and could be team learning at its best.

_____ 3. Reward "out of the box" thinking: individuals are normally risk-aversive, but working in teams often requires doing things that seem uncomfortable for certain personality types. Being personally exposed at times of risk taking for the good of the project or the team deserves recognition and reward. Make it big or make it small, but do it consistently and in a timely fashion. Make this a function of the team's "personal trainer"—get the training staff out into the team—manage training by "walking around." Make it a point to know when creative and collaborative thinking occur.

_____ 4. Give a lot of thought to what kind of rewards will motivate your particular employees. Here are some categories of rewards:

> *Blue ribbons*—inexpensive and enough to go around; reward "most improved team member," "best cheerleader," "best networker," "most valuable player," etc. Blue Ribbons can also be adapted to photos in a hall of fame, or features in the company newsletter.
> *Free lunch*—including items generally thought of as "travel and entertainment"; free lunches, a dinner club membership, sports tickets, concert tickets, ski weekends, a beach house for a week.
> *Toys*—grownup gadgets and hardware with a wow effect; faster computers, better fax machines, cell phones, laptop computers, car phones.
> *Privilege*—company perks generally reserved only for executives; a private parking space with a name plate, guest privi-

leges every Wednesday in the executive dining room, a direct phone/fax line, flextime, travel on the corporate jet.

*Investments*—stock options, advisory committee appointment, increased budget, more authority over how to allocate resources, higher company contributory percentage to 401K plans.

*Cold hard cash*—outright grants, bonuses, prizes.

# Team Training Checklist 5.3
## How Fewer People Can Do More Work

Trainers usually get involved early in team formation, often in designing and delivering training to the new team members in how to manage change. This kind of training often is group training, and often its immediate purpose is to help employees adopt a point of view that is "how to do more with less." Trainers obviously need to give a lot of thought to this, because often there are natural resentments among the trainees, as comfortable ways of doing things become challenged by team organization. Trainers need to focus on personal skill development that facilitates team growth—and its consequent better ways of working. Here are some ideas for topics to cover during this kind of training:

_____ 1. *Team versus individual goals.* Be sure that you allow each individual on the team to verbalize his or her personal goals; get it all out on the table before you facilitate definition of team goals.

_____ 2. *Negotiate a win-win.* During this kind of initial "change management" training, help the team set up win-win situations regarding their personal goals versus the team goals. People are miserable if they believe that they have to compromise too much by being on a team. Help them to get to the point where they can define the added value item(s)—that is, the truly new ways of working or delivering service—so that it doesn't seem like giving up some things as much as working together, as individuals, for that something new. Don't allow people to wallow in their fond memories of the way things were. Focus on the new, and negotiate to it from the individual's point of view.

_____ 3. *Do scenario-planning.* In the safe environment of training, engage the team in some "what if?" scenario development. Present actual challenges facing the team and real business problems in a workshop setting where trainees can develop solutions in the form of scenario A, scenario B, scenario C, asking all the time, "What if this were the case? What if we had these resources? What if these persons interacted?" etc. Scenario planning allows many individual needs and wants to become incorporated.

_____ 4. *Decision making.* Sensitize the team to various ways of making decisions. In business-the-old-fashioned-way, individuals didn't usually give much thought to how they made decisions. In teamwork, team members need to be helped to see the variety of decision-making models out there, and to know that there are many acceptable ways of making decisions. How things are decided often is a critical factor in how teamwork progresses and how its success is measured. Individuals need to know that it's okay to try out new ways of decision making in order for the work of the team to go forward.

Here are some more common models of decision making: majority rule, minority report, consensus, middling (going for the middle ground, compromising), do what the consultant says, do as I say (authoritarian rule with no discussion), follow orders (but with participant involvement and adaptation). Much of teamwork operates in what management experts call "the boundaries"—that is, the fringe areas where innovative thinking is critical to the team's ability to get things done. Policy and procedures manuals seldom get opened in boundary areas. What's more important to the conduct of business here is the definition of obstacles, constraints, or limitations to be considered. Doing more with less requires well-tuned thinkers who are psychologically free to experiment with different ways of making decisions and who are encouraged and supported to intentionally learn from their work.

# Team Training Checklist 5.4
## Checklist for Behavioral Feedback

Giving and receiving behavioral feedback is important to the initial creation, development, maintenance, and improvement of teams. It is hard to change one's way of doing things and to "internalize" new and often uncomfortable performance standards and work processes. Team members generally need training in both giving and receiving feedback. Each team member will both give and receive feedback many times during teamwork; good training early in a team's development should help everyone. Here are some tips for team members:

**TIPS FOR GIVING FEEDBACK**

_____ 1. Make your comments descriptive, not evaluative.

_____ 2. Describe specific behaviors that you have observed, not fuzzy impressions.

_____ 3. Don't accuse; start sentences with "I noticed" rather than "You did."

_____ 4. Watch your own body language; smile with your eyes, don't fold your arms in front of your chest, keep eye contact, don't slouch, be sincere.

_____ 5. Know yourself; don't get tangled up in bias and discriminatory comments.

_____ 6. Be conscious of self-esteem issues; don't push forward giving more feedback if it is being taken poorly. Think of better ways to say it next time around.

_____ 7. Remember to give positive feedback, too.

**TIPS FOR RECEIVING FEEDBACK**

_____ 8. Lock in on the person's eyes; actively listen to what is being directed at you.

_____ 9. Ask for clarification, point by point. It's easier to understand small observations and to make changes based on specific points.

_____ 10. Don't get defensive: go for the facts.

_____ 11. If you've had enough feedback, say so. Go at it again another day.

_____ 12. Decide what you can act upon to change, and prioritize your plans.

_____ 13. Turn feedback into action as quickly as possible.

_____ 14. Thank the giver of feedback; remember that all feedback is useful.

# Team Training Checklist 5.5
## Team Performance Checklist

Measurement of teams, like measurement of individual achievement, is an essential component of any systematic approach to the organizational development of teams. Training managers need to be involved in measurement of team performance in order to get the information you need for design and delivery of future training. Here are some tips:

_____ 1. Team performance depends on process "tuning." Devise some measurement forms and rating scale through which you can collect opinion data, expressed as numbers on a 7-point scale. Numbers are always easier to deal with than just words, especially on opinion items.

_____ 2. These are some of the processes that need to be measured:
- using resources
- communicating
- focusing and refocusing
- managing time
- making decisions
- solving problems
- interacting outside of the team

_____ 3. Getting quantitative data (as contrasted with qualitative data) is the foundation of measurement, including team measurement. These are some of the places to look for sources of quantitative data:
- better product yield
- fewer errors
- fewer quality defects
- fewer returns
- more sales
- better margins
- quicker delivery
- shorter development cycles
- fewer customer complaints
- more on-time targets met
- fewer safety infractions
- higher attendance
- more budgets met

_____ 4. Try to measure against both standards and a baseline of acceptable performance. Be realistic, and especially if you haven't had any experience with teams, be sure to involve team members in the creation of the standards document. Most people want teams to succeed and want to succeed as individuals in teams; getting their help with the process of setting baseline standards and stretch standards by which they themselves will be measured is just plain good business.

_____ 5. Find others who've had experience with teams and make a contact with them in the name of "benchmarking." Business magazines, web pages, and chat groups online are all good sources of individuals in other companies with experience. Don't be too idealistic at first: Go for the reality of standards and reflect this reality in your measurement instruments and procedures.

# Chapter 5 Forms
## To Manage Training for Teams

**LIST OF TEAM TRAINING FORMS**

- **5.1** Basics of Personality Type
- **5.2** Language Baggage
- **5.3** Process Improvement
- **5.4** "Capture the Flag"
- **5.5** Influence Linkages and Support Networks

# How to Manage Training for Teams 123

**Team Training Form 5.1**
**BASICS OF PERSONALITY TYPE**

> **How to Use This Form**
> 1. This form is a chart containing the key personality descriptors of several important thinkers. It is meant to be a team member's or trainer's job aid regarding the definition of type. References are indicated to direct the user to more complete information.
> 2. Use this as a handout after a team training session on personality or behavioral type.
> 3. Do not use personality typing for purposes of salary review, placement, hiring and firing decisions, or in any circumstance that could be misconstrued as bias or discrimination.

**Psychological Types.** Carl Gustav Jung (1875–1961), Swiss psychiatrist and analytical psychologist, popularized studies of extroversion and introversion. Among his monumental works are *Psychology of the Unconscious* (1912 and 1952); *Symbols of Transformation* (1952); and *Psychological Types* (1921). His works were translated into English in 1953, and remain the foundation for numerous related studies about personality and behavioral style. He identified the basic four psychological types—thinkers, feelers, intuitors, and sensors—and concluded that the entire population can be categorized into these basic psychological types, and no more; each individual falls predominantly into one of the four. The implication for teams especially, and for groups of all kinds, is that 75 percent of the population is psychologically different from each other—tough odds when collaboration and consensus are sought.

**Myers-Briggs Type Indicator (MBTI).** A currently popular American personality assessment instrument created and developed extensively over the past several decades by Isabel Briggs Myers and Katharine C. Briggs. An easy-to-score profile gives the MBTI taker a readout of his or her type profile, based on Jung-like scales. These are:

> **extroversion—introversion**
> **sensing—intuition**
> **thinking—feeling**
> **judging—perceiving**

An MBTI profile gives the results of the assessment in terms of sixteen combinations of these eight categories. It is widely used in companies and nonprofit agencies in many kinds of applications, such as coaching, counseling, career education, leadership development, and conflict resolution. MBTI materials are available from Consulting Psychologists Press, Palo Alto, California.

## 124 How to Manage Training

**Team Training Form 5.2**
**LANGUAGE BAGGAGE**

### How to Use This Form
1. Use this form when you need help in cooling down a heated exchange between team members. The words in bold type often carry with them a lot of semantic baggage, and are sometimes overused by zealous team leaders and trainers.
2. Go down the list of related words under each "loaded" word; find a less charged term to introduce into the exchange.
3. Add your own words; make the chart as big as you can.

**love**
respect
enjoyment
likability
empathy
understanding

**commitment**
trust
pledge
acceptance
agreement
trial

**leadership**
facilitation
leverage
guidance
responsibility
ownership

**share**
teach
compromise
collaborate
participate
explain

**align**
agree
position
focus
consent
cooperate

**support**
help
hear
understand
sympathize
advocate

## How to Manage Training for Teams

**Team Training Form 5.3**
**PROCESS IMPROVEMENT**

### How to Use This Form

1. Use these lists as a job aid to facilitate a team's understanding of process improvement, and their initiation of action to make process improvements.
2. Refer to Team Training Form 5.2 for suggestions of nouns (top row) and verbs (bottom row) to use in process-improvement exercises.
3. Add "...ing" words to key concepts and terms. Making the action active through the use of "...ing" helps individuals to see that action is what is needed in order to make *process* improvements.
4. This can also be used as a handout to team members during or after training, for their continuous reference on the job.

Here are some examples of how to get a team to focus on process improvement. The secret is to focus on the action word, the "...ing" word, getting the trainee to immediately begin thinking in terms of what he or she needs to do to make the process work better. For example:

| | |
|---|---|
| *eliminating* waste | *selecting* colleagues |
| *preventing* delays | *configuring* benefits |
| *consolidating* sign-offs | *teaching* others |
| *showing* respect | *getting* agreement |
| *demonstrating* enjoyment | *conducting* a trial |

By concentrating on the development of the "...ing" word—that is, by creating an action plan around that part of the process-improvement phrase—you will set yourself up to take action. In the examples below, it is tempting for team members to focus on the wrong part of the phrase, "vision," "outcomes," "dialogue," or "information." Action stops when you do this. Empowered employees take action. This exercise is a sure way to help employees move from a command-and-control old-style to a new team-based, empowered workforce style.

Here are some other ideas for process improvement. Add your own to the list:

| | |
|---|---|
| defining vision | monitoring outcomes |
| designing jobs | establishing dialogue |
| asking questions | practicing skills |
| creating solutions | assessing risks |
| analyzing problems | disseminating information |

# How to Manage Training

**Team Training Form 5.4**
**"CAPTURE THE FLAG"**

### How to Use This Form
1. This form is for you to use as you help team leadership set goals.
2. The form contains a list of points to cover as you discuss the team's goals with the team leader or, if the leader chooses, with the entire team. Make copies for all "players" to encourage dialogue.
3. The goal-setting process uses the metaphor of the children's game, "Capture the Flag," the object of which is to make small strategic moves to ultimately capture the enemy's flag and thus claim the territory.

1. Be realistic in setting goals.
2. Know what your resources are: time, money, people, skills.
3. Think short-term rather than long-term (no more than 6 months out).
4. Identify obstacles.
5. Line up alliances.
6. Set timelines and checkpoints.
7. Identify measures to verify progress.
8. Break down the goal(s) into several subgoals.
9. Define tasks associated with each subgoal.
10. Prioritize the tasks.
11. Reprioritize the tasks at each checkpoint.
12. Measure progress toward subgoals.
13. Quantify outcomes.
14. Reassess goals after measurements.
15. "Capture the flag!"

# How to Manage Training for Teams

**Team Training Form 5.5**
**INFLUENCE LINKAGES AND SUPPORT NETWORKS**

### How to Use This Form
1. Show team members how to continuously update this form and keep it at hand, ready to refer to at any time.
2. Use this in a training session on team maintenance and growth.
3. A sample completed row, included below, provides guidance.

*Sample:*

| name: *G. Monaco* <br> job title: *writer* <br> *(in p.r. organization)* | phone: *7152* <br> e-mail: *rev.com* | problem area/ *creation of a team newsletter, viz.* <br> focus of influence: *format for "Polish Our Stars" monthly column* | role: *designer, cheerleader, first writer* |
|---|---|---|---|

| name: <br> job title: | phone: <br> e-mail: | problem area/ <br> focus of influence: | role: |
|---|---|---|---|
| name: <br> job title: | phone: <br> e-mail: | problem area/ <br> focus of influence: | role: |
| name: <br> job title: | phone: <br> e-mail: | problem area/ <br> focus of influence: | role: |
| name: <br> job title: | phone: <br> e-mail: | problem area/ <br> focus of influence: | role: |
| name: <br> job title: | phone: <br> e-mail: | problem area/ <br> focus of influence: | role: |
| name: <br> job title: | phone: <br> e-mail: | problem area/ <br> focus of influence: | role: |

# Chapter 5 More Information on How to Manage Training for Teams

## Facilitating "the whole" as well as "the parts"

Teams have been around for a while now, and the business press and publishing establishment have begun publishing information about team failures and have suggested prescriptions for corrective actions or preventive measures against common traps. The experience of many businesses is showing us more focused and more appropriate approaches to the development of teams. We're moving beyond "feel good" workshops and Friday night beers to more solid and substantial ways of helping teams and team members to learn. The particular challenge for trainers is to address both the team as a whole and each individual in it during training needs assessment, design, delivery, and evaluation. Books listed in the Bibliography can provide more information on the current difficulties with teams. They should be used to provide a point of view regarding what's broken about teams and how to fix it. They should not be used as an indictment of the team movement. Teams are here to stay, probably for a long time.

In addition to job-related skills—that is, the skills required for each person to do his or her job—individual team members require the cognitive skills for making sense of organizational and corporate financial reports; the human relations skills for dealing with personnel problems within the team; written, oral, and online communication skills for maximizing the use of information within the team and between the team and outside organizations; and broader and more advanced decision-making and problem-solving skills for efficient and innovative teamwork. Trainers aren't used to dealing with the same individual trainees in such a variety of skills; team structures demand more of a trainer, as well as a more focused and deeper knowledge of individual learners.

Steven R. Rayner's book, *Team Traps,* lists some common team traps.* Trainers generally can be expected to be called upon to both fix and prevent some of these problems: a leader who's afraid to lead, no planning for team member replacements, broken trust and shattered loyalty by hurtful downsizing or reengineering, a team that's into its own little world, disgruntled and disruptive team members, degenerating work or social habits, uneven empowerment and contributions, no one's responsible, and uninformed and uncreative decision making. In dealing with these problems in a training context, trainers will find it difficult not to focus entirely on the individual. What makes the training challenging is the need to bring the whole into the parts, essentially elevating the business goals and corporate vision by helping the trainee to get beyond his or her local problem into a more global frame of reference.

---

*Steven R. Rayner, *Traps*. New York: John Wiley, 1996, p. 16.

## Changing the Corporate Mind-Set to Value Mistakes

Quality guru W. Edwards Deming said it first and best: "Drive fear out of the workplace." His work defined the issues in process quality improvement, and his "14 Points" about creating high-quality workplaces have been used by millions of followers throughout the world. His essential message was that there should be joy in work, that it is the manager's job to remove barriers to a worker's ability to be proud of his or her own work, and that learning on the job is everyone's work.

Deming and his followers advocate continuous system improvement as well as time for reflection and revision. Errors are your friends; it is okay, and in fact imperative, to learn from one's mistakes.

American business management developed in other directions, however, and Deming did most of his essential work in Japan. We adopted a bureaucratic and hierarchical model of organization, one that featured bosses who controlled work and workers who carried out what bosses decreed. We rewarded individual achievement. We used stopwatches and stood over workers with buzzers and flashing measurement devices. We tried always to minimize, hide, or put another spin on our mistakes. Max Weber and Frederick Taylor were our management heroes. It's hard now to think in terms of changing this way of viewing work, and to value experimentation, reflection, joy in discovery, and learning from mistakes. We probably have Deming to thank for our unease with the present training challenges inherent in working with teams.

### If You Have Limited Budget and Staff . . .

Focus first on individual "needs to know." Construct a learning needs chart for each team member and update it periodically. If you can work on only one change, work on changing the company-wide mind-set about the value of mistakes. Communicate, communicate, communicate—in every way you can think of! Post Deming's 14 Points everywhere around your company.

### If You Have Adequate Budget and Staff . . .

Involve team members in a teamwide, total participation design of a training program for the team. Assign a training staff developer and instructional designer to work with members of the team as individuals and as a team. Look in the training literature (*Training magazine, Training & Development, Human Resource magazine,* for a start) for models of team-developed training. Find consultants with experience to help you (ASTD Online is one source); find companies against whom you can benchmark. Contact the Malcolm Baldrige National Quality Award winners from the past five years (find them through the U.S. Department of Commerce in Gaithersburg, Md.). Go to the annual Baldrige Awards Conference or to national or regional conferences of ASTD. Check out the preconference workshops for intensive one-day immersion in issues of policy, procedure, design, and evaluation.

# 6

# How To Manage Coaching and Mentoring

In recent years, coaching and mentoring have received a great deal of attention as important teaching and learning processes. Companies and nonprofits have adopted coaching and mentoring in great numbers and with a variety of employee exposure and depth. Steven Berglas, professor and psychiatrist, estimates that by 2006 there will be 50,000 executive coaches alone, a number up from 2,000 just ten years earlier. (See the sidebar, "The Economics of Executive Coaching," *Harvard Business Review*, June 2002, p. 89.) Other forms of coaching have been around for a long time: peer training and "the buddy system," cross-training throughout a company, and apprenticeship. Mentoring, too, has become popular in the last decade as companies find that one-to-one attention to learning generally yields big results: motivation for higher achievement, skill development, and increased cultural understanding.

There are some basic definitions of coaching and mentoring. *Coaching* is seen as tactical, task-centered, behavioral, and action-oriented. It is generally a training experience of short duration. It is often done by a manager with his or her subordinate, but it is also commonly done by high performers with low performers at the same level in an organization. Executive coaching is a particular form of coaching that typically involves a coach from outside the company who works for a period of several months with an executive to develop job-related and interpersonal skills in preparation for advancement. *Mentoring* is generally conceived as a process that helps an individual manage change, define and solve problems, or make transitions. It usually features highly successful persons helping those who are new to the company or currently in another organization, looking for movement within the company. Both coaching and mentoring work best when there is a formal process in place for evaluation and feedback, resulting in new career plans or improvement in work processes.

**KEY MANAGEMENT ISSUES**

Here are some management issues you should consider when managing coaching and mentoring.

- **Skills, Relationships, and Best Practices.** In both coaching and mentoring it is critical to first identify the skills that need developing, relationships that need strengthening, and best practices that need to be adopted. It is important to define needs in terms of cognitive and behavioral skills as well as the emotional intelligence factors that need to be addressed. Coaching can support on-the-job learning, or it can be a follow-up to classroom training or workshop experiences. It can focus on one's present job or on a future job. Executive coaching, of course, concentrates on the executive's agenda, built upon the fundamentals of enhanced skills, performance capability, and personal development. Coaching and mentoring can be very effective ways of teaching more than the typical analytical skills and corporate procedures, addressing issues such as building morale, improving creativity, and inspiring teamwork. See the Appendix to this book for detailed information about skills, relationships, and best practices culled from training and psychological literature.

- **Diversity.** Mentoring has been a popular and successful training approach to help women and minorities overcome barriers to advancement. In many companies, mentors are assigned and a comprehensive program of diversity training through mentoring is implemented. In other cases, people who need mentoring are challenged to find it for themselves. This can mean acting assertively to contact someone whose work you admire, volunteering for project teams out of your immediate area of expertise, and seeking high-visibility assignments. Networking internally and externally with individuals who will teach you is another way to find your own mentor. Training managers have a responsibility to encourage formal and informal mentoring programs on behalf of women and minorities, who are still not at parity with white males in pay or advancement opportunity. Refer to the writings of Sheila Wellington and her staff at Catalyst, a New York City–based research agency dedicated to the advancement of women in business (catalystwomen.org) for more information on mentoring.

- **Stimulus, Facilitation, and Support.** Good coaching or mentoring programs especially need organizational involvement from the training department. A company-wide program needs internal visibility through newsletters, online and interactive information, video clips, rewards for successes, and so on. It needs promotion through internal information channels so that program goals are well known and program participants are identified. These measures can provide stimulus for participation and creativity.

Training managers also need to provide facilitation and support services for mentoring and coaching, including planning and design assistance for participants, matching services based on accurate information so that those involved can succeed, orientation training, and monitoring and evaluation guidelines. Training managers have a responsibility to help coaches and mentors with instructional design that fits the needs of those to be coached and mentored. The training department should be prepared to provide supplies, reference materials, job aids, task lists and competency guidelines, and training software and hardware as needed. Training staff need to be available to coaches and mentors as troubleshooters and clerical helpers.

■ ***Mutual Advantage.*** It is tempting to think of coaching and mentoring as one-way processes, of greatest benefit to the person being coached or mentored. Numerous studies of coaching and mentoring and articles in business journals go further than this, however, and talk of the mutual advantage of these kinds of learning processes.

One obvious situation of mutual advantage is that of cross-training, in which a company trains its key personnel to do the basics of other strategic jobs such as those in hotels, health clubs, fire departments, emergency rooms, retail stores, businesses using a large number of part-time workers, or other high-turnover, customer-intensive business. This kind of one-to-one coaching has benefits for the entire company as individuals are trained to handle each other's jobs in emergencies—something of mutual advantage to each trainee and to the company as a whole.

Coaching and mentoring can also create an atmosphere of continuous learning, benefiting both individuals and the company as a whole. Coaching can become a company's "core competency," intensifying employees' abilities to seek information, building stronger relationships and better teams, and broadening creativity through learning.

The only caution about coaching and mentoring, especially executive coaching, is that it be done by the right person—one who knows how to take the executive through needs analysis and who is humble enough to not impose shallow solutions to poorly defined problems. Training managers can become involved in a company-based, not coach-based, executive needs analysis and thereby have a better chance of facilitating a coaching program of mutual advantage to the executive and the company.

# Chapter 6 Checklists
## To Manage Coaching and Mentoring

The following checklists are written from the point of view of what the training manager needs to do in order to facilitate an orderly, meaningful, and productive coaching or mentoring learning process.

**LIST OF CHECKLISTS TO MANAGE COACHING AND MENTORING**

    **6.1**  Roles of Coaches

    **6.2**  Mentoring to Overcome Women's Barriers to Advancement

    **6.3**  Cautions About Coaching

    **6.4**  Management Support Checklist

    **6.5**  Feedback and Evaluation from the Coach or Mentor

# Coaching and Mentoring Checklist 6.1

## Roles of Coaches

The following list suggests some of the most common roles for coaches. Use it before you hire or assign coaches to more carefully define what kinds of coaching your employees need. This kind of analysis precedes development of competency or task lists.

_____ 1. Coach for skills development.

_____ 2. Coach for performance monitoring and development.

_____ 3. Coach for interpersonal skills development.

_____ 4. Coach for follow-up to leadership training workshop.

_____ 5. Coach for visibility within the company.

_____ 6. Coach for visibility outside the company.

_____ 7. Coach for communication skills development.

_____ 8. Coach for developing emotional strength.

_____ 9. Coach for developing assertiveness.

_____ 10. Coach for career planning.

_____ 11. Coach for implementing action.

_____ 12. Coach for solving problems.

_____ 13. Coach for learning to learn.

_____ 14. Coach for job redesign.

_____ 15. Coach for using new systems.

# Coaching and Mentoring Checklist 6.2

## Mentoring to Overcome Women's Barriers to Advancement

Pay and opportunity equity between men and women is still a persistent problem in American workplaces. Mentoring of women is often seen as a way of helping women overcome barriers to advancement. The corporate environment in American businesses seems to still be full of glass ceilings. The following checklist highlights the kinds of things this specific mentoring can do.

_____ 1. Sensitize top executives to accountability structures for women's advancement that are the same for men.

_____ 2. Break stereotypes about women's roles and abilities by devising internal visibility programs for particular women.

_____ 3. Identify internal networks and teams into which women can be introduced and facilitate their introductions.

_____ 4. Facilitate creation of a corporate-wide "Overcoming Women's Barriers To Advancement" committee or task force. Help them develop an agenda, monitor their progress, and be sure top executives know their results. Be sure that your protégés are part of this effort.

_____ 5. Review existing corporate functions such as recruiting, hiring, orientation, public relations, and career development to be sure that women's goals are well represented. Involve your protégés in review and analysis.

_____ 6. Help your protégés develop standards for corporate progress and get them involved in monitoring corporate efforts and reporting results.

_____ 7. Identify female role models for your protégés.

_____ 8. Identify gaps in your protégés' experience, knowledge, or skills and create plans to get rid of the gaps. Make your protégés individually and unquestionably promotable.

# Coaching and Mentoring Checklist 6.3

## Cautions about Coaching

There are many kinds of coaches available for all kinds of employees. Companies need to be aware of the coach's expertise and experience, and verify bios and references. This checklist applies to coaches who are brought in from outside the company. Use this checklist to heighten your consumer awareness before you sign a contract.

\_\_\_\_\_ 1. *Contact hours.* Be sure that you understand how much "face time" your coach will spend inside your company. Be sure that it is enough. If your coach also provides telephone calls and e-mail communication, be sure you know how those expenses are charged.

\_\_\_\_\_ 2. *Rock star image.* Be sure that you hire a coach for the ability to deliver what you need, not for a rock star or sports hero image alone.

\_\_\_\_\_ 3. *Quick fix.* Evaluate the potential coach's promotional materials for signs of a one-size-fits-all, quick fix kind of approach. Beware of "the five habits of . . ." or "the ten signs of . . ." or "the three things I've learned" kinds of simplistic approaches.

\_\_\_\_\_ 4. *Stuck in skills.* There's more than skill development, but coaching for skill development is the easiest kind of coaching and therefore sometimes the most commonly provided kind of coaching. Your employee might need other kinds of coaching that are not properly identified by a coach with a behaviorist approach. Verify that an adequate needs assessment has been done, and that the coaching plan is significant and appropriate to the need.

\_\_\_\_\_ 5. *Blindness to psychological problems.* A common problem with executive coaching in particular is that the one being coached has an underlying psychological problem that is the main reason for low performance. Coaches must be skillful enough to know when this might be the case and make referrals to competent therapists, not try to act like therapists themselves.

\_\_\_\_\_ 6. *Power grab.* It is easy for a successful coach to wield great influence throughout a company, especially at executive and upper management levels. There's a fine line between working to promote the person being coached and promoting the coach. Beware of the power grab; it does no one any good in the long run.

# Coaching and Mentoring Checklist 6.4

## Management Support Checklist

Use this checklist to remind yourself of how the training department can and should be helpful to coaches and mentors.

_____ 1. Provide orientation to the company for the coach or mentor.

_____ 2. Provide monitoring and evaluation standards, process guidelines, and timelines.

_____ 3. Provide access to training department archival materials and online resources that pertain to the coaching or mentoring assignment.

_____ 4. Provide access to content information from current training courses: objectives, job and task lists, media tools, and learner evaluations of courses.

_____ 5. Provide a "listening ear" for your coached or mentored employee to talk with you about how learning goals are being achieved. Schedule periodic sessions for dialogue.

_____ 6. Provide clerical help and phone coverage for your employee during coaching or mentoring sessions.

_____ 7. Provide resources about learning styles, emotional intelligence, hierarchy of human needs, and cognitive and behavioral psychology. (See the Appendix and Bibliography of this book for suggestions.)

_____ 8. Provide introductions to internal formal and informal networks that can be helpful to the coach/mentor and the employee in achieving learning goals that they have established.

_____ 9. Provide access to computers and appropriate software.

_____ 10. Provide privacy and comfort for coaching and mentoring sessions.

# Coaching and Mentoring Checklist 6.5

## Feedback and Evaluation from the Coach or Mentor

"How'm I doin'?" is a question that should be asked often. Good coaches and mentors will instill a sense of in-process (formative) evaluation and encourage both informal and formal evaluation sessions. Think of in-process evaluation as feedback, debriefing of specific learning sessions, and dialogue about successes and failures. This checklist can guide you through the evaluation process.

\_\_\_\_\_ 1. Create performance standards collaboratively; never make standards a surprise.

\_\_\_\_\_ 2. Tell the trainee why something was wrong and suggest an avenue for improvement.

\_\_\_\_\_ 3. Listen, guide, and facilitate: Let the trainee tell you what he or she is doing differently after coaching/mentoring.

\_\_\_\_\_ 4. Discuss strengths and challenges, with praise and suggestions for improvement.

\_\_\_\_\_ 5. Identify recurring patterns so that together you can evaluate whether these are good or bad for the company.

\_\_\_\_\_ 6. Encourage the trainee to think in terms of individualizing his or her interpersonal relationships with others throughout the company. Guard against "one size fits all" thinking and behavior.

\_\_\_\_\_ 7. Collaboratively create a development plan for your trainee based on your evaluation data and information.

\_\_\_\_\_ 8. Be sure to give your trainee a chance for self-evaluation, and synthesize that evaluation with your own evaluation of the trainee.

# Chapter 6 Forms
## To Manage Coaching and Mentoring

The following forms are included here to suggest formats and structures for the management of coaching or mentoring. They are meant to be suggestive of ways of thinking about the processes of managing associated with these individualized, one-to-one forms of teaching and learning that have become so popular in recent years.

**LIST OF FORMS TO MANAGE COACHING AND MENTORING**

- **6.1** Reasons for Coaching and Mentoring
- **6.2** Matching Mentor and Protégé
- **6.3** Coaching Skills
- **6.4** Cross-Training Planning Form
- **6.5** Success Factors Needs Analysis
- **6.6** An Individual Learning Plan

# How to Manage Coaching and Mentoring

**Coaching and Mentoring Form 6.1**
**REASONS FOR COACHING AND MENTORING**

### How to Use This Form
1. Use this form to do a quick overview of needs for either coaching or mentoring or both. Make this your initial overview document as you plan for creating a coaching or mentoring program in your company.
2. Make a list of the needs of your learner, that is, the job tasks or cultural attitudes that can best be learned by coaching or mentoring. List needs down the left column.
3. Then check the appropriate coaching or mentoring cell across from each listed need.

| Job needs | Coaching | Mentoring |
|---|---|---|
|  |  |  |
|  |  |  |
|  |  |  |
|  |  |  |
|  |  |  |
|  |  |  |
|  |  |  |
|  |  |  |
|  |  |  |
|  |  |  |
|  |  |  |
|  |  |  |
|  |  |  |
|  |  |  |
|  |  |  |

**Coaching and Mentoring Form 6.2**
**MATCHING MENTOR AND PROTÉGÉ**

### How to Use This Form
1. Develop a form for each person you are having mentored.
2. Begin by listing this person's unique needs down the left side of the form.
3. For each need, choose a mentor from either inside the organization or outside the organization. Write their names in the cell across from each need.
4. Make a decision about which mentors should be contacted. Present this list to the person to be mentored, asking for his/her input to the decision about whom to assign.

Name of person to be mentored: _____

| Unique needs | Internal | External |
|---|---|---|
|  |  |  |
|  |  |  |
|  |  |  |
|  |  |  |
|  |  |  |
|  |  |  |
|  |  |  |
|  |  |  |
|  |  |  |
|  |  |  |
|  |  |  |
|  |  |  |
|  |  |  |
|  |  |  |

**Coaching and Mentoring Form 6.3**
**COACHING SKILLS**

| How to Use This Form |
|---|
| 1. Use this form to help potential coaches figure out what they need to know about being a coach.
2. Give a form to each potential coach to use as a check sheet that allows you to develop an appropriate train-the-trainer program. The form is especially useful for employees who will take on the added job of being a coach.
3. Ask them to rate themselves on a scale of 1 to 5 according to their need to know in each category. |

1 = small need; 5 = great need.

Name of coach: _____

| Coaching skills | Rating 1, 2, 3, 4, 5 |
|---|---|
| Design of instruction to reflect employee's environment | |
| Use of cognitive and psychomotor hierarchies | |
| Use of learning strategies favored by adults | |
| Variety in progress through a learning experience | |
| Use of experience-based learning design | |
| Use of chunking, learning objects, and small steps | |
| Provision for searching and browsing | |
| Use of guided practice | |
| Use of multimedia | |
| Design of self-study opportunities | |

**Coaching and Mentoring Form 6.3 (continued)**
**COACHING SKILLS**

| Coaching skills | Rating 1, 2, 3, 4, 5 |
|---|---|
| How to ask good questions | |
| How to recognize a "teachable moment" | |
| Active listening skills | |
| Pacing instructional presentations | |
| Giving feedback | |
| Receiving feedback | |
| Stating objectives for learning | |
| Differentiating "describing" from "explaining" | |
| How to give learning cues | |
| How to teach by demonstration | |
| How to teach through stories and metaphors | |
| How to design and use job aids | |
| How to develop evaluation standards | |

# How to Manage Coaching and Mentoring

**Coaching and Mentoring Form 6.4**
**CROSS-TRAINING PLANNING FORM**

### How to Use This Form
1. Use this form to plan a cross-training program, a useful form of coaching in which peers generally teach each other the essentials of their respective jobs.
2. Identify the peer coach and decide when you want to do the training: options could be throughout the company on the same day, every Thursday, at the convenience of the participants, etc.
3. List the learning activities down the left column. Develop this list in collaboration with a high performer in the job for which you are cross-training. Add extra pages.

Job: _____
Coach's name: _____
Trainee's name: _____
Estimated total training time: _____

| Learning activity | Scheduled time/date | Completion date |
|---|---|---|
| 1. | | |
| 2. | | |
| 3. | | |
| 4. | | |
| 5. | | |

**Coaching and Mentoring Form 6.5**
**SUCCESS FACTORS NEEDS ANALYSIS**

---

### How to Use This Form

1. Choose no more than four major functions of the job—those which represent the most benefit to the company. List them across the top of the form.
2. Place a check mark or other notation (brief comment) in the appropriate cell opposite each success factor indicating the need for coaching/mentoring in each job function according to the factor being addressed.
3. After analyzing the patterns, write a brief narrative about this person's needs for coaching/mentoring. Attach a separate sheet for this if necessary. Use this as an initial planning document.

---

Name of person being coached/mentored: _____

Name of coach/mentor: _____

Narrative commentary on patterns of need: _____

_____

_____

| *Success factors* | *Major functions of the job* | | | |
|---|---|---|---|---|
| Employee relations | | | | |
| Public relations | | | | |
| Creativity | | | | |
| Oral/verbal expression | | | | |
| Written expression | | | | |
| Assertiveness | | | | |
| Self-confidence | | | | |
| Reasoning | | | | |

| | | | | |
|---|---|---|---|---|
| Organizing | | | | |
| Teamwork | | | | |
| Speed | | | | |
| Presentation skills | | | | |
| Math/number facility | | | | |
| Memory recall | | | | |
| Muscle coordination | | | | |
| Computer skills | | | | |
| Flexibility | | | | |
| Focus | | | | |

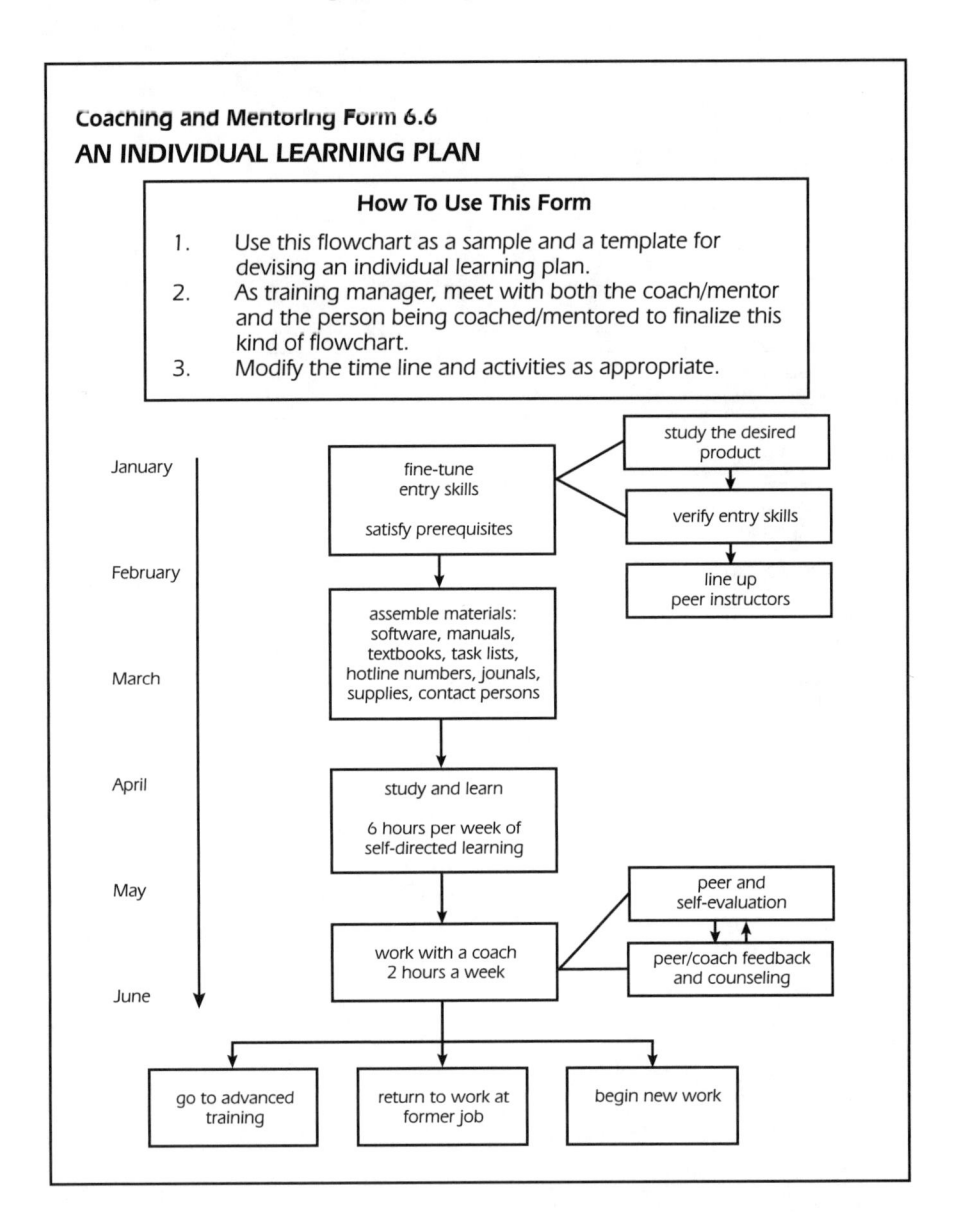

# How to Manage Training

**Coaching and Mentoring Form 6.6**
## AN INDIVIDUAL LEARNING PLAN

### How To Use This Form
1. Use this flowchart as a sample and a template for devising an individual learning plan.
2. As training manager, meet with both the coach/mentor and the person being coached/mentored to finalize this kind of flowchart.
3. Modify the time line and activities as appropriate.

| Timeline | Activity |
|---|---|
| January | fine-tune entry skills / satisfy prerequisites → study the desired product → verify entry skills → line up peer instructors |
| February | |
| March | assemble materials: software, manuals, textbooks, task lists, hotline numbers, jounals, supplies, contact persons |
| April | study and learn — 6 hours per week of self-directed learning |
| May | |
| June | work with a coach 2 hours a week ↔ peer and self-evaluation / peer/coach feedback and counseling |

→ go to advanced training | return to work at former job | begin new work

# Chapter 6
# More Information on How to Manage Coaching and Mentoring

## The Numbers Favor Coaching and Mentoring

Recently there have been numerous studies of the results of coaching and mentoring. We report on five of them in the following paragraphs. All of the studies demonstrate the value of coaching and mentoring in different ways.

■ *Retention and Staffing Report*, Manchester Inc., March 1999. An article by Jeff Barbian in *Training* ("The Road Best Traveled," May 2002, pp. 38–42) cites a survey from the report that polled 378 companies across the country to find out why they offer mentoring programs to their employees. The following percentages represent their reasons for mentoring:

- 73 percent of the companies mentored to retain employees
- 71 percent of the companies mentored to improve leadership/managerial skills
- 66 percent of the companies mentored to develop new leaders
- 62 percent of the companies mentored to enhance career development
- 49 percent of the companies mentored to put high-potential individuals in a fast career track
- 48 percent of the companies mentored to promote diversity
- 30 mentored of the companies percent to improve technical knowledge

■ *Center for Creative Leadership: Report on Retention and Report on Follow-Up Coaching.* The articles "The Road Best Traveled" by Jeff Barbian (*Training*, May 2002, pp. 38–42) and "In It for the Long Haul: Coaching Is Key to Continued Development" by Gina Hernez-Brooms (*Leadership In Action*, v.22 n.1, March/April 2002, pp. 14–16) cite the two 1999 studies by the Center for Creative Leadership (CCL) in Greensboro, North Carolina. The studies report on the value reaped by companies when they increased their employee retention during times of movement and diminished loyalty. Barbian's reference to CCL states that 77 percent of the companies studied reported that mentoring increased retention (p. 39). Hernez-Brooms' report notes that 75 percent of the companies that instituted follow-up coaching to leadership development programs said they had a sustained coaching-related positive change in behavior following the period of coaching (p. 16).

■ *Catalyst: Women of Color in Corporate Management—Three Years Later.* Catalyst, the New York City–based research and advocacy group for women in business, recently completed a three-year study of women of color and reported on it in their news release of July 16, 2002. The years covered by the study were 1998 through 2001. The study surveyed 368 women of color who, during the three-year period, intentionally found mentors, networked strategically, and took charge of their own careers.

Catalyst discovered that as of 2001, 58 percent of the women surveyed had developed mentor relationships, up from 38 percent in 1998. Percentage usage of mentors by group was: African-American women 62 percent, Latina women 52 percent, and Asian-American women 51 percent. Catalyst also found that 70 percent of the women who had a mentor in 1998 have since had a promotion, and the more mentors a woman had, the faster she advanced. The study also indicated that overall income of women of color was up 37 percent from 1998.

■ *ASTD: Two Mentoring Studies.* Jeff Barbian's article "The Road Best Traveled" (*Training*, May 2002, pp. 38–42) reports on the studies conducted by ASTD, based in Alexandria, Virginia. One of the studies reports that 75 percent of executives surveyed said mentoring played a key role in their careers; the other study found that mentoring and coaching combined increased managerial productivity by 88 percent, nearly four times as much as just training alone (p. 39).

■ *The Managers' Mentors: Mentoring Study.* This Oakland, California–based organization's study, also cited in the Barbian article, has a slightly different perspective. It was based on measurement of eleven essential job skills, and it revealed that persons who were mentored increased these skills by an average of 61 percent. The study also found that more than 60 percent of college and graduate students looked for companies that offered mentoring, thus giving those companies a recruitment edge ("The Road Best Traveled," *Training*, May 2002, p. 39).

## Executive Coaching Versus Psychotherapy

A final word needs to be said about what executive coaching is not: It is not psychotherapy. If executive coaching attempts to be built on personality defects (and not business skills), it fails. It also fails if it ignores personality defects.

Professor and psychiatrist Steven Berglas has written a cautionary article on this subject ("The Very Real Dangers of Executive Coaching," *Harvard Business Review*, June 2002, pp. 86–92). It is an article of case studies of executives who were mentored for the wrong reasons by the wrong kind of mentor, making matters worse and yielding nearly disastrous results. Executive coaches, in particular, must be sensitive to deeper personality problems and be ready to refer their protégés to appropriate

# How to Manage Coaching and Mentoring

therapists instead of trying to solve what are nonbusiness problems. Clearly linking mentoring and coaching to business strategy, and having clear program objectives and realistic expectations for all participants, are key first steps in identifying the business problems that can be solved by mentoring. Leave the psychiatry and psychology to those who are professionally prepared to serve clients in these ways.

Dr. Berglas brings the point home in a sidebar within his article that details the economics of executive coaching. He notes that often a coaching engagement lasts no more than six months; yet, in psychotherapy, it takes at least six months for the two parties to "say hello." He also suggests that executives are driven by time constraints and therefore would prefer to have an executive coach come to their workplace rather than have to leave the workplace to go to a therapist's office. Finally, he suggests that even the lowest-paid executive coach makes twice that of a typical therapist (p. 89). Executives and coaches are cautioned to do business together for the right reasons.

## If You Have Limited Budget and Staff . . .

If you know that you need to hire a coach or mentor, buy the best and engage him or her for a shorter time. Go for quality. Buy the best diagnostician. Check references, biographical information, and client lists. Don't be fooled by the words "management consulting" on a resume or in a company title. Make your decision after thoroughly checking if this is the kind of coach or mentor you want to hire.

Often you can get extra free training and coaching services from suppliers when you purchase or lease their equipment. Structure whatever "training time" they offer you as coaching time, to maximize the immediate learning effects that coaching provides. This can be especially helpful in one-to-one coaching on new computer hardware and software.

Look for professors in nearby colleges and universities that have "centers" or "institutes" in their research operations. Very often there will be grant money available for collaboration with businesses, and you can sometimes get free access to and involvement in their research studies and to university personnel who can function as coaches or mentors. Look to the community colleges and adult schools funded with public education funds for individuals who might be available as coaches.

Finally, refer back to the Performance Technology model (p. 311) and recall the list of options other than training for solving performance problems. In short, be sure that you have a training problem for which a training solution is required. Realize that there are other reasons besides lack of knowledge and skills that can cause poor performance. Too often, companies identify poor performance and immediately throw training at it, to the good of no one and the harm of many. Here is a list of options (other than training/coaching/mentoring) that can help to solve performance problems:

- Compensation and reward change
- Change in incentives and expectations
- Better documentation
- Better environmental conditions (air flow, lighting, privacy, etc.)
- Health and wellness programs
- Job aids or Electronic Performance Support Systems (EPSS) at the worksite
- Modification of work design/work processes
- Better or different supervision
- Better tools
- Modification of the consequences for poor performance
- Better information
- Job rotation
- Better identification of career goals

The message is to save training in any of its forms for solutions to training problems. Before embarking on an expensive coaching or mentoring program of any size, be sure to take a hard look at some other options for solving performance problems. If you have limited resources, this is your managerial—and your ethical—responsibility.

## If You Have Adequate Budget and Staff . . .

What can be a resource-intensive approach is using your own employees as mentors and coaches. Sponsor and organize a company-wide, in-depth program. This, of course, demands a sizeable chunk of your time as training manager to pull it all together, provide necessary training for coaches and mentors, facilitate implementation, and provide support. All of these are resource-intensive, especially the resource of your time, so be sure that the bottom line is in fact affected as positively as you think it will be.

Companies who do this report mixed results: Some say that a coaching atmosphere throughout the company pays off big in terms of bringing employees to a heightened awareness of learning possibilities on a daily basis; others say that coaches and mentors that are mismatched with those being coached or mentored do more harm than good in terms of both self-esteem and sustainable improved performance. Such a company-wide program run out of the training department requires corporate clout on the part of the training manager, so if you don't have it, figure out how to get it. Volunteer on important committees and teams, know your company's accounting practices and balance sheet, know your corporate-wide computer hardware, software, and Internet capacity, know who the movers and shakers are among employees in all departments, and know where the informal communities of practice operate.

Make executives understand that a learning organization needs resources: funding in the training department itself and a different way of accounting for learning while on the job. It's not easy to figure out how to account for a coach or mentor's time teaching or a learner's time learning. If you see these functions as separate from work, as the classroom training model has seen them for decades, you will trap yourself in irrelevancy. As the ads for Apple computers say, it's time to "think different."

Another essential part of any coaching or mentoring program is the needs assessment phase. In a company-wide program, this takes up more resources than a one-by-one as-needed kind of program. It is always tempting to try to shorten the needs assessment phase; and in this kind of program, doing that can be disastrous. As a first step in preventing a shrinking assessment, create standards for determining need. Involve a company-wide task force or team to set standards and help to promote the program. Develop checklists and forms to be given to each participant, so that the process gets started in a standardized fashion throughout the company. Create content development standards and templates so that teaching can be documented and become part of a corporate resource base. Create monitoring and administrative systems, and teacher and learner evaluation standards. Create opportunities for "show and tell" sessions, public relations, and company-wide celebrations of learning.

# 7

# How to Train for Innovation

In this chapter, I focus on how to assure the long-term viability of the training function in a company by shaping empowered employees with skills for lifetime employability. The key issues stem from the training program's relationship to business needs and its ability to serve employees' needs as continuous learners and innovators.

This chapter is for the training manager who believes that learning is an important and pivotal business function that contributes to profit and to a company's long-term health. The dual focus—that is, the corporate reaching out as well as the personal reaching in—is critical whether you are part of a large, midsize, or small company and whether you are on a limited budget or have adequate staff and financial resources.

The management issues and strategies discussed here are issues of "process"—of the way in which the training program as a whole integrates itself into the life of the business enterprise and into the personal lives of its employees. These issues and strategies are relevant only if training has been managed well, designed well, written well, delivered well, and analyzed and evaluated with applicability and growth in mind.

## KEY MANAGEMENT ISSUES

■ *Flexibility.* This is the issue of program responsiveness, or ability to change in order to provide the training people need and want. It's a question of whether the training operation is pliable enough to "go with the flow" of changing times to facilitate learning.

You should budget and staff for flexibility, avoiding getting tied to specific courses but following instead a flexible curriculum approach—that is, a range of training opportunities that build upon each other. It's also advisable to establish linkages with corporate planners and marketing organizations in order to keep up with new business directions.

The training department should be available to design and deliver courses in response to training needs created by restructuring, mergers, downsizing, relocation and dislocation, global expansion, and political, cultural, and environmental challenges. It should be able to respond quickly to gaps in the workforce and to special needs created by retirement of large numbers of people, by a growth in the number of entry-level jobs, by changing demographics, such as an increase in the number of foreign-born employees at all levels, by needs for literacy training, by demands of working mothers, or by an influx of part-time older workers. In short, your operation cannot be so static that it relies on a set group of consultants, vendors, or courses. Your communication sensors must be tuned in to sources of information within your company, and your staff, facilities, and budget must be flexible enough to flow with changing times.

Training can play an important role in responding to all these changes in the workplace, but only if it can remain flexible in its organization and in the ways in which it provides service. A flexible training program can help to shape a company's effective management of change.

■ *Learning to Innovate.* Flexibility, learning, and innovation are key ingredients of remaining employable in today's corporate atmosphere of challenge and change. Someone who's responsible for training, learning, and employee development—the training manager—needs to take on the task of facilitating employees' abilities to be creative and to help them learn to innovate. These days, every job description could start with the requirement to create and innovate, and employees could be held accountable for their creative acts in new ways of measuring that includes accumulation and manifestation of knowledge and implementation of new ideas. If knowledge resources resident in the employee base are a company's competitive advantage, then those in charge of learning need to find ways to help employees learn beyond their competencies and job skills in order to be able to continuously contribute to the company's and their own personal growth. Systems of control need to give way to systems of imagination and interpretation. Every day should be an opportunity to make nonobvious connections.

A recent book* by Lawrence Lessig, Stanford University law professor, talks about the "tragedy of the commons" in which resources held in common get overused and dry up. He makes the distinction between these kinds of tragedies of the commons and "nonrivalrous" resources that create no depletion. Lessig suggests that ideas and expression are examples of nonrivalrous resources and are the basis for an "innovation commons" that benefits all users. A 2002 ASTD "manifesto" states that "It's not how well managed the change, but how much innovation you can inspire" (*T+D,* January 2002, p. 7). Through year 2003, The MIT Sloan School of Management offers an executive series of courses on "Management, Innovation, and Technology"; The University of Chicago's Graduate School of Business offers an innovative course on New Product Development. Words like "breakthrough," "create," and "cutting-edge" are among

---

*Lessig, Lawrence, *The Future of Ideas: The Fate of the Commons in a Connected World.* Random House, 2001.

its descriptors. Other business schools and executive programs, too, are getting into the business of teaching employees at all levels to learn to innovate. Send for their brochures.

The business press frequently features stories of innovation. Two examples are presented here, showing how nonobvious connections were made and turned into action in product development. The July 14, 2002 *New York Times* ran a photo of a woman scientist holding a "cell phone tooth," a cell phone embedded in a tooth (p. 3). Discussion in the accompanying article talked about "genetic algorithms" and the cross-fertilization between disciplines occurring more frequently these days.* The August 12, 2002 *Business Week*† ran an article on Procter and Gamble's new "SpinBrush," including a racing-car model electric toothbrush for kids that runs on just $5 worth of batteries. The article applauds P&G for being willing to look beyond its own, nearly sacred marketing and distribution capability and transfer it out of the company in partnership with a very small start-up product developer. P&G was willing to experiment innovatively with its business models, no small endeavor for a large, culture-bound, traditional corporation.

The challenge for training managers should be clear: To keep your company competitive through its key resource, its people, you need to assure their employability through learning to innovate.

■ *Linkage.* It is of critical importance that training be visible to top management and that its outputs clearly contribute to business goals, and personal and organizational growth. This doesn't happen easily, because training is often seen as a necessary expense of business, not as a strategic competitive tool for accomplishing business ends.

The wise training manager devises ways in which to directly link training operations to other related operations of the business. Other managers, supervisors, and team leaders will probably not think to include you in policy or strategic planning discussions; they generally think of you in tactical terms, that is, they'll call on you to provide specific training to solve an immediate problem. It will be up to you to forge linkages at higher levels. The business of innovation is business as unusual.

There are two avenues you can take in this endeavor. The first is to establish operational relationships with the other major organizations in your reporting chain; that is, look at your organization chart, see who else reports to the same executive officer that you report to, and establish working relationships with them first. The other avenue is to establish operational relationships with organizations outside of your own organizational line. Here's how each avenue might work:

---

*Brown, Patricia Leigh, "Ideas and Trends: Blinded by Science," in *The New York Times,* July 14, 2002, p. 3.
†Berner, Robert, "Why P&G's Smile Is So Bright," in *Business Week,* August 12, 2002, pp. 58–60.

Within your own organizational line, you can:

1. Find out who in the personnel organization keeps track of the results of performance reviews. With their help, devise a reporting form that lists employees' and supervisors' stated needs for training as a result of performance reviews. Develop training documentation, in addition to salary increase documentation. Consider coding the training needs as either "knowledge" needs or "skill" needs, in addition to using organization identification coding.

2. Identify those members of the human resources managerial staff who administer benefits. Find out what employees are worried about—flextime, child care, health insurance, elder care, stock options. With the managers' help, review the information dissemination function of their jobs and isolate those functions that could be viewed as training tasks. Training can help employees to make better decisions regarding benefits; training can help people design effective programs; training can facilitate efficient choice, thereby improving both the work of the benefits administrators and of the training department.

3. Establish relationships with the groups who provide social activities for employees—dances, ski weekends, museum trips, concert parties, "sunshine" clubs for ill employees, support groups. Tap into existing organizations by asking these groups what training opportunities they might like the company to provide. Do this formally with a questionnaire of your own, by adding an item or two to one of their questionnaires or evaluation forms, or by an informal telephone call. Sometimes grouping employees by hobby or by social interest generates discussion about learning from a "relationships" point of view, which often has a direct impact on work problems and solutions, yet is articulated only when the social environment encourages it.

4. Seek input on perceived training needs from the medical organization. Persons who interview or log in employees who visit medical staff have an excellent database from which to illuminate training needs. Medical records might indicate a need for safety training, public health training, or mental health programs aimed at managing stress, developing assertiveness or overcoming prejudice against workers from ethnic or other minorities, and overcoming bias against gay workers or older workers.

Use all sources of information about training needs, expecially those that can provide current data and especially those groups in your own organizational line that can achieve greater cost-effectiveness by cooperating with you than by operating alone.

If you choose to work outside of your organizational line, you can:

1. Plug training into the corporate information, library, electronic mail, communications systems, Internet, Web site, and corporate intranet. Spread information about training opportunities around the company in as many places as you can think of. To many people, training means a chance for a better future. Training is often considered an "equal opportunity" in the context of employee rights; as an equal opportunity manager, be sure that information about training is disseminated equally to all employees. Truly offer something for everyone.

In some places, information functions are grouped in one part of the organization; in other places, each functional group handles its own information needs. Be sure that all the information channels in your company include up-to-date information about what's going on in training. Use the familiar marketing strategy of depending on channels to spread the word; you usually don't have to do it all yourself. You do, however, have to tailor your information to the deadlines and formats of your channels, so find out what these are and do what you need to do in order to make effective use of them to promote training opportunity.

2. Ask your accounting department how you should keep your records. Ask an accountant to show you how accountants calculate return on investment. If you make it easier for the accountants to do their job, they'll find it easier to understand how training works. Do your part to help these bottom-line types begin to see training as a mainstream and strategic part of the business.

3. Attend sales and marketing meetings to see how those departments project and forecast. See what drives them to perform well; see if training can help them accomplish their goals. Engage in regular discussions with marketing planners and with sales people to be sure that they understand how products and services of the company can be improved by the training that you provide. Try to get yourself assigned as a regular member of sales and marketing advisory groups and focus groups or as an ex officio member of staff. Get training goals and accomplishments written into marketing plans.

4. Be sure that corporate policy makers and the official corporate planning organization know the full scope of your training products and services. Be sure that they are aware of training's successes, especially as stated by key customers on evaluation forms or through other feedback. Develop your own training policy built upon the more general corporate policy, and seek the involvement of corporate policy gurus as you develop and implement your training policy. Create a training business plan that fits in with corporate planning goals.

5. If you have a "quality" or "quality assurance" department, ask the experts there for advice on how to build quality in for training. Members of

a quality department who have a background in "process quality"—as contrasted with "product quality"—can be especially helpful as you attempt to create standards for needs analysis and course design, delivery, and evaluation. You should create quality measures that are a spin-off of the corporate quality metrics. Be very sure that everyone understands that training is a central player and a strong corporate citizen when it comes to quality goals and measurements.

Only when you yourself see your role as larger than responding to immediate needs will you be able to begin to position training as a function with strategic corporate potential—and, fundamentally, it is this positioning that will guarantee training's longevity and, ultimately, your company's capacity to innovate, and your employees' employability.

■ *Career development.* In addition to having a solid foundation in business planning, training must be grounded in the benefits it provides to individuals on the job. Training has an important place in the process loosely called "career development."

Career development is related to training in several ways—creating motivation for accepting company values, building careers, providing up-to-date skills and knowledge as career positions become fulfilled and maximized, and helping to manage downsizing as careers are redefined. Across the workforce, training is the best hope for maintaining America's skill base.

1. *Training in motivation toward company values.* Every company has its own unique culture—open, closed, collegial, top-down, bottom-up, protective, sharing, bureaucratic, entrepreneurial, report-driven, or hands-on. Within this culture, there are distinctive values that are held in high esteem, such as respect for the individual, excellence in performance, achieving zero defects, viewing change as opportunity, and seeing diversity as strength. Individuals at work often need reminding about what these values are and about how to behave in order to act in accordance with them.

You are missing the boat in training if you don't anticipate these value-centered needs. One obvious place to provide this kind of training is during orientation programs for new or reassigned employees. Most people want to do a good job at work; sometimes they fail because they haven't tapped into the cultural mainstream fast enough.

It's not enough to tell people about the value system; most people need training in experiencing the values through role play, mentoring, case studies, or other interactive and facilitated group work. You should always be on the lookout for opportunities to design and deliver value-related training because it is generally directly related to personal effectiveness on the job, and that's what keeps people happy and productive. Training that can contribute to psychological health at work, fewer absences, fewer stress-related personnel problems, and increased productivity is training that will last. Employees who master the culture of one company and learn how to grow within it generally can more easily learn the culture of a new company, should they leave your employer. Trainers should not underestimate their contributions to the workforce at large.

2. *Training in building careers.* The role of training in building careers is probably its best understood reason for being. This is the kind of training that helps people learn new systems, master new machines, develop new skills, and transfer accumulated knowledge to new situations. It's the kind of training that keeps the wheels of progress running smoothly as each person does his or her job, and it's the kind of training that helps people prepare for lateral career moves as well as moves up the corporate ladder. It's this kind of training that helps people perform better in order to improve work. The need for such training often shows up on performance review documentation in feedback from multi-rater review processes, or in the objectives of business plans.

It is important to provide this kind of training with great care and to verify its relationship to personal goals through valid business goals. You should regularly establish the need for it with managers and advisory groups that include a large number of people. In this kind of training, the obvious personal career in the spotlight must share the stage with an obvious business objective. If training is careful to do this, it is likely to be embraced by the individual and applauded by the organization whose goals it furthers.

In recent years, training has had an every-growing role to play in helping employees deal with mergers and downsizing. Training has helped individuals look inward to "know themselves" and to plan step-by-step for their futures, either within the newly merged company or outside the company. Training has helped individuals identify leads for new positions, handle rejection along the way, and go after that new position with a personal and professional style that gets results. Training has helped people write business plans and marketing plans, clarify goals, and manage their own change through organizations in turmoil.

3. *Training in maintaining skills.* Most companies acknowledge that their most important and valuable resource is their employee base. Training departments are well-advised to maintain strong linkages with career development specialists on staff who analyze the numbers regarding salary grades, impending retirements, proportion of new hires to experienced staff, and other staff characteristics. While the accumulated wisdom of the staff may be growing, its knowledge base may also be getting stale, and new skill and knowledge needs may be surfacing. Be sure that you know what your company's "core competencies" requirements are; be sure you know what leads to high performance in your company.

It's important that training stay one jump ahead by providing opportunity for professional development through broadening—incorporating skills or knowledge about new ideas into the already solid base of experience represented by a more mature staff. Training is not only for the rising stars; it is also for the stars who are currently shining brightly!

You should try to develop a training program that is geared to the relative proportion of career building and career maintenance employees in the company. Alternatives to classroom instruction should be explored here; training through conferences and institutes, video-based self study, e-learning, field trips, and college-based programs are all possible ways to deliver training to persons who are settled in their careers. Many companies are afraid of losing their resident knowledge base as career employees leave.

It's easy to ignore this training audience because its contribution to the company has largely been made already. However, it still represents an enormous investment by the company and is a high-potential service provider. Delivering the right kind of training to this group can pay off handsomely because this group of people knows how the system works and how to get things done. Training's role here is to help maximize the contributions that can be made by your career employees by knowing how to fill in the gaps in their current knowledge and skills.

In recent years, training has played a critical role in helping the workforce define itself. All signals point toward an increase in the importance of this role in the coming years. You should be ready to serve individuals in the very important function of career development.

■ *Empowerment.* Empowerment cannot happen instantly just because everyone says it's a good thing. Slogan-driven efforts don't stick; employees need the ups and downs of learning in order for the personal and organizational changes that define empowerment to occur. The issues for training management here are those of building trust and overcoming fear, meeting each individual employee's skill-based and emotional needs for embracing empowerment, and designing and delivering training with corporate goals clearly as drivers of change.

Trainers must equally address the needs of top management and the newest staff support person, the highest-paid and the lowest-paid employee, salespersons, accountants, engineers, technical specialists—in short, all employees everywhere who make a company work. Trainers will be successful at this if they can keep the "one-to-one" teaching and learning paradigm in mind: classroom training is fine, but only if you keep the objective before you of facilitating the learning of one single person with unique learning needs.

The essence of empowerment is that one size does not fit all and that the power of one creative and innovative employee is tremendous.

# Chapter 7 Checklists
## To Help You Train for Innovation

Trainers these days are finding that their mission often is to facilitate change, first at the individual level and then at the organizational level. These checklists are reminders of important elements to include in your training for an empowered workforce, one whose individuals can remain employable as the workplace changes. As companies become less bureaucratic and less hierarchical, trainers are often called upon to work with all employees as the company moves through structural and cultural changes. These can be heady times for training managers, as the ability to learn on the job and from work itself becomes a strategic tool for business success. Training managers are finally getting their day in the sun: How you manage empowerment and train for innovation for all of your employees will translate directly into your own longevity as a critical component of business.

**LIST OF INNOVATION CHECKLISTS**

- 7.1 Trustbusters: Where to Look for Obstacles to Building Trust
- 7.2 Empowerment Slogans that Need to Be Turned into Action
- 7.3 The Empowering Manager's Guide to Good Behavior
- 7.4 A Top Twelve List of Don'ts for Empowering Managers
- 7.5 Employability Skills
- 7.6 Fifteen Ways to Learn on the Job from Work Itself
- 7.7 Fundamentals of High Performance
- 7.8 Organizational Indicators of Innovation

# Innovation Checklist 7.1

## Trustbusters: Where to Look for Obstacles to Building Trust

Being employed these days involves more than a paper contract between parties. At the root of employment is a social contract, often unwritten, that requires parties to this contract to behave in certain ways in interaction with others on the job. Much has been said in recent years about the value of a company's human resources; the term "human capital" has become part of our business vocabulary.

Key to the successful functioning of human capital for the good of all parties at work is the virtue of trust, seen as an active force that helps to govern relationships between persons in association with each other and that is viewed as an important foundation of innovation. The following checklist will remind you to actively train to build trust within your employee base. An employee who has learned to trust is more valuable to himself, herself, your company, and ultimately to the workforce at large.

Here's where to look for obstacles to trust:

_____ 1. **Support.** Objectively look at all support systems: accounting, computer systems, copying and mailing, telephone/fax/e-mail, personnel, clerical, etc. Are the interfaces between the requester of services and the provider of services based on trusting paperwork and human interactions? Are turnaround times and procedures realistic? Do service providers have a say in how they'd like to provide services? Did you ever ask any service provider to explain his/her job to you?

_____ 2. **Recognition.** All persons at all levels and in all kinds of jobs like to be recognized for what they do and for what they know. Look around and see if recognition is lopsided in your company; that is, are some categories of jobs or some particular individuals always getting the lion's share of recognition? Companies often need help in training employees to seek recognition and to give it to others who deserve it. Trusting relationships often depend on equal opportunity for recognition.

_____ 3. **Civic involvement.** Towns and cities in which companies are physically located have a stake in a company's success. Often local residents have given up significant "quality of life" matters to bring a business to their locale: extra traffic, extra police and fire personnel, shopping and parking hassles, lower tax rates and other municipal incentives for businesses in order to attract corporations, extra need for schools and other publicly supported services. Individuals who benefit from working in a town are sometimes well advised to think of themselves as corporate citizens who should give back to the town something of their workplace skills in order to help the town function better. Employability often involves mutual responsibility and demonstrated trust between the institutions of the municipality and the corporation. This can happen only when individuals at work take action on behalf of their companies to provide expertise that towns and cities often badly need. And sometimes, too, trust has to be earned. Managers in human resources organizations, including training managers, need to be proactive here.

_____ 4. **Association.** One sure way to evaluate a company's trust level is to look at how freely persons associate with each other on the job. Are there several assistants to get through before you get to the boss? Are there endless levels of voice mail? Do physical barriers impede access—doors? outer offices? private stairs? a maze of cubicle walls? separate buildings? Does your organization chart imply limited access? What can you change to encourage trust?

_____ 5. **Collaboration.** Are there rewards for seeking help, coaching, mentoring, one-to-one teaching, working in teams? If not, help to make "teamwork" more than a nice slogan and train employees in effective ways to collaborate.

_____ 6. **Listening.** Encourage folks to listen so that they hear; try to break the great American cultural habit of "speaking up" and talking fast. I have a friend who is often called a "Ready, Fire, Aim" kind of guy. Ken Blanchard says it this way: "Don't just do something, stand there" (*Empowerment Takes More than a Minute,* Berrett-Koehler, 1996). It's a matter of trusting the other person to be at least as wise and wonderful as you are. Listening builds trust, and it is often very hard to do. Training can help.

_____ 7. **Self-organization.** Help folks practice a "bottom-up" way of working, not a "top-down" way. People at work have very good ideas about the way in which their own jobs should be done. Get rid of rules that reinforce the top-down command and control way of organizing work. Train all employees in bottom-up approaches. Folks on the front line with customers or at the beginning of processes need authority and support to conduct their jobs the best way they know how for the good of the company.

_____ 8. **Continuous improvement.** Encourage everyone at all levels, in all kinds of jobs, to build quality in, not wait for it to be inspected out. Think of errors and mistakes as your friends, not your mortal enemies. Catch the problem early, as soon as you see it. Train all employees to feel and act responsibly about feedback, in all work processes and products and at all times.

Reward those who find errors the earliest; don't reward "cover your tail" behavior.

_____ 9. **Pride in skills.** Look for individuals who are proud of what they know and how they perform their jobs. Publicize, recognize, and reward the acquisition of new skills and the development of existing skills. Make known widely the high standards by which certain jobs are done; spread the good news and make it skill-specific. Facilitate acquisition of skills at all levels.

_____ 10. **Information.** Pay attention to information flow and content. Full disclosure should be the rule to live by—anything less ruins trust, and leads to frustration, annoyance, and anxiety. Help employees to understand their company and give them a foundation for continued employment, even in a shifting economy.

# Innovation Checklist 7.2

## Empowerment Slogans that Need to Be Turned into Action

A common obstacle to real progress is the human tendency to sloganeering. We love to hand out "the good words" in the form of vision cards for our wallets, posters in the hallways, and silver mottoes on our letterheads. It's tempting to think we've met our management responsibilities by handing out or handing down these pronouncements about what all employees should be or do. When it comes to empowerment, or the evidence of trust in employees by employers, we seem to have no lack of favorite slogans.

The real work of empowering individuals, of course, is a time-consuming, energy-sapping, mentally challenging network of actions, not wordsmithing. Real partnering with employees is about pain as well as profit. Following is a short list of some of our favorite slogans, those that appear on our posters as well as those that are spoken by employees and by managers.

Training managers are often on the front lines of responsibility for turning these into the real change that they imply. The operative word here is *action:* trainers need to be proactive in design and delivery of training that facilitates the realization of the good words that abound in our workplaces. Trainers, in fact, have a golden opportunity to be the primary change agents for empowering workplaces. In the case of each of these "good words," individuals need to learn how to be here and to practice behaving in ways to turn them into the desired action. Trainers have nearly limitless opportunities associated with each of these assumptions:

_____ 1. People are our most important assets.

_____ 2. The customer comes first.

_____ 3. You are now a team.

_____ 4. I am giving you this responsibility.

_____ 5. Downsizing automatically leads to empowerment.

_____ 6. Participation is the same as collaboration.

The following negative expressions are also commonly heard around workplaces on the road to empowerment. These assumptions, too, must be challenged.

_____ 7. Fear, anxiety, and mistrust are normal and inevitable parts of employment.

_____ 8. I just want to come to work to do my job.

_____ 9. Hourly workers should do what they're told; they don't get paid to think.

_____ 10. I'm a nice person and care about your kids; you should be nice to me at contract time.

# Innovation Checklist 7.3
## The Empowering Manager's Guide to Good Behavior

The trick for managers is to clarify what their job is and what the job is of the empowered employee. Both manager and subordinate need to respect each other's roles and functions in the organization. Much of the literature about empowerment focuses on the employee's role and new responsibilities, and often the role of the manager remains unclear. Trainers have the challenge of dealing with both ends of the empowerment pull—the manager as well as the employee.

Here's a checklist for managers, to help you see the best kinds of things you should be doing:

_____ 1. Be credible: Do what you say you will do. No name without the game.

_____ 2. Be fair: Create equal opportunity for success as well as for failure. Go beyond the letter of the law to the spirit of fairness. Don't just polish your stars.

_____ 3. Think in terms of "letting it out" when it comes to responsibility, not of "handing it out." Most people at work want to do a good job, be proud of their work, and take responsibility for their own results.

_____ 4. Provide support. Go get the resources employees need to do their jobs better. Ask them if you don't know exactly what they need. Find the tools, money, time, contact persons, information—whatever it takes for individuals to do their best work.

_____ 5. Coordinate work. You are the one with the big picture of the organization. It's your role to fit all the pieces of the puzzle together.

_____ 6. Communicate the big picture. Bring the whole into the parts; help all employees see the larger scene, the big picture of why they are working and how their jobs contribute to that big picture.

_____ 7. Treat persons as partners, not subordinates. Think in terms of individual relationships, one-to-one, what we can do together. Coach, facilitate, teach individuals to work more effectively with each other as partners and with you as a partner.

_____ 8. Encourage cross-functional work.

_____ 9. Encourage diversity to ensure breadth of ideas.

_____ 10. Place creative thinkers in supportive networks.

## Innovation Checklist 7.4
### A Top Twelve List of Don'ts for Empowering Managers

This checklist for managers says it another way—what the empowering manager should not do. Trainers might find this helpful as a lesson in a management training program.

_____ 1. Don't expect attitude change in a month or two. It takes time for experimentation and for trust-building behaviors to develop.

_____ 2. Don't hide bad news. Sharing means sharing everything.

_____ 3. Don't segment information and channel it only where you think it should go. Information is power—to everyone, not only to you.

_____ 4. Don't evaluate progress on smiles tests only. Devise new, valid, and reliable measures to systematically measure progress, and use feedback immediately to make adjustments to processes that don't work right.

_____ 5. Don't let people tell you only what they think you want to hear. Learn to accept problems as your friends; learn to allow employees to do the same.

_____ 6. Don't give feedback only when it's negative; positive feedback has great motivating power.

_____ 7. Don't let your words and actions slip out of alignment. For example, if you tell an employee that he or she is responsible for "protecting assets," don't rant and rave about the dirty toilets or the pile of broken machines in the corner. You can't expect employees to automatically see how a big goal like "protecting assets" translates into griping about small things: They'll think you talk big about empowerment but act in the same old small, petty, nitpicky way.

_____ 8. Don't focus only on the employee's relationship to the job. Formally, consciously, and systematically focus also on developing new and better relationships between employee and management and between employee and employee across the company. Trainers often think too narrowly in terms only of tasks of the job.

_____ 9. Don't throw a slogan over an old procedure and expect change. Create a better procedure first.

_____ 10. Don't take all the credit or all the blame: Empowered employees will share in both of these if you step aside and let them.

_____ 11. Don't stifle innovation by keeping it buried. Be sure it sees the bright light of day.

_____ 12. Don't keep top executives from knowing what kinds of innovative efforts are going on at lower levels.

# Innovation Checklist 7.5
## Employability Skills

Employability essentially means two things: competency in the core skills required for one's present job within a specific company, and competency in generic workplace skills that are marketable between companies. Focus and flexibility are required.

There are many ways to categorize employability skills. The way shown here gives training managers a clear view of groups of skills for which training programs can be designed. These categories can form the structure for training for employability.

\_\_\_\_\_ 1. **Knowing yourself skills,** including
- Knowledge of your work style
- Knowledge of and acceptance of your own personality characteristics
- Knowledge of your motivations
- Knowledge of your energy level
- Accurate assessment of your ambitions
- Ability to deal with stress, demonstrated by specific measurable behaviors
- Knowledge of the balance you require between home and work
- Knowing when to ask for help
- Self-assurance
- Integrity

\_\_\_\_\_ 2. **Demonstrating job competency skills,** including
- Cognitive skills
- Psychomotor skills
- Pacing, timing
- Accuracy
- Efficiency
- Big-picture view
- Dealing with details
- Business savvy
- Quality products and services
- Results

\_\_\_\_\_ 3. **Making decisions skills,** including
- Balance—knowing when to act, including when to hold back
- Scale and quantity—knowing how to seek enough information—the "necessary and sufficient" standard
- Organizing, categorizing
- Prudent risk taking
- Managing conflict
- Negotiating
- Innovating

4. **Relating to others skills,** including
    - Active listening
    - Flexibility with systems and processes
    - Mental agility
    - Empathy
    - Ability to influence others
    - Giving feedback
    - Receiving feedback
    - Acting upon feedback
    - Mentoring
    - Coaching
    - Facilitating
    - Sharing power
    - Leading
    - Following
    - Collaborating

# Innovation Checklist 7.6

## Fifteen Ways to Learn on the Job from Work Itself

These are key learning strategies that anyone can apply in order to learn from work. They are things anyone can do to enhance his or her own productivity as a learner. Trainers should be helping all employees to do these things as an organization of skilled learners takes shape. Remember that organizations of the future will depend on finely tuned learners; employability, and innovation, above all, will require conscious and continuous development and growth of individual learners.

_____ 1. **Stretch the limits of what you already know.** Play "what if" games with yourself as you focus on the tasks of your job.

_____ 2. **Think process.** Stand back and observe how you actually do things, and see if the way in which you do them can be improved. Here are some for starters: sorting, prioritizing, recognizing patterns, estimating, analyzing, synthesizing, translating, writing. Think in terms of "add, delete, or modify." Keep a log or a journal of "process improvements."

_____ 3. **Think results, not just outcomes.** Imagine—that is, actually describe to yourself—the possibilities for all kinds of results from what you are doing. Thinking "outcome" often limits one's probabilities to a much too direct way of thinking: a "this always comes out that way" kind of thinking ties one down to methods and procedures, the letter of the contract, adversarial relationships, and rigidity. Think, rather, in terms of longer-range benefits to many different persons and added value to many different products and services.

_____ 4. **Don't confuse learning about something with learning something.** In your quest for greater knowledge in the work you are doing, get quickly beyond lists, definitions, and descriptions. For example, when you access your computer's help screen, pass quickly to the item you need and try it out immediately. It's the experimentation, not the accessing, that leads to deeper learning. Learning about help is not the same as being helped. Apply this analogy to other situations in which you are seeking deeper knowledge. Get off the description and into the action as quickly as possible.

_____ 5. **Reflect.** Adopt a model, if you need to, in order to remember to reflect upon your thoughts and your actions. One model is the "Action/Reflection Learning" philosophy; another is the continuous improvement model of W. Edwards Deming:

"Plan, Do, Check, Act." Consciously build in the time for reflection.

_____ 6. **Think of work as hierarchies of tasks.** Everyone's work has easier parts and harder parts. Know your work so well that you can accomplish the easier tasks more quickly and better by intentionally knowing when you are doing them; tackle the harder parts with the assurance that they are merely a different configuration of tasks. Know what you need in order to perform all tasks well. Identifying the hierarchy of skills is a first step.

_____ 7. **Ask for help.** Know your limitations. Don't do bad work; ask for help.

_____ 8. **Engage in the disciplines of your work.** Think in terms of intrinsic motivation for work, not extrinsic motivation. Enjoy your relationship to what you do, not necessarily to some piece rate, some deadline, or some stopwatch. Each job has a certain rhythm, certain parameters and disciplines. Define these for yourself, and enjoy your engagement with them as you do your work. Intentional, engaged working usually is the most productive working.

_____ 9. **Identify and pursue gaps.** Don't be afraid to identify gaps in your information, your tools, your support, or any other input you believe you need in order to perform your job at peak capacity. Go after what you need.

_____ 10. **Be proactive.** Speak up. Be your own advocate. Seek strategic alliances with others who value your work anywhere you can find them.

_____ 11. **Remember your memory.** Adult learners have an excellent and often untapped resource for learning from work: memory. We often forget to call up our earliest experiences with thorny situations by focusing too much on the here-and-now or the immediate future. Adults have memory for such things as patterned response, sounds, tactile memory, spatial relationship memory, preferred learning style, concepts, and problem-solving approaches that stand ready and waiting to be used again in new situations. At work, we somehow often forget to integrate our past experiences with our present challenges. Simply remembering to use your memory is an excellent way to tighten up your competence as a learner.

_____ 12. **Think equally in terms of giving and receiving.** Think in terms of passing it on—pass the torch, or whatever metaphor works for you. That is, every time you learn something or get a new insight, pass it on to someone else. Keep the learning building by getting and giving, getting and giving.

_____ 13. **Respect followership.** Forget being a hero, empress, conquistador, or lone ranger. Learn to be a good follower, not only to be a leader. Discover the intellectual rewards in followership; widen and develop your sense of skilled observation, active listening, intuition, and integration of past incomplete knowledge with what is new.

_____ 14. **Bring the whole into the parts.** Try to always remain aware of the whole—the big picture—to which your specific work is contributing.

_____ 15. **Talk out loud** when solving a problem, especially when teaching someone else.

# Innovation Checklist 7.7
## Fundamentals of High Performance

During 1996, the American Society for Training and Development (ASTD) helped to define the concept of human performance technology and how its practitioners implement its tenets through various roles. Numerous ASTD publications have contained articles about performance improvement, written by staff and guest writers. The publication, *ASTD Models for Human Performance Improvement,* edited by William J. Rothwell (1996), is a particularly good source of information.

Throughout the ASTD literature, fifteen core competencies for trainers turned performance-improvement specialists are suggested and elaborated in many different ways. This is a brief listing of these competencies.* They are one way in which a training manager could begin to restructure his or her job in order to function as a more overt facilitator of performance improvement.

_____ 1. **Industry awareness,** including the ability to link the big picture to organizational goals and actions

_____ 2. **Leadership skills,** including skills in influencing others

_____ 3. **Interpersonal relationship skills,** focusing on collaborative skills of working with others to achieve common goals

_____ 4. **Technological awareness and understanding,** including experience as a user of new software, hardware, online services, and electronic performance support systems

_____ 5. **Problem-solving skills,** especially the analysis skills of identifying gaps in people's performance and facilitating the closing of them

_____ 6. **Systems thinking and understanding,** including an understanding of the effects of "double loop" systems

_____ 7. **Performance understanding,** including knowing the difference between activities and results

_____ 8. **Knowledge of interventions,** including demonstrated ability and skill at choosing and using a variety of personal and procedural interventions across the organization to close performance gaps

_____ 9. **Business understanding,** focusing on your company's specific way of doing things in order that you can affect business results, primarily the financial ones

*Adapted from William J. Rothwell, ASTD Models for Human Performance Improvement (Alexandria, Va.: ASTD, 1996).

_____ 10. **Organization understanding,** focusing on adopting a larger perspective on the definition of organization to include a multiinfluence, multigoal entity

_____ 11. **Negotiating and contracting skills,** including management of all contingent workers

_____ 12. **Buy-in and advocacy skills,** including facilitating change among all stakeholders

_____ 13. **Coping skills,** including flexibility, and handling stress and ambiguity

_____ 14. **Ability to see the "big picture,"** or going beyond the details of work

_____ 15. **Consulting skills,** including ability to see what stakeholders want and how best to facilitate achieving results for stakeholders

# Innovation Checklist 7.8

## Organizational Indicators of Innovation

Use this checklist as an "innovation culture" check in your company, before you develop a training program on learning to innovate. Work within your systems and processes to create the kinds of changes you'll need to form a foundation that supports innovation.

_____ 1. Individuals are allowed and encouraged to work outside their normal spaces and relationships of comfort.

_____ 2. Creative individuals are supported by management at all levels.

_____ 3. Creative individuals are not isolated, but rather are enveloped in communities of practice and influence networks so that innovative ideas can be raised without fear of employability reprisals.

_____ 4. Expectations are realistic; benchmarks of success are agreed upon by those involved.

_____ 5. Personal style differences are welcomed on creative projects, including styles that require structure and rules.

_____ 6. Innovation training is or will be available to all employees.

_____ 7. Innovations are recognized for their links to new business opportunities.

_____ 8. Funding to bring innovations to market is secure and separate from operational budgets.

_____ 9. Innovation programs have broad-based leadership.

_____ 10. Partners and collaborators within and outside of the company are involved early in innovation efforts.

_____ 11. Innovation programs focus on motivating and retaining employees as well as on attracting new customers.

# Chapter 7 Forms
## To Help You Train for Innovation

Forms in the following section are ready-made for your use as you train for innovation. A finely tuned, responsible, and empowered workforce is the only route to the future. Forms here are especially adapted to the fast pace of change in the workplace. They can be useful as you help to make learning the fuel that propels individuals forward, in your company and ultimately in all workplaces.

**LIST OF FORMS FOR INNOVATION**

- **7.1** Skills Matrix: What I Need and Where to Get It
- **7.2** Online Who's Who Skills Directory
- **7.3** "The Way I See It . . ." Journal
- **7.4** Process Quality Self- and Organizational Assessment
- **7.5** Wanted: Creative Workers—Am I One of Them?
- **7.6** Change Management Matrix: Trainer into Performance Consultant

## How to Train for Innovation

**Innovation Form 7.1**
**SKILLS MATRIX: WHAT I NEED AND WHERE TO GET IT**

### How to Use This Form

1. As trainers break out of their traditional roles of "dispenser of wisdom," "instructor," and "certifier of class attendance" into a more business-focused and cross-functional network of influence, you'll need to encourage each person on your staff to continuously self-assess his or her competencies and be responsible for getting the help needed to improve. This kind of form can help, as a weekly or monthly reminder, to take stock of one's own "employability" development and capacity for innovation.
2. Use this with trainers first, then have trainers use it with other employees.
3. Check one or more boxes across each row.

**Where to get it**

| Skill/knowledge needed | self-study/on-the-job | EPSS | informal learning group | wandering around | role model/mentor | videos | periodicals | books | professional association membership | conference | Internet; e-learning | seminar | college | new standards | coaching/mentoring | cross-training | external consultant | internal consultant | professional development center |
|---|---|---|---|---|---|---|---|---|---|---|---|---|---|---|---|---|---|---|---|
| 1 strategic planning techniques | | | | | | | | | | | | | | | | | | | |
| 2 leadership training | | | | | | | | | | | | | | | | | | | |
| 3 team-building skills | | | | | | | | | | | | | | | | | | | |
| 4 computer specifics | | | | | | | | | | | | | | | | | | | |
| 5 problem-solving techniques | | | | | | | | | | | | | | | | | | | |
| 6 how systems work | | | | | | | | | | | | | | | | | | | |
| 7 performance technology | | | | | | | | | | | | | | | | | | | |
| 8 intervention strategies | | | | | | | | | | | | | | | | | | | |
| 9 business finance | | | | | | | | | | | | | | | | | | | |
| 10 organization development | | | | | | | | | | | | | | | | | | | |
| 11 managing contingent workers | | | | | | | | | | | | | | | | | | | |
| 12 change-management skills | | | | | | | | | | | | | | | | | | | |
| 13 how to cope with stress | | | | | | | | | | | | | | | | | | | |
| 14 how to see the "big picture" | | | | | | | | | | | | | | | | | | | |
| 15 consulting skills | | | | | | | | | | | | | | | | | | | |

**Innovation Form 7.2**
**ONLINE WHO'S WHO SKILLS DIRECTORY**

### How to Use This Form
1. As persons at work become more collaborative, continuously demonstrating skills required for work in teams with customers, suppliers, and contingent workers, they need to begin to think in terms of what they can learn from each other and what they can teach each other. Use this form as a template for an online skills directory.
2. Make entry into the directory a responsibility of each employee. Gently force everyone to become teachers and learners.

_____
Employee's name

_____
e-mail address

_____
telephone number

My strongest job skills:
1
2
3
4
5

My recreational skills/hobbies:
1
2
3
4
5

Skills I'd like to learn in the next year:
1
2
3
4
5

## Innovation Form 7.3
### "THE WAY I SEE IT . . ." JOURNAL

#### How to Use This Form

1. Part of the innovation imperative is to help people articulate their views and accept the views of others—to "tell it how it is." Encouraging the use of a journal, either in notebook form with paper and pencil or online, is one way to do this. This exercise is especially helpful for persons struggling to work together in teams. This journal exercise can be a standard "assignment" with each training session on team building or empowerment. Designate a "collection" date for review of ideas.
2. Suggest that employees set aside 10 minutes each day—for example, right after lunch—to reflect on some key issue that's come up over the past 24 hours. Use a form similar to the one here, and encourage structured responses designed to lead the responder into his or her own intuition about their work.

_____  _____
Issue                                                                    Date

"The way I see it is this:

                                                                                    "

". . . and I think the reasons for it are:

                                                                                    "

". . . and this is what I'd do to change things:

                                                                                    "

**Innovation Form 7.4**
**PROCESS QUALITY SELF- AND ORGANIZATIONAL ASSESSMENT**

### How to Use This Form
1. "Building quality in, not inspecting it out" is the mantra of the process quality movement, and the most basic building block of remaining employed. This form suggests the skills and knowledge necessary for being a quality builder. These skills are based on the 1997 Malcolm Baldrige Quality Award standards in Employee Education, Training, and Development (Criteria booklet 5.2, p. 26).
2. Use this as a handout, a flipchart exercise, or a group exercise. Ask employees to decide for each skill whether the need applies to "me" or to "us" as a group. Vote by placing a check mark in each appropriate column.

|    | Skill | me | us |
|----|---|---|---|
| 1  | Evaluation skills | | |
| 2  | Customer-retention skills | | |
| 3  | Customer service skills | | |
| 4  | Benefit/cost ratio skills | | |
| 5  | Leadership skills | | |
| 6  | Communications skills | | |
| 7  | Teamwork skills | | |
| 8  | Problem-solving skills | | |
| 9  | Interpreting and using data | | |
| 10 | Process analysis skills | | |
| 11 | Process simplification skills | | |
| 12 | Waste-reduction skills | | |
| 13 | Cycle-time reduction skills | | |
| 14 | Error-proofing skills | | |
| 15 | Prioritizing skills | | |
| 16 | Safety assurance skills | | |
| 17 | Basic literacy and math skills | | |

## Innovation Form 7.5
## WANTED: CREATIVE WORKERS—AM I ONE OF THEM?

### How to Use This Form
1. Across the top of this form are four generally recognized characteristics of creative workers. Part of training's job is to help develop innovative workplaces; helping employees recognize creativity when they see it is a good first step in helping to build a creative workforce. Encourage all employees to intentionally be watchful for demonstrations of creativity; ask them to record their observations in the columns below each characteristic.
2. Sponsor a "creativity day" every Tuesday and encourage all employees to record their observations that day. Discuss the records at team or department meetings. Use names; identify and publicize the most creative employees for each week.

### Characteristics of creative persons

| Tolerance for ambiguity | Divergent thinking | Capacity to find order | Synthesis and evaluation |
|---|---|---|---|
| (ability to suspend judgment; thrive on diversity; generate ideas) | (ability to quickly connect ideas; flexibility in approaching new tasks) | (ability to seek organizing structures instead of having them imposed) | (ability to put information together and judge its worth; ability to objectify and act upon information) |

### Observable instances of creative behaviors

| _____ date | _____ date | _____ date | _____ date |
|---|---|---|---|
| _____ date | _____ date | _____ date | _____ date |
| _____ date | _____ date | _____ date | _____ date |

**Innovation Form 7.6**
**CHANGE MANAGEMENT MATRIX:**
**TRAINER INTO PERFORMANCE CONSULTANT**

### How to Use This Form
1. This worksheet will feel like an editor's job: in it, the trainer/analyst must isolate phrases and keywords from his or her actual job description (make a new one if your current one does not describe what you actually do). List these key phrases down the left side of the form.
2. Across the top of the form, the four roles of the performance consultant are stated. These are the four roles identified by ASTD. For each phrase from the actual job, check an appropriate box across the rows to indicate that you personally must change in this direction in order to move from trainer to performance consultant. Make brief notes to jog your memory later.

|  | Role 1: analyst | Role 2: intervention specialist | Role 3: change manager | Role 4: evaluator |
|---|---|---|---|---|
| " <br><br> " | notes: | notes: | notes: | notes: |
| " <br><br> " | notes: | notes: | notes: | notes: |
| " <br><br> " | notes: | notes: | notes: | notes: |
| " <br><br> " | notes: | notes: | notes: | notes: |

# Chapter 7
# More Information on How to Train for Innovation

## Spin-Offs from the Performance Debate

For several decades, trainers have been prodded, encouraged, and forced to break out of the often narrow world of classroom training and move into the mainstream of corporate contributors to the bottom line. As far back as the mid-1970s, writers such as Thomas Gilbert and Robert Mager were presenting models for analysis and development of training that used then strange-sounding phrases like "engineering worthy performance" and "performance gaps." These words were all very different from the trainer's world of "behavioral objectives" and "instructional technology."

Since the late 1990s, although trainers still prefer classroom training as the most often used venue to deliver training (it's still seen by many as the most cost-effective way to deal with groups of learners), they are finding themselves in the roles of corporate human resources growth facilitator and strategist in addition to that of classroom instructor and developer of individual learners. This is largely because of the influence of the human performance improvement language and perspective, which has grown considerably over the decades since its initial infusion into our thinking.

## Trainers Still Playing Catch-Up

It's not that trainers have taken the lead in playing this new role: In many cases it has been forced upon training managers especially, and on instructional designers to a lesser extent. Downsizing, decimation of training departments that has often accompanied overall downsizing, and the continued growth of using outside consultants, vendor-developed materials, and contingent trainers have all contributed to the motivation for those left on the corporate rosters to spread out, do more with less, and build influence within their newly configured corporations. Employability as a trainer these days demands a "performance engineering" perspective and a willingness to lead the design efforts at creating a higher-quality workforce—in short, to be innovative.

At the same time that the pressures to change are great, so are the numbers of new and relatively inexperienced persons who are coming into training jobs. As a field, we are still playing catch-up. Industry surveys by both *Training Magazine* and the American Society for Training and Development (ASTD) present the picture of the profession as one still solidly in the past but making strides to embrace new ideas and technologies for the future.

Trainers are, of survival necessity, looking beyond the narrower training objective to the broader corporate environment of societal influences, methods and procedures, and values and rewards to define their jobs. One of the spin-offs of the performance debate is the push for new job descriptions and new roles for trainers. Another imperative is that trainers help other employees to think more broadly too, and likewise take responsibility for their own employability and performance improvement, not just certification or accumulation of credits.

## Government Influences in Legitimizing Performance Standards

### 1997 Updates in The Malcolm Baldrige National Quality Award Criteria

The Malcolm Baldrige 1997 National Award Criteria booklet represented a turning point. It contains two pages of changes from the previous year's criteria. The National Quality Award has been awarded annually for ten years by the U.S. Department of Commerce, whose mission is to promote economic growth. These two pages, and the booklet's subtitle, contain a great deal of evidence of the perceived value of moving from training to performance technology.

Here are some of the more important excerpts regarding these changes in criteria:

- *from the first paragraph, p. 31:* "The Criteria continue to evolve *toward comprehensive coverage of strategy-driven performance*, addressing the needs and expectations of all stakeholders. . . . The Criteria for 1997 strengthen the systems view of performance management, and place a greater focus on company strategy, organizational learning, and better integration of business results." (p. 31, emphasis mine)

- *from Human Resources Development and Management, p. 32:* "Item 4.1 from 1996, Human Resource Planning and Evaluation, has been eliminated. The important planning included in this item is now *integrated within overall company planning* as mentioned above under Strategic Planning." (p. 32, emphasis mine)

- *from Human Resources Development and Management, p. 32:* "Item 4.2 from 1996, High-Performance Work Systems, now becomes Item 5.1 and is titled Work Systems. Although this item retains its focus on high performance, its title is changed *to avoid the appearance that its purpose is narrower*—high-performance work teams." (p. 32, emphasis mine)

- *from Business Results, p. 32:* "Item 7.4, Supplier and Partner Results, has been expanded to include company costs and/or *performance improvements due to supplier and partner performance.* This is an added measure of the effectiveness of the relationship and the linkage to important results." (p. 32, emphasis mine; suppliers and partners are increasing in numbers around training organizations)

- *from Business Results, p. 32:* "Item 7.5, Company-Specific Results, is a new Item. . . . Results appropriate for Item 7.5 include *improvements in and performances of* products, services, and processes; productivity; cycle time; regulatory/legal compliance and related performance; and new product and/or service introductions. . . ." (p. 32, emphasis mine; this is a very broad view of performance, grounded here in the quality framework of "building quality in")

Of special interest, too, is the subtitle of the criteria booklet: "Criteria for Performance Excellence." In previous years, there was no subtitle; the booklet simply was called "Criteria."

## Baldrige 2001 First-Time Award to Innovative Chugach School District

The small, remote, 214-student Chugach School District in Anchorage, Alaska was the first Baldrige award winner in the education category. Most of the widely dispersed students come to school by aircraft. A school breakfast program flies 300 miles to the school and arrives frozen. District programs go from preschool to post-secondary education, serving students up to age 21. District Superintendent Richard DeLorenzo led his staff and community to craft a program of education focused on the individual student, and did away with traditional credit hours and grade levels.

DeLorenzo is surely an innovator. He is quoted in an interview in the August 2002 issue of *Quality Digest*\* as saying that education in America is mired in mediocrity and routine, and lacks focus. He attributes his district's success to the fact that they took everything apart and built it back up again. He used a quality systems approach of plan, do, evaluate, and refine, and overlaid it with a strong vision and future focus. He calls on the Baldrige to incorporate these elements in all future standards for the award in the education category. DeLorenzo can be reached through his foundation, the Reinventing Schools Coalition, through his website at chugach.schools.com, or by phone at 907-522-7400.

That the Chugach School District won the first award in education, although the category had been in existence for several years in the Baldrige, is also a sign that business as usual in education may not be toler-

---

\*Green, Robert, "2001 Baldrige Award Winner Profile: Chugach School District," *Quality Digest*, August 2002, pp. 46–47.

ated, and that business as un-usual is worthy of acclaim. Chugach can inspire training designers, managers, and learners at work.

## The Bureau of National Affairs Reports Recommendations of the 20th Century Fund

In the fall 1996 issue of *BNAC Communicator,* an article contained the recommendations of a task force on retraining the American workforce. These recommendations came from a bipartisan effort to identify and suggest ways to compensate for the gaps in workplace training. Numerous studies show rather consistently that executives, high-level managers, and computer users get more training than other categories of workers. The BNAC article estimates that "the private sector would need to invest $160 billion if all companies were to emulate firms that place a high priority on strengthening the abilities of their employees."

The essence of the report is that bridging the gap suggested by the figure above requires a fundamental shift in the way companies think about training. These gap-filling measures would have to occur in the change to a commitment to enhancement of abilities of all employees, a narrowing of government training programs for the unemployed to focus only on skills that are in demand, and the requirement of all workers "to exert the effort required to improve their value in the job market." One of the specific recommendations is "consideration in government contracting for companies that develop high-performance work organizations and upgrade the skills of their employees" (p. 4).

The message is clear that on all fronts, if you want to stay employed in the twenty-first century, you'd better figure out what you need to know, and then go for it.

### If Have Limited Budget and Staff . . .

Get on the mailing list to receive the Malcolm Baldrige National Quality Award annual mailings. They're free. Pay attention especially to the short section in the criteria booklet on changes from the previous year's criteria. These areas of change will give you a good overview of the direction of "process quality" and should spark your imagination about how to design a good program incorporating change. The specific criteria in the Human Resource Development category will give you some guidelines for developing your own specific training programs. The address is:

United States Department of Commerce
Technology Administration
National Institute of Standards and Technology (NIST)
Route 270 and Quince Orchard Road
Administration Building, Room A537
Gaithersburg, MD 20899-0001
Telephone: (800) 975-2036; e-mail: oqp@nist.gov

Or fall back on your library search skills. Browse the Web beginning with quality.nist.gov. You'll be surprised at where this might lead you. Spend a few days in the library of your local college. Read all of the business periodicals for ideas; take a notebook to jot down ideas about empowerment and process quality improvement, as well as specific ideas about how to stay employed. Read case studies; follow up with phone calls. Identify one creative thinker, and encourage his or her efforts at innovation.

## If You Have Adequate Budget and Staff . . .

You might want to attend the NIST annual conference of winners, usually held in winter in the Washington, D.C. area. The Conference Board in New York City also frequently has conferences of Baldrige winners. There's no substitute for talking, eyeball to eyeball, with people who've lived through the change process. Plan to spend about $1,500 per person in conference fees.

Several media companies also produce audio and videotapes of Baldrige winners and of other conferences, such as the ASTD conferences and those of the Society for Human Resource Management, (SHRM). A set of tapes can run in the hundreds of dollars, but it's permanent and cheaper than airfare. Start with Audio Archives International, 800-747-8069, or with Mobiltape Company Inc., 805-295-0504.

If you really get serious about driving change, apply for the Baldrige Award. It's an expensive deal, but it is guaranteed to shake things up and get people thinking in new ways. Hire consultants to help, or get started yourself by using one of the many analysis and evaluation software packages advertised in *Quality Progress* magazine. Plan to spend at least $600 on software, and be prepared for additional licensing fees. Find out what courses and programs on creativity and innovation are being offered in colleges and universities. Go for high-level offerings, where you will meet leaders in the field. MIT's two-day program currently costs $2,600; University of Chicago's five-day program costs $5,750. Other university programs throughout the country are similarly priced. E-learning programs are beginning to be available, with various pricing structures.

# 8

# How to Support Learners on Their Own

All over all kinds of companies, people are learning on their own and seeking out others to learn with them. This kind of learning is not a coaching relationship, but rather is a self-directed, self-motivated engagement with learning. It is sometimes called on-demand learning, just-in-time learning, or plain on-the-job training. By whatever name, it requires that you as training manager get involved with learners on their own with support of various kinds.

Some suggest the training department adopt a counseling role: helping the individual learner make a list of what he or she needs to know both for business and personal success; suggesting options regarding the means or avenues through which to learn; identifying subject matter experts and other key individuals from whom the individual can learn; helping the individual to measure the impact of individual learning; and figuring out who needs to receive a report about the individual's learning progress. These are all evolutions of the traditional Instructional System Design (ISD) model, with an overlay of particular kinds of facilitation and communication skills. Designs for learning, expert instruction, and groups of learners are still part of learning on one's own, but they have evolved beyond the classroom while still keeping it as a viable option. The bottom line is: The goal of training management should be to support expert learners.

**KEY MANAGEMENT ISSUES**

There are some key management issues you should keep in mind as you plan to support your learners.

■ *Taking Charge.* Learners on their own need to know how to take charge of their own learning. They need to practice "metacognitive" strategies in which they first define the big picture of what they need to know, starting with something larger than the task list that often gets stuck in behaviorism. Training managers can help individuals do this.

A simple way to think of this is to differentiate between concepts and data. Conceptual organizers come first and define a job or task within a connection of ideas. Dealing with only the data or tasks of a job can often feel like the short answer test or list of dates to memorize in junior high school history class. The data always make more sense within a strategic conceptual framework based on the individual's personal need to know. It matters where the learner puts his or her locus of control. Learners on their own need to be assertive in searching for new knowledge, and training managers need to support them as they do this.

Learners on their own also need to be reminded to reflect on what they've done or on something new that they've learned. Here, too, training managers can be the catalyst for a learner's taking time for reflection. Often the training manager can function as a sounding board for reflective discussion. Often the training department can set a company-wide tone of respect for experimentation and seeking, a tone that can motivate the learner to learn more. Higher-order learning involves intentional linking of current learning experiences with past experiences; it means that learners need to be encouraged to continuously reconstruct learning on previous experience. Training managers can intervene to reinforce this linking, just by asking questions and challenging the learner to reflect. Training managers can also organize training departments to work with individual learners in new and creative ways.

- ■ *ISD and Self-Directed Learners.* The Instructional System Design (ISD) framework for building a course has been around for decades and is still very much in use for classroom instruction. Its steps of needs assessment, design, development, implementation, and evaluation have mutated and evolved to describe the learning environments of communities of practice, coaching and mentoring, and e-learning. Hundreds of consulting companies focus on ISD, and hundreds more companies look for more and better ISD experts.

There's a role for ISD in supporting learners on their own, too. In a company that values and supports learners on their own, the training manager will focus on a discovery model of learning, not a deliver and transfer model. Self-directed learning is not designed, per se, as is a course presented in lecture or seminar format. It is, however, responsive to pre- and post-tests of various sorts, both formal and informal. Training managers can help learners on their own to devise simple and effective means to analyze their learning gaps before a learning experience, and to evaluate how those gaps were filled when the learning experience concluded. Adult learners are known to appreciate knowing where they stand; evaluation and feedback are important elements of support for learners on their own.

It has been said that a typical classroom training session consists of about 70 percent designed instruction, consisting mostly of declarative and procedural information. In self-directed learning, that 70 percent should change to 30 percent, with a new 70 percent devoted to critical thinking skills of seeing the big picture, how to elaborate on knowledge and experience, how to integrate what one sees and experiences, and how to link new understandings with previous experience, construct new knowledge, and solve problems. In elementary schools, high schools, universities, and workplaces, learners on their own need to learn how to think differently. Training managers can be helpful by focusing on the middle three functions of ISD—design, development, and implementation—to be sure that the company's learning environment supports these functions for the self-directed learner.

Learners on their own need to develop some basic skills for learning to learn. These include: gathering data and information about one's self, identifying what success at learning will look like, identifying how best to learn what needs to be learned, determining who else must become involved, making it happen, and documenting progress and accomplishment. These are all variations on traditional Instructional System Design—variations that de-emphasize the "sage on the stage" model of workplace learning.

■ *Internet Tools.* There is no doubt that the Internet has opened a huge new resource for learners on their own. The most obvious thing to say about using the Internet for learning is that it is the best source of data and information. Learning online is still not the preferred learning system for skills development or problem solving—that works better in real-world demonstration, practice, and collaboration. The criticism is still that too many self-paced e-learning courses are just "pages of text dumped on the Web" (Patti Shank in "No More Yawns," *OnlineLearning*, May 2002, p. 22). But for data and information, for important and essential foundations of learning, the Internet is the medium of choice. A company can save enormous amounts of time and money by posting essential information on the Internet instead of taking up classroom time, as in the past, with an instructor who simply dispenses information. As in all training, the challenge for managers is to assess your options in delivery and implementation and fit the medium of instruction with the message of what needs to be learned. The trick for training managers is to not get overcome by salespersons with bells and whistles that you know won't work for your learning needs.

In cases where the Internet is used for interaction and collaboration, there are some important design considerations to build person-to-person relationships into the learning. These include:

- Providing a help button or virtual coach
- Building in interactive practice exercises
- Providing for and encouraging feedback from coaches and between learners
- Providing navigation training so that everyone can use all features
- Building learning supports around familiar online habits: e-mail, chat, and instant messaging
- Encouraging e-learners to explore the fringes, find new and diverse learning partners, and experiment with sources outside their usual patterns and influence

- Creating a system for self-monitoring and learning evaluation
- Building in time for learning on the job, on company time

There are also e-learning content issues that training managers need to address. Learners online need to know how to browse and branch through content, how to repeat lessons or parts of lessons, how to use or ignore multimedia, how to communicate with fellow learners, and how to print material for later study. Training managers also need to provide online learners with training in use of Learning Management Systems, Learning Content Management Systems, and Learning Objects. If you use online coaches, be sure that they are well matched to those they coach, and that they can establish credible and productive personal and professional e-learning relationships. These are all process issues to take learners through content in a way customized for each individual learner. They are different from the processes of the familiar model of classroom learning. And best of all, they can be used as motivators for continuous learning.

- ***Variations in Ways to Learn.*** Learners learning on their own do so for a variety of reasons. Training managers have a responsibility to envision the options for learning that fit the company's mission and business plan and the individual learner's needs. These are some of the reasons for learning on one's own: a job assignment far away from the center of things; career change; job change and the need for immediate new skills; flextime and working from home; certification; CEUs; graduate school across the country; sabbaticals. In each of these situations, some option for self-directed learning is appropriate. Training managers need to help learners design learning environments and provide challenges and motivations for learning to happen. Training managers need to remember the wide resource of learning tools and systems available to support the variety of learners and learning situations on their own: coaches, mentors, communities of practice, teams, videos, DVDs, audiotapes, CD-ROMs, workbooks, textbooks, databases, widely distributed systems, e-learning programs, and classrooms. Working with learners on their own, in all the variation that comes with them, can be a most exciting and satisfying job. Creating a learning curriculum rather than a training curriculum is a place to start—a learning curriculum in which achievement and contribution are expected and valued.

# Chapter 8 Checklists
## To Support Learners on Their Own

The following checklists help you to support learners on their own by facilitating their ability to be self-directed and take charge of their own learning, by giving you some help with the new ways of thinking about Instructional Systems Design (ISD), by helping you maximize the use of Internet tools for them, and by helping you encourage and support variety in the way individuals learn.

**LIST OF CHECKLISTS TO SUPPORT LEARNERS ON THEIR OWN**

- **8.1** Checklist for Learning to Learn Skills
- **8.2** Baldrige Information and Analysis Self-Assessment Tool
- **8.3** Setting Yourself Up for Learning, or, How to Use Information
- **8.4** Active Processes for Moving Beyond Data
- **8.5** Individual Learning Designs Anchored in ISD
- **8.6** Checklist of Learning Benefits of "On Your Own"

# Learners on Their Own Checklist 8.1
## Checklist for Learning to Learn Skills

Use this checklist as a job aid for learners, that is, all your employees who will be involved in a self-directed program of learning on their own. You can coach them through these items, or simply give employees checklists to be used each time they engage in learning on their own. This checklist can also be adapted as an office poster.

**FOR MY INTERACTION WITH THE LEARNING OPPORTUNITY**

_____ 1. What do I want from this learning opportunity?

_____ 2. What will it look like when I learn it?

_____ 3. What skills or knowledge do I need to acquire on the way?

_____ 4. What and where are the resources I need?

_____ 5. What's in my way? What are the barriers to learning?

_____ 6. What abilities do I already have to bring to this learning opportunity?

_____ 7. What plan do I need to accomplish it?

**FOR MY PERSONAL COMPETENCY AS A LEARNER**

_____ 8. I am flexible and resilient in difficult situations.

_____ 9. I am open-minded to change.

_____ 10. I help to motivate others.

_____ 11. I practice leadership through communication and persuasion.

_____ 12. I act responsibly, accepting both criticism and praise.

_____ 13. I value diversity by seeking out others not like myself.

_____ 14. I follow the rules or work within the system to change them.

_____ 15. I know how to find, process, and evaluate information.

_____ 16. I monitor my own progress and make corrective actions where needed.

# Learners on Their Own Checklist 8.2
## Baldrige Information and Analysis Self-Assessment Tool

This checklist is adapted from an assessment tool for leaders developed by the Malcolm Baldrige Quality Award Foundation. More information can be found on The Baldrige National Quality Program Web site: quality.nist.gov. The National Institute of Technology and Standards, Technology Administration, U.S. Department of Commerce administers "The Baldrige." Individuals who use this checklist are urged to rate themselves on a five-point scale from strongly disagree to strongly agree on each item.

Strongly disagree   1   2   3   4   5   Strongly agree

_____ 1. I know how to measure the quality of my work.

_____ 2. I know how to analyze the quality of my work to see if changes are needed.

_____ 3. I use these analyses for making decisions about my work.

_____ 4. I know how the measures I use in my work fit into the organization's overall measures of improvement.

_____ 5. I get all the important information I need to do my work.

_____ 6. I get the information I need to know about how my organization/company is doing.

_____ 7. I am recognized for my work.

_____ 8. I can make changes that will improve my work.

_____ 9. I am encouraged by my boss to advance my career.

_____ 10. I am encouraged to uncover errors and use them to improve things.

_____ 11. I am valued for my competencies and skills.

## Learners on Their Own Checklist 8.3

### Setting Yourself Up for Learning, or, How to Use Information

The proliferation and accessibility of information because of computers and the Internet have challenged training managers and learners to develop more finely tuned skills for dealing with information to learn at work. These skills include refining the skills of analysis, synthesis, and evaluation, as well as the skills of differentiating the kinds of and sources of information. Companies that are creating content databases and who facilitate online learning are being challenged like never before to place information at the fingertips of those who want to learn on their own. This checklist contains some of the main elements in making information work for you. As a self-directed learner, it's your responsibility to help get these things if they're not in place.

_____ 1. My company has updated content databases from both internal and external sources: employee research studies, new laws, conference reports, etc.

_____ 2. My company has online information that allows me to connect with other employees around the company and throughout the world.

_____ 3. My company has databases that show me where to find more offsite opportunities for learning on my own: conferences, university courses, seminars, libraries, certification programs, etc.

_____ 4. This information is relevant to my learning needs.

_____ 5. This information is reliable and valid.

_____ 6. This information stands on its own; it does not compete with similar information.

_____ 7. This information is free of bias and/or sales pitch.

_____ 8. This information will not hurt anyone.

# Learners on Their Own Checklist 8.4
## Active Processes for Moving Beyond Data

This checklist uses some of the concepts of cognitive psychology to help you get beyond data. Use the checklist as a job aid for yourself as you counsel or facilitate the work of learners on their own in your company. Or, give the checklist to all learners to check themselves as they work through a learning experience on their own. These are "active" mental processes that facilitate learning:

_____ 1. Attending/isolating something from its surroundings or context

_____ 2. Focusing

_____ 3. Sequencing

_____ 4. Recognizing patterns

_____ 5. Integrating

_____ 6. Scanning

_____ 7. Selecting

_____ 8. Regulating

_____ 9. Storing

_____ 10. Retrieving

_____ 11. Elaborating

_____ 12. Inferring

_____ 13. Organizing

_____ 14. Translating

_____ 15. Summarizing

_____ 16. Visualizing

# Learners on Their Own Checklist 8.5
## Individual Learning Designs Anchored in ISD

Traditional Instructional System Design (ISD) is the system generally used by instructional designers to create courses. It has been used in classroom training for decades, spawned graduate programs, and defined consulting companies over the years. The advent of individual online learning, coaching, mentoring, and all forms of just-in-time learning has necessitated a rethinking of the classroom-based processes of traditional ISD. This checklist has a listing of some of the changes to ISD that better suit the needs of individual learners.

_____ 1. Designing for individuals, using goal-oriented skill objectives

_____ 2. Building in plenty of variety in learning paths (That is, don't make the learning experience a linear, boring disaster.)

_____ 3. Setting the learning experience within a larger context, so that the learner comprehends his or her place in the bigger scheme of things

_____ 4 Providing for ways to jump in and out of the learning situation without penalty (Don't make learning on one's own a repeat of the classroom delivery model with preprogrammed break times.)

_____ 5. Reinforcing accomplishment by providing intense sessions of short duration

_____ 6. Encouraging active learning, experimentation, and practice

_____ 7. Avoiding e-learning programs that frustrate the learner because of downloads that take forever or that branch to insignificant information

_____ 8. Supporting learners' choices (Demonstrate that you value their efforts and learn from them.)

_____ 9. Avoiding Power Point overload or media extravaganzas that waste time

_____ 10. Focusing on continuous motivation through feedback, reward, and encouragement (Learning by one's self can be lonely: Show your learners that you care about their successes in learning.)

# Learners on Their Own Checklist 8.6
## Checklist of Learning Benefits of "On Your Own"

This checklist identifies some of the benefits that learners on their own get from learning this way. Encourage your learners to add more and to share the list with others. Use it to launch a "Learning on Your Own" program in your company.

_____ 1. Sensitivity to the work of others

_____ 2. Capacity for sharing

_____ 3. Expectation for achievement

_____ 4. Self-confidence

_____ 5. Acceptance of challenge

_____ 6. Career development

_____ 7. Learning just-in-time

_____ 8. Awareness of resources

_____ 9. Focusing on essentials

_____ 10. In-process feedback and evaluation

# Chapter 8 Forms
## To Support Learners on Their Own

The forms in the following section can help you facilitate the process of learners learning on their own. They can be used in helping to set up individual learning programs, or they can be used in moving particular learners forward.

**LIST OF FORMS TO SUPPORT LEARNERS ON THEIR OWN**

- **8.1** Individual Learning Plan
- **8.2** Self-Evaluation for Needs Assessment
- **8.3** Resources that Enable Performance
- **8.4** Where to Look for Learning Opportunities
- **8.5** Using 360-Degree Feedback for Individual Learners

**Supporting Learners on Their Own Form 8.1**
**INDIVIDUAL LEARNING PLAN**

> **How To Use This Form**
> 1. Use this form as a planning document when working with an individual to set up a customized learning plan.
> 2. Meet one-to-one with each individual learner to review each item. Encourage the individual to make notes about each item.
> 3. After dialogue about the elements of planning, ask the learner to create a plan addressing all elements.

| Needs assessment | Notes |
|---|---|
| 1. I understand the company's goals and business mission. | |
| 2. I know how my personal goals fit with the company's goals. | |
| 3. I can identify any gaps between (1) and (2). | |
| 4. I can identify steps to take to fill those gaps. | |
| *Content and process* | |
| 1. I can identify what resources I need to succeed. | |
| 2. I can identify the methods by which I learn best. | |
| 3. I know how to measure my progress and success. | |
| 4. I can develop a realistic schedule for learning. | |
| 5. I have a plan for transferring learning to my job. | |

**INDIVIDUAL LEARNING PLAN**

| Need | Content | Process | Date |
|---|---|---|---|
| | | | |

# How to Support Learners on Their Own

**Supporting Learners on Their Own Form 8.2**
**SELF-EVALUATION FOR NEEDS ASSESSMENT**

### How To Use This Form

1. This form is for learners to be able to feed evaluation data back into a needs assessment for the next learning experience. It closes an ISD loop for individual learning.
2. Use this form as a self-evaluation tool after a self-directed learning experience.
3. Rate yourself on a scale of one to five, where one equals very strong evidence of skill not being present, to five which equals very strong evidence of skill being present.
4. After completing the rating scale, fill in the narrative section for a broader evaluation.

Learner's name: _____ Date: _____

Brief description of the learning situation: _____

When filling out this form, ask yourself the question: "As a result of this learning experience, what do I need help in?"

| Capabilities/competencies | 1 | 2 | 3 | 4 | 5 |
|---|---|---|---|---|---|
| 1. Assertiveness | | | | | |
| 2. Creativity | | | | | |
| 3. Organization | | | | | |
| 4. Planning | | | | | |
| 5. Decision making | | | | | |
| 6. Problem solving | | | | | |
| 7. Inclusivity | | | | | |
| 8. Political savvy | | | | | |
| 9. Written communication | | | | | |
| 10. Oral communication | | | | | |
| 11. Patience | | | | | |

| Job-related skills (add others as appropriate) | | | | | |
|---|---|---|---|---|---|
| 1. Usage of technology | | | | | |
| 2. Presentation skills | | | | | |
| 3. Product knowledge | | | | | |
| 4. Usage of information | | | | | |
| 5. Customer knowledge | | | | | |
| 6. Supplier knowledge | | | | | |

**NARRATIVE EVALUATIVE COMMENTS, BASED ON DEMONSTRATED LEARNING**

- What are my strengths?
- Where do I fit best in the company?
- How do I perform?
- What should my contributions be?
- What are the surprises I discovered about myself?
- What three things will I work on improving during the next quarter?

1.

2.

3.

## How to Support Learners on Their Own

**Supporting Learners on Their Own Form 8.3**
**RESOURCES THAT ENABLE PERFORMANCE**

### How to Use This Form
1. Use this form with the preceding Form 8.2 as part of the front-end analysis that comes before an intentional learning experience.
2. One way to approach this form is to think of the barriers to your current learning experience; then, complete this form according to where you need to concentrate on finding the resources you need for your next learning experience.

|  | *Where to look/whom to contact* |
|---|---|
| 1. Computer manuals |  |
| 2. State legislation |  |
| 3. Federal legislation |  |
| 4. Online communities |  |
| 5. Web resources |  |
| 6. Offsite course/seminar |  |
| 7. Supplier |  |
| 8. Spreadsheet/financial reports |  |
| 9. Contracts |  |
| 10. Marketing plans |  |
| 11. Wall Street |  |
| 12. Research reports |  |

**Supporting Learners On Their Own Form 8.4**
# WHERE TO LOOK FOR LEARNING OPPORTUNITIES

### How To Use This Form

1. Use this form after you've determined your learning needs.
2. List the needs across the top, in the slanted boxes. Focus on no more than 6 needs. Fewer is better.
3. Place a checkmark in the appropriate box to help you design just the right self-directed learning opportunity.

My learning needs

| Where to look for learning opportunities | | | | | | |
|---|---|---|---|---|---|---|
| 1. People who have a job like mine | | | | | | |
| 2. People who have a different job from mine | | | | | | |
| 3. Identified problems with no apparent solution | | | | | | |
| 4. New employees | | | | | | |
| 5. Old-timers | | | | | | |
| 6. R&D work | | | | | | |
| 7. Cross-cultural work | | | | | | |
| 8. High-visibility, high-stakes work | | | | | | |

# How to Support Learners on Their Own

**Supporting Learners on Their Own Form 8.5**
**USING 360-DEGREE FEEDBACK FOR INDIVIDUAL LEARNERS**

### How to Use This Form

1. The evaluation process known as 360-degree evaluation has been popular for the last decade. It is seen as a way of encouraging organizational flexibility and future focus. There are, however, some constraints that can minimize its usefulness for individual learners. This form contains this list of constraints.
2. As training manager, you need to assess the organizational temperament for effective, or ineffective, use of 360-degree evaluation. Use a simple range line, marking the line on a yes-no continuum. Then decide whether it can be a useful evaluation and needs assessment tool for you.

|   | Yes: Constraint is present | No: Constraint is not present |
|---|---|---|
| 1. No obvious demonstration of value of learners on their own | | |
| 2. Penalties for experimentation | | |
| 3. Little value placed on feedback; employees seldom seek it | | |
| 4. No respect for differing opinions | | |
| 5. Lack of interdependence and working relationships between organizations | | |
| 6. Too much talk; too little action regarding values, mission, and alignment of personal and corporate goals | | |

# Chapter 8
# More Information on Supporting Learners on Their Own

## Knowledge Work, Just in Time

One keen observer once said that all employees should be given the opportunity to be knowledge workers, not task workers; that the entire environment of work should be designed for learning (Xerox Institute for Research on Learning). Work at the Institute for Research on Learning (IRL) in Menlo Park, California, has focused on learning that integrates knowledge into the life of communities and enables the individual learner to learn by intentionally choosing with whom to engage. IRL researchers have talked about "learning as an act of membership," an act of acceptance that leads to engagement and empowerment. Their perspective is that "knowing depends on engagement in practice," and that failure to learn comes from exclusion from participation (*IRL Perspective: Seven Principles of Learning* brochure, 1990).

In 2001 at a "Future Search Conference" ASTD identified one of the new trends in training and workplace learning as the "increasing demand for just-in-time learning" (reported in *T+D*, June 2002, p. 52). ASTD's authors Robert S. Weintraub and Jennifer W. Martineau in the article "The Just-in-Time Imperative" (*T+D,* June 2002, p. 52) also say that learning is primarily the result of experience and collaboration. To these catalysts they add observation and reading, all four together defining the context for learners on their own. All four define the essential ways in which a learner gains knowledge on his or her own, and describe how learners build a company of continuous learners.

## Paying Attention

When I was researching material for another book, I interviewed the CEO of a small manufacturing company about his training policies and practices. He told me that it was simple: His challenge to all employees was simply to "pay attention." We then walked through the shop floor where people were working—and learning, just in time. All over the factory, there were small groups of two or three people huddled over a machine or manual or in animated discussion about an immediate work problem.

No one paid any attention to us; we were definitely out of their learning loops. The CEO's message about paying attention to the what, why, and how of the job was so simple, effective, and right. In addition to the right message for this particular working community, the individual workstations were scattered throughout one large room, and books and manuals were easily accessible to anyone, creating opportunities for individuals to seek information and to collaborate with colleagues to solve a problem or clarify a situation. The message to "pay attention" was a challenge to be a continuous learner. The company, Sterling Engineering of Winsted, Connecticut, has produced three generations of community leaders, created hundreds of local jobs, and has had prized government contracts from World War II through the present space program.

Paying attention, of course, works two ways. Both the person paying attention and the person functioning as a one-to-one trainer need to be good communicators and to think flexibly and creatively to solve the problem at hand. CEOs, organization development specialists, human resources leaders, learning officers, and training managers need to think in terms of the skills and challenges required to be an effective and productive learner on one's own. Employees need demonstrated assurance that they will be supported when they leave their workstations to find what they need to know across the shop or office, or from a book on someone else's desk. They need proof that the CEO cares about seeing them learning—and doesn't care about their seeing the CEO.

## Small Groups and the "Little People"

Training managers in companies of continuous learners need to refine the lecture/slide show of the standard classroom to think, rather, in terms of the social aspects of learning as they apply to both large groups and small groups of learners. Especially, training managers need to create an atmosphere and the means for individuals to be continuously challenged and rewarded for learning.

Training managers need to realize that the "little people" count. Melanie Wells tells the story of the online auction house E-Bay's big vendor show at the Anaheim Conference Center in the summer of 2002 ("D-Day for E-Bay," *Forbes*, July 22, 2002, pp. 68–70). Five thousand people who sell their wares on E-Bay were there to *learn* what was new and get autographs from the CEO. As Wells said, "E-Bay doesn't want to lose its 'folksy flea-market feel' even as it becomes a mass marketer; E-Bay has to *learn* how to move beyond the small-timers without abandoning them." This is no small task for a company with 46 million users in twenty-seven countries and 325 million page views per day. Flexibility, communication, and critical thinking are surely the requirements for E-Bay's multitude of individual vendors and for E-Bay's management through this time of learning, transition, and growth. E-Bay's learning concerns mirror those of many other companies.

### If You Have Limited Budget and Staff . . .

Take small steps. Work with a handful of motivated learners to establish the formal and informal structures you'll need to support them. Pay special attention to needs assessment documents, even if they are simple lists of skill needs. Start small, achieve some successes, promote these successes, and gradually add more learners.

### If You Have Adequate Budget and Staff . . .
Hire instructional designers to evaluate your current learning opportunities: classroom courses, e-learning efforts, and self-directed learning currently going on. Know what is working from a learning point of view; be sure that the evaluation criteria for the training operation are based on learning, not on numbers of "butts in chairs." Instructional designers can be very helpful in working with individual learners to make the most of their motivation and self-direction.

Focus on feedback and flexibility. Create a working environment in which creativity and experimentation are valued; give visibility to individuals who identify and solve problems, who resolve conflicts, who devise new or better work processes. Work hard to improve communication skills and accessibility to information for all workers. Think differently about time; learning on one's own can be in small bits or in large chunks. It is hard to account for; develop monitoring and evaluation systems with the help of an evaluation consultant. Create a company-wide program of skill and competency-building that supports learners on their own.

# 9

# How to Assess Training Needs

Needs assessment is an area of training management that has a reputation for raising the blood pressure of many a training manager. The reasons for this are rooted in lack of understanding about what needs assessment is, about the standards for doing it right, about the effects it has on those it touches, and about the ways in which it consumes many dollars' worth of analysis time and time spent by employees away from the job.

This chapter provides you with some guidelines for understanding training needs assessment and for doing it properly.

## KEY MANAGEMENT ISSUES

■ *Starting Training at the Beginning.* Training managers are generally under considerable pressure to produce training now, or maybe tomorrow. Customers from outside your company who want you to design and deliver courses for them, as well as internal customers—other departments in your own company—seldom believe that your professional staff can do a better job than they themselves can do of defining just what kind of training they really need. Most customers believe that training begins with the first encounter between students and instructor.

Training managers, however, know that what seems to be the beginning is not the beginning. Good training begins with several days or weeks of investigation aimed at identifying precisely what needs to be taught. This period of investigation is known as **needs assessment,** and it is absolutely critical to designing and delivering training.

The training manager faced with a customer who insists that he or she knows exactly what the training need is, what training is required, and how it should be structured is in a tough position. At issue is, How does the real customer, the person paying the bill, relate to the persons receiving the training? How can those trainees provide legitimate input to the design of the course? And how can you be sure that your customer has defined that training need correctly?

The wary training manager realizes that training never starts at what seems to be the beginning. Customers who attempt to force you into creating quickly what they say they need should be suspect. You owe it to yourself to get behind the scenes as fast as you can so that the training that you ultimately design and deliver is in fact the training that the trainees—and the customer—need.

■ *Finding Discrepancies.* "Discrepancy" is a word you will come to love. It is the outcome that you seek as you do your needs assessment. A list of discrepancies between optimum performance and actual performance is the list that takes your training designers into the next phase of training. Training needs are based on performance discrepancies that can be addressed by new skills and knowledge. That's what training is made of, and that's what you should look for as you do your needs assessment. And when a lack of skills or knowledge is not the cause, do not attempt to solve the problem by "throwing training at it." Define the cause and solve the problem with another kind of intervention.

■ *Crossing Organizational Boundaries.* Isolating the training problems often requires you to cross organizational boundaries. This happens, for example, when you start with the results of poor performance. If you focus only on an employee's efforts, you limit your search only to the organization in which that person works. A better way to uncover the true nature of a training need is to focus on the results of performance, which probably have an effect on many different organizations and can be quantified in many different ways—hours, items, frequencies, dollars.

By opening your needs assessment to all of the organizations that are affected by a particular performance, you have a better chance of developing a network of key contact persons with a stake in the outcome of training. These persons can provide valuable help in zeroing in on the exact nature of the required training.

Interacting with other organizations in search of true training needs requires your best political sense in dealing with people and the corporate culture. This part of needs assessment tests your managerial skills!

■ *Choosing a Methodology.* Most training needs assessments are accomplished by person-to-person interviews conducted either over the telephone or in person or by questionnaires sent by interoffice mail or electronic mail. Valuable additions to the standard interviews and surveys are departmental self-study, work observations, document reviews, job analysis, and task analysis. Each method of study has its advantages and disadvantages. Your task as a training manager is to keep your options open regarding methodology, so that no potential source of information is inadvertently overlooked because of what seems to be a time crunch or a narrow choice of methodology.

An associated challenge is to conduct needs assessment with fairness, objectivity, dispassionate emotions, and timeliness. Results must be gathered with technical skill and reported in a way that is understandable to all concerned persons. As a training manager, you need to monitor carefully possible validity problems associated with the methodology you have chosen if your results are to be credible and taken seriously. Often what appears to be a training need turns out to be a problem of communications, incentives, or organizational structure. Using the right methodology for training needs assessment can help you solve all sorts of performance problems and, not incidentally, produce the best possible kind of training.

# Chapter 9 Checklists
## For Needs Assessment

In this section you'll find checklists to help you define the dimensions of your needs assessment, to plan the actions you'll need to take, and to structure your results.

A group of forms follows these checklists. Use them after you've reviewed the checklists if you need specific tools for investigation, documentation, or communication.

**LIST OF NEEDS ASSESSMENT CHECKLISTS**

- **9.1** General Guidelines for Success
- **9.2** Staff Self-Assessment Readiness Check
- **9.3** Where to Look for Companywide Contacts
- **9.4** Drivers of Change ("Triggers")
- **9.5** Help in Finding Performance Discrepancies
- **9.6** Guidelines for Investigation Methodology
- **9.7** Job Analysis Checklist
- **9.8** Task Analysis Checklist
- **9.9** Defining Needs Assessment Results
- **9.10** Cost-Benefit Analysis
- **9.11** Rationale for the Training Proposal

# Needs Assessment Checklist 9.1
## General Guidelines for Success

Read this checklist before you begin specific planning. These items provide a framework for success, while you are still in the "thinking about it" stage of needs assessment.

\_\_\_\_\_ 1. **Define your objectives.** Are you intending, for example, to identify individual employees, define problems with work processes, pinpoint systems confusion, find supportive data to measure training's impact, get input to long-range plans, justify budget expenditures, quantify productivity, analyze specific intellectual or physical skills? Be sure that you and your staff are all very clear about the objectives of the needs assessment.

\_\_\_\_\_ 2. **Estimate resource expenditure during needs assessment.** Estimate how much time will be taken up by persons asking questions and by those answering questions. Estimate the costs of time spent in meetings, creating questionnaires or other instruments, analyzing results, preparing documentation, giving feedback. Before you begin, know what your commitment of time and money will be. Scale your needs assessment to the size of the commitment you are able to make. Identify staff who will do the various needs assessment tasks.

\_\_\_\_\_ 3. **Identify a measurement and evaluation specialist who can advise you.** This person should be able to help you design your data-gathering instruments and show you ways of documenting and presenting needs assessment results.

\_\_\_\_\_ 4. **Anticipate the benefits of needs assessment in terms of positive energy for change.** Be prepared to suggest new directions in program development, new avenues for communication, and new possibilities for personal growth. Be ready when employees come to you with enthusiastic ideas related to the needs assessment.

\_\_\_\_\_ 5. **Identify which employee groups should receive—and give—feedback.** Be sure to include all those who will be touched by the results of needs assessment. Plan your company politicking strategy before you begin to design your needs assessment.

\_\_\_\_\_ 6. **Use a variety of data-gathering methods, so that you get good numbers and honest opinions.** Surround the performance issues with as much variety as possible in order to elicit responses from a variety of employees.

\_\_\_\_\_ 7. **Start well in advance.** As soon as you hear rumblings of a request for training, begin thinking about time up front for needs assessment.

_____ 8. **Be careful of your language.** Don't use the term "needs assessment" if you believe that it will conjure up images of big spending. Be creative—use other words, such as "design specs," "up-front effort," "research," "review of training background," "verification of training problem," or "cause analysis."

# Needs Assessment Checklist 9.2
## Staff Self-Assessment Readiness Check

Use this checklist to help you assess the receptivity of a group of employees—your own staff or the staff of a department that has requested training—to analyzing their training needs in a systematic way. A self-assessment can save you time, but it shouldn't be undertaken if you have reason to believe that it can't be done honestly or with objectivity.

Use this checklist yourself or give it to your training requestor to use with the requestor's staff.

_____ 1. The staff has some experience in working together; that is, it is not an organization whose culture is bound up in individual cubicles.

_____ 2. The staff is willing to work together on training issues. There is evidence of interest in making training better than it is.

_____ 3. You have assured those who participate in needs assessment that the results will be used in a positive way and that deficiencies in performance will be tied to training only and not to compensation.

_____ 4. Every individual on the staff has had training or experience in giving and receiving feedback from peers.

_____ 5. You are willing to promote the idea of self-assessment, although it takes time from regular work.

_____ 6. You believe that asking people what they need to know or need to know how to do will yield useful information.

_____ 7. You have a high performer in the organization who can help you design the questions.

_____ 8. You are willing to accept the results of employee self-assessment, even if they differ from management's point of view.

_____ 9. You or your designee are ready to facilitate employee group meetings and address problems that arise during self-assessment.

# Needs Assessment Checklist 9.3
## Where to Look for Companywide Contacts

Scan this checklist to broaden your field of vision as you seek key contact persons who can assist with needs assessment activities. Look for key contacts here:

\_\_\_\_\_ 1. Your peer managers throughout the company

\_\_\_\_\_ 2. Personnel department specialists who do interviewing and who write classified advertisements

\_\_\_\_\_ 3. Accountants

\_\_\_\_\_ 4. Secretaries

\_\_\_\_\_ 5. Senior programmers and systems analysts who often have to do one-to-one training of new hires

\_\_\_\_\_ 6. Corporate planners

\_\_\_\_\_ 7. Technical writers

\_\_\_\_\_ 8. Editors and public relations specialists

\_\_\_\_\_ 9. Supervisors

\_\_\_\_\_ 10. Individual employees

\_\_\_\_\_ 11. Team members

\_\_\_\_\_ 12. Customers

\_\_\_\_\_ 13. Suppliers

# Needs Assessment Checklist 9.4
## Drivers of Change ("Triggers")

Needs assessment is often launched by some kind of trigger—an identifiable event, memo, law, high-visibility person, or report that drives change. It is helpful to identify that driver of change before you set about designing a needs assessment.

\_\_\_\_\_ 1. Customer complaint or request

\_\_\_\_\_ 2. New policy

\_\_\_\_\_ 3. New boss or new boss's boss

\_\_\_\_\_ 4. New work assignment

\_\_\_\_\_ 5. New technology breakthrough

\_\_\_\_\_ 6. New piece of equipment

\_\_\_\_\_ 7. New system

\_\_\_\_\_ 8. Financial report

\_\_\_\_\_ 9. New legislation—federal, state, or local

\_\_\_\_\_ 10. New lobby group

\_\_\_\_\_ 11. Performance appraisal

\_\_\_\_\_ 12. Noncompliance report

\_\_\_\_\_ 13. Accident or on-job injury

\_\_\_\_\_ 14. Publicity

\_\_\_\_\_ 15. Report of task force

\_\_\_\_\_ 16. Action of a clique or ad hoc group

\_\_\_\_\_ 17. Union contract

\_\_\_\_\_ 18. Change in benefits

\_\_\_\_\_ 19. New building

\_\_\_\_\_ 20. New business; new customers

\_\_\_\_\_ 21. New teams

Also consider these more delayed triggers—changes, to be sure, but ones for which you have more advance warning:

\_\_\_\_\_ 22. Changed proportion of contingent workers

\_\_\_\_\_ 23. Merger

_____ 24. Downsizing
_____ 25. Changes in organizational structure
_____ 26. High turnover
_____ 27. Changed diversity of the workforce
_____ 28. Need for succession planning
_____ 29. Retirement
_____ 30. New business venture or product line
_____ 31. International expansion
_____ 32. New focus on quality

# Needs Assessment Checklist 9.5
## Help in Finding Performance Discrepancies

Using discrepancy analysis in needs assessment allows you to either quantify or define the discrepancy so that it can be measured. A discrepancy analysis looks at the drivers of change as they affect the state of what should be versus the state of what actually is.

This checklist contains tools that can help you find discrepancies quickly and painlessly.

_____ 1. Define all the "what should be's" that result from a specific driver of change.

_____ 2. Describe the current state associated with each "what should be." Use key contact persons to help define what actually is happening in terms of performance.

_____ 3. Analyze the difference between the desired state and the actual state. Decide if you can solve the problem—the discrepancy—by some means other than training.

_____ 4. Get rid of all solutions that are not training solutions. Pass on the solutions to whomever can implement them most effectively, but stay actively involved in the solution.

_____ 5. If training will solve the discrepancy, continue with an in-depth needs assessment involving a job and/or task analysis as a predesign activity feeding into training design.

_____ 6. Use criteria of acceptance performance in numerical terms if possible. Percent accomplished or percent needing help are suggestions. For each task of "what should be" performance, identify a number representing the extent of the discrepant performance.

_____ 7. Ask for help from high performers as you develop a task list and define optimal performance. Trust the people who work for you; they know best what the standards of good performance are.

# Needs Assessment Checklist 9.6
## Guidelines for Investigation Methodology

Err on the side of too much communication about needs assessment methodology. Describe, explain, show examples, ask for feedback—in short, do all you can to make the forms and methods of information gathering as simple and clear as possible. With this general and basic admonition, you can use the following checklist to develop the tools you need to get the job done.

_____ 1. Design instruments that yield unambiguous results. Word questions carefully so that answers are easy to tally.

_____ 2. Plan to administer the instrument at the same time of day for all respondents. Don't let the administration of needs assessment get in the way of valid and reliable responses. Give all respondents an equal chance to answer questions thoughtfully, when they're not tired or in a hurry.

_____ 3. Know who will need a report of needs assessment results; keep those persons or groups informed about the procedures and timing of needs assessment activities as they occur. Don't wait until the end to begin to bring those persons into the process.

_____ 4. Ask focused "open" questions, so that you don't get only yes or no answers. Keep the focus on improving the way a job is performed; don't focus on an individual's personality shortcomings.

_____ 5. Write clear instructions for the person conducting an interview or the person filling out a questionnaire.

_____ 6. If you use a rating scale (1, 2, 3, 4, 5), be sure that all numbers or choices go the same direction, that is, be sure that all items have the scale going from 1 to 5 and not sometimes 5 to 1. Check the logic of the instrument.

_____ 7. Ask a colleague to review your finished draft of a needs assessment instrument to be sure that it says what you think it says. Be sure the instrument is valid.

_____ 8. Structure any data-gathering activity or form with great care so that results can be easily and consistently recorded and subsequently analyzed.

_____ 9. Use a variety of methods for gathering information, even in a one- or two-day needs assessment. Look at documents, do interviews, send out questionnaires, work with experts to set standards, observe users, talk with supervisors, talk with workers, talk with customers, talk with executives, talk with support staff, talk with vendor reps, and encourage self-assessments.

# Needs Assessment Checklist 9.7
## Job Analysis Checklist

Job analysis is the basic step in designing training that will make a difference in the way work is performed. Job analysis is the "secret ingredient" that makes training the agent of behavior change and that distinguishes training from the simple process of dispensing information.

Use this checklist to determine a structure for the job analysis that fits your needs.

\_\_\_\_\_ 1. Break down the performance in question into major responsibility areas. Use the job description as an initial guide.

\_\_\_\_\_ 2. Categorize these responsibilities as people responsibilities (e.g., greet each client by first name), data responsibilities (e.g., total accounts receivable daily), or things responsibilities (e.g., water the office plants); that is, list the job responsibilities according to the people-data-things focus of each one.

\_\_\_\_\_ 3. With the help of the person doing the job in question, assign each category a rough percentage that reflects how much of the job it accounts for. This will give you a picture of what the job actually is and allow you to design only the training you need.

\_\_\_\_\_ 4. Draft a questionnaire or interview schedule that addresses the nature of the job. Use closed questions (simple answers, descriptions) to get the facts and open questions (complex answers, explanations) to get opinions. Put the closed questions first in a group, and conclude with a section of open questions.

\_\_\_\_\_ 5. Consider organizing an expert observation session in which a would-be expert uses a checklist to record observations about what the expert does differently from the ordinary worker. Get the regular worker involved as an auxiliary needs assessor, directly observing the high performance. Structure the observation checklist with the help of the expert to be observed.

\_\_\_\_\_ 6. Solicit opinions and beliefs about the job and about working conditions in order to identify problems that can be improved by interventions other than training (e.g., better chairs, less glare, more clerical support, new software, or different incentives). Identify those problems that are not solvable by training, so that when you get around to designing the training you are right on target.

# Needs Assessment Checklist 9.8
## Task Analysis Checklist

Task analysis, which follows job analysis, deals with the smallest elements of behavior on the job. It uses task lists to build training lessons and exercises. Without a task list to guide you, you probably will not design skill-building learning.

This checklist indicates the most likely sources of information about the tasks of a job:

_____ 1. Direct observation of a person doing the job

_____ 2. Videotaped observation

_____ 3. Interview with a person doing the job

_____ 4. Interview with a worker's supervisor

_____ 5. Interview with an expert doing that job

_____ 6. Log of usage of equipment required for the job

_____ 7. Data on periodic reports required on the job

_____ 8. Past performance review documents

_____ 9. A person's training history

_____ 10. Self-assessment reports

_____ 11. Responses to mailed questionnaires

# Needs Assessment Checklist 9.9
## Defining Needs Assessment Results

After you've found out what the training problems are, you are ready to take the first step at planning the training. Plans involve goals or targets, prioritized actions, measurement milestones, dates, and designation of persons responsible for implementation.

Use this checklist to double-check your needs assessment process so that your results are definable in a way that leads directly to planning:

_____ 1. Your discrepancy list of performance problems can be addressed by training. Give it one more check to be sure that the identified problems are based on knowledge or skill deficiencies.

_____ 2. You either have or can get the resources to solve the problems facing you.

_____ 3. If you need to purchase the resources (equipment, consultants, new staff) to solve the problems, you have started the ball rolling in terms of corporate politics and signed approvals.

_____ 4. You have translated each performance discrepancy into a specific training solution (for example, make a videotape showing close-up assembly to distribute to all line workers; design a two-hour workshop on prevention of carpal tunnel syndrome and neck and back stress; send six supervisors to a one-day vendor-delivered course on how to give performance feedback).

_____ 5. You have prioritized the training solutions with their associated performance problem so that you know what to tackle first.

# Needs Assessment Checklist 9.10
## Cost-Benefit Analysis

Needs assessment gets people nervous because they think it will take up a lot of everybody's time, eating up dollars in productive time away from the real work of the business.

The training manager often can abort this kind of thinking before it becomes full-blown by issuing a memo regarding the benefits of training as soon as the performance problems have been identified. Tying specific benefits to the estimated costs of developing and delivering training can often silence even the staunchest critics. Talk to people in terms of dollars and cents to balance the sometimes jargon-filled information about learning and productivity. Money is the language of business; the sooner you adopt it as the language of training, the better your chances of success as a training manager.

Use this checklist to focus on a cost-benefit analysis for training solutions.

_____ 1. Identify a list of training outcomes (for example, faster turnaround, higher frequency counts, fewer lines of code, fewer accidents, more sales closings, less time on maintenance calls, more errors found earlier).

_____ 2. Assign a dollar value to each outcome per month and per year. Use the annual figure as the projected benefit value of training.

_____ 3. Determine the costs associated with designing and developing the training. Include professional and support staff salary and benefits, expressed as person-days of time spent on this particular training. (Benefits costs are often expressed as a percentage of salary. Check with your personnel director to find out what the current figure is for your company—usually it's 15 to 30 percent. Factor in the benefits figure after you figure out the salary figure.)

_____ 4. Include an overhead figure with the design and development costs.

_____ 5. Figure the delivery costs for this particular training. Include classroom supplies, printing and binding, rental or purchase of videos or slides, and hospitality costs.

_____ 6. Include the cost of the instructor's salary and benefits or consultant fee, the instructor's travel and lodging expenses, and rental of a hotel room or conference center.

_____ 7. List the estimated "loss of business opportunity" cost if necessary—that is, the estimated cost of not having a person on the job but in training instead. Bringing the instructor to the students cuts down on this cost.

_____ 8. Compare the costs to the benefits on an annual basis. That is, factor in a cost multiplier if the training has to be repeated periodically throughout the year in order to realize even greater benefits. Be sure that costs are fairly counted.

_____ 9. Most of all, for your own use, do the cost-benefit analysis early in the needs assessment to see whether the training is as worthwhile as you originally thought or if you need to come up with more efficient or cost-effective ways to design and deliver it.

For example, many managers feel that bringing in a consultant for a flat per diem rate or per seminar rate is a good way to do training from a cost point of view. However, early in the needs assessment, you should compare the printed list of topics in the consultant's seminar with your stated needs and see if some of the topics could be eliminated and the seminar shortened to fit your own needs better. At issue is effectiveness, not just cost.

Another place to examine cost-effectiveness is in the choice between classroom training and on-the-job training. Always consider the trade-off between time that trainees spend away from work in class and the potential benefit of keeping them on the job, albeit at somewhat lower productivity than normal. Don't be fooled by the seemingly painless format of a classroom to deliver training—sometimes it hurts to take someone off the job to attend class. Consider, too, the potential attitude improvement that might occur through on-the-job training. Consider using videos and computer-based training, which can be more efficient than classroom training. Consider embedding an electronic performance support system (EPSS) within individual workstations. Consider enrolling students in online courses. Think about options early in needs assessment, before you begin expending resources in course design, development, and delivery.

# Needs Assessment Checklist 9.11
## Rationale for the Training Proposal

Circumstances in your company might be right for preparing your needs assessment report in the form of a training proposal. This document contains all the usual financial justifications and planning milestones one would expect with a proposal, but it also contains sections of narrative text that describe and explain the trainee population, the reasons training is needed, and the nature of the training itself. It also contains elaborations on how the training department can accomplish the training it envisions. It is a slightly salesy document.

If you need to convince several key persons of the value of the training you propose, perhaps you should consider writing a proposal. This checklist provides guidance regarding items you should include, such as:

_____ 1. A strong, burning statement on how this proposal will solve a specific training problem.

_____ 2. Description of the target trainee audience. State who the immediate audience will be and what the annual audience is likely to be.

_____ 3. Statement documenting the capability of your current staff to create this training.

_____ 4. Description of the course or program to be developed.

_____ 5. Cost-benefit analysis.

_____ 6. Learning objectives for trainees.

_____ 7. A time line for development and delivery.

# Chapter 9 Forms
## For Needs Assessment

Forms on the following pages provide guidelines and structure for the key elements of needs assessment.

**LIST OF NEEDS ASSESSMENT FORMS**

- **9.1** Self-Assessment Skills Inventory
- **9.2** Self-Assessment Group Discussion Guide
- **9.3** Key Contact Chart
- **9.4** Performance Discrepancy Form
- **9.5** Guide to Closed and Open Questions
- **9.6** People-Data-Things Job Analysis
- **9.7** Task List by Job Responsibility
- **9.8** Cost-Benefit Summary

**Needs Assessment Form 9.1**
**SELF-ASSESSMENT SKILLS INVENTORY**

### How to Use This Form
1. Give one of these forms to each employee in the potential trainee group.
2. Ask each person to complete the form independently by a certain date, at which time the results will be discussed in a group.
3. Instruct each person to list the skills required to do his or her particular job and then to check the appropriate column, "Need Help" or "Do Not Need Help."

Name _____

Job title _____

| List of required skills | Need Help | Do Not Need Help |
|---|---|---|
| 1. | | |
| 2. | | |
| 3. | | |
| 4. | | |
| 5. | | |
| 6. | | |
| 7. | | |
| 8. | | |
| 9. | | |
| 10. | | |
| 11. | | |
| 12. | | |
| 13. | | |
| 14. | | |
| 15. | | |

**Needs Assessment Form 9.2**
**SELF-ASSESSMENT GROUP DISCUSSION GUIDE**

### How to Use This Form

1. Follow the procedures for facilitating peer discussion as you discuss the self-assessments your potential trainees performed on Form 3.1.
2. The goal of the discussion is to complete a master self-assessment need-to-know chart, using information compiled by the group.
3. The need-to-know chart then becomes the foundation for creating training based on the skills with which employees need help.
4. Remember that persons in this group all have the same job title.

Procedures for facilitating peer discussion using the individually completed Skills Inventory Form 5.1.

1. Choose a moderator and recorder for the group.
2. Hold the discussion meeting in a comfortable place.
3. Provide refreshments.
4. Ask participants to introduce themselves by first and last name, telling one other thing about themselves such as what previous job they had or how long they've been with the company.
5. Draw the chart below on a blackboard or flipchart. Fill it in as you get each person's input from the forms.
6. Ask the recorder to make a paper copy of the chart when it is complete. Photocopy and distribute it to each participant.
7. Begin with each employee's name (first name is enough). When the meeting is over, ask participants to give you their forms.
8. Across the top of the chart, write in any skill identified as one with which the employee needs help.
9. List all names, followed by additional skills, and tally marks in appropriate columns to complete the chart of the skills with which people need help.
10. Keep discussion going if difficulties are brought up. Probe for reasons why people are having trouble with certain skills. Learn as much as you can about skill deficiencies.

| | TARGET POPULATION NEED-TO-KNOW CHART | | | |
|---|---|---|---|---|
| Name of Employee | Skill #    : | Skill #    : | Skill #    : | Skill #    : |
| • | | | | |
| • | | | | |
| • | | | | |
| • | | | | |

**Needs Assessment Form** 9.3
**KEY CONTACT CHART**

### How to Use This Form
1. Record important information about any person who can be helpful to you as you engage in any needs assessment activity. Be sure to get the title correct.
2. Keep the form up to date; don't overlook anyone at any level in the company or the customer's company. This list will come in handy as you implement this and other training programs. Take the time in the beginning to get accurate details (spelling of names is especially important—remember, you're in a people business).

| | Name | Title | Organization Name | Boss's Name | Telephone |
|---|---|---|---|---|---|
| 1. | | | | | |
| 2. | | | | | |
| 3. | | | | | |
| 4. | | | | | |
| 5. | | | | | |
| 6. | | | | | |
| 7. | | | | | |
| 8. | | | | | |
| 9. | | | | | |
| 10. | | | | | |
| 11. | | | | | |
| 12. | | | | | |
| 13. | | | | | |
| 14. | | | | | |
| 15. | | | | | |
| 16. | | | | | |

**Needs Assessment Form 9.4**
**PERFORMANCE DISCREPANCY FORM**

### How to Use This Form
1. Use this form to express in brief what is driving the need for training and to identify the performance problem that must be addressed.
2. Think carefully whether that problem can best be solved by a solution other than training. If this is the case, leave the "Performance Discrepancy and Suggested Training" box empty. Write down what you believe to be the nontraining solution and pass on the form to someone who can handle that nontraining solution.

Change driver:


Description of desired performance (what should be):


Description of current performance (what is):


PERFORMANCE DISCREPANCY AND SUGGESTED TRAINING:


Nontraining solution:

**Needs Assessment Form 9.5**
**GUIDE TO CLOSED AND OPEN QUESTIONS**

### How to Use This Form
1. Use these guidelines to design questionnaires and interview schedules for one-to-one administration.
2. Use both types of questions during needs assessment. Closed questions are easier to answer, so you may want to ask this kind of question early in the interview or on the questionnaire. Answers to open questions provide elaboration and the opportunity to express feelings.
3. As you design forms for questions, also design forms for answers. Structure your asking in a way that makes recording answers easy and systematic. You'll ultimately improve communication if you think of questions and answers at the same time during the design phase of needs assessment.

Typical closed questions used during needs assessment:

1. How long have you been in this job?
2. What tools and equipment do you use on the job?
3. What job-related courses have you taken?
4. What job-related certification do you hold?
5. Are you a union member?     Which union?

Typical open questions used during needs assessment:

1. What changes could be made in your job description to reflect the true nature of what you do?
2. What circumstances, people, or equipment most affect your ability to perform your job well?    Why?
3. What is your opinion of the performance appraisal system currently in place here?
4. How would you change the working environment or working conditions to improve performance here?
5. What kind of training would make your job easier?

**Needs Assessment Form 9.6**
**PEOPLE-DATA-THINGS JOB ANALYSIS**

### How to Use This Form
1. Use this form as a first step in job analysis.
2. In discussion with an employee or in review of documents (job descriptions, performance reviews) break down the responsibilities of the job into the appropriate categories—people, data, things—according to the primary focus of that specific job responsibility.

Job being analyzed: _____

PEOPLE responsibilities

- 
- 
- 
- 
- 
- 

DATA responsibilities

- 
- 
- 
- 
- 
- 

THINGS responsibilities

- 
- 
- 
- 
-

**Needs Assessment Form 9.7**
**TASK LIST BY JOB RESPONSIBILITY**

### How to Use This Form
1. Use this form as a first step in task analysis that will lead you into designing training lessons.
2. From the job analysis that precedes this, determine the major responsibility areas and list them on this form. It can be a people-data-things breakdown or any other method of delineating job responsibilities.
3. Think in the smallest elements of work—filing, coding, lifting, looking, writing, posting, calculating.
4. Express these small elements of work as tasks, listing a group of tasks that are associated with each job responsibility area. Begin each with an active verb.
5. Assign a difficulty rating to each task, placing a check mark in the appropriate column beside each task.

|  | difficulty index |||
|---|---|---|---|
|  | easy | medium | hard |

Job responsibility area:

Tasks

- 
- 
- 
- 

Job responsibility area:

Tasks

- 
- 
- 
- 

Job responsibility area:

Tasks

- 
- 
- 
-

**Needs Assessment Form 9.8**
**COST-BENEFIT SUMMARY**

### How to Use This Form
1. Use this form as a summary document for informational meetings and as a discussion guide.
2. Keep detailed complete financial records in your file.

Brief description of proposed training:

Value of proposed training $ _____

Cost to develop this training

    Salary         $ _____
    Benefits      $ _____
    Expenses    $ _____
                                                   $ _____

Cost to deliver this training

    Salary         $ _____
    Benefits      $ _____
    Expenses    $ _____
                                                   $ _____

Statement of relationship between costs and benefits:

# Chapter 9
# More Information on Needs Assessment

## Dealing with the Time Crunch

Chances are that by the time you get a request for training, the performance problem that led to that request has become very complex. Well-meaning managers throughout the company often come to training to solve their problems before they've adequately figured out what their problems really are, and it's possible that good solutions can be found, without requiring training.

As a trainer, you know from experience that everyone loses when training is hurriedly thrown at a problem that is not a training problem, and you may well feel torn between your wish to satisfy your customer's immediate need and your awareness that training for the right reasons takes time to design.

You'll need to convince your customer that trainers have to be involved in doing the necessary needs assessment. There are some basic ways to help your customer see the value of taking just a little more time before training begins:

- Repeat the old adage AN OUNCE OF PREVENTION IS WORTH A POUND OF CURE. Customers can often see the wisdom in this analogy.
- Talk about building quality into the design process. Use the language of quality assurance to remind your customer that you'd like his or her input at various stages of development, including setting the goals for this training and identifying the target audience.
- Remind your customer that training is not just a pretty face doing a presentation for a captive audience. Training that sticks after the class has ended is training that is carefully crafted around specific objectives for learners.
- Suggest to your customer that designing training is like designing an advertising campaign: The goal is changed behavior at the end of it. You need to be absolutely sure what the behavioral goals are for this group of trainees. The content and the person are related by the expectation of behavioral change for the good of the company. You need to be sure that you're teaching the right things.
- Talk about customizing each training experience—but not too much. You'll need to balance the "carrot" of the special just-for-you course with the "stick" of taking too much time in development. Focus on the idea that a training experience that is precisely on target saves hours of design and classroom time in the long run. Custom courses can be delivered in less time than generic off-the-shelf courses with extraneous or superficial information in them.

- Get help wherever you can. Enlist the support of secretaries, other managers, personnel specialists, graphic artists, and others outside your department who can help you gather information about having an impact on your budget. You'll be surprised at how helpful people can be, because training is one of those things that most people like and see as a benefit of employment. The clue here is to be organized and to give people clear requests and easy ways in which to report their findings.

## If You Have Limited Budget and Staff . . .

There are, of course, times when all the negotiating in the world won't help and you're stuck having to design and deliver training in what seems to be an impossible amount of time. When this happens, in the name of needs assessment you can still do this:

- Conduct a telephone interview with each trainee prior to class to find out where he or she needs the most help. Record the responses on a chart to give to the instructor as soon as possible. Use a phone bank and several interviewers if the class is large.

- If you have a computer network for electronic mail, send a questionnaire about training needs to each registered trainee and ask that it be returned to your instructor by electronic mail. Make it simple and focused on help with skills.

- Before training begins, ask your instructor to call at least three persons with a stake in its outcome to obtain their opinions about what the performance problems are. Provide the list of contacts.

- Take fifteen to thirty minutes at the beginning of training to record the needs of group members on a flipchart or blackboard. Ask them what their personal goals are for this training, or what skills they need special help with. Another way to ask for this information is to say, "What do you hope to get out of this training?" Be sure to get a response from each trainee, and record each answer for all to see. One person's response often helps another person to respond more accurately. Adjust the training content and schedule to address these stated needs.

## If You Have Adequate Budget and Staff . . .

Take the time to get the customer and potential trainees involved in the detailed descriptions of training needs. Guide them through self-assessments and definitions of performance discrepancies. Have small-group meetings that include potential trainees, instructors, instructional designers, and the person paying the bill for training.

Spend some money on graphics to help get your message of training needs and benefits across to interested parties. Take the time to talk with the people who will be positively affected by a better trained workforce, and include their points of view in your presentations.

Write articles for newspapers and company newsletters about training needs, costs, and benefits. Spread the message of training and how it's done right. Highlight the payoffs—with dollar figures if you can.

Communicate the message that quality costs less when it is designed in at the beginning of the process; time spent assessing needs at the beginning of training design is time well spent because it is an investment in the quality of the ultimate training product. Tie training into the quality initiatives of the corporation.

Develop a training proposal document, structured according to the guidelines in Needs Assessment Checklist 9.11, and circulate it widely among managers in related departments. Use the proposal to demonstrate that training is a proactive department with profit and customer service in mind. Show the world that training means business.

# 10

# How to Design and Write Training

Making training stick is the goal of all managers who are part of the training enterprise—both the managers who send employees to class or who commit time and resources to on-the-job training and the training managers who are responsible for designing and delivering the best training possible.

Managers today have little tolerance for the "nice to knows" of knowledge and skills; they are interested in well-trained employees who can make the leap from engaging in training to engaging in better work as swiftly and as sure-footedly as possible. In addition, employees themselves have little interest in plodding through activities that are at best tangential to their jobs. In short, the training experience must be designed to allow maximum transfer to the work of individuals as they cross the bridge from trainee to trained worker.

The key management issues in designing training for maximum transfer to work center around two basic areas: (1) your role as coordinator and facilitator, and (2) the nature of the design for learning, that is, the way the course is built. Your coordination and facilitation functions occur primarily before and after training; the training design issues are addressed as you interact with and guide your instructional designers, writers, and subject matter experts.

## KEY MANAGEMENT ISSUES

■ *Meeting Your Customers' Needs.* Think of your trainees as customers who have chosen training as a tool for accomplishing a business purpose. All those who design and deliver training should understand what that business purpose is before the training is planned. Transfer to the job happens more effectively if trainers know what the trainee's job is; as a training manager, be sure that you put in place analysis and information mechanisms that will enable your designers to learn what business reasons your trainee customer had for choosing training.

- **Setting Expectations.** Create opportunities to express your expectations for training. Make it clear to your designers, instructors, and support people that you expect certain standards to be followed and that you expect monitoring, evaluation, and feedback from your trainees once they have completed training. Go out of your way to close the loop between learning and productivity.

    Create opportunities for your trainees' supervisors to express their expectations as well. Be known as a manager who has high yet realistic expectations that good training will directly improve the business. Get people thinking that their grasp can in fact match their reach. Never underestimate the role of belief in determining achievement. The wise training manager formalizes and institutionalizes the verbalization of expectations—what people hope for as they enter training and what they hope for as a result of training—and involves both the trainees and their supervisors in this process. Transfer happens better when organizations are ready for it.

- **Learning to Learn.** Part of your mission in creating transfer is to encourage your adult student to realize that there are many avenues to learning and that the admonition "know thyself" is a very important suggestion. Many adult students have learned to mimic learning; that is, they read the manuals and do the exercises as if they were learning when in fact they are not. Transfer happens more efficiently when the adult student realizes that one approach to a problem is not yielding results and that another approach is indicated—that there are options for learning and that the learner is in control of exercising those options. You should build methodology options into the design of courses and counsel instructors to help trainees learn to learn.

- **Recognizing Different Learning Styles.** Closely related to the issue of learning to learn is the issue of learning style. Much has been written in recent years on the ways personality differences affect how individuals learn new information and new skills. Questions of learning style must be considered as course planners design course content, course exercises, and the choices of delivery modes for instruction. Be sure that you engage your staff in discussions about the best way to deliver instruction, as well as about the best way to present content and learning objectives for any given course.

    Be sure that your training isn't inadvertently designed to appeal to only one learning style. Trainees who are uncomfortable while learning or who just go through the motions of learning because they're basically on a different wavelength are not very likely to transfer any new skills to the job.

- **Understanding Taxonomies.** Training design is greatly helped by the training manager's understanding of taxonomies, groups of related concepts organized in a hierarchy—low to high or high to low. Designing training for transfer requires that you organize learning in certain work-related areas into hierarchical categories for acquiring knowledge or skills.

These groupings of learning concepts assist in the development of training by providing frameworks around which to build instruction. Because of the hierarchical nature of taxonomies, you need to ensure that lower-level skills are mastered before higher-level skills are introduced. Transfer is facilitated when learners can achieve and demonstrate competence in a hierarchy of skills, beginning with the lowest. Your course designers and instructors should always be aware of the taxonomy under which they are operating—where they've been and where they're going—in order to transfer to "take."

■ *Nurturing.* Once the training is completed, the training manager can become involved in some structured support activities to help ensure that what was learned in class can continue to be accomplished on the job.

The most common of these supports is periodic structured feedback from trainee and supervisor to training department, rotation assignments and cross-training, structured monitoring at three months and six months, mentoring, coaching, and peer support. The training manager should design and nurture these supports to training so that the learning that happened during training can be applied to the job through a development thrust that commits the entire organization to improvement through training.

■ *Packaging.* Putting it down on paper is one of the essentials of training. Even with a trend toward video- and computer-based training, trainees still expect to learn with the assistance of written language. It is, of course, important that training exercises and lessons be written with language that facilitates learning, language that is spare and lucid. It is also important that all of the support writing about training—the catalogs, the newsletters, the press releases, the electronic bulletins, the policies, the graphics and aids to training, and the sign-up information—use written language effectively.

This chapter provides guidance in managing the writing of training. In it, you'll find tools to help you initiate the writing activities for which your organization is responsible and to help you evaluate the training writing of others.

■ *Author vs. Producer.* When you create courses, you must first decide exactly who will do the writing. Will you try to employ an expert in the course subject to write the lessons? Can you find such a person—that is, someone who is a subject matter expert, who is interested in designing a course, and who can write? Will you try to hire experts in course design—that is, persons with graduate degrees in instructional technology who understand how people learn and who can turn other folks' ideas into course manuals? Will you try to staff your writing operation with some combination of the content expert and instructional designer? Or will you hire only instructional designers whose job it is to seek out the content experts in other organizations and work with them on a temporary or interview basis? Will you arrange with other managers who have the subject matter experts you need to rotate the experts in to your organization while the course is being written?

How will you get the ideas into course manual format? Will the person who writes the course also do the word processing, or will you employ a staff of production persons to do the final copy and printing? Will you go the route of buying instructional design software and personal computers for course authors? Will you train authors to use PCs to create courses? Will you employ editing staff? Will you employ technical writers? Can you borrow editing staff and tech writers from the corporate pool? Or will you purchase any of these services from outside vendors? Staffing course writing boils down to who will write and who will produce a course. How you matrix all of the competencies you need among this writing staff is a major challenge to the training manager.

■ ***Course and System Standards.*** Regardless of who creates a course, you are responsible for providing quality standards in language conventions, instructional design, and finished format. As a training manager, you must provide your writing staff the standards they'll have to follow when they author and produce your courses.

■ ***Dissemination.*** How much and what kind of dissemination activity you want as a support for training is also one of the major issues facing a training manager. Some of the issues you must sort out are the balance between paper and online dissemination, whether to use an internal newsletter to promote and report on training events and trends, and whether to do external information dissemination, such as community task forces, relationships with local colleges, and newspaper articles. In all of this, who will be responsible for writing the information to be disseminated? If you hire a full-time technical writing and editing staff, can they also do these general dissemination functions? Do you need a specialized training marketing and promotion staff?

# Chapter 10 Checklists
## To Help with Design and Writing

This section contains a variety of checklists to guide you in creating training and organizational situations that encourage the rapid transfer of newly learned skills and knowledge to the job. These checklists will show you how to "get it down on paper"—or disk.

Use these checklists as you plan your development of training. They will be useful as you work with your instructional designers, instructors, writers, and subject matter experts and as you meet with and select vendors to provide course design and documentation services to you. They will also help you plan follow-up activities to determine the value of training to your company.

The forms that follow the checklists provide you with a more graphic representation of some of these ideas and constitute ready-to-use aids as you get into the actual work of designing and writing training.

**LIST OF TRAINING DESIGN CHECKLISTS**

- 10.1   Designing Training for Customers
- 10.2   Setting Training Expectations
- 10.3   Designing Training for Adult Learners
- 10.4   Overcoming Constraints on Transfer
- 10.5   Fostering Learning to Learn
- 10.6   Dealing with Learning Styles
- 10.7   Building Learning Taxonomies
- 10.8   Categorizing Types of Transferable Skills
- 10.9   Focusing on Results
- 10.10  Continuous Enabling Through Organizational Development

**LIST OF WRITING CHECKLISTS**

- 10.11  Policy Development Guidelines
- 10.12  What to Look for in a Vendor's Proposal
- 10.13  When and How to Promote (Not Just Design and Deliver) Training
- 10.14  Catalog Design Checklist
- 10.15  Writing Competencies for Course Authors
- 10.16  Elements of a Course

**10.17** Authoring System Checklist for Instructional Design Software

**10.18** Trainee Manual Development Checklist

**10.19** Instructor Manual Development Checklist

**10.20** Writing Checklist for Computer-Based and Interactive Video Training

# Training Design Checklist 10.1
## Designing Training for Customers

In order to design training for transfer, you must first be wholeheartedly committed to understanding the needs of your customer—the person paying the bill for the training you deliver. Never design training or purchase a vendor course because you *think* it is just what everyone ought to know.

The best-kept secret in training management is that training is a business. Those managers who take the time to figure out what their customers really need can reap all the normal benefits of designing and delivering a business service that is cost-effective and profitable. Managers who think they know exactly what those folks need before asking them, or who buy "bells and whistles" for their "state-of-the-art" look, or who simply respond "yes, of course" to a colleague waving money in their faces will be sadly disappointed both with the quality of learning that takes place and with the amount of repeat business from customers who do not hesitate to tell them that training is mostly a waste of time and money.

Here are some simple checkpoints to jog your thinking and planning for designing training for customers:

\_\_\_\_\_ 1. You know the names of the persons paying the bill for training.

\_\_\_\_\_ 2. You know the names and job responsibilities of trainees.

\_\_\_\_\_ 3. The person paying the bill has told you the business reasons for choosing training.

\_\_\_\_\_ 4. As a training manager, you agree with these business reasons.

\_\_\_\_\_ 5. If you don't agree, you have exercised your responsibility as a corporate representative to suggest a nontraining approach to solving your would-be customer's problem.

\_\_\_\_\_ 6. You have adequate evidence that your customer has done some upfront analysis of the business reasons driving the need for training.

\_\_\_\_\_ 7. You have the results of needs analysis in time to build them into the design of training to meet those needs.

\_\_\_\_\_ 8. The training evaluation form includes at least one item regarding the application of training to the trainee's specific work assignment.

# Training Design Checklist 10.2
## Setting Training Expectations

There are two major objectives regarding training expectations: (1) to make your expectations regarding training design, production, and delivery known to your staff and vendors, and (2) to have your peers communicate their expectations for training among the employees who report to them. Call them standards, guidelines, values, employee development goals, training milestones, corporate training requirements, or whatever term conveys your belief that certain kinds of measurable improvements will result from the training experience.

This checklist will help you plan for and communicate these expectations:

_____ 1. You have a standards document regarding course design and course delivery.

_____ 2. You have taken the time to discuss this document with your staff and solicit their support for it.

_____ 3. You know that this document is followed faithfully by your internal training development staff and by all vendors and consultants that you hire to design or deliver training.

_____ 4. This document is written in clear language and is attractive, easy to use, and accessible to your staff.

_____ 5. You periodically review this document with your staff in order to incorporate changes based on their experiences with it.

_____ 6. You have production guidelines, formats for training manuals, and a project management system to track the production of a course.

_____ 7. Your staff is committed to producing training products in a timely fashion. Measurements are in place and being used, so that your information is accurate.

_____ 8. Incentives are in place to reward cost-effective products and production efforts.

_____ 9. You have offered assistance to supervisors on how to discuss training expectations with employees and how to document expectations so that they are useful in planning employee development opportunities.

_____ 10. You know what the supervisors expect in terms of new or improved skills and knowledge. You have talked with them about realistic time lines.

_____ 11. You know what trainees expect from the training experience itself.

_____ 12. You know how trainees expect to improve their work as a result of training.

_____ 13. You have shared expectations information with your instructors, or, if your instructors are the primary information gatherers regarding trainee expectations, they have shared these with you.

# Training Design Checklist 10.3
## Designing Training for Adult Learners

This checklist is meant to refresh your memory about how adult learners differ from children in school. You might want to share it with your instructors as a refresher for them, too.

_____ 1. Be sure that trainees know how their work fits into the totality of work. Be sure that instruction describes the big picture. Inspect the beginnings of your course documents to be sure that instruction is designed to enable trainees to see their work in relationship to all work of the business.

_____ 2. Be sure that trainees understand the requirements of the new skill—that is, give trainees a simple list of competent behaviors you expect them to exhibit after they've been through training.

_____ 3. Anticipate that trainees will come to training with some gaps in prerequisite knowledge. Have reference documents, user manuals, and job aids available during training for those who might need to catch up.

_____ 4. Demonstrate by your actions—the tone in which the course is written and the respect with which the instructor interacts with trainees—that the training department appreciates the past successes of trainees and will work with them to continue to build on their experiences.

_____ 5. Present training as a solution to problems. Conduct training in a way that engages trainees in working out solutions. Give trainees opportunities to problem-solve individually as well as in small groups. Give them clues and ideas, but let them work through the problems.

_____ 6. Provide feedback often during learning time. Adults like to know that they "got it"; if they didn't get it, they like to know what steps to take in order to do it right.

_____ 7. Build in plenty of practice time, and be sure that it is "instructed" practice time, so that trainees realize their successes and failures and can learn from them in a controlled situation.

_____ 8. Hand out some record or reminder of learning—a trainee manual, a course outline, a workshop agenda, a job aid—to take back to the job. Give them a crutch to reactivate their memories after training is done.

_____ 9. Give trainees a chance to evaluate their training, making suggestions for improvement.

# Training Design Checklist 10.4
## Overcoming Constraints on Transfer

Another way to think about designing for transfer is to focus on the negatives, that is, to zero in on the constraints and challenges to transfer. Often these negatives manifest themselves as poorly designed, off-target training, poorly delivered training, poorly timed training, training for the wrong people, or training that never should have been developed in the first place. Focus on the constraints involving content, money, and people.

This checklist will help you plan to meet the challenge of constraints on transfer:

_____ 1. Encourage your designers to think small. A goal that is too lofty, projections that are unreasonable, plans that are unrealistic, and objectives that can't be measured are enemies of transfer. Work for successive approximation—that is, accumulating small successes toward a larger goal in learning.

_____ 2. Anticipate problems. Expend time and energy in the structured exercise of problem definition: Define resource deficiencies, assess risks, attach dollar costs. Don't be too quick to jump to solutions. Correct evaluation of inputs shortens the process to outputs and makes those outputs of higher quality.

_____ 3. Initiate action. Get rid of the notion that training is "service." Be proactive, not reactive. Devise ways to solicit and demonstrate top management support for training through accounting channels, systems channels, marketing support, or organizational restructuring. Go for it; don't wait till it's handed out!

_____ 4. Identify sources of help. Be especially concerned with organizations whose work must be done well before training can be done. Examples are software developers, system documentation groups, information systems groups, graphic support groups, and technical writing groups. Cajole these significant others into committing their resources in a timely fashion so that you can create good training without wasting development time or heading down wrong avenues.

_____ 5. Generalize the goals of training to the trainee's job environment early in the course. Elaborate and reinforce the general applicability of new skills and knowledge. Encourage the trainee to "stretch" in thinking about the job. Prepare answers to lots of "why" questions.

_____ 6. Put feedback, monitoring, and follow-up procedures in place before training ever begins.

_____ 7. Assemble all peripherally related information ahead of training. Communicate its availability and introduce it to trainees at appropriate times.

# Training Design Checklist 10.5
## Fostering Learning to Learn

"Strategies" is a favorite word among educational psychologists. They use it to mean the ways in which we think in order to improve the effectiveness, thoroughness, and efficiency of intellectual processes. Cognitive strategies help us think about thinking and learn to learn.

The best writing about teaching adults suggests that adult students like to be in control of their learning. Learning can be a means to improved self-esteem and a sense of confidence on the job. Fostering learning to learn is a challenge to training managers because often adult learners can't recognize the learning strategies they're using. The training experience should build in opportunities to help trainees define their strategies and to control their use.

Here's a checklist to help you get started fostering learning to learn:

_____ 1. Your courses are designed with plenty of practice exercises, case studies, and business examples so that trainees can work on real problems that mean something to them during training. Course design facilitates their control of decisions during learning. (Be suspicious of training driven by overhead transparencies—often a tip-off that the course is designed basically as a lecture, with little control yielded to trainees).

_____ 2. Your instructors have a commitment to being facilitators of learning, not dispensers of wisdom. This should be documented in the end-of-course evaluation forms from trainees as well as through your own direct observation of how the instructors maneuver individual trainees into "working it out" in their own ways.

_____ 3. Your instructors are willing to turn over control of the learning situation to the learners. You've seen them do it.

_____ 4. Your courses allow time within the training period for individuals to work at their own best speeds. Additional tasks are built into the course to keep the early finishers busy.

_____ 5. Your courses are designed with a variety of avenues for learning, e.g., forming hypotheses, breaking down a problem into subproblems, starting with the finished product and figuring out the steps required to get there, building a bigger whole out of learning small bits of information, learning and applying rules, coding, using analogies, throwing a problem onto the table and giving cues, summarizing, picking out main ideas, reflecting on results, demonstrating new skills.

_____ 6. Your instructors are adept at giving feedback on the process of learning—i.e., on telling trainees how they're doing as they

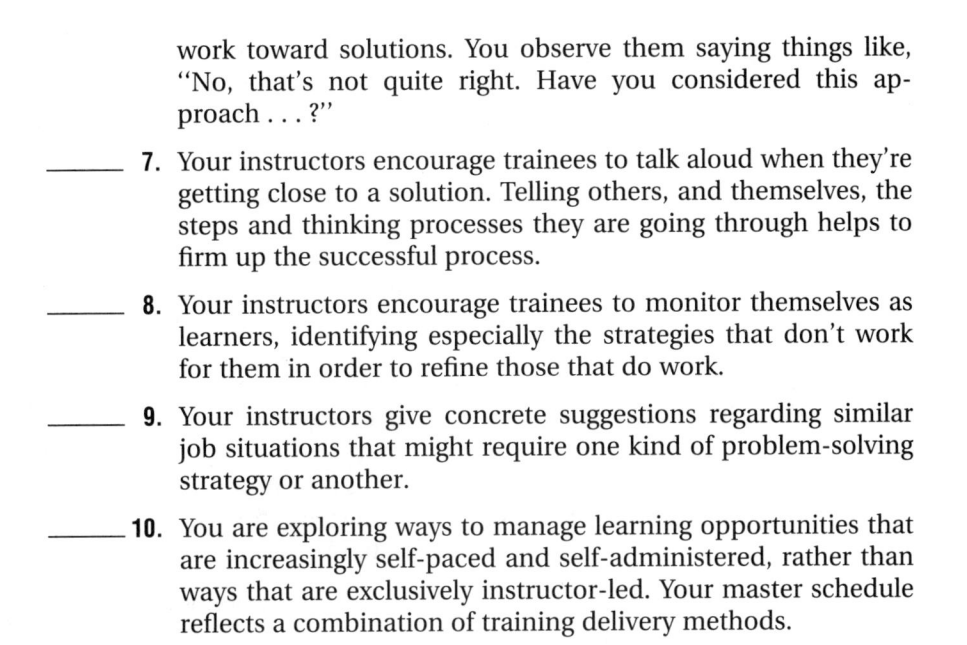

# How to Design and Write Training 253

work toward solutions. You observe them saying things like, "No, that's not quite right. Have you considered this approach . . . ?"

_____ 7. Your instructors encourage trainees to talk aloud when they're getting close to a solution. Telling others, and themselves, the steps and thinking processes they are going through helps to firm up the successful process.

_____ 8. Your instructors encourage trainees to monitor themselves as learners, identifying especially the strategies that don't work for them in order to refine those that do work.

_____ 9. Your instructors give concrete suggestions regarding similar job situations that might require one kind of problem-solving strategy or another.

_____ 10. You are exploring ways to manage learning opportunities that are increasingly self-paced and self-administered, rather than ways that are exclusively instructor-led. Your master schedule reflects a combination of training delivery methods.

## Training Design Checklist 10.6
### Dealing with Learning Styles

Personal learning style is related to an individual's values, family influences, personality, and past successes. A learner generally exhibits preference for different learning styles according to what has to be learned; while a person may prefer visual information, working models, or any of a range of modalities, he or she probably prefers to learn different things differently.

This checklist will help you to design and deliver your training to accommodate the most common preferences in learning style:

_____ 1. Present information that appeals to "left-brained" preferences—i.e., sequential, logical, organized information that requires reasoned analysis to understand.

_____ 2. Present information that appeals to "right-brained" preferences—i.e., nonverbal stimuli, impulsive, simultaneous, messy information requiring intuition and synthesis to understand.

_____ 3. Build in opportunities for divergent thinking—generating hypotheses, being creative, and solving problems using the concept of what might be possible.

_____ 4. Build in opportunities for convergent thinking—gathering evidence, documenting, and solving problems by figuring out observable necessary components.

_____ 5. Teach students to look for patterns—in verbal expression, in visual information, in situations in which touching, hearing, or smelling are important to the job.

_____ 6. Teach students to understand analogies and use them to foster understanding of new concepts and skills.

_____ 7. Build in opportunities for quiet individual work as well as noisy group work.

_____ 8. Encourage team problem solving in small groups so that trainees can learn from each other and can develop experience working with learners of varying style preferences.

_____ 9. Train your instructors to learn to listen for clues to a person's preferred style—e.g., "I see," "I believe," "I hear," "I figure," "I can prove."

_____ 10. Appreciate that in the same class you'll have students on the same issue who'll always want to ask you "what" and others who will always want to ask you "why," and that both approaches are equally valid. Be sure your instructors are prepared to satisfy each kind of question—sometimes coming from the same person.

_____ 11. Build in opportunities for individuals to exercise the various kinds of memory involved in human information processing—the short-term memory of present information delivered by current sensory inputs, the information store of past experiences in long-term memory, and the process of associating the present and the past. Be sure that training is consciously designed and delivered to support both short-term and long-term memory.

_____ 12. Build in the opportunity for trainees to plan as well as to "shoot from the hip."

# Training Design Checklist 10.7
## Building Learning Taxonomies

Adults seem to learn best by connecting new information to previous information. This is true for information inherent in processes, not only that in facts. Because of this, using hierarchies to mold instructional design and to form the foundation for presenting instruction is a good idea. Teaching basic skills first helps trainees to integrate the new learning into their former learnings and enables you to progress to higher-level skills.

This checklist will guide your thinking about building taxonomies in order to assist your trainees in transferring learning:

_____ 1. You have structured the learning objectives according to a well-ordered plan, such as lowest or easiest to highest or most difficult skill.

_____ 2. You have analyzed what you intend to teach for its intellectual (cognitive) skill components as well as its hands-on (psychomotor) skill components. Each group of skills has a range of easy to difficult.

_____ 3. You have considered your trainees' comfort levels during the training experience and realize that each trainee has a psychological need to be protected, safe, at ease, and valued during learning.

_____ 4. You recognize that each trainee has a different priority regarding the application of training—some will need to use the new skill tomorrow, whereas others will not need to use it until next month. You have made an attempt to find out what this hierarchy of urgency really is.

_____ 5. You have consistently tried to describe before you explain; you tell what the rules are, then tell why to use them; you verify that concepts have been mastered before you expect your trainees to solve problems or exercise mature judgment.

_____ 6. You pay attention to the very first stages of learning—how trainees respond to stimuli, especially visual and auditory stimuli, recognizing that each person learns at a different rate, even at these early stages of learning.

_____ 7. You understand that positive steps can be taken to assist the trainee to remember—that is, memory-enhancing skills are hierarchical and have to be taught.

_____ 8. You have reviewed the works of familiar taxonomy builders, including Bloom, Gagne, Gardner, Guilford, Hall, Mager, Maslow, Piaget, Simpson, Sternberg, Coleman, and others.

# Training Design Checklist 10.8
## Categorizing Types of Transferable Skills

Much has been written about the need today for flexible, original, intellectually agile employees—people from all levels of schooling and ethnic backgrounds and in all job assignments who can contribute their individual and collective expertise to the workplace. Organizationally, companies engage in cross-training, in which workers learn new skills that can be applied to several key areas of the business, and broadening assignments flourish—from mentoring programs to intra-company transfers and rotations. Regardless of native language or job assignment, employees are expected to be fluent in reading, writing, computation, and problem solving.

This checklist will help you to focus on the categories of transferable skills and to design learning for them:

_____ 1. Think about whether you want the new skill to be transferred intact (as in learning to log on to a computer) or to be a stepping-stone to learning-related skills (for example, learning to type, which can be transferred to learning part of the keyboarding skills required in desktop publishing).

_____ 2. Think about the work survival skills at your particular company. These might be following rules, using tools, dealing positively with time pressure, being a member of a team, writing reports, or analyzing spreadsheets. These are skills that the entire company values and uses at all levels of employee; they are thus transferable from job to job. They need to be learned well.

_____ 3. Focus on general communication skills—listening, speaking, writing. Teach them everywhere.

_____ 4. Focus on general mathematics skills—computing, accounting, estimating, budgeting, projecting, solving equations, using statistical measures of central tendency and dispersion, analyzing and creating graphs. Teach these everywhere.

_____ 5. Focus on general character traits—curiosity, cooperation, initiative, persistence, competency, sharing. Help employees at all levels to develop skills that demonstrate these traits.

_____ 6. Focus on reasoning skills—generating alternatives, making inferences, classifying, generalizing, using rules, planning, reshaping ideas, evaluating. Look everywhere for opportunities to teach these.

_____ 7. Focus on manipulative skills—sensory acuity, focus, eye-hand coordination, dexterity, repetitive accuracy. Watch for the numerous unexpected occasions when these kinds of skills must be taught together with communication or reasoning skills. Don't ignore these!

_____ 8. Focus on the skills involved in learning to learn—locating information, accessing information, recognizing patterns, taking stock of one's "place in the program," collaborating with others, seeking help.

# Training Design Checklist 10.9
## Focusing on Results

Skills learned in class transfer more readily to the job when instruction itself—the trainer interacting with the trainee—focuses on the results of training.

The following checklist will help you guide your instructors to focus on results:

_____ 1. Start each training session with an expectations dialogue. Find out what each trainee wants to get out of this session of training. Teach accordingly.

_____ 2. Tell trainees what the learning objectives of the course are, so they have an advance mental organizer about where you're going with the process of instruction and where you hope they will end up in terms of learning accomplishments.

_____ 3. Seize every opportunity during instruction to get trainees to talk about how this particular lesson applies to their particular work. Encourage trainees to talk their way into imagining how the job will be enhanced through this new skill.

_____ 4. Give generous and specific cues to trainees who might be slow to see the transfer possibilities. Suggest the corporate pay-offs—in sales, quality, market share, customer service, overseas penetration, profit—as they relate to what that individual trainee has just learned. Interject your belief about the uses of new information and skills, and ask other trainees for results-oriented comments.

_____ 5. Design your trainees' supervisors into their training somehow. Invite them in toward the end of a workshop to listen to a trainee's presentation; give the supervisor a structured feedback form to be used face-to-face with a trainee during training. Get the results perspective from the supervisor built into course design and delivery.

_____ 6. Adult learners like to know where they stand in terms of achievement. Be sure that they know what the learning tasks are, the standards by which they will be judged, and the instrument (checklist, rating scale, oral feedback criteria) by which results will be documented. Give trainees a chance to monitor and rate themselves and each other.

_____ 7. Plan a formal follow-up to training three months and six months after training to collect data on the results of that specific training. Establish timelines, quality, and quantity standards for success.

_____ 8. Communicate results widely. People appreciate knowing about real-life case studies that relate to them. Information empowers.

# Training Design Checklist 10.10
## Continuous Enabling Through Organization Development

People at work like to be "in" on things. They like to express their opinions, talk about how they did it, and control the way they learn. They prefer figuring things out to being told what to do. You can encourage transfer by making your organization one that enables and empowers people. This checklist will guide you.

_____ 1. Create forms and provide time for regular and valued feedback both ways—to employees from you and from employees to you.

_____ 2. Create visibility opportunities for employees at all levels to "show and tell" what they are doing well.

_____ 3. Give rewards (trips, days off, bonuses, certificates, trophies) for outstanding work processes, services, and products.

_____ 4. Continuously touch base with supervisors regarding their assessment of upcoming skill needs.

_____ 5. Create an open-door reality—encourage all employees to tell you what they want from training. Get out of your office and talk with people. Don't rely on the catalog or bulletins that signify one-way information.

_____ 6. Vary your delivery modes. Do as much on-the-job training as possible, develop peer training, use CBT and videodisc, encourage self-help approaches.

_____ 7. Fine-tune your information supports—be sure information necessary to enhancing training is attractive, plentiful, and accessible. Check this at regular intervals.

_____ 8. Get management buy-in at various levels before you embark on any kind of major training. Be sure that the organization is "well-oiled" before you commit major resources.

# Writing Checklist 10.11
## Policy Development Guidelines

As you create a training policy statement, keep foremost in your mind that you are explaining the *why* of training more than the *what* of training. Policy is management's way of providing guidance for employee action. Based on company goals and business strategy, policy tells employees how to deal with recurring situations about which there might otherwise be some general misunderstanding.

These guidelines will help you to develop training policy.

\_\_\_\_\_ 1. Don't create too many policies. Communicate in other ways when actions to be taken are obvious, situation-specific, or constrained by time pressures.

\_\_\_\_\_ 2. Drive policy creation by an overarching, recurrent theme, such as quality, productivity, involvement, personal development, career growth, customer satisfaction.

\_\_\_\_\_ 3. Whenever new management procedures are adopted, recheck any existing policies to see if updating is required. Examples are reduction in force, merged organizations, or new product lines.

\_\_\_\_\_ 4. Review any existing policies whenever new legislation affecting the company, such as a raise in minimum wage, new affirmative action/EEO laws, new safety laws, or new environmental laws, is adopted.

\_\_\_\_\_ 5. Before you write policy, touch base with all operations managers who will be affected by your policy to be sure that you're using language that they understand—that is, no training jargon, no sweeping generalizations, no meaningless clichés.

\_\_\_\_\_ 6. Review recent course evaluations from former trainees as a reality check on your ideas. Write policy that is sensitive to your customers—your trainees.

\_\_\_\_\_ 7. Be sure to include in your policy a clear reference to the person/group responsible for carrying out the policy—that is, who is expected to interact with whom in implementing this guide for action.

\_\_\_\_\_ 8. Give your policy a liberal dose of the words "commitment" and "belief."

\_\_\_\_\_ 9. Know the source or catalyst (event, person, change) for your policy. Don't just dream up something that sounds good. Writing policy is a business endeavor, not an exercise in creative writing.

# Writing Checklist 10.12
## What to Look for in a Vendor's Proposal

Using this checklist will help you evaluate a vendor's proposal. Often, choosing a reputable outside service provider or consultant is a cost-effective way to get the specific training services you need. The wise manager, however, is cautious.

The following questions, which focus on how the proposal is written, will help you in making a good choice:

_____ 1. As you leaf through the proposal, does there seem to be too much "boilerplate"? Does the proportion of solid planning specifics to nice-to-know platitudes seem a bit small?

_____ 2. Does the proposal start with a clear recognition of your training problem, not with a litany of wonderful things the vendor has done for others?

_____ 3. Does the proposal reflect your company's outlook on business? Does the vendor understand your business culture? This should be obvious on page 1 of the proposal.

_____ 4. Do you know exactly *what* the vendor proposes to do for you? Look for nouns in the proposal—things that can be measured, inspected, revised. Be careful that the verbs in the proposal convey concrete information and that actions are not so high-sounding that they can't be done.

_____ 5. Are the outcomes of the proposal clearly identified? Look for verbiage about when, how much, and what kind of results this vendor will provide.

_____ 6. Are you convinced? Look for a short section of believable information about the vendor's expertise. Be sure that it's relevant to what you need.

_____ 7. Does the proposal hang together? Look for tight logic. Be sure that this is a proposal to you only and not a "cut and paste" job that might get sent around to other companies.

_____ 8. Is the cost information inclusive and reasonable? Be sure that the language and numbers leave no doubt and no surprises. Check the timetable for checkpoints and completion dates; compare these with cost information.

# Writing Checklist 10.13
## When and How to Promote (Not Just Design and Deliver) Training

It is never enough to simply write good training. Because training is usually regarded as peripheral to the essential operations of business, it's a good idea to promote training, not just design and deliver it. Even the most perfectly designed training benefits from a carefully implemented promotional effort. A good promotional campaign builds expectations of success, communicates "big picture" information about specific training opportunities, and generates interest in future training programs.

These guidelines will help you to develop a training promotion plan.

\_\_\_\_\_ 1. The business reason for the specific training is clearly stated. Build your promotional materials from this.

\_\_\_\_\_ 2. Lead time has been calculated. You've considered:
- time to write articles
- staff to write articles and do camera work
- printing and production time
- distribution time
- response time

\_\_\_\_\_ 3. Your plan uses a variety of media to get your message across. Examples are:
- brochures
- bulletins, announcements
- newsletters
- press releases
- electronic mail, electronic bulletin boards, Web sites
- videos

\_\_\_\_\_ 4. You have a management employee watching out for special opportunities to promote training. Examples of these opportunities are:
- new product introduction
- installation of new equipment
- adoption of new systems
- organizational change
- procedural change
- individual career accomplishment made possible by training
- training success by a department or group
- legislation with an impact on training
- changes in community institutions that affect your employees or the training operation—new university programs, new adult education schools, changed state certification requirements, new business editors or reporters at the local newspaper

\_\_\_\_\_ 5. Before you write anything, prepare a "5W" list: who, what, when, where, why. These are the facts about training that your readers will want to know.

# Writing Checklist 10.14
## Catalog Design Checklist

Your catalog is a reference document. It should be written in a very structured way, giving equivalent information about each course or seminar that you offer.

As a manager, you should provide your course authors with a standard format to use in preparing a catalog entry for their courses. Get the catalog entry from each course author about two-thirds of the way through writing the course. Strive for consistency, brevity, and user-friendliness in the design of your catalog.

These are the structures to include in a standard catalog description of a course:

_____ 1. Course number and name

_____ 2. Title of the curriculum in which the course resides (for example, management training, quality curriculum, secretarial curriculum, sales curriculum, customer service curriculum

_____ 3. Narrative course descriptions (in sentences)

_____ 4. List of learner objectives for the course as a whole

_____ 5. List of major topics of content

_____ 6. Desired audience or level of the course

_____ 7. Required prerequisite courses or skills

_____ 8. Delivery mode (for example, small group, interactive videodisc, correspondence, teletraining)

_____ 9. Duration of the course

_____ 10. Location, if it is a standard location

# Writing Checklist 10.15

## Writing Competencies for Course Authors

Choosing someone to write a course is a difficult job because it's hard to find a person who has content knowledge, who is interested in working in the training department, and who is a competent writer. You are most likely to find someone with the first two qualities only.

The difficulty of finding qualified writers should not deter you from your search. A writing competency checklist can be useful to you as you interview potential course authors and can provide a skills improvement list for the person you choose.

Here is the list of writing competencies for course authors:

_____ 1. Fluent expression of ideas

_____ 2. Mental flexibility as an organizer of content

_____ 3. Superior vocabulary in the subject, coupled with the ability to simplify or expand

_____ 4. Differentiated use of description and explanation

_____ 5. Uncomplicated sentence structure

_____ 6. Correct grammar, punctuation, spelling, agreement

_____ 7. Preference for active voice

_____ 8. Natural use of action verbs

_____ 9. Ability to match writing style to instructional methods

_____ 10. Thoroughness in providing references

_____ 11. Logic skills in amassing and classifying information, finding patterns, generating alternatives, sequencing, and prioritizing

_____ 12. Ability to write within a given course design structure

# Writing Checklist 10.16
## Elements of a Course

A course does not simply dispense information. A course exists in order to help learners acquire new skills or knowledge and to change their way of doing their work. Course structure, therefore, must include ways to facilitate behavioral changes.

The essential elements of a course are:

\_\_\_\_\_ 1. Learner objectives

\_\_\_\_\_ 2. Outline of the content

\_\_\_\_\_ 3. Lessons

\_\_\_\_\_ 4. Handouts

\_\_\_\_\_ 5. Audio and visual aids

\_\_\_\_\_ 6. Exercises and assessments

Each course element can be designed and written as separate documents, and can be reviewed by peers or managers as it is developed to build quality into the writing process. As a manager, be sure that your course writers know the standards for each course element and that they work on each element with equal commitment to adherence to those standards. Use this brief checklist to monitor the course development process.

# Writing Checklist 10.17

## Authoring System Checklist for Instructional Design Software

You may be able to take advantage of instructional design software if you have compatible hardware and course writers who can work easily on the computer. In this arrangement, the instructional design or format of the course is embedded in the software, thereby minimizing your need for instructional design staff.

Use this checklist to verify the clarity of authoring system software:

_____ 1. A variety of structuring tools is available within the software.

_____ 2. There are templates for standard features of the course.

_____ 3. The system allows new content (updates) to be added easily.

_____ 4. The software is receptive to system enhancements such as videodisc, expert systems, scanners, scoring, and reporting features.

_____ 5. Trainee evaluation features are valid and appropriate for adult learners.

_____ 6. User interface is friendly—logical, easy, with abundant and meaningful help screens.

_____ 7. Graphics editing and screen editing are included.

_____ 8. You agree with the design standards built into the software.

# Writing Checklist 10.18
## Trainee Manual Development Checklist

The trainee manual is your customer's record of service provided. It must be easy to use and relevant to the customer's need, and it must "feel right" as the user uses it. It will probably reside on the trainee's bookshelf back on the job and be used as a reference document for at least several months after training; therefore it must pass the tests of good writing and good packaging.

The following checklist will help you to develop good trainee manuals:

_____ 1. Focus on doing. (Understanding will follow.)

_____ 2. Organize into clearly defined lessons. Present information in small chunks.

_____ 3. Define new terms. Be concrete.

_____ 4. Use short sentences.

_____ 5. Write in active, direct style.

_____ 6. Be consistent in heading and subhead conventions.

_____ 7. Label diagrams and charts clearly and consistently.

_____ 8. Describe succinctly. Avoid wordiness.

_____ 9. Teach step-by-step procedures.

_____ 10. Give the "big picture" first.

_____ 11. Use examples and case studies. Include many opportunities for trainees to relate their experiences to the course material. Allow time for demonstrations, discussion, trial and error, and simulations.

_____ 12. Use nonexamples, or explanations of "what it isn't."

_____ 13. Build in time for feedback.

_____ 14. Use friendly language.

# Writing Checklist 10.19

## Instructor Manual Development Checklist

No matter what size the training staff is, each instructor should have an instructor guide manual from which to teach the course. It's a good idea to keep a library copy of each course's instructor manual and to give each instructor a personal copy that can be marked up.

The instructor manual must have in it the exact pages—with the exact pagination—as the trainee manual. In addition, the instructor manual includes other information of specific interest to the instructor.

This extra information includes:

_____ 1. List of audiovisual and computer equipment required

_____ 2. List of audiovisual materials (slides, overheads, flip charts, markers) required in this course

_____ 3. Answers to exercises; solutions to lab sessions

_____ 4. List of handouts and references

_____ 5. Suggested timing of each lesson

_____ 6. Instructional design suggestions for alternatives in presenting lessons

_____ 7. Tips on proven methods of delivering instruction

_____ 8. Instructions regarding use of e-learning lessons and "blended" training.

# Writing Checklist 10.20

## Writing Checklist for Computer-Based and Interactive Video Training

Training managers often find themselves in the middle of a media explosion. Authoring system advances, graphics capability enhancements, and technological innovations in media hardware and software of all sorts present exciting and sometimes bewildering challenges to the training budget. Younger trainees who grew up in the multiple information processing environment of television at home and at school often expect training to be delivered in a lively, colorful, image-rich medium. They have learned to learn by processing graphic and written information simultaneously.

Training managers must know the difference between bad and good electronic media delivery systems. Evaluating the way in which these media-based courses are *written* is a good start. These guidelines will help.

_____ 1. Check the quality of online graphics. Often poor graphics limit learning. Look for poor resolution of line, limited or faded color, poor labels, screens that are too busy, irrelevant movement or design.

_____ 2. Check the ease of search through lessons. Be sure that the trainee can easily and quickly locate information—previous and upcoming—by some means other than electronically paging through every line, which produces eye fatigue and causes lack of interest.

_____ 3. Look for lucid presentation style. Be sure that course logic is very apparent and consistent. Topics must be easy to access.

_____ 4. Look for more "whats" than "whys." Computer-based learners are generally looking for what to do, especially when they call up help screens. Be sure the what is emphasized and that the why is minimized.

_____ 5. Look for good writing: complete sentences, consistent labeling, short sentences, active voice. Aim for only two or three eye fixations per line.

_____ 6. Look for a lack of screen clutter—about seven points, ideas, principles, instructions per screen.

_____ 7. Look for reading ease. This is achieved by normal use of upper- and lowercase letters. Use of all capital letters slows reading.

_____ 8. Look for a brief narrative overview of each lesson.

_____ 9. Look for trainee control through choices, branching, appropriate feedback, corrective responses, and high-level exercises for faster learners.

_____ 10. Know what you want. Be sure that you have compatible equipment. Here are some options:
- audiotape
- audiotape with trainee manual/workbook
- videotape
- videotape with trainee manual/workbook
- videodisc
- videodisc with trainee manual/workbook
- interactive videodisc
- computer-based training programs (CBT)

# Chapter 10 Forms

## To Help You to Manage Design and Writing of Training

The forms in this section will help you to manage the design of training for maximum transfer to work. Delivery issues are considered as they affect the design of the training experience. Forms are provided to help you "get it down on paper."

Some of the forms will take you into the organizational issues surrounding performance to make your planning and design efforts pay off more quickly. Other forms will help you focus on the instructional design process as it facilitates learning. Together, the forms will provide the foundation for maximizing the transfer of skills from the protected training environment to the real world of productive work.

**LIST OF TRAINING DESIGN FORMS**

- 10.1   Customer Contact Sheet
- 10.2   Components of Training Design
- 10.3   Creating Objectives that Push Performance
- 10.4   Components of Classroom Training Delivery
- 10.5   Employee's Training Opportunity Profile
- 10.6   Training Problem Analysis Worksheet
- 10.7   Organizational Support Time Line
- 10.8   Survival Skills Hierarchy
- 10.9   Training Transfer Follow-Up Questionnaire
- 10.10  Follow-Up Feedback Form

**LIST OF WRITING FORMS**

- 10.11  The Structure of the Policy
- 10.12  Catalog Entry Format
- 10.13  Public Relations Article Structure
- 10.14  The Learner Objective
- 10.15  Lesson Plan
- 10.16  Classroom Trainee Manual
- 10.17  Self-Study Trainee Workbook
- 10.18  Instructor Manual

**Training Design Form 10.1**
**CUSTOMER CONTACT SHEET**

### How to Use This Form

1. Use this form to document your initial contact with a potential customer—telephone or face-to-face.
2. Keep a stack of blank forms within easy reach of your telephone.
3. Use this form during or immediately after the contact with the person (probably a supervisor or other manager) who will be paying the bill. (Keep talking until you find out exactly who that person will be. Be sure that you are listening to the _real_ customer.)
4. When completed, this form provides input information for your training staff member who will be in charge of needs assessment. Pass on a copy to that person.

Date _____ Customer's telephone/e-mail _____

Customer's name and title _____

Customer's organization _____

Customer's address _____

Customer's statement of the training problem _____

_____

_____

_____

_____

Brief description of target trainee audience (job title, numbers of trainees, customer's idea of probable duration of training, target date by which trainees must be trained, etc.) _____

_____

_____

_____

_____

_____

_____

Date of next meeting to verify training need _____

Training staff responsible for needs assessment _____

**Training Design Form 10.2**
**COMPONENTS OF TRAINING DESIGN**

> **How to Use This Form**
> 1. Use this form as a guide for managing the design elements of a course through the process of development.
> 2. If you're new at managing training, use these completed forms as planning documents for future development, noting especially the discrepancies between actual and target dates.

|  | Target Date | Actual Date |
|---|---|---|
| 1. Verify training objectives and content with subject matter expert. | | |
| 2. Achieve consensus among all significant parties on learning objectives. | | |
| 3. Achieve consensus among all significant parties on best mode of delivering this course: CBT, video, classroom, hands-on workshop, etc. | | |
| 4. Verify content scope and sequence of topics with customer. | | |
| 5. Check course visual aids for clarity, accuracy, consistency, and completeness. | | |
| 6. Set production schedule and get commitment from all involved organizations (customer, advertising, graphics, writers, programmers, instructional designers, instructors, registrars, etc.) | | |
| 7. Label/number and set the course within its proper place in the training curriculum and catalog. | | |
| 8. Promote the course through appropriate channels. | | |

**Training Design Form 10.3**
**CREATING OBJECTIVES THAT PUSH PERFORMANCE**

### How to Use This Form
1. Refer to this chart when you select objectives for learning. Use your imagination to enlarge the lists.
2. Commonly used verbs are listed alphabetically in two sections: (1) examples of those used to develop cognitive (thinking) skills, and (2) examples of those used to develop psychomotor (hands-on) skills.
3. When you review training design documents, be sure that lower-level skills come before higher-level skills. Transfer occurs more readily when low-level skills are mastered before higher-level skills are introduced.
4. When you analyze objectives, be sure that they are followed by evidence of training for high-level skills if the objectives contain high-level verbs. Be sure that the course unfolds in a logical way in terms of its design for learning. This is especially important in online learning design.

| Low-level skills | Mid-level skills | High-level skills |
| --- | --- | --- |
| COGNITIVE ||| 
| define | ask | classify |
| describe | compute | conclude |
| identify | explain | differentiate |
| label | generalize | extrapolate |
| list | illustrate | formulate |
| name | relate | judge |
| recall | rephrase | plan |
| recognize | translate | summarize |
| ▪ | ▪ | ▪ |
| ▪ | ▪ | ▪ |
| PSYCHOMOTOR |||
| feel | connect | build |
| hear | cut | calibrate |
| place | depress | demonstrate |
| see | insert | isolate |
| sit | lift | modify |
| smell | mark | operate |
| stand | remove | reconstruct |
| wait | straighten | simulate |
| ▪ | ▪ | ▪ |
| ▪ | ▪ | ▪ |

**Training Design Form 10.4**
**COMPONENTS OF CLASSROOM TRAINING DELIVERY**

> **How to Use This Form**
> 1. This form outlines the essential components of training delivery that foster transfer.
> 2. Use this form in one of three ways:
>    a. as a discussion document between you and your instructor(s)
>    b. as a guide to topics to include in a "train the trainer" workshop
>    c. as an evaluation guide during your observation of an instructor during a field test of a course

1. **Preparation.** The instructor is obviously "on top of things." The instructor knows the objectives, is well-versed in content at mastery level, has handouts and media organized.

   Observation/comments:

2. **Planned start.** The instructor has a structure for the first fifteen minutes of class. This includes opening remarks to establish credibility in a nonthreatening way, interactions that help trainees feel comfortable, "advance organizers" that help set the mental stage for the main points of the course, exercises that yield critical information about what each trainee expects to get out of the course.

   Observation/comments:

3. **Lessons.** The instructor presents information in short segments—about fifteen minutes each. During this time, the instructor describes, explains, uses examples, analogies, tells what "it isn't" as well as what it is, uses diagrams and demonstrations, asks and answers questions.

   Observation/comments:

*(continues)*

**Training Design Form 10.4 (continued)**

4. **Formative Evaluation.** As each trainee learns new concepts or skills during each lesson, the instructor tells the trainee how s/he is doing. Good instruction is always done against a standard, and good instructors are always aware of the standard as well as the individual's proximity to it. (This is why we keep the class size small and write in branching and feedback to CBT lessons.)

   Observation/comments:


5. **Continuous Feedback.** The instructor seeks feedback from trainees and immediately uses it, being especially adept at modifying a lesson to include up-to-the-minute information of relevance to a trainee's work and individual concerns. The instructor interacts continuously with individual trainees visually and verbally, especially reinforcing generalized skills.

   Observations/comments:

**Training Design Form 10.5**
**EMPLOYEE'S TRAINING OPPORTUNITY PROFILE**

### How to Use This Form
1. The end result of this form is a twelve-month plan for training that you suggest for an individual employee. The suggestion to engage in training should be presented as an opportunity of employment—an opportunity for personal improvement and for contributions to the company—never as a "punishment" for lacking certain skills.
2. In order to present the opportunity profile in the right way, base it on a job analysis. One kind of job analysis is suggested here.
3. Create the chart in consultation with your employee (and counsel supervisors to do the same). Keep a copy and give a copy to the employee.

Employee's name _____ Date _____
Employee's job title _____
Desired job within 24 months _____

### Job Requirements

| People Skills | Data Skills | Things Skills |
|---|---|---|
| ∙ | ∙ | ∙ |
| ∙ | ∙ | ∙ |
| ∙ | ∙ | ∙ |
| ∙ | ∙ | ∙ |
| ∙ | ∙ | ∙ |
| ∙ | ∙ | ∙ |
| ∙ | ∙ | ∙ |

### 12-month Training Opportunity Chart
(Check quarter in which training is recommended)

| Course title | Jan–Mar. | Apr.–Jne. | Jly.–Sep. | Oct.–Dec. |
|---|---|---|---|---|
|  |  |  |  |  |
|  |  |  |  |  |
|  |  |  |  |  |
|  |  |  |  |  |
|  |  |  |  |  |
|  |  |  |  |  |

**Training Design Form** 10.6
**TRAINING PROBLEM ANALYSIS WORKSHEET**

### How to Use This Form

1. Use this form as a guide to dialog about the nature of a problem that you believe can be solved by training.
2. This form can be especially helpful if you have no time for a more thorough needs assessment. Completing this worksheet with your customer, instructional designer, or instructor—or all three together—can help you get off to a good start.
3. The essence of this form is structured thinking, focused area by area, on describing the current problem situation, defining the desired situation after training, and defining the specifics of an action plan to get from where you are to where you want to be.

Effective problem solving looks at problem definition separately from solution definition. Training for transfer, then, makes the action plan operational.

---

Describe the problem situation

Define the desired situation

State causes of problem situation

- 
- 
- 
- 
- 
- 

List constraints to achieving desired situation

- 
- 
- 
- 
- 
-

**Training Design Form 10.6 (continued)**

ACTION PLAN

What has to be changed? _____
_____
_____

- 
- 
- 
- 

Is it worth changing? _____
Describe the key training solutions _____
_____
_____

- 
- 
- 
-

# How to Design and Write Training

**Training Design Form 10.7**
**ORGANIZATIONAL SUPPORT TIME LINE**

### How to Use This Form
1. Keep a chart of keywords by month in order to remind yourself of the organizational supports per course that you need to have in place that month for effective training development.
2. Use the "notes" section to elaborate.
3. Use these keywords as a start. They list the kinds of support you'll need:

   **executive, marketing, accounting, computer systems, writing, graphics, printing and binding**

Course title _____

| January | February | March | April | May | June |
|---------|----------|-------|-------|-----|------|
|         |          |       |       |     |      |

Notes: _____
_____

| July | August | September | October | November | December |
|------|--------|-----------|---------|----------|----------|
|      |        |           |         |          |          |

Notes: _____
_____

## Training Design Form 10.8
## SURVIVAL SKILLS HIERARCHY

### How to Use This Form
1. Use this as a discussion guide for meetings with your training staff prior to designing a course or hiring a vendor. Assign an order of priority to each item in each of the four categories.
2. Be sure that you have an established training need.
3. With your staff, prioritize the survival skills needed to be a valued employee in your company. Add other skills. (Don't be surprised at your priorities!)
4. Whatever they are, use this skill list to design training to provide employees with the highest-priority skills.

**Priority**

<u>Problem Solving Skills</u>
- fact finding
- making inferences
- classifying
- recognizing patterns
- defining options
- modification
- analysis
- synthesis
- adoption
- 
- 
- 

<u>Intellectual Skills</u>
- mental flexibility
- originality
- depth of knowledge
- breadth of knowledge
- fluency of verbal/oral expression
- fluency of written expression
- math skills
- thinking on one's feet
- 
- 

**Priority**

<u>Organization Skills</u>
- following rules
- working independently
- working collaboratively
- generating information
- helping others
- using computer networks
- mastering time pressure
- giving feedback
- receiving feedback
- 
- 

<u>Personal Skills</u>
- being on time
- taking initiative
- being a follower
- being a leader
- driving quality standards up
- minding one's own business
- being friendly
- being accessible
- 
-

**Training Design Form 10.9**
**TRAINING TRANSFER FOLLOW-UP QUESTIONNAIRE**

**How to Use This Form**
1. Use this form some interval after training, for example, three weeks, three months, six months—one form for each trainee.
2. Send it out to trainees with a return stamped envelope, or do a face-to-face or telephone interview.
3. Use Form 10.10 to compile results from all Forms 10.9.

Course title _____ Date given _____

1. How soon did you use your new knowledge/skills? _____
   _____

2. What elements of training have been most useful on the job? _____
   _____

3. What elements were least useful? _____
   _____

4. What constraints (money, time, support, equipment, systems, schedules, etc.) have you encountered that prevent you from using what you learned? _____
   _____
   _____

5. How would you modify the training to make it more useful? _____
   _____
   _____

6. What organizational changes would help the application of this training? (coaching, peer training, job rotation, mentors, monitoring, reports, supervisor training, support staff, rewards, materials, equipment, spaces, etc.) _____
   _____
   _____

**Training Design Form 10.10**
**FOLLOW-UP FEEDBACK FORM**

> **How to Use This Form**
> 1. Use this summary document with your instructional designers to make course revisions that will enhance transfer.
> 2. Use this information to make organizational changes that can support training and transfer.
> 3. This form summarizes data from Form 10.9.

1. Average time for using new skills _____

    Range of times for using new skills _____

2. Most useful elements _____
   _____
   _____

3. Least useful elements _____
   _____
   _____

4. Constraints on transfer _____
   _____
   _____
   _____

5. Suggested modifications to training _____
   _____
   _____
   _____

6. Suggested organizational changes _____
   _____
   _____

**Writing Form 10.11**
**THE STRUCTURE OF THE POLICY**

### How to Use This Form

1. Use language throughout the sections of the policy statement to show that training is assertively committed to implementing corporate directives.
2. Look for opportunities to tie training to the corporate vision, mission, goals, and quality thrust. Training ties in well with assembly and manufacturing productivity, distribution intervals, communications, safety, and customer service.
3. Be as specific as possible so that your statement of policy is believable and charts a clear course of action.
4. Begin your policy statement with the name of your training department, program, or course—that is, use it as the subject of the first sentence that you write.

---

**COMMITMENT STATEMENT**
one or two sentences

**BELIEFS**
several sentences

**THE POLICY IN BRIEF**
"Therefore, we will . . ."

**EMPLOYEE CHALLENGES**
several bullet items

**TRAINING PROGRAM OBLIGATIONS AND RESPONSIBILITIES**
several bullet items

**Writing Form** 10.12
**CATALOG ENTRY FORMAT**

### How to Use This Form
1. Give this form to your course instructor or course writer to complete.
2. Allow sufficient time for editorial review of completed forms from various sources. Consistency is critical in order to give each course an equal marketing advantage.

---

course number                                course title

name of curriculum in which this course is found

Course Description:

| Objectives for the Trainee: | Major Topics: |
|---|---|
| ■ | ■ |
| ■ | ■ |
| ■ | ■ |
| ■ | ■ |
| ■ | ■ |
| ■ | ■ |

Target Audience:

Prerequisites (knowledge, skills, experience, courses):

Instructional Delivery Mode (self-paced, computer-based, lecture, etc.):

Course Length:

---

This form originally appeared in *Training Program Workbook & Kit*, by Carolyn Nilson, copyright 1989. It is reprinted by permission of the publisher, Prentice-Hall, Inc., Englewood Cliffs, N.J.

**Writing Form 10.13**
**PUBLIC RELATIONS ARTICLE STRUCTURE**

### How to Use This Form

1. This is standard journalistic article structure. Use it to write articles for newspapers, department newsletters, or radio and TV features about your training events or newsworthy personalities.
2. "All the news that fits, we print" is a rewrite of a popular newspaper industry slogan. It applies to the reality of promotional or public relations writing—that is, often space requirements dictate how much of your article gets printed. This is why journalistic structure recognizes this fact of public relations publishing life and saves the least important information for last.

JOURNALISM'S INVERTED PYRAMID

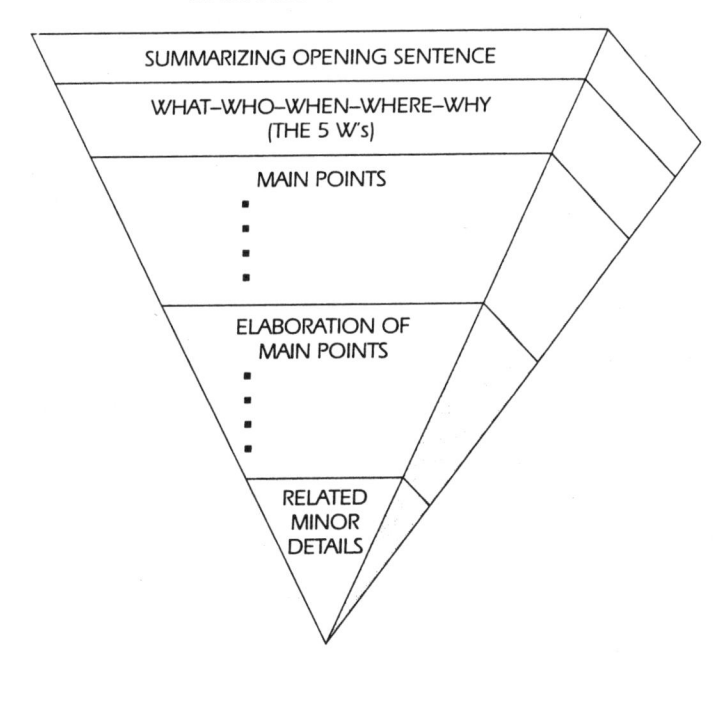

- SUMMARIZING OPENING SENTENCE
- WHAT–WHO–WHEN–WHERE–WHY (THE 5 W's)
- MAIN POINTS
- ELABORATION OF MAIN POINTS
- RELATED MINOR DETAILS

**Writing Form 10.14**
**THE LEARNER OBJECTIVE**

### How to Use This Form
1. Write all behavioral objectives so that the learner knows what to do.
2. Write each objective so that it can be taught and learned in about fifteen minutes. Be reasonable. Be nontrivial.
3. Before you write an objective, verify to yourself that what you intend to say has a clear business purpose. Be careful of "nice to knows" and of learning for its own sake. "Bottom line" is your focus.
4. Use this threefold format to develop a learner objective.

| Do this: | To this: | In this amount: |
|---|---|---|
|  |  |  |

Examples

| Call up | the HELP screen | at the start of each new menu. |
|---|---|---|
| Analyze and correct | ten sentences with faulty subject-verb agreement | with 100 percent accuracy, using the answer key if necessary. |
| Tell | your partner | what the last three steps are. |

# How to Design and Write Training

**Writing Form 10.15**
**LESSON PLAN**

### How to Use This Form
1. Use this lesson plan format to plan each fifteen-minute segment of learning.
2. In long courses, staple the lesson plans together in logical units, modules, or two-hour time blocks. Give each logical unit a name. Use lesson plans to structure your course logically.
3. Write in outline form, limiting each lesson to one page.

Lesson title: _____

Purpose of this lesson: _____
_____

Materials needed for this lesson:
_____   _____
_____   _____

Learner objectives for this lesson:

1. _____
   _____

2. _____
   _____

Content outline for this lesson:

1. _____
   a. _____
   b. _____
2. _____
   a. _____
   b. _____
3. _____
   a. _____
   b. _____

**Writing Form 10.16**
**CLASSROOM TRAINEE MANUAL**

> ### How to Use This Form
> 1. Use this as a quick guide for development or critique of a trainee manual.
> 2. This form is for the manager who has created trainee manuals before but who wants a refresher regarding the key elements of content and format. These elements are organized in a hierarchical fashion.

FORMAT
  User-friendly
    Clean, Uncluttered
      Consistent (tabs, headings, typefaces, graphics, labels)

Notes:

---

ORGANIZATION
  Units/Modules
    Lessons
      Chunks

Notes:

---

FOCUS
  Job-related
    Practical applications
      Pros and Cons
        How to

Notes:

*(continues)*

**Writing Form 10.16 (continued)**

STYLE
  Direct and to the point
    Short sentences
      Easy things first

  Notes:

**Writing Form 10.17**
**SELF-STUDY TRAINEE WORKBOOK**

### How to Use This Form

1. Use this form in any kind of situation in which the trainee learns alone. The environment can be interactive e-learning, interactive videodisc training, a video- or audiotape presentation, or an old-fashioned book-based correspondence course. Each of these kinds of self-study should include a trainee workbook.
2. The key in writing this kind of trainee manual is accessibility of information, because in self-study, the trainee, not the instructor, controls the sequence and depth of information.
3. The following chart suggests the pieces that must be in place in the self-study workbook. They can also delineate responsibilities for a writing team creating a self-study workbook.

---

USER-FRIENDLY FORMAT: tabs, indexes, glossaries, cross-references

Writing problems/solutions regarding format:

---

BASIC AS WELL AS ENHANCED CONTENT: clearly marked sections so that trainees know what's required as well as what's in-depth content (for those who want to know more about a subject)

Writing problems/solutions regarding content:

*(continues)*

**Writing Form 10.17 (continued)**

OBVIOUS INSTRUCTIONS: boxed, highlighted, bold type, consistent and clear word order (verb first), same placement in each lesson

Writing problems/solutions regarding instructions:

PRACTICE EXERCISES: with solutions in a separate section of the manual

Writing problems/solutions regarding practice exercises:

REMEDIAL EXERCISES: options in presentation of material (for example, graphics rather than text; case study rather than lists) in case trainees "don't get it" with the first reading

Writing problems/solutions regarding remedial exercises:

**Writing Form 10.17 (continued)**

REFERENCES: books, reports, videos, people

References to be sure to include:

A "HELP" CONTACT PERSON ON CALL, WITH PHONE NUMBER AND E-MAIL: instructor, instructional designer, expert performer

Name and contact information for HELP person:

**Writing Form 10.18**
**INSTRUCTOR MANUAL**

### How to Use This Form
1. These are the most common styles of instructor manual. Choose one that fits your preferred way of teaching.
2. Always keep the trainee manual intact, including the same page numbers.

A. NARRATIVE OPTION

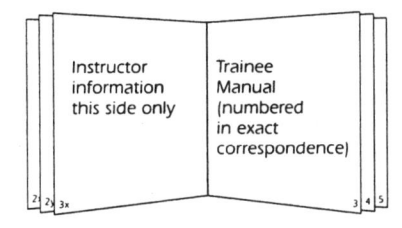

Problems:
- Pagination can be cumbersome using "XYZ" tag for the instructor page.
- Manual is large and heavy.

B. HIGHLIGHT OPTION

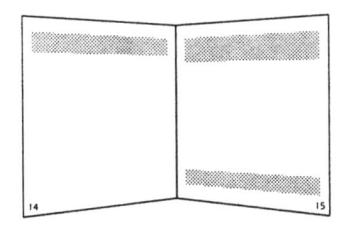

Problems:
- Smaller type size or wide margins must be used for both manuals in order to fit in the instructor highlights.
- Trainee manual doesn't look the same because of interspersed highlights.

C. TWO-MANUAL OPTION

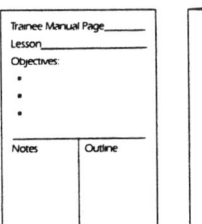

Problems:
- You have two manuals going at once.
- Inexperienced instructors find the outline format too skimpy.

# Chapter 10
# More Information on How to Design and Write Training

## Synthesis and Summary of Basic Instructional Design Literature

The following pages contain summaries of the thinking of learning experts whose work forms the historical basis of taxonomy building in education and training. The references in this section have been carefully chosen for their direct application to achieving transfer and to building performance competency.

## Conventions of Grammar and Usage for Training Documents

This section contains a list of the basics of English grammar and language usage employed in training manuals, handouts, visual presentations, reports, and memos.

1. **Be direct.** Use spare language, and say what you mean.
*Instead of this:* Implement the following procedure as necessary in as timely a manner as possible.
*Write it this way:* Send your report to room HC66 by August 10.

2. **Use the active, not the passive voice.** Use subject-verb-object order. (Often this means present tense, not a form of past tense. Check yourself by looking at the verbs.)
*Instead of this:* A major system upgrade is expected next week.
*Write it this way:* We expect a major system upgrade next week.

3. **Use one- and two-syllable words wherever possible.**
*Instead of this:* If more personnel will be required to implement the assignments, kindly notify this department.
*Write it this way:* If more people are needed to do the tasks, please contact us.

4. **Use gender-neutral language.**
*Instead of this:* It's critical that the manager personally visits his employees at the job site.
*Write it this way:* It's critical that managers personally visit employees at the job site.

5. **Use parallel structure.**
*Instead of this:* Elements of teaching are planning, researching, and to deliver information.
*Write it this way:* Elements of teaching are planning, researching, and delivering information.

## Preferred Punctuation for Training Documents

Because training documents are often procedural in nature or contain instructions or hierarchical lists, the conventions of punctuation vary somewhat from standard editorial punctuation, which is geared more toward narrative writing.

Training documents use bullets and dashes liberally. They often do not contain periods at the ends of ideas; often they do not contain complete sentences. They use commas and modifying words very sparingly. Training documents go for the main words—strong action verbs and precise nouns.

If your company has a technical writing department or a style manual, use the standards they set as a basis for training documentation. Technical writers and editors can help you modify their general writing standards for your training documents; build your training documentation standards and conventions on your company's existing style manual.

The following chart includes guidelines for using punctuation (the "Use" column) and the most common errors (the "Do Not Use" column). Use these conventions in addition to the punctuation conventions typically found in standard grammar textbooks.

| Use | Do Not Use |
|---|---|
| **Period** | |
| 1. After each listed item that forms a complete sentence | 1. After single words or phrases in a bullet list |
| 2. Within parentheses when the parenthetical expression is a complete sentence | 2. Within a parenthetical expression that is not a complete sentence |
| 3. At the end of sentences | 3. At the end of steps, outline items, or procedures that are not sentences |
| **Comma** | |
| 4. Following items in a series | 4. Between season and year or before zip code |
| 5. Following the year in a month-day-year sequence in a sentence | 5. Between month and year; in military date format |

6. To set off nonessential phrases

6. Whenever your speech pattern seems to "feel" like a comma (writing is a visual medium governed by rules of written language)

**Colon**

7. To introduce a list

7. In the middle of a sentence to introduce a series

**Bullets**

8. To list items of equal importance

8. Before steps or procedures that are prioritized (use numbers instead)

**Capital Letters**

9. For titles and main headings

9. In instructions (using all caps impedes understanding)

10. For critically important words in text, such as STOP, CAUTION, DANGER

10. In text of explanation or description (write the way people are used to reading, that is, use upper and lower case)

## Headings, Labels, and Margins

### Headings
Headings in a training document must be logical and must make sense. Most training documents contain several levels of headings; most headings are printed in **bold type**. This is one way to do headings:

**CENTERED ALL-CAP MAIN HEADING**

**First Subheading at Margin (with space above and below)**

**Second subheading indented (with period at end).**

## Labels

### Drawings
Use the same type that you use in the text describing the drawing. Photo-reduce the drawing label to fit; cut and paste it (actually or electronically) on the drawing. Label horizontally, parallel with the top and bottom of the page. Don't slant labels. Use slanted lines or arrows if necessary, but not slanted words.

### Tables
Label tables at the top. Use chapter and sequence number identifiers as well as title information, for example, Table 2.5 . . . , Table 2.6. . . .

### Figures
Some prefer to label figures at the bottom. Use chapter and sequence number identifiers as well as title information, for example, Figure 1.2 . . . , Figure 1.13. . . .

### Modules in Manuals
If you write your manuals in modules that are lifted out of the course and taught in isolation, you should number each module as if it were a complete document; start each module at page one, even those modules in the middle of the course. It's also a good idea to put the title of the module at the top of each page of a modularized course. Here's an example:

| **ROLES AND RESPONSIBILITIES** | page 4 |
|---|---|

The text or lesson outline begins below this line.

## Margins
Allow a margin of at least one inch at the top, bottom, and sides of documents. If a document, such as a manual, is to be bound, allow a $1^{1}/_{2}$-inch left margin to accommodate binder rings or other mechanical processes of binding.

In trainee manuals, be sure that type is clear and that white space abounds. If your manual is chock full of words—lots of explanations and narrative text—leave 2-inch margins all around. Type all instructor and trainee manuals using double space or space-and-a-half settings on your keyboard.

## Typeface for Manuals and Other Printed Training Material

Typographers generally believe that a typeface with serifs is easier to read on the printed page than a sans serif typeface. Most books, newspapers, magazines, catalogs, and other printed matter designed for mass reading use serif typefaces, and it is generally accepted that reading comprehension is aided by the use of serif typefaces in training materials.

However, in printed matter designed to promote, advertise, attract attention, or artistically represent letters, any typeface that serves the purpose—serif or sans serif—will do. There are hundreds of type styles from which to choose. As a training manager, you should be aware that your choice of typeface can have an effect on readability and on the message that's being put forth on the written page.

## Screen-Projected Writing

There are some specific guidelines for writing words for projecting on screens, such as computer-generated words, words on videotapes, films, or slides, and words on transparencies. As a rule, you should:

- Write letters that can be seen easily from the back of the room in which you intend to project them
- Make letters with a solid or near-solid line
- Keep the projected image uncluttered in both line and meaning
- Restrict the number of messages to no more than seven per screen

These guidelines apply to all forms of media that project words. In addition, there are some specific considerations that are unique to each medium. These are detailed below.

### Computer-Generated Words

Resolution of line is a key issue, especially in computer-generated words, because there's wide variety in printer quality and software programs that govern the density of the printed line. When you have to project computer-generated words, as you often do in courses on computer applications, view the projected words before you "go public" to be sure that the line density is thick enough for adequate instruction. You don't want the white dots within the lines of a letter to detract from the trainee's ability to read the letter to the extent that the typography interferes with learning. Don't make your trainees expend energy trying to figure out what the letters are; save their strength for figuring out the content. The small letters that are acceptable on your CRT may not be at all acceptable when they are blown up on a screen.

Another issue with computer-generated words that are projected on a screen is contrast. Again, what may be strong contrast of light and dark or of colors on a CRT may seem very faded when the letters are enlarged and projected on a screen. Remember that your CRT editing screen is many, many times smaller than the screen you'll need for projection to a classroom of trainees. When you get a powerful projection light through your computer-generated image, the words may not be as visible and as obvious as they were on the 9-inch screen behind your keyboard.

Check out these potential projection problems before you choose computer-generated words for training. If you do have projection problems you simply have to live with, try to compensate by having good sight lines from each trainee seat, a darkened area near the screen, or a printed job aid or handout that summarizes the poorly projected information.

## Words on Videotapes, Films, Slides, and CD-ROMs

These media are similar in that a camera usually generates the image that gets projected. These are media of choice when pictures tell a better story than words.

Often, the cameras used to take these pictures are far better at taking photos at three feet, five feet, thirty feet, or infinity feet than they are at taking pictures of words. Many times, however, words are desirable in a training video, film, or slides. In such cases, you need a camera with a close-up lens or text copying capability; another possibility is to splice a separately generated "words" piece of tape, film, or slide into your presentation. Especially if you plan to produce your own training video, film, or slide show, be sure that you have the equipment you'll need to get the words in if you need them; otherwise, supplement the picture show with a carefully coordinated manual.

## Words on Transparencies

Words on transparencies generally can be read at a maximum distance of thirty-five feet. For ease of reading at this distance, a projected letter has to appear about $1^{1}/_{4}$ inches in height on the screen.

If there is plenty of white space around labels and titles, and plenty of space between lines, you can get away with setting your type size at eighteen points for phrases of text and bullet lists. Set main titles in 24-point type.

For ease of reading, use a sans serif type style that is not too tall in scale or too thin in line density. Helvetica typeface is a standard style that meets these guidelines. There are many other sans serif typefaces that are similar in design. Stay away from fancy styles and the use of script; as the type is enlarged and photocopied as part of the production process, the serifs often do not reproduce well, get partially cut off, or reproduce less densely than the body of the letter. When this happens, the meaning of the letter is incomplete to viewers, who are accustomed to the balance of the letter with its serifs intact.

If you intend to write your own transparencies "on the fly" during a training session, practice writing on transparency acetate in 18-point and

24-point size before you try doing it in front of a trainee. Be sure that you use nonpermanent washable pens in case you make an error.

### If You Have Limited Budget and Staff . . .

This design information will serve as a quick reference for your cursory assessment and planning the instructional design of the courses you offer. It provides you with the briefest brief on educational psychology. Writing guidelines for resource-limited operations can help you save time and money too.

Hire one good technical writer, agree on writing standards and guidelines for all of the various training documents you intend to write, and distribute the document standards to anyone who functions as an author of training material for you.

Divide the content editing from production editing. Because you are the training manager, it probably makes sense for you to do content editing. Give your technical writer the production editing tasks (grammar, usage, format, printing), allow enough time, and good luck!

If you have to create new training documents, invest in an instructional design authoring system and teach subject matter experts to use it to write courses in that system's standard format. If you can find an authoring system that you like and it runs on the computers you already have, chances are that you'll end up with a pretty good course by helping the content experts through the strict structure of the system format.

Get what you can from the vendor in terms of training, but hire an instructional design consultant for a brief time to work with content experts if you need to. It's a lot cheaper to borrow subject matter experts and buy a consultant for a short time to create a course than it is to maintain a staff of instructional designers, researchers, and writers who have to go off and interview subject matter experts in order to get raw material for a course.

If you're really on a tight budget, use flip charts and acetates that you can run through your office copier for your visual aids.

### If You Have Adequate Budget and Staff . . .

You'll want to read some more and study in depth. References in this section, the Appendix, and in the Bibliography can lead you further into investigation of problem solving, skills hierarchies, learning styles, and studies of memory, intelligence, cognition, information processing, systems' discipline, change management, and performance technology.

Training that is designed and delivered in accordance with an understanding of systems thinking and learning hierarchies is training that can be expected to transfer more readily to work. These taxonomies can also be used as a foundation for setting quality standards in course design. Managers with development organizations and a staff of instructional designers will find this section a useful building block for quality improvement.

In this section, I introduce and summarize twelve relevant areas of thought that training professionals most frequently tap into when they design, deliver, and manage training that leads to peak performance on the job. (More complete discussions of key writers on this subject are in the Appendix.) These twelve areas include:

- problem solving
- cognitive skills
- psychomotor skills
- motivation and human needs
- adoption and management of change
- brain lateralization and learning style
- memory
- conditions of learning
- multiple intelligences or frames of mind
- the learning organization
- 8-step program for creating change
- performance technology

Within each area, a graphic representation of the taxonomy introduces the topic and the writer. Taken together, these graphics provide a quick and easy-to-use reference or job aid to creating training for transfer. Figures below are presented with the most advanced level of the hierarchy at the top.

If your budget is solid and your future secure, maintain a full writing and editorial staff. Separate the various editorial tasks, distributing documents among the staff according to the level of editing that must be done. Have a production editing group whose responsibility is to produce finished manuals—formatted, printed, and bound in sufficient quantity and with consistent quality.

Assign to a graphics editor responsibility for checking all visual presentations and materials that complement training lessons and for maintaining a library of training visuals. Staff a training marketing function with writers who have some background in public relations, publishing, or journalism; give someone the job of checking all outsiders' slides, overheads, or video presentations to be sure that they meet your standards for clarity, visibility, and relevance.

If things are going well for you, beef up your support staff of training specialists—persons with a bent toward good writing and clear thinking who can maintain catalogs, write bulletins, do master scheduling, send out registration confirmations, run conferences, coordinate vendors, supervise equipment maintenance and repair, maintain libraries, summarize evaluation forms, and prepare reports. Increase your training support staff so that you save your professional staff of course authors and instructional designers for the higher-level work that they do best.

Create your own courses. Buy the best printer that's on the market; get copies of the best graphics software and a person who knows how to use it to its fullest capacity. Produce or purchase the production of training videos and high-quality slides; run your own video production lab and video library.

## Problem Solving

Most of the literature on problem solving is characterized by the philosophy "divide and conquer." That is, success in solving problems comes from breaking down the problem into smaller problems and solving them in a systematic way.

Most problem-solving literature treats solution finding separately, suggesting methodology for the study of solution options that ultimately leads to the behavior change that represents the solution to the problem.

Many training problems can be approached from a problem-solving framework. Many topics within courses can be presented within this framework, too. Figure 10.1 represents the most common elements of problem solving, beginning with the first element, problem definition.

**Figure 10.1. Elements of problem solving.**

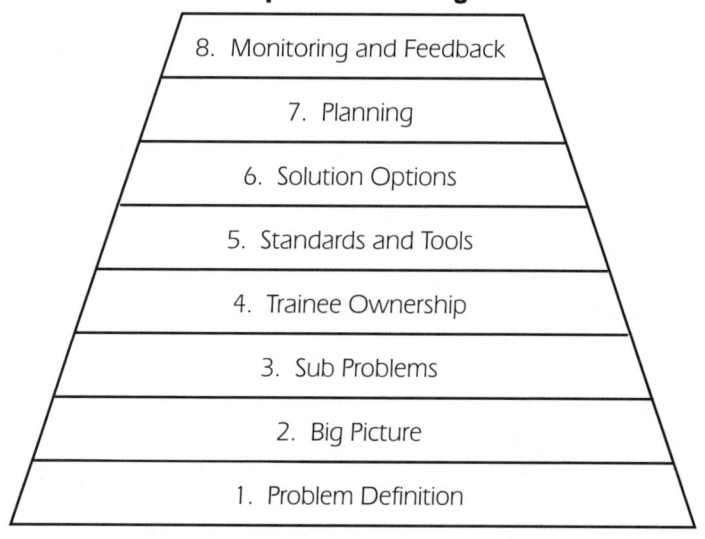

8. Monitoring and Feedback
7. Planning
6. Solution Options
5. Standards and Tools
4. Trainee Ownership
3. Sub Problems
2. Big Picture
1. Problem Definition

*Source:* D. T. Tuma and F. Reit, *Problem Solving and Education: Issues in Research and Teaching.* Hillsdale, N.J.: Lawrence Erlbaum, 1980.

## Cognitive Skills

Cognitive skills are those elusive ways of thinking that demonstrate knowing; the mental gymnastics that label us as "smart" or "sharp" or "scholarly" or "apt." These are the kinds of skills that take us beyond simply taking in information; because they are skills, they can turn our information gathering into action. Trainers who aim for "working smarter" pay attention to trainees' development of cognitive skills. Figure 10.2 presents the hierarchy of cognitive skills, from basic knowledge at the lowest level to evaluation at the highest.

**Figure 10.2. Cognitive skills.**

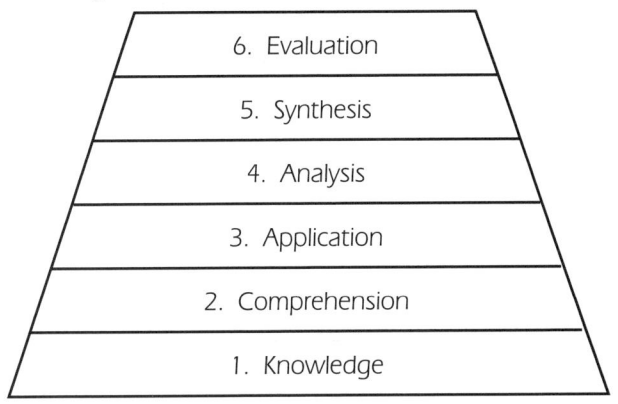

6. Evaluation
5. Synthesis
4. Analysis
3. Application
2. Comprehension
1. Knowledge

*Source:* B. S. Bloom, ed. *Taxonomy of Educational Objectives: Handbook I: Cognitive Domain.* New York: Longman, 1954/1980.

## Psychomotor Skills

Training to develop psychomotor skills has been the staple of industrial training in the United States for many decades. Psychomotor skills training is immediately obvious and easily measured training for doing—the kind of training that teaches the trainee to use a tool correctly or to perform actions in a certain predictable way. It is training for using one's muscles, or "motor" responses.

Figure 10.3 represents a hierarchy of skills required for competent psychomotor performance, beginning with skill of perception.

**Figure 10.3. Psychomotor skills.**

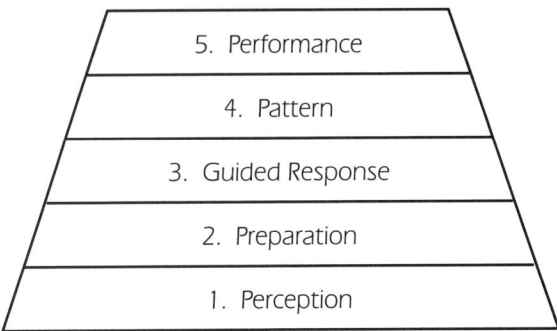

5. Performance
4. Pattern
3. Guided Response
2. Preparation
1. Perception

*Source:* E. J. Simpson, *The Classification of Objectives, Psychomotor Domain.* Urbana, Ill.: University of Illinois, 1966.

## Motivation and Human Needs

In order to teach people to believe something or to want something, trainers pay attention to motivation. Several kinds of business functions have as their purpose motivating people—clients, subordinates, potential customers, new employees, "career" employees, and sales or product development teams. Doing this kind of training well takes skill—and some understanding of the psychology of human needs. Figure 10.4 presents the classic view of Maslow's Hierarchy of Human Needs.

**Figure 10.4. Maslow's Hierarchy of Human Needs.**

5. Self-Actualization
4. Esteem
3. Love and Belonging
2. Safety
1. Physiological Needs

*Source:* A. H. Maslow, *Motivation and Personality,* 3rd ed. New York: Harper, 1987.

## Stages of Concern Regarding Adoption of Change

If we believe that education and training lead to changed behavior at work, we must pay attention to the times when trainees are most receptive to change. Many writers in organization development and educational psychology have presented models for change management, but few have presented a model at a personal level that can be effectively used in a training context. Figure 10.5 is such a model.

**Figure 10.5. Stages of concern.**

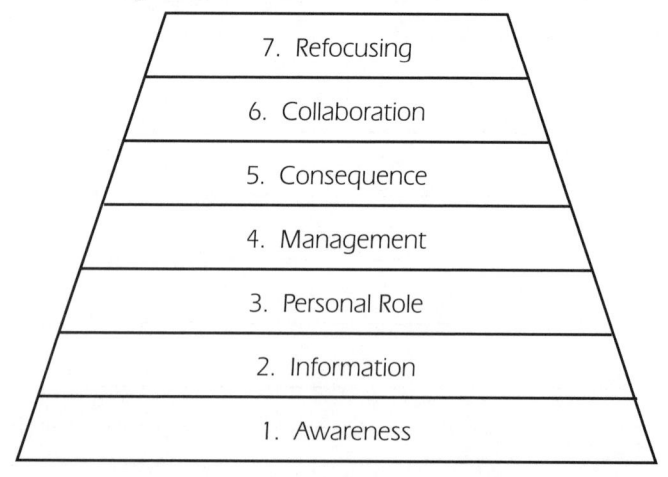

7. Refocusing
6. Collaboration
5. Consequence
4. Management
3. Personal Role
2. Information
1. Awareness

*Source:* G. E. Hall, *Concerns Based Adoption Model.* Austin, Texas: R&D Center for Teacher Education, University of Texas, 1973.

## Brain Lateralization and Learning Style

In recent years we have come to accept the notion that certain kinds of mental operations are more prominent in one half of the brain or the other. "Left brain/right brain" studies have given trainers a whole new way of thinking about the design and delivery of training that appeals to each part of the brain. Figure 10.6 is a presentation of the commonly accepted brain hemispheric activities.

**Figure 10.6. Left brain, right brain.**

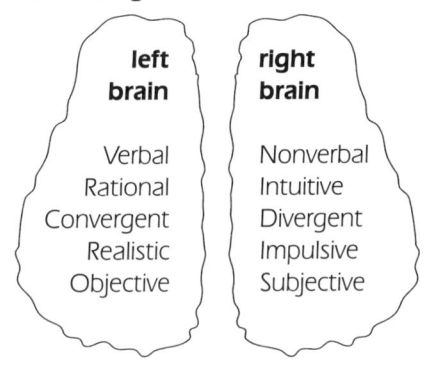

| left brain | right brain |
|---|---|
| Verbal | Nonverbal |
| Rational | Intuitive |
| Convergent | Divergent |
| Realistic | Impulsive |
| Objective | Subjective |

*Source:* S. P. Springer and G. Deutsch, *Left Brain, Right Brain.* San Francisco: W. H. Freeman, 1981.

## Memory

Advances in the study of human and computer information processing, as well as new work in gerontology, have increased our understanding of how memory functions. Training for transfer incorporates training that increases the effectiveness of memory. Figure 10.7 suggests a common view of the components of memory.

**Figure 10.7. Memory.**

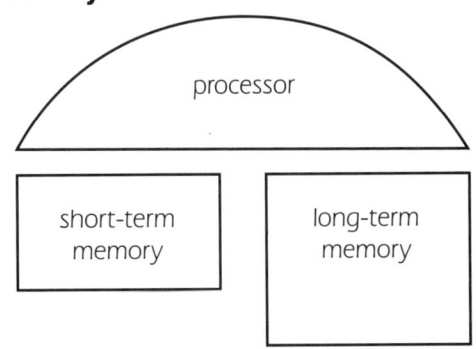

processor

| short-term memory | long-term memory |

*Source:* M. W. Eysenck, *A Handbook of Cognitive Psychology.* London: Lawrence Erlbaum, 1984.

## Conditions of Learning

Our public school teachers often talk about children's "readiness" to learn such things as reading, spelling, and math concepts. In adult education, too, there is "readiness"—in this example, the "conditions" of learning.

Figure 10.8 presents a classic model for learning of increasing complexity based on a hierarchy of conditions of readiness.

**Figure 10.8. Conditions of learning.**

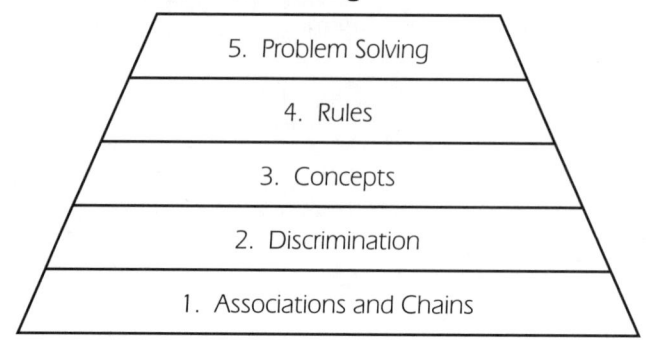

```
        5. Problem Solving
         4. Rules
          3. Concepts
        2. Discrimination
     1. Associations and Chains
```

*Source:* R. M. Gagne, *Conditions of Learning.* New York: Holt, Rinehart & Winston, 1977.

## Multiple Intelligences or Frames of Mind

For as long as educational psychology has been around, scientists have been attempting to categorize intelligence. This line of investigation is important for trainers because it reinforces what every trainer knows—that adults in learning situations vary greatly and are very individual in how they learn and in what they can learn best. Figure 10.9 represents some of the kinds of intelligence people may have, in the view of researchers in this field.

**Figure 10.9. Frames of mind (multiple intelligences).**

| |
|---|
| Linguistic Intelligence |
| Musical Intelligence |
| Logical-Mathematical Intelligence |
| Spatial Intelligence |
| Bodily-Kinesthetic Intelligence |
| Personal Intelligence |

*Source:* H. Gardner, *Frames of Mind: The Theory of Multiple Intelligences.* New York: Basic Books, 1985.

## The Learning Organization

As work has become more and more knowledge-intensive (head work rather than hand work), organizational structures and visions both must become focused on learning as a strategic process. MIT professor and corporate consultant Peter Senge is credited with coining the term "learning organization" and of popularizing it throughout the 1990s. Figure 10.10 represents the five disciplines that he believes are necessary for success as a learning organization. Of all, the "fifth discipline," systems thinking, he says is the most important, because it is here, in systems thinking, that we find a discipline for seeing the worldview, for recognizing patterns and interrelationships, wholes rather than only parts.

**Figure 10.10. The five disciplines.**

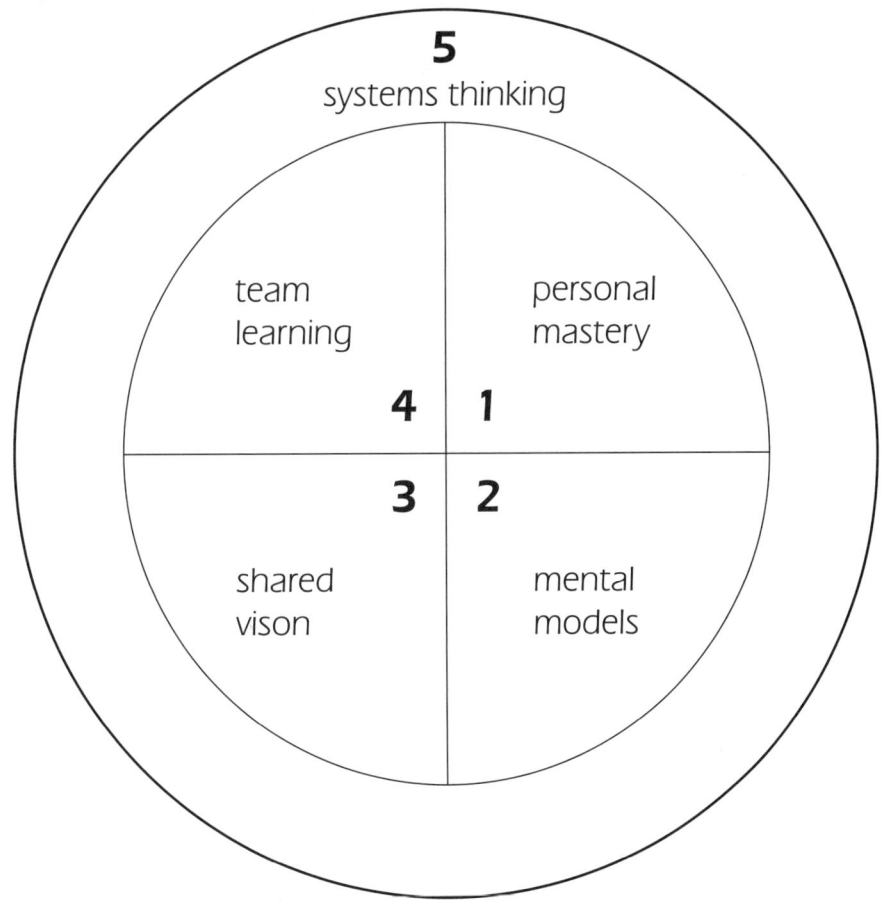

```
              5
        systems thinking

   team              personal
   learning          mastery
              4   1
              3   2
   shared            mental
   vison             models
```

*Source:* Peter Senge, *The Fifth Discipline.* NY: Doubleday Currency, 1990, and Senge et al., *The Fifth Discipline Fieldbook.* NY: Doubleday Currency, 1994.

## Organizational Change

Innovation and creativity have become goals in not only product development but also in organizational development as the "reengineered" companies of the 1990s struggle to succeed after surviving structural changes.

Many companies are trying to become newly cohesive and focused in order to compete in a changed business environment. John P. Kotter, a Harvard professor and consistent writer on the topic of organizational change throughout several decades, has an 8-step program for creating change, one that recognizes the importance of both strong leadership and empowered followers. It is outlined in Figure 10.11.

**Figure 10.11. 8-step program for creating change.**

1. Establish a sense of urgency.

2. Create the guiding leadership coalition.

3. Develop a vision and strategy for realizing it.

4. Communicate the vision for change.

5. Empower people at all levels for broad-based action.

6. Allow short-term wins; make them happen.

7. Consolidate gains.

8. Institutionalize and formalize new approaches that work.

*Source:* John P. Kotter, *Leading Change*. Boston: Harvard Business School Press, 1996.

## Performance Technology

As trainers function within organizations as learning consultants, the traditional Instructional System Design (ISD) model becomes broader. No longer can trainers expect to simply design and carefully craft a course or a series of lessons: trainers now must think more "organizationally," in terms of behavioral causes and results, not just specific learning objectives. Figure 10.12 shows the components of performance technology and represents a broader view of design. Trainers should pay special attention to the two vertical boxes, "Cause Analysis" and "Intervention Selection." Instructional designers will recognize some elements of ISD in this new framework.

**Figure 10.12. Performance technology model.**

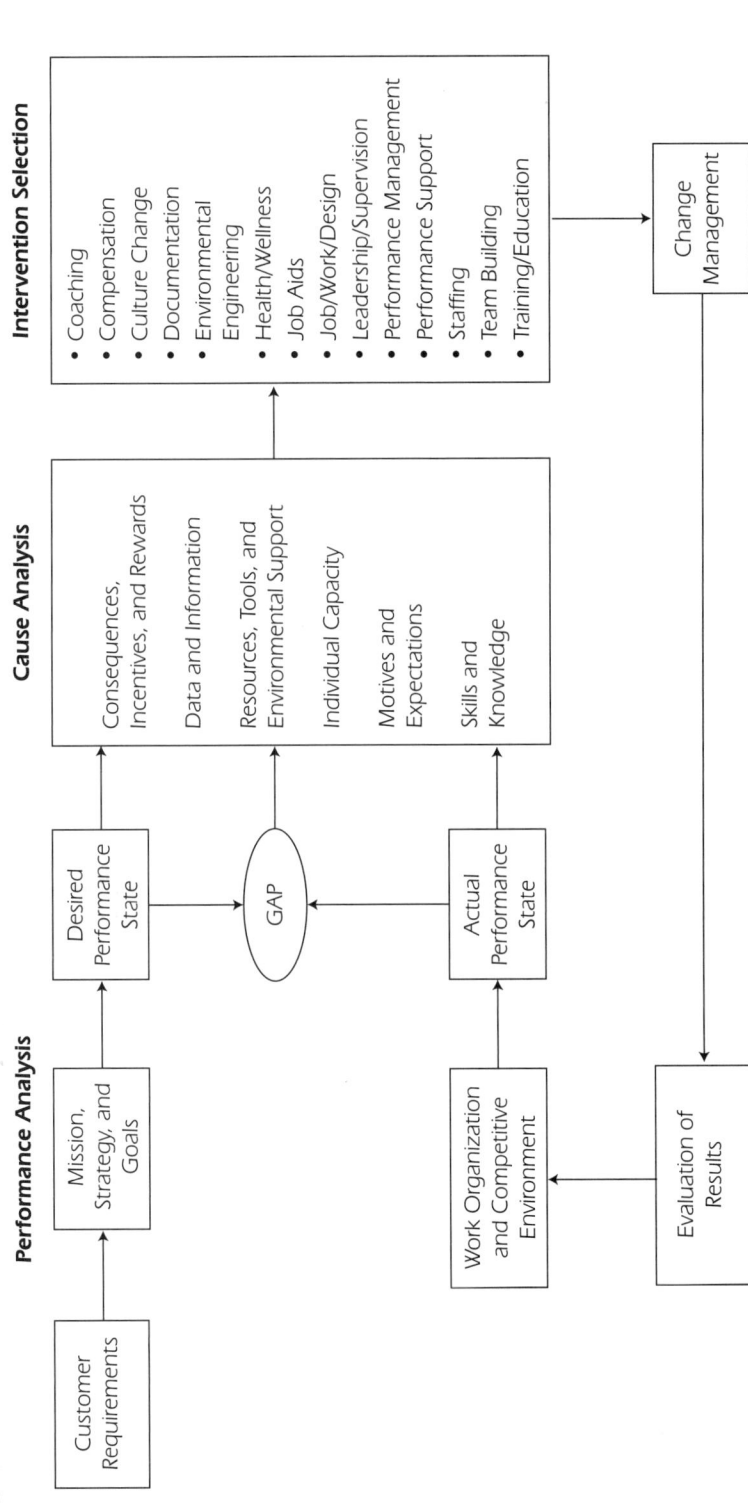

**Performance Analysis**

Customer Requirements → Mission, Strategy, and Goals → Desired Performance State → GAP ← Actual Performance State ← Work Organization and Competitive Environment

**Cause Analysis**

- Consequences, Incentives, and Rewards
- Data and Information
- Resources, Tools, and Environmental Support
- Individual Capacity
- Motives and Expectations
- Skills and Knowledge

**Intervention Selection**

- Coaching
- Compensation
- Culture Change
- Documentation
- Environmental Engineering
- Health/Wellness
- Job Aids
- Job/Work/Design
- Leadership/Supervision
- Performance Management
- Performance Support
- Staffing
- Team Building
- Training/Education

→ Change Management → Evaluation of Results → (back to Work Organization and Competitive Environment)

*Sources*: W. A. Deterline and M. J. Rosenberg, *Workplace Productivity: Performance Technology Success Stories*. Washington, D.C.: International Society for Performance Improvement, 1992; published in W. J. Rothwell, *ASTD Models for Human Performance Improvement*. Alexandria, Va.: American Society for Training and Development, 1996. Reprinted with permission of ISPI, the International Society for Performance Improvement, Washington, D.C.

# 11

# How to Implement and Deliver Training

In this chapter, the management and administrative tasks associated with the delivery or presentation of training are presented. There are numerous sources of information on the methods and techniques of delivering training; this chapter is not about methodology. Instead, it presents an organized way to look at managing the instructional function of training. Good design and good delivery techniques are part of this and are the subjects of more thorough investigation elsewhere. See, for example, Knowles (1984), Mitchell (1987), Nilson (1992, 1996, 1997), Rothwell (1996), and the publications list of the American Society for Training and Development (ASTD).

The delivery of training, or the process of instruction, involves the organization of external events and stimuli so that these actions help people learn. This means that the training manager must cope with the many tasks of developing the organization of trainers and training support people so that the organization itself is set up to facilitate workers' learning about various aspects of their jobs and the company.

The way in which training managers manage the delivery of instruction makes all the difference in the world in how easily, how thoroughly, and how effectively employees learn.

**KEY MANAGEMENT ISSUES**

- *Designing the Instructor's Job.* How you design the job of instructor depends on the background and experience levels of the persons who teach your courses. Will you expect instructors to handle their own advertising, scheduling, registration, and billing, that is, do you need to find instructors who are also good public relations people and excellent paperwork coordinators? Is it reasonable to expect that someone who is an expert in a certain subject and who can teach that subject to others is also an efficient clerk? Can you afford to staff your instructional team with only subject matter experts? Can you afford not to?

Will you expect your instructors to function as curriculum managers and developers in the broader subject area of their courses? Will they have to be your resident experts in a range of similar courses? Or will you simply maintain a staff of curriculum managers and have them hire expert instructors, either from within the company or from outside, as demand dictates? Will you choose "electronic" instructors embedded in EPSS systems?

Will you expect your classroom instructor to make arrangements for refreshments during class sessions, for taking trainees to lunch, and for entertaining trainees after class? Do you have a budget for this and a procedure for detailing such expenses? No matter which way you go in this issue, be sure that you know what's going on and that you tell your instructors ahead of time what's expected of them in this regard.

All of the foregoing considerations fall generally into the category of job design for the instructional staff. Have these issues clearly thought out before you embark on an ambitious training program.

■ *Training the Trainer.* As a manager, it is your responsibility to be sure that each of your instructors knows your beliefs about training delivery and can deliver instruction the way you want it to be delivered.

Getting your points across to your instructional staff is loosely called "training the trainer." There are many seminar and consulting firms that specialize in generic train-the-trainer courses and workshops, and plenty of individual consultants who can develop customized programs for you. Develop and teach your own train-the-trainer program, or hire an outside vendor to work with you on the task of training your trainers.

Naturally, training the trainer is easiest if you must train only your own regular staff of instructors. It gets considerably more complicated when you hire outside vendors to deliver courses for you; these folks come already trained to be trainers, and generally they are not at all interested in going through your train-the-trainer course. Outsiders may or may not understand your approach to training or be able to do it the way you envision, so be careful.

It is your responsibility to make a list of the things you want your instructors to know and to be able to do. If you intend to do the train-the-trainer training yourself, be sure that the items on your list can be taught, learned, and transferred to the classroom or training environment and that you know how to do the training that needs to be done; realize that this particular "trainee" audience—your own instructors—is probably the most difficult audience you'll ever face. Managers often find that this is one course that is worth going outside for!

If you intend to hire an outside workshop provider or individual consultant to work with you, use your list of train-the-trainer topics in your initial discussions with that outsider. Any good train-the-trainer vendor can readily adapt her workshop to fit your needs.

In addition to the content of the train-the-trainer course, you need to give some thought to the characteristics of various kinds of trainers and exactly what constitutes quality performance by each. There are many avenues to learning—experimentation, analysis, synthesis, categorization, memorization, reinterpretation, unlearning. Some kinds of instructors and instructional situations favor one avenue over another.

As a manager, you must sort out in your own mind the special differences that set apart each kind of instructor. The following list gives you a starting place for developing quality checklists for various kinds of trainers:

- The subject matter expert as trainer
- The vendor as trainer
- The technician as trainer
- The programmer as trainer
- The hot line answerer as trainer
- The team member as trainer
- The presenter as trainer
- The facilitator as trainer
- The supervisor as trainer

- *Selecting a Delivery Mode.* You should consider all options before deciding how to deliver training. Today, there is a myriad of ways to present instruction, some having high instructor visibility, some having low instructor visibility, some done in a classroom setting, and some done through an interface between a person and an electronic device (keypad, CRT, microphone, telephone transmitter, camera).

The following five classifications constitute the basic methods of delivering training:

- **Team:** Team members teaching each other and learning as a team
- **Group:** Large and small classrooms, seminar, workshop, small group, one-to-one training, peer training
- **Individual:** Computer-based training/programmed instruction/CD-ROM, self-study manuals and correspondence courses, video- or audiotape, interactive videodisc, online
- **Distance:** Any training characterized by trainees who are separated from their instructors, generally linked by telephone lines, satellites, or a computer network
- **"Other":** A wide assortment of training delivery structures in which the instructor's work is secondary and the instructional designer's work is primary, such as training conferences and conventions, field trips, simulations, and job aids

In some of these delivery options, the instructor functions as a coordinator and not as a "stand-up" presenter at all; in some, the instructional designer's role is the primary and most apparent building block facilitating delivery. Some of these options require more obvious and finely tuned stand-up presentation skills; some require a more intimate and facilitative instructional delivery style.

In addition, certain kinds of content suggest certain delivery modes. You should look carefully at the range of delivery options available and match up the content, the preferred delivery mode, and the best instructor you can find for the job. Never assume that training should be taught in a classroom with a single instructor up front and coffee and donuts in the back.

■ ***Obtaining Delivery Feedback.*** Most training managers seek feedback from trainees on how the course went—the usefulness of the course, trainees' comfort level in the training space, and the quality of instruction. Most training managers use this feedback to make changes in those areas in which constructive criticism was received.

There are two other areas of feedback that are often overlooked in the development of better training delivery. One is feedback from the instructor, and the other is feedback from a well-trained third-party instructional evaluator who observes an instructor at work with trainees. Trainees are not the only ones with a valuable perspective on the way a course was delivered. Consider adding a more comprehensive trainer evaluation component to your program by delivering feedback forms for instructors and for third-party evaluators.

# Chapter 11 Checklists

## To Help You Manage the Implementation and Delivery of Training

Use the following checklists to focus on the management issues associated with training delivery.

Following the checklists are forms to help you manage training delivery more effectively.

**LIST OF TRAINING DELIVERY CHECKLISTS**

- 11.1 Topics in a Train-the-Trainer Course
- 11.2 Vendor Instructor Evaluation Checklist
- 11.3 Quality Checklist for Instructional Support Media
- 11.4 When to Use a Job Aid Instead of Training
- 11.5 When to Choose the Big-Ticket Items—Computer-Based Training (CBT) and Interactive Videodisc (IVD)
- 11.6 Checklist for EPSS Use
- 11.7 What to Expect from Training via the Internet
- 11.8 Checklist for Setting Up a Training Intranet
- 11.9 Checklist for Setting Up One-to-One Instruction
- 11.10 Preparation Checklist for Classroom Training
- 11.11 Distance Training Checklist
- 11.12 Checklist of Items You Might Forget When Planning a Conference

# Training Delivery Checklist 11.1
## Topics in a Train-the-Trainer Course

This checklist contains the basic elements you need to include in a train-the-trainer course. They apply to all such courses, whether it's one you design yourself, one that an outside consultant helps you design, or a seminar or workshop to which you consider sending your instructor. Use this checklist to focus on course development for training in which the instructor is to be present, face-to-face with the trainee. The training should cover:

_____ 1. Preparation responsibilities, including:
- paperwork such as advertising, registration, and writing the catalog entry
- ordering the right size binders, photocopying handouts, communicating with the printer regarding format and numbers of course manuals
- choosing and ordering refreshments for trainees during training
- scheduling design reviews of course units or modules if the course is a new one or has been extensively revised
- placing the course in the master schedule
- developing a daily course agenda

_____ 2. Options in presenting the course to trainees, including:
- one-to-one instruction
- groups and teams
- labs and experiments
- the trainer's role in individualized instruction
- how to teach using case studies
- role plays and simulations
- demonstrations
- lectures

_____ 3. Physical setup of the classroom, including:
- environmental comfort—lights, heat, air
- quality of tables and chairs
- organization of tables and chairs
- electrical hookups (number, convenient placement, safety)
- sight lines for projected information
- computers and computer support

_____ 4. Hospitality and creature comforts during training, including:
- location of rest rooms
- location of lounges and smoking areas
- location of telephones
- location of message center
- location of copying machines

- location and number of personal computers
- location of food and drink
- location of emergency and medical help

_____ 5. Writing and using lesson plans, including:
- format
- timing
- objectives
- specific media needed for each lesson

_____ 6. Choosing and using instructional media, including:
- graphic and typestyle guidelines
- use of line, color, motion, sound
- separating medium and message, that is, ensuring that media support, not supplant, the content

_____ 7. Teaching techniques, including:
- using questions and answers
- active listening
- giving feedback
- managing conflict
- yielding control to trainees; getting it back again
- building on trainees' experience
- using examples
- teaching to objectives
- using guided practice, tests, and formative evaluation
- using manuals and aids effectively

_____ 8. Personal presentation strategies, including:
- movement
- eye contact
- proximity
- what to do with your hands
- what to do with your feet
- effective use of your voice

_____ 9. How adults learn, including:
- motivation
- learning styles
- responsibility

# Training Delivery Checklist 11.2
## Vendor Instructor Evaluation Checklist

There are times when it is practical and cost-effective to use an outsider to deliver training. Here's a quick review of the points to check out before you engage a vendor instructor:

_____ 1. The vendor's course outline exactly meets your needs. If it doesn't, hold up the contract until the vendor revises the generic course to fit your exact needs. Get it in writing.

_____ 2. The vendor has been in business long enough to satisfy your desire for credibility.

_____ 3. You are provided with names and phone numbers of former clients of this vendor who purchased similar courses.

_____ 4. You have spoken personally with enough of the vendor's former trainees to have gotten you a fair picture of the vendor's effectiveness at teaching this particular course.

_____ 5. Your vendor agrees to meet with you or your staff as many times as you require during any design or development stages. (You are ready to pay for this time to assure that you get the right course and to assure that all of your needs are met as the course is finalized.)

_____ 6. The vendor provides you with evaluation forms filled out by former trainees if you ask for them.

_____ 7. The vendor's experience and credentials are satisfactory to you.

# Training Delivery Checklist 11.3

## Quality Checklist for Instructional Support Media

There are three essential questions you should ask regarding the role of instructional media in facilitating instructional delivery. They are:

- Does my choice of media support good instruction, not attempt to substitute for poor instruction?
- Does my choice of media help trainees accomplish their objectives for learning; that is, are all instructional media supports tied in closely with the intent and desired business outcomes of the course?
- Is my choice of media cost-effective—that is, will I have enough trainees over the expected life of the media to warrant the expense now? Am I cautious about the "whiz-bang effect" of certain media, and have I weighed pros and cons of expense and effect as I decided on media? Is this choice easy to use during lessons?

With these considerations in mind, here are some specifics to look for as you evaluate instructional support media:

_____ 1. Image size

_____ 2. Dot patterns of computer-generated words

_____ 3. "White space" around words, phrases, and graphics

_____ 4. Messages unconfounded by extraneous graphics

_____ 5. Ease of electrical hookup

_____ 6. Clarity, pace, waver, color in film and video

_____ 7. Compatibility with hardware

_____ 8. Maintenance records and available troubleshooters

# Training Delivery Checklist 11.4
## When to Use a Job Aid Instead of Training

Sometimes it is cost-effective to neither buy nor make a course but to use instead a device known as a job aid. A job aid, which is designed to replace training, is generally used without an instructor; the instructor's role is incorporated in the aid's design.

Typical job aids are wall charts, models, tent cards, templates, stick-on instruction panels, if-then charts, and flow charts.

These are typical reasons you might want to use a job aid instead of training:

_____ 1. The learning task involves a heavy dose of memorization and can be facilitated by having cues or answers close at hand.

_____ 2. The learning task involves following procedures in a very specific way and can be facilitated by having those procedures spelled out simply and clearly where they are needed.

_____ 3. Learning can be speeded up by examination of a working model as the individual trainee's needs require.

_____ 4. The learning task represents complicated generic information needs or critical procedures that are best learned at the trainee's own speed from materials that can be referred to often.

_____ 5. Enough trainees need to use the job aid to make its printing, assembly, production, or manufacture worthwhile; that is, the job aid is not likely to become obsolete.

_____ 6. The job aid can be available and accessible to those who need it.

_____ 7. The content of the training adapts well to a graphic or abbreviated presentation.

# Training Delivery Checklist 11.5

## When to Choose the Big-Ticket Items—Computer-Based Training (CBT) and Interactive Videodisc (IVD)

CBT and IVD can save you time and money in the long run—the very long run. The fundamental question you must ask yourself is, "Do enough trainees need this course presented in this way to make the initial investment pay off over time?" If the answer is yes—that hundreds of trainees need this information presented this way—then by all means opt for these big-ticket ways to deliver instruction. One rule of thumb is that there should be about one hundred trainees per course per year to make the development or purchase of CBT or IVD worthwhile. Another way to look at it is to determine the value of downtime and business opportunity lost if critical employees have to be taken off the job and put into classrooms and compare the result with the cost of CBT or IVD.

In addition to the answer to the "numbers" and "dollars" questions, there are other delivery issues that you should consider before you choose CBT or IVD:

_____ 1. **Programming excellence:** Has there been an instructional design check to balance the programmer's way of looking at instruction?

_____ 2. **Easy access:** Is the trainee interface with the computer menu- or "windows"-driven so that moving around in the course is easy, bypasses extraneous information, and is nontrivial? Is access to lessons extremely user-friendly?

_____ 3. **Help screens:** Has the instructor's point of view been considered in designing help screens?

_____ 4. **Hotline:** Is an instructor available at the information end of the hotline?

_____ 5. **Hardware "transparency":** Is the course so well designed that the computer hardware seems transparent to the trainee (that is, the hardware is easy to use and doesn't get in the way of learning)?

_____ 6. **Equipment:** Do you have enough of the right equipment to accommodate all instructional software, videos, and necessary peripheral devices to make learning happen the way it was intended to happen for all the trainees who want to use it when they want to use it?

_____ 7. **Space:** Are your CBT and IVD training spaces arranged so that individual trainees can comfortably learn in them?

## How to Implement and Deliver Training

_____ 8. **Updates:** Do you have in place a trainee feedback process and a staff to make corrections in programming, content, filming, and instructional design?

_____ 9. **Responsibility:** Do you have an instructor and an instructional designer in charge of your CBT and IVD courses? Trainees are responsible for their own learning, but management is responsible for making it happen.

# Training Delivery Checklist 11.6
## Checklist for EPSS Use

EPSSs (Electronic Performance Support Systems) are used as a combination instructor and instructional delivery medium in a handful of companies. *Training Magazine*'s 1996 Industry Report (October 1996) noted that EPSSs in use then were both "rare" and rather "rough approximations" of their potential. *Training* reports that only about 5 percent of organizations have developed EPSS systems, except in companies of 10,000 or more employees where EPSS usage is as high as 15 percent. Most trainers agree that the technology is out there to make good on the EPSS vision of providing a new paradigm for learning—one that features self-directed learning precisely at the time it is needed, one that considers new ways of structuring problems and their solutions, and one that entices the learner to seek and find information in its many forms through the touch of a keypad. EPSS can be all at once a coach, a teacher, a field trip, an evaluative reinforcer, a multifaceted job aid, and a reference librarian.

Here are a few things to consider regarding your possible use of an EPSS:

_____ 1. Consider your available development time and resources: in-house development staff, consultant help, dollars for services, salaries, training, software, and hardware.

_____ 2. Be sure that your need for training won't go away before you get your EPSS up and running. For example, think about new product obsolescence, customer loyalty, stability of your employee workforce, etc.

_____ 3. Investigate do-it-yourself software for creating performance support programs. Collaborate with your brightest computer whizzes to help you choose software that truly meets your company's needs before you get in touch with salespersons. Look into authoring systems, software shells, and hypertext and hypermedia technologies. New products are coming to market quickly, but you must be knowledgeable about what you want to accomplish before you sign on the dotted line or enjoy that nice lunch with the salesperson.

_____ 4. It's hard to retrofit an EPSS into an existing (old) computer network or isolated group of desktop PCs. Think more in terms of either creating a whole new system of performance support yourself, or of hiring a consulting organization to create one for/with you. A bunch of CD-ROMs won't do it. Avoid the costly learning mistake of trying to retrofit new EPSS technology onto old instructional designs.

_____ 5. Be prepared to facilitate people's thinking away from their traditional belief that the classroom with an instructor up front is the best way to deliver all training. Be prepared to encourage people to accept responsibility for their own learning, to be active rather than passive participants in all of their learning decisions.

# Training Delivery Checklist 11.7
## What to Expect from Training via the Internet

The Internet is an excellent information resource, and, according to many current studies, it is used by about half of all employees. Careful, professional learning design on the Internet and World Wide Web is, however, still in its infancy. Web sites proliferate, but few are designed with learning in mind. Chat rooms, e-mail, and other communication venues are popular on the Internet, but these deliver the most elementary ingredients of learning—simply basic information (some would say an overload of information). It takes the will of the learner plus a structured approach to what to choose and how to learn in order for learning to occur.

This checklist can be your reality check for training via the Internet:

_____ 1. Much of the free information you find on the Internet will be words. Graphics require bigger and faster computers and often strain the communication lines. Think carefully about how you learn best: if it's not through word-intensive reading facing a computer screen, maybe you'd better not get too involved with this delivery system.

_____ 2. What you say on the Internet through newsgroups, chat rooms, and e-mail should be said carefully. Publishing laws regarding copyright protection of others' original work, protection of your company's intellectual property, and protections guaranteed by the Communications Decency Act apply to online exchanges of information. Be careful of biased remarks, off-color comments of a sexual nature, and words that could be deemed libelous. Expect to be monitored.

_____ 3. Online learning is serious business; off-task elements like jokes, silly banter, and playing with the technology should be used sparingly. Expect dollars and cents accountability of your time spent online.

_____ 4. Organized learning institutes and online universities are available and are generally conscientious about providing good instructional design and support services, including persons to telephone for help. Expect more of these to be available.

_____ 5. Be ready for "pay-to-play." As new courses and other learning opportunities come online and more people become developers of Web pages, expect to have charges assessed for usage. Entrepreneurs have been trying hard to find ways to do business on the Internet. As always, "buyer beware." Be sure that you are not buying pure entertainment or simply information masquerading as training.

## Training Delivery Checklist 11.8
### Checklist for Setting Up a Training Intranet

An intranet is based on information from a single source such as one company's database of employee, customer, product, policy, and work process information. Intranet documents can be created and managed by users themselves without the administrative effort of IT staff. Intranets can quickly and effectively tie together a company's diverse employee population. They are especially useful in companies with widely scattered sales forces, service representatives, and employees residing in other countries. Corporate intranets generally have built-in links to Internet resources. Training opportunities designed for intranets can and often do make use of full Internet resources as needed. As in using the Internet for training, using an intranet requires that the user be aware that information is only the first important ingredient in learning: an approach to problem solving, decision making, prioritizing and evaluating information, and motivation to learn all must also be present for any delivery mechanism to succeed.

Here are some typical applications for training using an intranet:

_____ 1. Personalized biographical/resume information can be easily stored and shared, often increasing a group's motivation to get to know fellow employees better.

_____ 2. Standards documents, job specs, glossaries, and product information can be made available to all employees as they need the information.

_____ 3. Corporate news and information, and policy and personnel changes can be quickly communicated to all employees, giving more people a sense of empowerment through knowledge.

_____ 4. Conferences online can put people together across buildings and across oceans. Discussions, question and answer sessions, and feedback from experts can all become part of an employee's natural communication patterns, leading to learning.

_____ 5. Formally structured courses with graphical links to video resources can be custom-designed for employees, tapping into just what an individual needs to know in order to perform better at his or her job. Intranet software is beginning to be available to facilitate the customization and personalization of learning opportunities. The magazines *PC World* and *PC Magazine* frequently contain comprehensive articles about intranets.

_____ 6. Intranets allow employees throughout a company to work on the same project simultaneously and interactively, in teams or as individuals, usually to great cost savings in terms of travel and frequently to higher levels of creativity and productivity.

This kind of online collaboration often fuels divergent thinking as the whole of the effort becomes greater than its parts. Opportunities to work together and to learn together are made possible by intranets.

# Training Delivery Checklist 11.9

## Checklist for Setting Up One-to-One Instruction

Refer to these guidelines whenever you or someone you designate must do one-to-one instruction. These ideas will be helpful in any kind of on-the-job apprentice and peer training, as well as in supervisor-to-employee training. Mentoring and coaching can also be guided by these seven points:

_____ 1. Cover the regular job of the person who will function as the one-to-one instructor. Assign a responsible backup person while the training is taking place.

_____ 2. Designate a comfortable training place and keep other employees out of it during training.

_____ 3. Choose a method of teaching that fits what needs to be learned. (Don't automatically do a viewgraph presentation for just one trainee. Think in terms of guided practice, working through a simulation, or analyzing business cases, instead.)

_____ 4. Allow time for the instructor to create training materials—lesson plans, handouts, job aids, study guides.

_____ 5. Let both the instructor and trainee know whether or not mastery levels or other performance data need to be taken and recorded during training and reported later.

_____ 6. Be sure that instructor and trainee know what constitutes acceptable performance for the trainee during the course. Have the instructor write down these performance standards and share them with the trainee.

_____ 7. Establish a beginning and an end to one-to-one training.

# Training Delivery Checklist 11.10
## Preparation Checklist for Classroom Training

The training manager can help the classroom instructor by providing the administrative amenities and supports that make trainees feel comfortable. It's usually enough for the instructor to have to get the course together—you can facilitate a good delivery of classroom instruction by paying attention to the following:

_____ 1. Give the names of enrolled trainees to the instructor several days ahead of class.

_____ 2. Give the instructor all the forms that you need for your records—charge-back accounting forms if that's the way you do your billing, attendance forms, certification forms or grading forms if you use these, evaluation forms, and so on.

_____ 3. Give the instructor clear directions about how to use these forms and when you need them.

_____ 4. Provide refreshments for the class if the instructor wants them. Be sure that you know when the instructor intends to break in the morning and in the afternoon and when lunch is scheduled.

_____ 5. Be sure that the instructor knows how to regulate room temperature.

_____ 6. Be sure that media equipment and supplies are in working order and adequate for the instructional intent.

_____ 7. Be sure that computers are online for the class and that student identification numbers are reserved.

_____ 8. Provide the instructor with phone numbers of persons on your staff who can troubleshoot media and computer problems.

_____ 9. Provide empty tables for the instructor to use for supplies, reference materials, and handouts.

_____ 10. Show the instructor the location of a copy machine and telephone.

# Training Delivery Checklist 11.11
## Distance Training Checklist

Distance training is training in which the instructor is separated from the trainee—training that generally happens in a location remote from the source of instruction, often via telephone lines or video. Managers of field operations—branch offices or regional sales offices—often choose distance training as a cost-effective and efficient delivery method. Other managers, too, choose distance training when business considerations require that trainees be positioned in remote locations.

Consider these points when you consider distance training:

_____ 1. The course content can be broken down into one-hour modules and spread out over several days. This is necessary because the trainee in a remote training room probably can't afford the time away from the job that a normal classroom training format requires and probably can't focus on learning for much longer than one hour without the instructor actually being available. The content must be learnable even if its components are separated by time.

_____ 2. If you use a classroom for group training, be sure that a site coordinator is available to handle questions about the course content as well as troubleshoot transmission problems.

_____ 3. Be sure that training materials are of high quality and are available at the remote site. Be sure that the site coordinators know the procedures for getting completed workbooks and administrative forms back to you.

_____ 4. Focus distance courses on content that is immediately relevant to the trainee's job if possible.

_____ 5. Be sure that your instructor practices interacting with trainees over telephone lines. Some instructors can't handle the anonymity of teletraining or the problem of remembering individual trainees when they can't interact with them face to face.

_____ 6. If your instructor plans to use graphics, especially computer-generated graphics, be sure that the receiving site has adequate receiving equipment. Be sure that you practice the transmission of graphics before you run the training.

_____ 7. If you expect your remote trainees to interact with the instructor, be sure that they know how to do this. Be sure that either your instructor or your site coordinator reviews the proper procedures with them at the start of training.

# Training Delivery Checklist 11.12

## Checklist of Items You Might Forget When Planning a Conference

Running a training conference is one good alternative to offering classroom training. A conference can be an effective way to focus on some of the "process" issues that can be addressed only by delivering training to a group. Some of these issues are the interaction among trainees, the choices trainees make when confronted with options, and the way trainees select from a "smorgasbord" of choices and integrate those choices for the benefit of the company.

You can facilitate good choices that benefit both the individual and the company by planning and running a tight conference. Here are some suggestions for attending to details you might be tempted to overlook in your haste to finalize your program:

_____ 1. Write down several conference objectives for the trainees. Think of conference attendees as learners, and state the objectives as you would state objectives for courses.

_____ 2. Assign a responsible person to each of the major areas of program, food, facilities, and administration. Encourage each person to delegate responsibilities within each area, with a start date and end date to each task responsibility. It's easy to think of the conference as only program and food; you'll get through the details better if you create a separate responsibility category of facilities and administration, too.

_____ 3. There are several areas that are easy to forget: parking, publicity prior to the conference (newspaper, radio, TV, in-house), a way for conferees to get and to send messages, escort/transportation for conference speakers, a pre-conference hotline to handle questions, a "clean up" mailing list with no duplicates, publicized graphics and display standards for exhibitors, a reliable procedure for recording attendance at small-group sessions, feedback forms for conference speakers and small-group session leaders, an available copy machine, extra media supplies (acetates, slides, bulbs, extension cords), and planned conference follow-up with speakers and with attendees.

# Chapter 11 Forms

## For Managing Training Implementation and Delivery

Forms in this section will help you make decisions about and manage the delivery of training in various modes—self-study, one-to-one study, and group study. Feedback and evaluation forms are provided to help you gather information about how your courses are presented and what makes a good instructor. A master scheduling template is also included.

**LIST OF TRAINING DELIVERY FORMS**

- 11.1  The Master Schedule
- 11.2  One-to-One Training Decision Factors Chart
- 11.3  Classroom Training Decision Factors Chart
- 11.4  Delivery Components in CBT Lessons
- 11.5  Dry-Run Trainee Feedback Form for Classroom Training
- 11.6  Dry-Run Trainee Feedback Form for Self-Study
- 11.7  Performance Review for Classroom Instructor

## How to Implement and Deliver Training

**Training Delivery Form 11.1**
**THE MASTER SCHEDULE**

### How to Use This Form

1. Create a master schedule only when your full program of courses is identified and consistently labeled. Course numbers have to make sense to potential trainees as they look at the master schedule.
2. Post the master schedule for a three-month period. It's hard for employees to plan further ahead than this; things change around the training department too.
3. Make the master schedule poster-size and display it in a prominent area (reception area, cafeteria, lounge, etc.).
4. At the bottom include a key to abbreviations.
5. Organize the master schedule by curriculum areas, such as sales, personal computers, technical skills, supervisors.
6. Indicate by horizontal bars in the "days of the month" section when and where the course will be taught.

---

Curriculum | Course Number | Course Name | Days of the month
1 2 3 4 5 6 7 8 9 10 11 12 . . .
Room A
Room B

Curriculum | Course Number | Course Name | Days of the month
1 2 3 4 5 6 7 8 9 10 11 12 . . .
Room A

Curriculum | Course Number | Course Name | Days of the month
1 2 3 4 5 6 7 8 9 10 11 12 . . .
Room C

**Training Delivery Form 11.2**
**ONE-TO-ONE TRAINING DECISION FACTORS CHART**

### How to Use This Form
1. Focus on an individual employee as you decide whether to choose one-to-one training. Enter the person's name, telephone number, and job title on this form.
2. With this specific person in mind, place a check mark in the appropriate column. "Yes" checkmarks indicate that one-to-one training delivery is advisable.

Employee's name _____ telephone _____

Employee's job title _____

| | Not Applicable | No | Yes |
|---|---|---|---|

Business goals

1. Personalized PC training is mandated
2. Productivity goals require presence on the job site
3. Agreed-upon MBO (management by objectives) still need to be fulfilled
4. Management decision to migrate to CBT and IVD within two years; needs transition help

Organizational environment

5. New hire requires acculturation
6. Merger affects job design
7. Costs of off-site training are prohibitive
8. You or your designee can do the training

Personal needs

9. Performance review indicates skill/knowledge lack in relation to similar employees
10. Return from leave of absence indicates need for catch-up skills/knowledge
11. Out of town/overnight travel is not possible for personal reasons at home
12. Tasks to be learned are unique to this person or this person's job

**Training Delivery Form 11.3**
**CLASSROOM TRAINING DECISION FACTORS CHART**

### How to Use This Form
1. Focus on the learning environment. If it seems ideally suited for learning in a group, proceed.
2. State the name of the course and its probable location at the top of this form.
3. With this setting in mind, place a check mark in the appropriate column. "Yes" checkmarks indicate that group training is advisable.

Course title _____

Probable course location _____

| | Not Applicable | No | Yes |
|---|---|---|---|
| 1. The learning is structured around group dynamics. | | | |
| 2. Trainee interaction is desirable to propel the course forward. | | | |
| 3. An excellent instructor is available. | | | |
| 4. A design team (subject matter experts, instructional designers) is available if you must create the course yourself. | | | |
| 5. There's enough lead time to get the course materials ready and printed. | | | |
| 6. A review team of "similar students" is available prior to giving the course to be sure all constituencies will be adequately served by this course. | | | |
| 7. The training room is comfortable, convenient, and properly equipped to accommodate this course. | | | |
| 8. Trainees and their supervisors are willing to invest time away from the job in order to attend class. | | | |

**Training Delivery Form 11.4**
**DELIVERY COMPONENTS IN CBT LESSONS**

### How to Use This Form
1. Use this form as a guide to examination of individual lessons in a CBT course. It is especially useful as you evaluate an off-the-shelf CBT course prior to purchase.
2. Use it beside your keyboard as you step through each lesson. Record your comments in the comments column. Make corrections or accommodations prior to giving the course to individual trainees.
3. Skim the course online so that you have an accurate view of the length (e.g., three screens, ten screens) of each lesson. Be sure that the timing is good for your particular training situation.

Course title _____

Lesson title _____ # of screens _____

| Process information | Comments |
|---|---|

Process information
  1. Objectives can be learned via CBT.
  2. Mechanics of moving around are elegantly simple.
  3. Instructions are clear; format is consistent.

Content/text
  4. Objectives parallel the content presentation.
  5. New content is presented from simple to complex.
  6. Content options are given through branching.
  7. Content is relevant, necessary, sufficient.
  8. Text is lean, easy to follow.

Graphics
  9. Related information is chunked together.
  10. Plenty of "white space" surrounds chunks.
  11. Information flows like reading, from left to right, top to bottom.
  12. Tables, figures, icons, animations are consistently and adequately labeled.

Tests/practice exercises
  13. Test questions relate to objectives.
  14. If timing is a success indicator, guidelines are stated and timing feedback is provided.
  15. Responses can be easily changed by trainee.
  16. Trainee controls when to begin testing.
  17. If self-scoring is desired, answers are given.
  18. Scoring standards are provided.
  19. Scoring results are easily accessed.

**Training Delivery Form 11.5**
**DRY-RUN TRAINEE FEEDBACK FORM FOR CLASSROOM TRAINING**

### How to Use This Form
1. Use this form with a new course or a greatly revised course or with a new instructor for an existing course.
2. In these situations, take the time to dry-run the course in front of sample trainees who are very much like the "paying customers" for this particular course. Strive for representation, not necessarily the exact number of trainees (i.e., you don't need twenty-five trainees).
3. Ask each sample trainee to provide feedback to help your instructor and course designers to correct any problems before the course goes public. Ask for narrative feedback.

1. How was the flow of the course? Were any topics out of sequence? How would you rearrange the topics?
   _____
   _____
   _____

2. What were the instructor's strengths? What actions and approaches helped you to learn?
   _____
   _____
   _____

3. What were the instructor's weaknesses? How could they be improved?
   _____
   _____
   _____

4. What improvements in the classroom would you suggest in order for trainees to be more comfortable and to support learning?
   _____
   _____

5. What kind of instructional follow-up to this course would you suggest as you return to your job?
   _____
   _____

**Training Delivery Form 11.6**
**DRY-RUN TRAINEE FEEDBACK FORM FOR SELF-STUDY**

> **How to Use This Form**
> 1. Use this form to evaluate new or greatly redesigned self-study courses, such as correspondence courses, video courses, CBT courses, and IVD courses.
> 2. Ask an instructor or frequent user of self-study courses to be the sample trainee who fills out this form.
> 3. Set up the sample trainee in a training environment and allow enough time for that person to take the entire course so that you get a complete picture. (Remember that the course itself functions as the primary instructor in self-study. Therefore you need to schedule enough evaluation time for your sample trainee to address instructional design issues as well as delivery issues inherent in the self-study format.)
> 4. Ask for narrative comments. Use the feedback to improve the delivery structure of the course.

1. As you skim through the course, do you find the topics in the right order? How would you change things around to be better? _____
_____

2. As you skim through the course, does the scope, design, and format seem interesting? Does self-study seem to be a good way to present this training? Why? _____
_____

3. At some point during the course, ask for help (use a hot line number, call up an instructor-contact, use a help screen, etc.), and report on what happened. We are interested in the quality of help. _____
_____

4. How good are the instructions? Why? _____
_____

5. Are lessons at the right level—not too easy, not too hard? What do you believe is the level of this course? _____
_____

6. Are the exercises and tests helpful? Why? Why not? _____
_____

**Training Delivery Form 11.7**
**PERFORMANCE REVIEW FOR CLASSROOM INSTRUCTOR**

### How to Use This Form
1. Use this form as a guide to assembling and reviewing all of the relevant information you need to do an effective performance review of a classroom instructor.
2. This form can also be used as an aid to designing the various kinds of data-gathering documents you need all during your training year.

Information source                             Exact quotes or summaries

1. Trainee evaluation forms

2. Forms this instructor filled out to evaluate courses

3. Training days per year in class

4. Written complaints from any source

5. Written commendations from any source

6. MBO statements and reports

7. Personal performance goals and accomplishments

8. Attendance record

# Chapter 11
## More Information on Training Implementation and Delivery

Information in this section is presented in a detailed way to help you focus on some principles and techniques of instruction. It is a training manager's brief, designed to give you some insight into behaviors and methods that should be practiced by your instructional delivery staff.

## What Motivates Adults to Learn

As the U.S. population has been aging since the 1970s, we have seen an increase in researchers and spokespersons for adult learning theory. Numerous studies and books have been published in recent years on the subject of adult learners. The fields of education and of developmental psychology regularly include material on how adults learn in their publications and professional association meetings.

Training managers should look for evidence that the delivery philosophy and methodology of their instructional staffs are based on the latest findings about adult learning. The following list of characteristics is synthesized from what we currently know about adult learners. Use it as a guide for discussion with individual instructors as they tell you about the design, development, and delivery of their courses.

### Fundamental Motivational Characteristics of Adult Learners

- *Adults want to know why they need to learn something.* If you can make them see exactly how this new skill/knowledge will make life easier for them (i.e., more profitable, fewer hassles, more productive, fewer meetings, more quality time for tasks), your job of teaching will be much more effective.

- *Adult learners like to feel that "I'm in charge here."* At work, most adults are trusted to make many important decisions many times in any one hour of the working day, and they quickly develop an "in-charge" relationship with their job and their job site. They generally carry this "self-possession" attitude into the training room. Good instructors structure the delivery of instruction to capitalize on this very positive attitude and do not revert to old models of instructional delivery that treat students like dependent children. Good instructors maneuver the learning situation to allow and even encourage trainees to take charge.

- *Adult learners need others to know the legitimacy of their experiences.* All adults who show up in training programs have huge successes behind them. They have managed successful life events, they have exerted influence over a variety of other people, and they have a string of work-related accomplishments behind them. They will not tolerate being made to look foolish or inadequate in front of their peers in the classroom situation. The good instructor takes whatever time is needed to assure each class member or trainee that his or her specific experience—life event or job accomplishment—is valuable in the context of the present training challenge. Good instructors take the time to listen to the cues that trainees invariably are happy to provide.

■ *Adult learners are motivated by "doing it."* They demand relevant objectives and clear instructions. They like to know the standards and criteria for success, and they like to know that they can "tick off" the requirements one by one as they satisfy them. The wise instructor delivers instruction by providing plenty of "how'm I doin'?" feedback to individual trainees throughout the course.

## A Model of Delivery Steps That Lead To Mastery

The model of instructional delivery in Figure 11.1 helps lead learners to learning success. It can be adapted to many training situations in which skills or new information must be learned.

**Figure 11.1. Instructional delivery model.**

| |
|---|
| Define or describe the task to be learned. Establish interest and mental readiness to learn. |
| Tell trainees why this needs to be learned. Give several solid business reasons that most trainees can relate to. Focus on the big picture—profitability, market share, quality, job security, efficiency. |
| State specific objectives for the learner. Be sure that trainees agree with what you say. Be flexible and ready to adapt the way you said it to include the way they want it said. Ask trainees if there are any other objectives that are unique to them. |
| Specify what the standards and criteria for success are. Do you require 100 percent or will four out of five correct solutions be adequate for training success? Most trainees will want to perform at peak capacity because higher pay and job security are generally related to high performance. Be sure that you communicate at the beginning of training what the highest level of performance/understanding is in this new subject. Standards of performance should always be tied to the objectives for learning. |

Teach content in small chunks. Use any appropriate medium—video, viewgraphs, case studies, role plays, examples, nonexamples, etc. Aim the content at the group as a whole.

Model success after a chunk of content. Show trainees how this bit of information can make a specific job easier, how the application of this principle or formula can improve productivity or yield, etc. Demonstrate time savings by following this procedure. Show quality in product by using these new skills. Get trainees to think that if you can do it, so can they.

Guide trainees in a practice session. Suggest a problem situation that trainees can solve using the new skill/knowledge. Give plenty of cues and facilitative help.

Turn trainees loose in an independent practice session where they are more on their own—the workshop concept rather than the seminar concept. Make the problem to be solved a generic business problem, or ask each trainee to define one for himself or herself.

Check to see if trainees got it. Do this by informal questioning, walking around the room to see how the practice is going, being available as a resource to a small group, etc. Engage in formative evaluation, designed to spot learning problems as the process of practice unfolds, before a small incorrect approach becomes a roadblock to future learning. Ask trainees how they think they're doing.

Vary the practice exercises until each trainee has achieved success at some level. Give trainees feedback about their progress relative to the agreed-upon objectives for learning. Tie the progress toward mastery at the end of training to the objective at the beginning.

Suggest related higher-level problems for trainees who are faster learners.

## The Instructor's Personal Presentation Primer

This section contains helpful hints regarding an instructor's personal style. Obviously, personality differences exist among excellent instructors. However, there are some presentation skills that can be used effectively by all instructors to facilitate learning. These presentation skills go beyond the skills one needs to do a good "information show" or convention speech. It's a good idea to observe your instructors or potential instructors to be sure that these teaching skills are part of their bag of presentation tricks. Trainees always see through and discredit the presenter who only puts on a good show.

Good instructors should be able to:

- Set a realistic and somewhat flexible agenda; hold lunch break and quitting time sacred
- Encourage trainee participation and know how not to become defensive or intimidated by an attempted takeover
- Teach constantly to agreed-upon objectives; once is generally not enough
- Listen for cues to learning breakthroughs; reinforce trainees who take learning risks; encourage others at critical learning times
- Provide reviews and summaries often
- Help trainees focus on specific learning tasks; point out "the good stuff" on which attention should be directed
- Go slowly and deliberately with instructions; be patient
- Use clear, consistent language; leave the jargon in the textbooks
- Be friendly, personable, approachable; move around the room
- Be a facilitative leader, willing to share information and to lead learners forward to effective discovery and mastery
- Give personal and useful feedback to trainees; receive and apply feedback from trainees

## If You Have Limited Budget and Staff . . .

Even if you are a limited training operation, there are some things on which you should not compromise. These are (1) breadth of courses; (2) depth of content coverage; (3) quality of training staff; and (4) quality of training materials. These four areas of noncompromise are considered further:

1. **Breadth of courses.** Offer a variety of courses in the areas of the business that are important to your company, for example, supervisory training, sales and customer service training, or accounting and financial training. If you can't afford to hire staff instructors, rent training videos in the general subjects and coordinate a self-study program using these tapes. Prepare some introductory material, keep the tapes for a two- or three-day (minimal) period; carefully schedule people into the self-study training area, and prepare them in a friendly and personal way. Help them focus on the important parts of the tape through your preparatory materials.

Save the specialized course topics for individualized treatment, such as sending one or two people to a regional seminar or running a "shadowing" program in which trainees work next to an expert in that specialized topic for a period of time. Think in terms of on-the-job training, peer training, and other person-to-person training that does not require an employee whose only job is that of instructor.

2. **Depth of content coverage.** Never sacrifice depth of content because you can't find an instructor who can deliver that truly special subject. Train your subject matter expert to be a trainer. If you can't do the train-the-trainer course yourself, find a one- or two-day train-the-trainer workshop given by a vendor or, better yet, hire a consultant for one or two days to work at your site with that subject matter expert. Chances are that you can find a subject matter expert who would enjoy becoming a trainer for a group of people eager to learn about what he does; use the expertise of your company's staff, and add to that expertise the skills required to be a trainer. Allow the subject matter expert time to practice and to develop confidence that she can do the job of training. Make the training assignment a temporary one for the subject matter expert.

3. **Quality of training staff.** Excellent training support employees—graphic artists, registrars, administrative assistants—can provide enormous help to instructors by having all of the materials and paperwork associated with courses ready when the instructor needs them. Save your instructor dollars for time the instructors spend with trainees by keeping the quality of your training support staff high.

4. **Quality of training materials.** Buy a good personal computer, excellent desktop publishing software that has the ability to create 18- and 24-point type size, and a laser or laser-quality printer, and produce your own manuals, newsletters, and viewgraphs. Create the materials yourself if you are a good writer, or hire one top-notch technical writer to create and produce your training materials. Avoid cut-and-paste jobs taken from many sources. Set your writing and production standards high, and control the output by putting a writing specialist in charge.

### If You Have Adequate Budget and Staff . . .

If you are lucky enough to have a generous budget, a full-time staff, and receptive top brass, there's a lot you can do to facilitate delivery of training services. Among the options available to you are these:

1. **Maintain a staff of instructors.** Organize around the major business areas such as executive and management training, supervisory training, R&D training, sales and customer service training, financial training, cross-cultural training, clerical training, literacy training, and safety training. Place an instructor at the head of each curriculum area, and assign an instructional designer assistant to each area as well.

2. **Delegate the responsibility of finding and maintaining suitable instructors within that business area to the head instructor.** This often means that courses are taught by qualified vendors working side-by-side with your own employees. Stress coordination and communication; keep your instructional staff well-informed about company policies and procedures so that a consistent front is presented to all trainees.

3. **Consider formalizing a field testing process for all courses that have been heavily revised or that are being offered for the first time in your company.** Set high standards of development and delivery or revision and feedback so that your instruction is as good as it possibly can be. If you use a combination of in-house and outside instructors, insist that both go through the same formal, rigorous course validation process.

4. **Provide information.** Publicize outstanding work. Send your best staff for updated professional development workshops, especially those that focus on skills and new electronic delivery systems. Pay staff dues to join professional associations. Subscribe to training journals and magazines, and make a library of current training books available to them. Provide them with online research services.

5. **Listen to your instructors.** They provide invaluable feedback from trainees regarding the perception of folks "out there" about how the company is doing. Trainees know the weak spots, and they often share enormously useful planning information with instructors. Make it a point to speak to instructors after training to get their informal assessment of how things are going. Value instructors as a communication channel, and seek their comments and analyses in both informal and formal ways.

6. **Use instructors to do what they do best.** Initiate an internal train-the-trainer program, led by your own outstanding instructors, so that any employee can learn instructional skills. Upgrade your staff with new skills and pass them on.

7. **Hire a consultant** knowledgeable in instructional design and evaluation to help you create electronic performance support systems (EPSS) to be used on the job.

8. **Facilitate teams.** If your workforce is organized in teams, assist team leaders to become instructors. Adapt what you know about group learning to your team context.

9. **Develop training standards for corporate intranet use.** Encourage your workforce to seek training online, but help them be "intentional" about their learning.

10. **Insist on being involved in planning for Internet and intranet services.** Be sure that your company maximizes its opportunity to be a learning organization by using only high-quality online learning. Evaluate e-learning programs carefully.

# 12

# How to Evaluate Training

Training managers who see training as a system are generally convinced that continuous feedback helps propel the training function in a company. The management tasks of stating your values, setting standards and developing policies, and monitoring how work is progressing all provide the inputs to the process of evaluating training. Getting evaluation results you and your people can count on and use are the output goals of evaluation.

When you begin to think about developing a strong evaluation component for your operation, think first about how to categorize what you do and what parts of your operation can be looked at separately, without confounding or confusing the way you look at the other parts. For example, you can isolate these typical training operational elements fairly well and evaluate each in a systematic, organized, nonconfusing way:

- The training program as a whole
- Training projects
- The training staff
- Training manuals and materials
- The curriculum
- Individual courses
- Students
- Exercises and tests
- Special team-based training

You want to focus your evaluation so clearly that the results can easily be used to improve that part of your operation. To do this, you need to evaluate each discrete part of training according to standards set for that part, so that the process of evaluation is fair, relevant, and important and so that you're not mixing apples and oranges as you perform your evaluation.

### KEY MANAGEMENT ISSUES

- ***Accuracy.*** Be sure that the specific subject of evaluation is definable, has clear parameters, and can be described correctly and completely.

Be sure that you're going after the right information so that your evaluation results make sense.

- **Ethics.** Be aware as you conduct your evaluation that your conduct will be subject to questions of bias, balance, fairness, nondisclosure, freedom of information, protection of subjects, conflict of interest, credibility, and concerns of general propriety. Design any evaluation with ethical considerations foremost. Review these safeguards with someone you trust before embarking on your evaluation.

- **Practicality.** Be sure that everyone involved in an evaluation can see the point of going through all the data collection, observations, and cost that generally go along with it. Schedule your evaluation at a time when your business can tolerate the extra time that evaluation activities might consume. Or better yet, build evaluation time and expense into all facets of your operation. Be sure that evaluation outcomes have a fairly good shot at making a positive difference to the subject of the evaluation.

- **Usefulness.** Be sure that everyone who will be affected by the evaluation process and results receives the results in a timely and clear fashion. Be sure that information is disseminated with care and that communication channels are open before you report the evaluation results. Don't run the risk of "shooting the messenger." Be sure that the results are usable—that they are collected, documented, and presented in such a way that they can be turned into action for the benefit of business.

- **During.** The issue of "during" is the issue of whether to conduct evaluation activities as work progresses, that is, doing evaluation in a natural setting as projects or courses unfold. This kind of evaluation is known as formative evaluation and is often preferred because of its immediacy.

- **After.** The issue of "after" is the issue of whether to wait until after work is finished to do the evaluation. This kind of evaluation, which seems to be more scientific, is known as summative evaluation. It is often preferred because of its controllability.

- **360 Degrees.** 360 Degree Evaluation, or 360 Degree Feedback as it is often called, is an evaluation process that features primarily peer review of performance and includes performance review by other stakeholders and colleagues. It is a multisource, multirater kind of evaluation that is focused on how a person has done his or her job. It is not a salary review. It frequently features checklist or narrative reviews of team members, subordinates, support staff, supervisors, and sometimes even customers. Many of the checklists and forms in this chapter are appropriate to use in 360 Degree Evaluation.

  As in any multirater evaluation program, with 360 Degree Evaluation it is important to use valid and consistent evaluation instruments—that is, the same checklist for all constituents—so that the person or thing (project, program, training materials) being evaluated can receive tabulated evaluation results that are valid. It's important not to "mix apples and oranges" during multirater assessments of all sorts. Accurate and useful results must be the goal.

■ ***Levels of Performance.*** In recent years it has been common to see "Kirkpatrick's 4 Levels" of evaluation in the professional literature about training. For many years, trainers and training managers worried only about continuing to fill up classrooms with more and more variety of training. We often got salary increases as training managers by the proof of higher numbers of students and more crowded weekly schedules of classes in our training centers. Conscientious training managers also worried about evaluating progress toward objectives for learning during class, and we devised ways to do "pretests" and "posttests" of our trainees, thus being able to show our bosses and our trainees' bosses that our training made a difference.

Times changed, however, and we needed an evaluation model that recognized the benefits—real dollars and cents benefits—of training as it affected business goals and company profits. Kirkpatrick's 4 Levels seemed to fill this need. Donald Kirkpatrick, a professor from Wisconsin, and others especially from the mid-1980s to the present began talking loudly about the outcomes and the cost-effectiveness of training. During this period, too, the emphasis shifted from what was learned in corporate classrooms to how a person performed on the job after training.

Kirkpatrick articulated these levels of the effects of training, and urged trainers everywhere to evaluate each level in order to justify the resources spent on training:

| | | |
|---|---|---|
| Level 1 | Reaction | (how they liked the training experience) |
| Level 2 | Learning | (if they learned new knowledge, skills, attitudes) |
| Level 3 | Behavior | (if they acted differently back on the job) |
| Level 4 | Results | (how profits or production increased after training) |

■ ***Benchmarking.*** The process known as benchmarking grew out of the Total Quality Management movement, spurred on by the criteria for the Malcolm Baldrige National Quality Award, which includes a requirement for benchmarking by companies seeking the award. Benchmarking is the process by which a company seeks good ideas from other companies in order to make changes. Benchmarking usually involves a team visit to an outstanding company or department within a company in order to set benchmarks of quality against which to measure one's own progress toward similar goals.

Training is often an operation that is benchmarked. Many of the checklists and forms in this chapter can form the basis for asking benchmarking questions. Any standards document is a good place to begin.

# Chapter 12 Checklists

## To Help You Plan Evaluation

This section of the chapter contains three kinds of evaluation checklists for managers:

- Program evaluation checklists
- Checklists for courses
- Checklists to determine if trainees have learned anything

Use these checklists at the start of planning and evaluation, during the evaluation to stay on track, or after the evaluation to help refocus your objectivity as you reexamine the items in the checklist.

The forms that follow the section of checklists provide you with ready-to-use tools as you engage in the evaluation processes that are right for your own situation.

**LIST OF EVALUATION CHECKLISTS**

| | |
|---|---|
| 12.1 | Overall Program Evaluation |
| 12.2 | Training Project Evaluation |
| 12.3 | Evaluation Documentation |
| 12.4 | Evaluating Training Staff |
| 12.5 | Evaluating Team Learning |
| 12.6 | Evaluation of Training Materials |
| 12.7 | Doing a Dry Run/Field Test of a Course |
| 12.8 | Course Evaluation for Trainees |
| 12.9 | Course Evaluation for Instructors |
| 12.10 | Formative Evaluation Checklist |
| 12.11 | Evaluation of Tests |

# Evaluation Checklist 12.1
## Overall Program Evaluation

As you evaluate your overall training program, be sure that you emphasize the benefits training provides to the company as a whole—to its profitability, its provision of quality services and products, and its viability within your local community and the larger business world. In order to do this, you must be sure that your training operations are organized and documented in a way that facilitates getting the information that will help you see how you're carrying your weight of corporate responsibility.

Check these items before your overall training program evaluation begins:

\_\_\_\_\_ 1. Standards exist to define an adequate training program.

\_\_\_\_\_ 2. Operational guidelines exist.

\_\_\_\_\_ 3. Standards reflect the actual program.

\_\_\_\_\_ 4. Operational guidelines include current special projects.

\_\_\_\_\_ 5. Corporate accounting practices reflect the way training does business.

\_\_\_\_\_ 6. Training facilities and equipment information is current.

\_\_\_\_\_ 7. Training files are up-to-date.

\_\_\_\_\_ 8. Advertising and promotional materials are grouped together and accessible.

\_\_\_\_\_ 9. Training cost data are available.

\_\_\_\_\_ 10. Training program goals are realistic.

\_\_\_\_\_ 11. Your training organization chart and job descriptions are current.

\_\_\_\_\_ 12. Key contact persons will be available during planned evaluation activities.

\_\_\_\_\_ 13. Roles of evaluator and employees are clarified.

\_\_\_\_\_ 14. Your expectations regarding the frequency, timing, and format of communications and reports are clarified.

\_\_\_\_\_ 15. The evaluator's credentials and acceptance in your company have been verified with anyone at any level who might possibly object.

\_\_\_\_\_ 16. The evaluation time line is realistic.

# Evaluation Checklist 12.2

## Training Project Evaluation

Training operations are often organized into projects. This happens because training is a responsive business function, changing to accommodate new needs for understanding, information, and skills. Training projects come and go; it's always wise to evaluate a project in order to be accountable to the customer, the demographic shifts, the turn of economics, or the business development that created the need for the project in the first place.

Check these items as you prepare to evaluate a project:

_____ 1. Each project has a beginning and an end.

_____ 2. Each project has objectives—yours and the customer's.

_____ 3. Projects are defined accurately.

_____ 4. Project scheduling information is up-to-date—planning and projected schedules as well as actual schedules.

_____ 5. Responsibility lines are clearly drawn.

_____ 6. Cost data are complete and cover salary, materials, equipment, purchased services, overhead, travel, and sales.

_____ 7. Project accountability structures exist for cost, content, and communication.

# Evaluation Checklist 12.3

## Evaluation Documentation

Evaluation documentation comes in two varieties—that which you routinely collect in the course of your many operations and that which is specifically designed to record and report information during the processes of evaluation. Pay attention to both kinds of documentation as you engage in program evaluation.

Consider these:

\_\_\_\_\_ 1. A list of training files and their contents is current and available.

\_\_\_\_\_ 2. Your evaluator knows what kind of results documentation you expect and when you want it.

\_\_\_\_\_ 3. You have specified what style of writing (e.g., outline, complete sentences, graphs, slide copy, case examples) you want for your results documents.

\_\_\_\_\_ 4. You've considered audiotape, videotape, and computer input/output as documentation possibilities, in addition to written reports and notes.

\_\_\_\_\_ 5. You have checked all documentation instruments (e.g. questionnaires, interview schedules, checklists, experimental designs, tests) that your evaluator intends to use before evaluation begins.

\_\_\_\_\_ 6. You and your evaluator have agreed on the list of persons to be questioned regarding training information.

\_\_\_\_\_ 7. You have notified all persons with whom your evaluator will interact in order to facilitate the collection of data.

\_\_\_\_\_ 8. You and your evaluator have agreed on the list of persons who will receive evaluation reports, in what format each person's report will be presented, and when the reports will occur.

\_\_\_\_\_ 9. You have built in enough time for people to respond to evaluation results. You have established an atmosphere that is open to feedback, and you have planned for feedback to occur.

\_\_\_\_\_ 10. You are committed to using the results of evaluation and have designed your evaluation documentation with this commitment in mind. The practical design of your documentation makes it easy for results to be used for program improvement.

# Evaluation Checklist 12.4
## Evaluating Training Staff

No one is more important to the success of your training program than your staff. They deserve to understand what you expect of them and how well they're meeting your expectations. They deserve to be able to build their careers while working for you to accomplish your goals. Staff evaluation is done for many reasons—to determine merit pay increases, bonuses, ranking, promotion, transfer, downsizing, career development, change in job responsibilities, or any other reason that you believe will improve the way you run training.

When doing any kind of staff evaluation, consider these items:

\_\_\_\_\_ 1. Your evaluation objectives are clear to your staff.

\_\_\_\_\_ 2. You have reviewed rights of persons to be evaluated in the following areas: law, ethics, courtesy, and common sense. Your evaluation design reflects these considerations.

\_\_\_\_\_ 3. You have checked your corporate personnel policies and practices to be sure your training staff evaluation is not in conflict with general corporate evaluations.

\_\_\_\_\_ 4. You have specific objectives and procedures for staff evaluation and have shared these with your staff.

\_\_\_\_\_ 5. You have communicated in writing your commitment to confidentiality and protection of sources.

\_\_\_\_\_ 6. You have given your staff fair notice regarding the timing and procedures of evaluation.

\_\_\_\_\_ 7. Job descriptions are current and realistic.

\_\_\_\_\_ 8. Performance standards are specified for discrete groups of employees and for individuals where that is appropriate. (The same standards probably do not apply for all staff.)

\_\_\_\_\_ 9. Your staff evaluation design includes provision for staff to respond in writing to evaluation results as part of permanent records of the training department.

# Evaluation Checklist 12.5

## Evaluating Team Learning

With the proliferation of types of teams with a wide range of operational goals in today's workplaces comes the need for evaluation of the "learning work" of individuals in the team and of the team as an entity.

Teams of all sorts need members to develop their interpersonal skills such as listening, responding, and participating; their leadership skills such as mentoring, facilitating, and influencing; their support skills such as providing services and contributing to the work of the team; and their cognitive or mental skills such as innovative thinking, ability to solve problems, and fine-tuning their decision-making processes. Training managers will be called upon to design evaluation programs and measurement instruments that address how the team learned in these various areas of skill development. Here are some guidelines for developing evaluation of team learning:

_____ 1. Key evaluation questions to the actual tasks of teamwork.

_____ 2. Evaluate both the content and the processes that are necessary for teamwork.

_____ 3. Get consensus from team members as to who will evaluate them and how the results will be used.

_____ 4. Communicate often with team members about the standards for team performance. Be sure that each person being evaluated knows what the standards are for individual performance within the team and for performance of the team as a whole.

_____ 5. Use a variety of measures: rating scales, surveys, observation, analysis of data, interviews, open-ended written questions, etc.

_____ 6. Involve those to be evaluated in the development of measurement instruments.

_____ 7. Create easy-to-read feedback forms and data summary sheets to report results.

# Evaluation Checklist 12.6

## Evaluation of Training Materials

Your training materials should be evaluated according to standards that specify content, instructional design, and graphic design. It's a good idea to devise a way for the instructional materials used in courses, conferences, and seminars to be evaluated during their development as well as after they have been presented to trainees.

Consider these items:

\_\_\_\_\_ 1. Standards exist for content of training materials.

\_\_\_\_\_ 2. Standards exist for instructional strategy.

\_\_\_\_\_ 3. Standards exist for style, graphic presentation, and production of training materials.

\_\_\_\_\_ 4. Materials standards cover manuals, books, handouts, curriculum, guides, catalogs, brochures, newsletters, job aids, slides, overheads, films, tapes, and online training materials.

\_\_\_\_\_ 5. Standards cover training products (videotapes, slides, manuals, guides) purchased from vendors or through mail order catalogs.

\_\_\_\_\_ 6. Readability level is considered.

\_\_\_\_\_ 7. Policies are clear regarding bias and stereotypes.

\_\_\_\_\_ 8. Printed material interfaces with electronic media are considered in the development of evaluation standards.

\_\_\_\_\_ 9. Standards applied to trainee manuals focus on the uses of learning.

\_\_\_\_\_ 10. The forms used to evaluate training materials record data in an efficient way that makes resulting modifications of materials easy and cost-effective.

\_\_\_\_\_ 11. There is enough time after evaluation results are received to make changes to training materials before they are used again with trainees.

# Evaluation Checklist 12.7
## Doing a Dry Run/Field Test of a Course

Field testing is the process of running through your proposed training with an audience that is very similar to the target audience for which the training was designed. Field testing allows you to see whether your training "teaches right." Training is like a play—it has to be presented or experienced in order to have meaning, and it needs a dress rehearsal to be sure that all of the elements of success are designed well and can function together.

Consider these items when you field test a course or other training event:

_____ 1. Any separate training event (course, seminar, workshop, conference, videotape showing) has separate guidelines for preview or field test prior to its use with paying customers.

_____ 2. A sample audience for the specific training event has been identified so that the field test can be accomplished with an audience that adequately represents the true audience.

_____ 3. Field test evaluation forms have been developed for use by the sample audience during field testing.

_____ 4. The location, environment, materials, and equipment of the field test are very similar to those of the actual training.

_____ 5. The sample audience has been requested to provide evaluation input in a structured way during the field test. They know this before they attend.

_____ 6. The evaluator instructs the sample audience before the training event begins in how to document their comments and coordinates the comments of the sample audience.

# Evaluation Checklist 12.8

## Course Evaluation for Trainees

The person to whom training is presented is the best person to tell you if that training was any good. In order for you to have a baseline for analysis across all trainees who took that course, trainees must respond in a structured way, either by completing a questionnaire that you administer one-to-one or by filling out an evaluation form distributed by the instructor near the end of the class. Don't forget to leave time or space on a form for a trainee to elaborate or explain a response.

Be sure that these kinds of items are included in the evaluation:

_____ 1. Difficulty of accomplishing the stated objectives

_____ 2. Clarity of expression of the objectives

_____ 3. Relevance of content to the trainee's job

_____ 4. Completeness of content

_____ 5. Sequence of topics

_____ 6. Opportunity to learn through exercises and practice

_____ 7. Quality of handouts and course materials

_____ 8. Comfort of the training facility

_____ 9. Ease of use of equipment required during training

_____ 10. Instructor's style

_____ 11. Instructor's preparation

_____ 12. Applicability of new skills/knowledge to the job

_____ 13. Would you recommend this training to others? Who? Why?

# Evaluation Checklist 12.9

## Course Evaluation for Instructors

Don't overlook your instructor's opinion about the quality of the course that he or she has just taught. Often the instructor is not the person who wrote the course; in such cases, the instructor's evaluation can give you invaluable feedback about "how the course teaches." Your instructor's opinions are very useful as you modify and update courses and the learning spaces in which they're given.

Be sure to allow time or space for the instructor to explain responses and offer suggestions for improvement.

Consider these items when you ask your instructor to evaluate a course:

\_\_\_\_\_ 1. Adequacy of student prerequisite knowledge and skills

\_\_\_\_\_ 2. Appropriateness of learning objectives

\_\_\_\_\_ 3. Appropriateness of instructional delivery techniques

\_\_\_\_\_ 4. Completeness/accuracy of course content

\_\_\_\_\_ 5. Organization of course content

\_\_\_\_\_ 6. Quality of handouts and manuals

\_\_\_\_\_ 7. Ease of use of equipment

\_\_\_\_\_ 8. Adequacy of facilities

\_\_\_\_\_ 9. Administration support (promotion, registration, billing)

\_\_\_\_\_ 10. Scheduling and length of course

\_\_\_\_\_ 11. Accuracy of catalog description of the course

# Evaluation Checklist 12.10

## Formative Evaluation Checklist

The best and most useful kind of achievement measures are those that allow students to show the instructor how much they've learned at many different points during the course. This is called "formative" evaluation and is contrasted with the "summative" evaluation or end-of-process measurement sometimes done at the end of a course (college final exams are summative).

Formative evaluation involves checking, verifying, and confirming and is often done quickly and informally by question and answer as the course is being taught. A good instructor typically does this kind of trainee evaluation several times during each fifteen-minute segment of class time. Formative evaluation, also known as "in-process" evaluation, encourages restructure of training as it goes along.

As a manager of training, you can check your courses for these considerations that affect formative evaluation:

_____ 1. The course is designed to encourage trainee participation.

_____ 2. The instructor has a reputation for getting trainees involved.

_____ 3. The course content seems complete and logically outlined.

_____ 4. Course objectives are clear and can be measured.

_____ 5. There are three to six logical breaks per hour in the course. These may signal logical times for trainee evaluation. The course is written to encourage feedback from instructor to trainee at the end of learning sequences.

_____ 6. The instructor can give you examples of the kinds of evaluation questions he or she might use and point out sections of the course where evaluation might occur.

# Evaluation Checklist 12.11

## Evaluation of Tests

If you choose to do more formal testing of trainees and use multiple-choice or fill-in-the blank tests either on paper or online, be sure that the test questions are valid—that is, that you are testing what the course contained and the instructor taught.

Here are some guidelines for evaluating tests:

\_\_\_\_\_ 1. Each test item is specifically related to the course.

\_\_\_\_\_ 2. The wording of each item is very clear.

\_\_\_\_\_ 3. The test is not too easy or too hard. All items are consistent with each other in difficulty.

\_\_\_\_\_ 4. All test items are important to the trainee's job.

\_\_\_\_\_ 5. All test items are free of biased language.

\_\_\_\_\_ 6. The test as a whole has been tried out on a group of "fake" students and revised if necessary.

# Chapter 12 Forms
## To Help You to Evaluate Training

The forms, charts and structured documents on the following pages provide useful tools for engaging in the various forms of evaluation required in the training operation. These include evaluation of program, staff, materials, courses, tests, and trainees.

**LIST OF EVALUATION FORMS**

- **12.1** Authorization to Begin Evaluation
- **12.2** Training Program Standards
- **12.3** Project Monitoring Form (Formative Evaluation)
- **12.4** Program by Objectives Evaluation Report (Summative Evaluation)
- **12.5** Departmental Self-Study Problem Analysis Chart
- **12.6** Training Staff Evaluation Form
- **12.7** Criteria for Evaluating Training Materials
- **12.8** Field Testing
- **12.9** Course Evaluation Form (Trainee)
- **12.10** Course Evaluation Form (Instructor)
- **12.11** Evaluation of Tests
- **12.12** Skill Observation Form

**Evaluation Form** 12.1
**AUTHORIZATION TO BEGIN EVALUATION**

> **How to Use This Form**
> 1. Fill in the identifier information. Carefully identify the subject of the evaluation. Specify no more than five objectives. Verify these with any significant other person, e.g., your boss or key staff members.
> 2. Assemble the initial working documents to pass on to your evaluator, and note the date on which you do.
> 3. Decide who else should see this form. List their names on the form. Copy this form and circulate it to those who will be affected.

Subject of evaluation _____

Objectives of evaluation:

- 
- 
- 
- 

Evaluator _____ Authorized by _____

Start date _____ Final report due on _____

Interim reports due _____

Documents provided:

| date | document |
|------|----------|
| ____ | Training Program Standards |
| ____ | Organization Chart |
| ____ | List of Training Files |
| ____ | List of Key Contact Persons |
| ____ |  |
| ____ |  |

Copies to: _____
_____

**Evaluation Form 12.2**
**TRAINING PROGRAM STANDARDS**

> **How to Establish Training Program Standards**
> 1. State your philosophy of training. Begin with "We believe that . . ."
> 2. Define what you mean by "program." Put it in the larger context of development of human resources, employee productivity, and quality of services and products. List your program's major components.
> 3. Specify operational objectives by using percents, fractions of deviation, customer requirements, tolerance levels, mastery targets, etc.
> 4. Describe the processes you intend to follow as you manage the department. Consider separately needs analysis, design and development, presentation/implementation, monitoring, and feedback.
> 5. State your commitment to evaluation. Include a time line, specify a format, and state the uses you intend for evaluation results.

1. Philosophy of training


2. Definition of the training program
   - 
   - 
   - 

3. Operational objectives
   - 
   - 
   - 
   - 
   - 

4. Process standards


5. Evaluation

**Evaluation Form 12.3**
**PROJECT MONITORING FORM (Formative Evaluation)**

### How to Make a Project Profile

This is a graphic summary of a specified time during which a project has been implemented—e.g., two weeks, one month, six months. It is a monitoring tool to be used by an evaluator to summarize observations, interviews, and document reviews that form the backup support data to this profile. It can easily be made into an overhead transparency, PowerPoint presentation, or chart to focus discussions in staff or task force meetings.

To complete the profile, place an X on the scale line at the appropriate point for each item. Connect the Xs vertically to form a line profile.

Project title _____

Period of evaluation _____

                                                              no                        yes

<u>Project Performance</u>
1. Products/deliverables are available according     _____
   to specifications.
2. Inputs to the project are sufficient, e.g.,       _____
   information, software, support.
3. Project acceptance by client is apparent.         _____

<u>Project Management</u>
1. Schedule is being met.                            _____

2. Feedback is adequate.                             _____

3. Project staff is effective.                       _____

4. Costs are justified.                              _____

5. Financial records are current.                    _____

<u>Evaluator's Comments</u>:

**Evaluation Form 12.4**
**PROGRAM BY OBJECTIVES EVALUATION REPORT (Summative Evaluation)**

### How to Use This Report Form

1. Have a stack of these forms, one for each objective of the program being evaluated. Fill in a different objective on each form.
2. Notice that the form is divided by a dotted line. The top half is information that you and your evaluator should fill out together before evaluation begins. The bottom half is for the evaluator to fill out as a result of evaluation activities.
3. "Findings" describe.
4. "Conclusions" synthesize and tell why.
5. "Recommendations" suggest what to do.

Objective #_____ "_____"

What to look for when evaluating this objective

- 
- 
- 

Best procedures to follow

- 
- 
- 

Where to get help

| people | documents |
|--------|-----------|
| •      | •         |
| •      | •         |
| •      | •         |

- - - - - - - - - - - - - - - - - - - - - - - - - - - - - - - - - -

Findings:

Conclusions:

Recommendations:

**Evaluation Form 12.5**
**DEPARTMENTAL SELF-STUDY PROBLEM ANALYSIS CHART**

### How to Use This Chart
1. Modify the left column to reflect your current needs.
2. Work with your program standards document and reports such as end of course evaluations, budgets, and consultant contracts as you complete the "if . . . then" columns, line by line. (Examples are shown in the first block.)
3. Make a copy of this chart for each key staff member. Meet periodically with your staff and together fill out the chart, reaching consensus in each category.
4. Focus on a specific problem in each category, e.g.:

| Operational Category | If . . . . . | Then . . . . . | Person Responsible |
|---|---|---|---|
| **Courses** | | | |
| Executive | only 10% trained | change rewards | John |
| Supervisory | 6 complaints re: length | delete 1-1/2 days | Shirley |
| Operations | need new SPC course | find qualified vendor | Chuck |
| Clerical | 3 new hires | need training by 8/10 | Jane |
| **Support** | | | |
| Supplies | blank VHS tape is gone | order 3 cases | Jane |
| Materials | manuals need new logo | talk to graphics dept. | Jane |
| Equipment | | | |
| . . . | | | |

*(continues)*

**Evaluation Form 12.5 (continued)**

| Operational Category | If . . . . . | Then . . . . . | Person Responsible |
|---|---|---|---|
| **Courses** | | | |
| Executive | | | |
| Supervisory | | | |
| Operations | | | |
| Clerical | | | |
| **Support** | | | |
| Supplies | | | |
| Materials | | | |
| Equipment | | | |
| Facilities | | | |
| Overhead | | | |
| **Purchased Services** | | | |
| Consultants | | | |
| Artists | | | |
| Vendors | | | |
| **Department Expense** | | | |
| Travel/ Entertainment | | | |
| Conferences | | | |
| Books/ Subscriptions | | | |
| Courses | | | |

**Evaluation Form 12.6**
**TRAINING STAFF EVALUATION FORM**

### How to Use This Form

Caution: This is a personnel evaluation, a legal document for permanent file. Use this form with great care.

1. Be sure that the employee knows the performance goals and the time targets for accomplishing them at the beginning of each evaluation period (one year, six months, three months, etc.).
2. Be sure that the employee knows at the beginning of the evaluation period the times and functions for which he/she will be held accountable.
3. If you use a generic staff evaluation form, be sure you have the option of customizing it to reflect accurately the duties and responsibilities of training. Check any modifications with your personnel officer.
4. Be sure to give your employee a chance to put in writing his/her accomplishments according to the performance goals and time targets.
5. Be sure your employee has a chance to sign the form in agreement or disagreement with your evaluation. Provide space on the form for employee explanation.
6. Be sure that the employee's job description matches the evaluation form.
7. Expand the sections of this form into as many pages as you need.

1. Evaluation period: _____

2. Performance goals and time targets for the evaluation period:

                                                                                 <u>date</u>

- 
- 
- 
- 
- 

3. Supervisor's highlights of employee's accomplishments (break down into technical accomplishments and human relations accomplishments). Attach a separate page for the employee's statement of accomplishments.

*(continues)*

**Evaluation Form 12.6 (continued)**

---

4. Areas for improvement

5. Plans for career growth (on the job development, external opportunities, company-sponsored training)

6. Skills summary

    An X in the appropriate column indicates an overall evaluation of training skills.

    NA  Not Applicable
    U   Unsatisfactory
    F   Fair
    S   Satisfactory
    E   Exceeds Expectations
    O   Outstanding

    | | NA | U | F | S | E | O |
    |---|---|---|---|---|---|---|
    | 1. Initiative | | | | | | |
    | 2. Teamwork | | | | | | |
    | 3. Content contribution | | | | | | |
    | 4. Customer relationships | | | | | | |
    | 5. Communications | | | | | | |
    | 6. Task management | | | | | | |
    | 7. Resourcefulness | | | | | | |
    | 8. Time management | | | | | | |
    | 9. Accuracy | | | | | | |
    | 10. Giving feedback | | | | | | |
    | 11. Self-monitoring | | | | | | |

**Evaluation Form 12.7**
**CRITERIA FOR EVALUATING TRAINING MATERIALS**

### How to Use This Form

1. Use this form to evaluate any support materials to be used during a lesson. Such items include manuals, job aids, photocopied handouts, PowerPoint slides, overhead transparencies, case studies, videotapes, online examples, reference books, and texts.
2. Evaluate together all of the materials associated with a course. Or evaluate all items in a category together, such as all overheads, all videotapes, all texts.
3. Rate each item with a value in each column. Give concrete suggestions for improvement for any "U" and "M" designations.
4. Give detailed feedback to persons who can most easily make corrections. Correct problems as soon after evaluation as possible. This "formative evaluation" catches errors early and corrects them before they are compounded. It also saves the embarrassment and expense of having upper management or trainee customers find mistakes at the end of the development process.
5. Be sure that copied sources have been credited. Don't violate any copyright laws.
6. This form works well with a team approach to evaluation. Give each team member a form to complete individually. Then get together as a team to discuss commonalities and discrepancies.

Key to rating:
    U  Unsatisfactory                       S  Satisfactory
    M  Minor changes required       E  Excellent quality

Categories for rating:

| | |
|---|---|
| Graphics: | Image size, "white" space, clean lines, consistency, use of color, labeling |
| Content: | Completeness, scope, accuracy, relevance |
| Instructional Value: | Clear relationship to learning objectives, necessary level of material matched to the level of course content |
| Readability: | Difficulty, grammar and syntax, word use, vocabulary |

*(continues)*

**Evaluation Form 12.7 (continued)**

Place the appropriate letter, U, M, S, or E in the appropriate cell of the matrix. Provide specific references in the "Correction Suggestions" column to speed up revision time.

| Item Evaluated | Graphics | Content | Instructional Value | Readability | Correction Suggestions |
|---|---|---|---|---|---|
| 1. | | | | | |
| 2. | | | | | |
| 3. | | | | | |
| 4. | | | | | |
| 5. | | | | | |
| 6. | | | | | |

**Evaluation Form 12.8**
**FIELD TESTING**

### How to Use This Form
Provide this form for use by observers of field tests or trial runs of a new course.

1. Have at least three persons act as course evaluators, sitting in on the field test of the course. These persons can be students taking the field-tested course. Another option is for all students taking the field-tested course to function as evaluators. (If you want them to do this as well as be students, be sure to ask them ahead of class to be sure that they feel comfortable in the dual role.)
2. Meet with the evaluators, instructor, and course designer immediately after the field test to review evaluation results. If you, the training manager, can't be present to chair the meeting, delegate someone to do the job for you, be sure that there is someone in charge of the evaluation and someone taking notes to facilitate changes. Set yourself up for efficiency as you enter the revision process. Evaluation feedback is a critical step in the field test. Build in the time on the last day of the field test course to give and receive the feedback.
3. Seek feedback as soon as the course is finished; don't let people leave the room until you have it. Make corrections to the course speedily. Allow at least one week for corrections after the field test and before the actual course begins. Involve enough of the right people in the field test so that you get valid and constructive criticisms.

Instructions: Place an X in either the "S" or "U" column. Explain any "U" evaluation by suggesting corrective action.

|  | S Satisfactory | U Unsatisfactory | Corrective Action Suggested |
|---|---|---|---|
| **Course Environment** | | | |
| Media | | | |
| Software | | | |
| Equipment | | | |
| Learning space | | | |
| Light, heat, air | | | |
| Hospitality | | | |
| **Course Design** | | | |
| Objectives | | | |
| Content | | | |
| Organization | | | |

*(continues)*

**Evaluation Form 12.8 (continued)**

| | | | |
|---|---|---|---|
| Tests, exercises | | | |
| Manuals | | | |
| **Instructional Methods** | | | |
| Rapport | | | |
| Explanations | | | |
| Command of content | | | |
| Interactions | | | |
| Respect for students | | | |
| Timing | | | |
| | | | |

**Evaluation Form 12.9**
**COURSE EVALUATION FORM (Trainee)**

### How to Use This Form
1. Distribute forms to all trainees in the course. Do this at a logical break in the instruction—about two hours before the end of the course.
2. Tell trainees that you appreciate their thoughtful responses in their role as evaluator. Thank each one as the completed form is turned in to you.
3. Make it clear that putting their names on the form is optional. What you really want is their opinions about the quality of the course, including specific suggestions for improvement.
4. Allow adequate time—at least twenty minutes. Stop class a little early if necessary to get a careful response. Encourage "additional comments."

Instructions:
Place an X in the column 1,2,3,4 to represent your evaluation of each item.

Negative 1 | 2 | 3 | 4 Positive

Learning Objectives
 1. Appropriate, learnable, pitched right
 2. Organized to facilitate learning
 3. Clearly stated
 4. Exercises helped accomplish objectives

Content
 5. Accurate
 6. Current
 7. Adequate in scope
 8. Sequenced properly

Course Setting
 9. Comfortable
10. Quality materials and visual aids
11. Adequate equipment

Instructor's Delivery
12. Course agenda and timing of lessons
13. Engaging presentation style
14. Respectful of trainee contributions
15. Preparation and expertise

Relevance to the Job
16. Course content relevance
17. Relevance of instructional techniques
18. New skills useable right away

*(continues)*

**Evaluation Form 12.9 (continued)**

19. New skills will save time
20. New skills will save money
21. Your confidence level to use this training on your job

**Additional comments and suggestions for improvement:**
_____
_____
_____
_____

Would you recommend this course to others?   Who?   Why?
_____
_____
_____
_____

**Evaluation Form 12.10**
**COURSE EVALUATION FORM (Instructor)**

> **How to Use This Form**
> **Don't Overlook This Form**
> 1. Remember that part of good learning is good teaching. At the end of a course, your instructors should be formally asked for their evaluation of how the course "teaches." Improvements from an instructor's perspective can often yield big results in terms of improvement of learning.
> 2. If the instructor is in a hurry to leave the classroom, don't insist that he/she stay to complete the form. Give your instructor a week to do it at a more reflective and more leisurely pace.

Instructions:
Check the Yes or No column after each item. Please explain your response, offering suggestions for improvement.

| | No | Yes |
|---|---|---|

1. **Prerequisites.** Did all trainees have adequate course entry skills/knowledge?
   Explain: _____

2. **Objectives.** Were all trainees able to achieve the learning objectives?
   Explain: _____

3. **Content.** Was content adequate and structured well?
   Explain: _____

4. **Delivery.** Did you have any instructional delivery problems?
   Explain: _____

5. **Materials.** Were handouts, manuals, and aids of good quality?
   Explain: _____

6. **Equipment.** Was equipment adequate and in good working condition?
   Explain: _____

7. **Facilities.** Were facilities comfortable and supportive to teaching and learning?
   Explain: _____

**Evaluation Form 12.11**
**EVALUATION OF TESTS**

### How to Use This Form

1. Think about what kind of test will best represent the content and skills you've designed into your course. Your options are many; some common ones are listed below.
2. Decide when you want to administer a test—at the end of each unit, in small doses every fifteen minutes, at the end of a three-day course, etc.
3. Check for validity—be sure your objectives for learning and your tests of those objectives are actually covered in the course. Be dispassionate and very analytical as you examine the test questions against the content of the course.
4. Be sure that the test is not too easy or too hard. Be sure that you give individual trainees the opportunity to meet or at least to approach your standards.
5. Decide how to notify trainees of the test results. Tell them ahead of time; create no surprises for trainees or their supervisors. Remember that obtaining useful results is the key.
6. Build in time for scoring. Aim for immediate feedback to trainees. Get help in administering the test or in scoring if you need it.

Formats of test items are listed alphabetically:

| Format of Test Item | Hard to Score | Easy to Score | Notes on Test Administration |
|---|---|---|---|
| 1. Case study | X | | |
| 2. Demonstration | | X | |
| 3. Direct question | | X | |
| 4. Drill and practice | | X | |
| 5. Fill in the blank | | X | |
| 6. Lab exercise | | X | |
| 7. Multiple choice | | X | |
| 8. Simulation | X | | |
| 9. Troubleshooting | X | | |
| 10. Written narrative | X | | |

**Evaluation Form 12.12**
**SKILL OBSERVATION FORM**

### How to Use This Form

1. This is a specialized form for testing an employee on the performance of some skill. It is used by an evaluator who records what he/she observes.
2. This kind of rating is useful at points of transition from one job classification to another and at the end of skills training. It can also be useful for analysis of training needs to indicate current skill performance before training begins.
3. Use this form in conjunction with a task list that includes each individual task that has to be done correctly in order to master the skill under scrutiny.

For example:

| Task | Cues to Good Performance | Rating 1 2 3 | Observer's Comments |
|---|---|---|---|
| 1. Locate cursor | 3 or fewer eye movements | 2 | Spent too much time in upper right quad |

Key: 1 = Unsuccessful; requires more training
2 = Right idea, but needs practice
3 = Proficiency demonstrated correctly

| Task | Cues to Good Performance | Rating 1 2 3 | Observer's Comments |
|---|---|---|---|

1.

2.

3.

4.

5.

# Chapter 12 More Information on How to Evaluate Training

## Program, Projects, Material, or People

Evaluation of training, no matter what evaluation subject is chosen, can be expected to result in an improvement, perhaps even an innovation. This change may come in the form of cancellation, continuation, modification, promotion, installation, purchase, sale, recycle, transfer, or other decision involving the initiation—and therefore the management—of change.

Do not engage in evaluation lightly. You do yourself and your organization a big disservice if you go simply for the smiles test at the end of a course, an automatic safe across-the-board salary increase for jobs well done, a token update or cosmetic change to your training materials only when they seem a little shabby, or a new budget based only on a percent increase over last year's budget.

Plan evaluations with rigor, carry them out fairly, and implement the changes they produce with efficiency and care. Good evaluation management pays off.

## The Nature of Standards

Evaluation of anything—programs, courses, conferences, materials, facilities, people—is a systematic process for determining worth. By nature, evaluation looks at forces and business functions that compete for corporate resources and establishes as accurately as possible the worth of the object in question.

Therefore, accurate and adequate quality standards for the object itself—the conference, the course, the videotape, the media library, the staff position of instructional designer—and for the process of conducting the evaluation are of the utmost importance. The best way to assure good standards is to listen to your customers or users and to your staff.

## Kirkpatrick's 4 Levels

Donald L. Kirkpatrick, professor and consultant, was national president of the American Society for Training and Development (ASTD). He is a widely respected voice on the subject of evaluation of training, and has consistently been writing, speaking, and putting his thoughts into action on the subject. He tells the reader in *Evaluating Training Programs, The Four Levels* (San Francisco: Berrett-Koehler, 1994) that he first wrote about "the four levels" in 1959; it has not been until recently, however, that his ideas have been widely accepted throughout the training community. See Figure 12.1.

**Figure 12.1. Kirkpatrick's 4 levels of evaluation.**

> 1. Reaction—i.e., evaluation of trainees' reaction to training
> 2. Learning—i.e., evaluation of knowledge, skills, attitudes gained
> 3. Behavior—i.e., evaluation of changes in behavior on the job after training
> 4. Results—i.e., evaluation of financial impact on business goals

Perhaps the quality movement has had something to do with a change of focus for trainers; perhaps economic downturns, reengineering, and downsizings have provided the drama necessary to drive change. Whatever the reasons, Kirkpatrick's levels have become, in the last decade, an important foundation block for building a strong evaluation component to your training management.

Above all, Kirkpatrick urges evaluators to look beyond activities and to the business outcomes of training. Numerous articles and studies in the professional training literature document dialogue about getting to evaluating levels three and four. There are even some new studies that talk about level 5, or about variations to Kirkpatrick's four levels. The latest ASTD and *Training Magazine* surveys indicate that we're making slow progress, especially in evaluating level 4, or the business results of training. It's hard to measure the immediate results of learning, and it's even harder to document those results in terms of dollars made or saved.

Some strategies often given for doing this are: indicate with numbers the alignment of performance measures and standards with corporate strategy; show with dollars the linkage between training programs and courses and business objectives; show with percentages the increase in customer satisfaction with services and products in correlation with better trained sales and customer service personnel or better trained engineers and product developers; show with numbers the effects of higher performance levels; show with numbers and percentages that more employees have higher level skills than they did before training.

Kirkpatrick by all means says don't give up evaluating at the lower levels 1 and 2, those two familiar and comfortable levels of "smiles sheets" and training feedback forms, and the measurement of new knowledge, skills, or attitudes (KSAs) learned during the training session. Supporters of his also urge followers to be brave and assertive, recognizing and using correlation as well as causation, qualitative investigation, and quantitative investigation. The main point in all of the deliberation about "the four levels" is for trainers to get out of narrow thinking that has tended to keep trainers hidden behind "objectives," and into the broader and riskier strategic thinking of managers in most other business operations. Kirkpatrick's contribution, in the long run, may be as much that of an evangelist as a theorist. His 1994 book referenced above is worth reading because it is a classic in the field of training management.

## Who Should Be an Evaluator

At about the same time you decide to do an evaluation, you should have a good idea of who will be the evaluator. If the evaluation is being imposed on you, perhaps as part of a routine annual management evaluation or by a program audit triggered by a merger or a lawsuit, you may not have any choice about who your evaluator will be. On the other hand, if you initiate the evaluation, you will choose the person or persons who will be your evaluator.

One of your most important decisions is choosing the right person to do the evaluation. Often, an evaluation team is a good choice. The person or persons who evaluate your operation must first of all be competent to conduct the evaluation in all its parts—data identification, data collection, data analysis, statistics, use of measurement tools such as questionnaires and interviews, and presentation of results. Your evaluator must be trustworthy and acceptable to the people whose jobs might be on the line as a result of evaluation.

Be sure your evaluator has had experience with implementing the standards you've developed for the evaluation subject. If you're evaluating instructor manuals, for example, be sure that your evaluator has had experience developing and using instructor manuals; if you're looking at the total training operation, be sure that your evaluator has been a training manager and has firsthand knowledge of what it takes to make a training operation go. Don't make the mistake of hiring an outsider with a big name if that person's reputation has not been made precisely in the field of the subject of your evaluation, and don't choose an evaluator whose only claim to fame is that he or she has mastered the politics of your company and seems to be the current shining star of the corporation. Check out your probable choice with the folks who report to you and who will undoubtedly be affected by what that evaluator does and says. Be sure your evaluator has superior facilitation, documentation, and communication skills, and take the time to explain and demonstrate exactly how you want your evaluation done.

## Evaluation Terminology You'll Need to Know

There are some basic terms of measurement and statistics that you should be familiar with as you interpret evaluation results and share them with others in your company.

- ***Statistics.*** Statistics is the mathematics of making sense out of collections of data. Statistics often organizes large amounts of disorganized information into understandable and usable numbers; in this sense, it has a summarizing, abbreviating, or condensing function. Using statistics to report the findings of analysis or assessment helps people to comprehend the results of evaluation, the trends of job performance, and the relationships among elements of organizational life; reducing information to simple numerical relationships provides efficient input for decision making and planning—and for "big picture" presentations to upper management.

It's important to remember that data are not information, and information is not behavior. Only the effective *use* of data provides a tool for building a training program—and it's the training program that can ultimately change behavior.

These are the statistics most often used to describe and represent the training operation:

- Statistics—means, medians, modes, and standard deviations—that summarize information through measures of central tendency, dispersion, and measures of variability.
- Statistics that help you place a value on discrepancies. These kinds of statistics are often expressed as probabilities or suggest the effect of one situation upon another. They test the significance of specific effects.
- Statistics that help you see relationships, often expressed in terms of correlation, regression, factor analysis, and matrices and tables.

- ***Measurement terms.*** Closely related measurement terms are those associated with development and use of scales and with the interpretation of performances based on norms or other criteria.

*Varieties of scales.* Scales are commonly used to represent a range of recorded opinion. Good scales provide a range of choices, are logically differentiated, and are equally weighted. Examples are: 5, 4, 3, 2, 1; often, sometimes, never; A, B, C, D, F; plus . . . minus.

Always pay attention to the direction of the scales presented to trainees during evaluation; that is, be sure that the responses lead the respondent's thinking in a consistent fashion, low to high, negative to positive, or poor to excellent. Always provide opportunity for the respondent to explain choices on a scale. Some people find it hard to zero in on only one point on a scale; the rigidity of a scale has to be tempered by freedom of response.

*Norm-referenced performance.* Norm-referenced performance evaluates individual performance against that of a selected group of people. The level of individual performance is often expressed either as a percentile, as a position on the normal curve, or in relation to the average or mean score. For example, if the average score on a typing test given to all persons at your salary-grade level in your department is 60 out of a possible 100 and your score is 80, you scored 20 points above the norm.

*Criterion-referenced performance.* Criterion-referenced performance measures individual performance in relation to a standard, or criterion. Criterion-referenced scores are often expressed as "performing according to standard" or "not performing according to standard." Scores are often expressed in yes or no terms and include the degree of discrepancy from the criterion. A criterion-referenced test is made up of many individual criterion-referenced test items. Here's an example: Assume the mechanic who fixed your flat tire tightened only two of the four bolts that attach your hubcap. That mechanic performed to only 50 percent of the criterion for attaching hubcaps while fixing flat tires. He did not perform according to standard.

## Using Your PC to Generate Evaluation Reports

Making sense of evaluation data is one way to enjoy your personal computer's graphics software. Always keep in mind that training improvement is your goal and that evaluation results should help you achieve that goal. If you have PCs available for use in training management, get yourself a good clear user manual and interpretation counsel if you need it.

Then, armed with your trainee's check marks, frequency counts, correct and incorrect responses, and ratings, choose a statistical representation (e.g. regression line, pie chart, bar graph, mean, or standard deviation) for your evaluation data. Remember that the use to which you put your evaluation results will be the ultimate test of your managerial effectiveness; perform an evaluation only to clarify decision making and facilitate improvement.

Analyzing your evaluation data by using personal computer graphics can help you understand your results and more quickly focus on obvious areas for improvement.

## If You Have Limited Budget and Staff . . .

If you're the only staff member in your operation, talk to one or two of your favorite customers. If you have no customers yet, talk to someone you trust at your level in your company. Jot down in outline form what standards you believe you should follow—for a course, a conference, job performance, instructional delivery—and bounce your ideas off that other person. Don't set standards in a vacuum; the more your standards are verified and recognized, the more empowering they become. Aim for the best quality. Just because you're small doesn't mean you have to be underpowered.

Get someone from your own company—someone who is not in direct competition with you for a share of the corporate budget and who has experience with service functions—to review your program, course, or whatever it is you want evaluated. Offer to do the same to him or her at some later date. Provide documents for that person to review in his or her office, or schedule the event to be evaluated so that it's convenient for that person to attend. Design and print the results forms yourself, and provide your evaluator with all the instruments and evaluation tools to do the job.

Tabulate results by hand, paying special attention to measures of central tendency, especially the mean and median. Feed back the results to those who were evaluated as soon as possible. Follow up the results with an action plan for training improvement.

### If You Have Adequate Budget and Staff . . .

If you're lucky enough to have a sizable training staff and multifaceted training operation, get the whole staff involved in setting or periodically verifying your standards. Recognize that the people who are actually responsible for course authorship, course delivery, sales, media production, conference administration, and facility management are the ones who are most familiar with the realities of making the training business work. They know what's good—and what's reachable.

Get them involved in standards setting through quality teams, task forces, workshops, or questionnaires. Arrange for your staff to get direct input from customers and former trainees. Let the world—and especially your staff—know what you all believe in and what you're working toward.

Choose an evaluator from outside your company—perhaps from a consulting firm specializing in evaluation of operations similar to yours. Consider hiring an evaluation team if your job is large and if you could benefit from several points of view. The objectivity and resources of a third party can help to assure accuracy, thoroughness, and fairness.

Consider doing a self-study prior to hiring an outside evaluator. Your focus on verifying standards, synthesizing, summarizing projects, weeding out useless information, and pulling files together will help save evaluator's time and expense and will prime you and your staff for focused contributions during the evaluator's time with you. Benchmark your evaluation program against several other companies' programs.

Tabulate results by hand, and then enter the variables into whatever graphics system you've chosen. Bounce ideas off one or two colleagues who were among those evaluated to get a good idea of which graphs and charts will be most useful.

Write a paragraph or two of graph interpretation for each graph, and add it to the graph as an attached sheet. Photocopy the graphs and interpretations and distribute them to all concerned. Make overhead transparencies of graphs, and use them in a Results Workshop. Assign improvement tasks at the conclusion of the workshop.

# Appendix
# Models for Individual and Organizational Learning

The following pages contain a selective review of the writing of learning experts whose work has formed the architecture of the fields of education, training, learning, and human performance. These ideas are essential to the process of transfer from learning situation to job. They are especially useful to the training manager in designing and delivering training to achieve high performance.

Key references are included in the following areas: systems thinking, balanced scorecard, Six Sigma—quality, performance technology, situated learning, communities of practice, problem solving, cognitive skills, psychomotor skills, hierarchy of human needs, stages of concern about innovation, habits of successful people, diversity, advancement of women, right brain/left brain, psychological types, memory, conditions of learning, self-study, frames of mind, and emotional intelligence. A working knowledge of these critical areas can provide practical guidance for those charged with creating training that transfers to the job, that improves performance, and that facilitates continuous learning. Models for individual and organizational learning are summarized here.

Literature cited in this Appendix represents a wealth of information culled and synthesized especially for the training manager who must show results of training beyond the evaluation form completed by employees at the end of the course. Text in this Appendix includes the cited author's framework plus this author's commentary regarding its usefulness in achieving the transfer of learning to better performance on the job.

## Systems Thinking

### Key References
Argyris, Chris. *Knowledge for Action: A Guide to Overcoming Barriers to Organizational Change.* San Francisco: Jossey-Bass, 1993.

Senge, Peter. *The Fifth Discipline: The Art and Practice of the Learning Organization.* New York: Doubleday Currency, 1990.

Senge, Peter et al. *The Fifth Discipline Fieldbook: Strategies and Tools for Building A Learning Organization.* New York: Doubleday Currency, 1994.

The work of Harvard professor Chris Argyris (Business School and School of Education) in the 1980s has had an obvious effect on the work of "learning organization" guru Peter Senge. Argyris's thinking is characterized by a systems approach to organizational change through "double loop" effects. The model of double-loop learning is especially useful in understanding how groups work and learn as groups. These are some of the foundations of Argyris's thinking:

1. **Learning occurs whenever errors are detected and corrected.** That is, if you want to build an organization of learners, don't punish people when they make a mistake: punish them if they don't correct the mistake. Find errors fast and fix them fast.

2. **Defensiveness leads to overprotectiveness and is antilearning.** A better choice is to exercise productive reasoning that meets problems head on and solves them. Learning occurs when that protective, self-serving wall is penetrated through productive reasoning.

3. **Double-loop learning** is that which is used to break out of the overall values-actions-consequences system of organizational development to solve a smaller problem within the system. Double-loop learning is that act of penetrating the self-serving wall.

Peter Senge's work has been predominantly centered at Massachusetts Institute of Technology (MIT)'s Center for Organizational Learning at Sloan School of Management. His earlier work (1990) has been supplemented by a newer (1994) book of practical exercises and case studies of implementation of his earlier theories. Both books are constructed on Senge's "5 Disciplines" or lifelong programs of study and practice through which individuals can systematically build learning organizations. These five disciplines are:

1. **Personal Mastery:** Learning how to know and articulate what is best for ourselves, and learning how to encourage all others to do the same.

2. **Mental Models:** Thinking about, reflecting upon, clarifying, and improving our internal thought patterns and how we view the world; knowing ourselves so well that we realize exactly "where we're coming from" on issues.

3. **Shared Vision:** Using our points of view to contribute to constructing a group vision; sharing images, principles, and plans for achieving a better future.

4. **Team Learning:** Learning new skills of expression and collaborative work habits so that the group intelligence is truly greater than the intelligence of the individuals in it.

5. **Systems Thinking:** Thinking differently so that interrelationships are cultivated and plans are made with system effects in mind; seeing wholes instead of parts; getting rid of, forever, the old office game of optimizing your own position at the expense of everyone else.

# Balanced Scorecard

### Key Reference
Kaplan, Robert S. and Norton, David P. *The Balanced Scorecard: Translating Strategy into Action.* Boston: Harvard Business School Press, 1996.

Kaplan and Norton have made a major contribution to the implementation of linkages between measurement and accountability in all areas of business. They developed the idea of a scorecard of a company's core measures in these essential areas:

financial,
customer, and
learning and growth.

Measures are defined in each area; for example, in the "core learning and growth" area, the measures might typically include:

employee satisfaction,
employee retention, and
employee productivity.

Each scorecard contains cells for documentation of goals and measures of objectives to accomplish those goals. Organizations create scorecards for themselves to link rewards with documented accomplishment, to present clear evidence of resource needs, and to demonstrate their own particular learning needs. A simplified model of a scorecard looks something like this.

| *Strategic objectives* | *Strategic measures* |
|---|---|
| Financial | |
| ■ | |
| ■ | |
| ■ | |

| Customer | | |
|---|---|---|
| ■ | | |
| ■ | | |
| ■ | | |
| Learning and growth | | |
| ■ | | |
| ■ | | |
| ■ | | |

Refer to Kaplan and Norton's articles in the *Harvard Business Review* archives, and to the reference cited here for more information.

## Six Sigma—Quality

### Key References

Lowe, Janet. *Welch: An American Icon.* New York: John Wiley and Sons, Inc., 2001.

Stamatis, D. H. "Guidelines for Six Sigma Design Reviews—Part One" in *Quality Digest,* April 2002, pp. 27–31.

Six Sigma is an enduring part of the quality literature; it is a statistical term for products that have a 99.9998 percent quality perfection rate. It was developed at Motorola in 1985, adopted over the years with fanfare by Honeywell, Allied Signal, General Electric, and many others. Six Sigma requires analysis, testing, measurement, and application of results to both products and processes. It can be applied to course development and to the process of managing the training operation.

Six Sigma design reviews can be especially useful in instructional design where a course is created and systematically reviewed by peers and stakeholders during the development process. Peer-to-peer learning is fundamental to Six Sigma design reviews. The basic Six Sigma glossary follows the general "plan—do—check—act" quality system and includes:

DMAIC: Design, Measure, Analyze, Improve, Control
DCOV: Define, Characterize, Optimize, Verify
PMT: Program module teams
QSA: Quality system assessment.

## ISO 9001:2000

### Key Reference

Whittington, Larry. "Ten Tips for Moving to ISO 9001:2000" in *Quality Digest,* April 2002, pp. 49–53.

ISO 9000 in its various evolutions is an international set of standards recognized by users as an expression of quality in products and processes. The ISO 9000:2000 family of standards are available for purchase online at *www.qualitypress.asq.org*. Like the other system and process control models we have outlined in the previous pages of this Appendix, ISO 9001:2000, the latest version, can provide a quality management model for the training operation. These are the essentials:

1. *Plan:* Analyze customer requirements, for example, needs of learners, and set objectives that will achieve the results you want. Establish a quality policy statement.

2. *Do:* Implement the processes defined in the "Plan" phase. Focus on providing appropriate resources—human, technological, and financial.

3. *Check:* Monitor, measure, document, and report results—of training product development and of processes used in managing the operation.

4. *Act:* Focus on continuous improvement of all training products and processes, using results of previous measurement activities. Strive for better performance in both individuals and work processes.

# SCORM

### Key Reference
Welsch, Edward. "SCORM: Clarity of Calamity?" in *OnLine Learning*, summer 2002, pp. 14–18.

SCORM stands for Sharable Content Object Reference Model. It is a set of standards developed in 1997 by the United States Department of Defense as an attempt to coordinate, standardize, and prevent duplication of course content and learning systems resident in the geographically dispersed Department of Defense. The Department of Defense began the project by establishing the Advanced Distributed Learning (ADL) initiative, a collaborative effort between government, industry, and academe. ADL's change was to focus on the "interoperability" of learning management systems, learning tools, and course content. See *www.adlnet.org*. Reusable Learning Objects (RLO) is the goal of development, according to SCORM standards. They are meant to give the e-learning community assurance that time and money are not being wasted by incompatible systems and parts. Annual "Plugfest" conferences/workshops facilitate sharing of user stories and information, and highlight areas for revision of SCORM standards.

These are the major requirements of a SCORM–compatible system for learning:

Content reusability
Content accessibility
Content durability
Content interoperability

## Performance Technology

### Key References
Robinson, Dana Gaines, and Robinson, James C. *Performance Consulting: Moving Beyond Training.* San Francisco: Berrett-Koehler, 1995.

Rummler, Geary A., and Brache, Alan P. *Improving Performance: How to Manage the White Space on the Organization Chart, 2nd edition.* San Francisco: Jossey-Bass: 1995.

Changes in the function of the training manager are most often described by using the word "performance." The Robinson and Robinson book is a popular, easy-to-read explanation of the differences between a training management approach and a performance consulting approach. It is a useful set of tools for moving from training to performance, valuing and enhancing what is best in a training approach, yet moving beyond that. Briefly, the Robinsons give you a number of "maps" for moving from a focus on employees' learning needs to employees' performance needs. They are careful to define terms:

1. **Business Need:** That which is required to carry out the operations of the business.
2. **Performance Need:** That which a person is required to do on the job.
3. **Training Need:** The knowledge, skills, values, and attitudes that people need to learn from a particular training program or experience.
4. **Work Environment Need:** That which must be adapted or fixed in order to provide a supportive environment for high performance.

They make the point in many different ways that the performance consultant is responsible for identifying these four kinds of needs and working with individuals and organizations to take active steps to address all of these needs.

The Rummler and Brache book is an update to an earlier work (1990) of the same title, often credited with clarifying and thus furthering the "process improvement" movement in organizations. A key point that these consultants make is that it's just as important to pay attention to improvement of processes between departments or groups in an organization as it is to your own department's processes. Rummler and Brache urge the reader to view their company as a system, with such features as resources, inputs, processing capabilities, outputs, markets, customers, shareholders, and competition. In short, improvements can be made at

# Models for Individual and Organizational Learning

numerous influence points within such a system in order to affect individual and organizational performance. Their work follows the important groundbreaking work of Thomas Gilbert, who wrote *Human Competence: Engineering Worthy Performance* in 1978 (McGraw-Hill).

The nine performance variables upon which Rummler and Brache's book elaborates are:

1. **Goals:** Organizational goals, process goals, and job goals,
2. **Design:** Organizational design, process design, and job design, and
3. **Management:** Organizational management, process management, and job management. These are the nine variables that can each become a lever to make change that can have impact on the system as a whole.

A performance technology model is found on page 311.

## Situated Learning

### Key Reference
McLellan, Hilary (ed.). *Situated Learning Perspectives.* Englewood Cliffs, NJ: Educational Technology Publications, 1996.

The idea of "situated learning" was first given public view in the late 1980s. It grew primarily out of research into the nature of cognition and the design of learning experiences being conducted in Palo Alto at Xerox Corporation's learning research center. Principal researchers were John Seely Brown, Allan Collins, and Paul Duguid. Other researchers Suchman, Striebel, Lave, Resnick, and Shoenfeld have also published heavily in the field. The McLellan book is a contributed work, full of dialogue about the developing theoretical base of situated learning. The periodical *Educational Technology*, by the same publisher, contains current articles from many of the authors listed above, and others, and is a good source of new ideas in the field.

Some of the key elements of situated learning are:

1. **Knowledge is "situated" in context:** Real-world applications are where knowledge is found.
2. **Learning advances through collaborative social action.**
3. **Reflective thinking must accompany experiential learning.**
4. **One-to-one relationships are important:** Engaging in coaching and passing on stories are important ways to teach and learn.
5. **Learners learn to think about thinking:** Articulation of problem solving and reasoning processes fosters knowledge of self that is critical for finely tuned learning and successful collaboration with others.

6. **Technology is an essential support:** It expands the scope, power, and flexibility of learning resources.

# Communities of Practice

### Key Reference
Wenger, Etienne, McDermott, Richard, and Snyder, William M. *Cultivating Communities of Practice.* Boston: Harvard Business School Press, 2002.

Etienne Wenger has been a leader in developing the concept of "community of practice." This recent book, in collaboration with McDermott and Snyder, demonstrates how to cultivate and nurture these work groups, how to assess their value, and how to prevent them from falling apart.

The authors differentiate Communities of Practice from teams, which they define as a group of individuals committed to a goal, within products that are deliverable and processes that are measurable and accountable. The authors make the point that a Community of Practice is not necessarily defined by its tasks; a Community of Practice is defined by its fundamental commitment to exploring its domain and sharing the relevant knowledge that it discovers. Training managers and team leaders can be facilitative of the formation and the work of Communities of Practice.

Three basic elements are necessary for cultivating a community of practice:

- ***Define Domain.*** Decisions need to be made regarding what the group really cares about and how these issues are connected to the organization's business strategy.

- ***Build Community.*** All of the people-nurturing elements are part of this foundation of Communities of Practice: developing trust, communicating, dealing with conflict, and balancing members' needs.

- ***Develop Practice.*** Becoming proactive about knowledge sharing, sponsoring learning activities, and being a continuous resource for persons within and without the Community of Practice are elements of developing practice.

The authors list six principles for cultivating a Community of Practice:

1. Design for evolution.
2. Open a dialogue between inside and outside perspectives.
3. Invite different levels of participation.
4. Develop both public and private community spaces.

5. Focus on value.
6. Create a rhythm for the community.

# Problem Solving

### Key Reference
Tuma, D. T. and F. Reif. *Problem Solving and Education: Issues in Research and Teaching.* Hillsdale, N.J.: Lawrence Erlbaum, 1980. These are the essentials of problem solving. If you are designing for transfer, structure your teaching in this manner:

1. **Problem Definition.** Define the problem by sorting out the relevant and irrelevant information surrounding the problem situation. Identify and describe the small elements that define the problem.

2. **Big Picture.** Set the problem within the big picture of results or effects. Help trainees to see why this problem is important to business.

3. **Subproblems.** Break the problem down into parts, logical definitions of subproblems. Organize and categorize.

4. **Trainee Ownership.** Relate one or more subproblems to each trainee. Early in your strategy, get trainees to feel a personal relationship to a well-defined piece of the larger problem.

5. **Standards and Tools.** Generalize the problem and all of its subproblems to a standard. Make it clear what the acceptable or optimum level of performance or production is. Provide numbers, percents, frequencies, or other criteria for success. Provide the measurement instruments and enunciate the steps of the processes that will be used to work through the problem to achieve the standard. Give each trainee a real live measurement tool to examine and refer to during problem solving.

6. **Solution Options.** Develop a list of possible solutions to the problem, focusing on specific options for each subproblem. Encourage broad thinking, inferring, making analogies and comparisons, projecting, withholding judgment, and brainstorming as the possibilities are defined. As in problem definition, discard irrelevant information as you focus on all of the relevant possibilities.

7. **Planning.** Choose which solution(s) to pursue, and make a plan. Use charts, matrices, models, diagrams, formulas, time lines, procedures, statistics, scripts, samples, and simulations. If trainees do not have the skills to use these planning devices, teach the necessary skills prior to engaging in problem solving.

8. **Monitoring and Feedback.** Create a timetable and reporting structure to monitor the solutions. This can be forms-driven, in which case you'll need to create monitoring and feedback forms. The best way to assure continued progress is to assign monitoring responsibilities to specific individuals, provide them with the tools to do their jobs, and make it clear that the solution, not the individual, is being monitored. Focus on procedures and results, not a person's personality or style of operating. Provide feedback to all concerned parties so that the problem-solving process can be improved. Highlight and disseminate widely what works; learn from what doesn't work.

## Cognitive Skills

### Key Reference

Bloom, B. S., ed. *Taxonomy of Educational Objectives: Book 1, Cognitive Domain.* New York: Longman, 1954/1980. Bloom's work at the University of Chicago has demonstrated that lower-level cognitive objectives must be mastered before higher-level ones can be attained. In training, it is important to know at what objectives you are aiming, so that your teaching is focused at the right level. Entire courses can be designed to accomplish the very lowest-level objectives—or the very highest. Courses can also be designed around a combination of objectives.

These are the levels, from low to high, as suggested by Bloom:

1. **Knowledge.** Knowledge includes knowledge of specifics, terminology, facts, ways of dealing with specifics, sequences, classifications, categories, criteria, methods, principles, and structures. Knowledge involves the recall of specifics. Knowledge objectives frequently emphasize the process of remembering. Skills include: defining, identifying, recalling, recognizing, naming, stating, reciting, labeling, and listing.

2. **Comprehension.** Comprehension represents the lowest level of understanding. It refers to a type of understanding in which the individual knows what is being communicated and can make use of the material without necessarily relating it to other material or seeing its fullest implications. Comprehension involves the skills of translation, interpretation, and extrapolation. Other comprehension skills include illustrating, rephrasing, restating, representing, and explaining.

3. **Application.** Application involves the use of abstractions in concrete situations. Abstractions may be in the form of rules, formulas, ideas, or principles that need to be remembered and used. Skills include applying, generalizing, relating, developing, using, translating, computing, solving, and producing.

4. **Analysis.** Analysis involves breaking down or decoding communication into its constituent elements in order to reveal or clarify its parts. Analysis can apply to elements, relationships, procedures, roles, or organizational principles. Skills include distinguishing, deducing, contrasting, differentiating, categorizing, classifying, arranging, and summarizing.

5. **Synthesis.** Synthesis is combining elements to form a whole, in such a way that they constitute a structure not clearly there before. This can involve development of a written or verbal communication, production of a plan, or derivation of a set of abstract relations, such as hypotheses. Skills include writing, telling, composing, producing, combining, synthesizing, creating, formulating, strategizing, and planning.

6. **Evaluation.** Evaluation involves the use of a standard to make judgments about the value of materials and methods for given purposes. It includes quantitative and qualitative judgments about the extent to which materials and methods satisfy criteria. Skills include judging, assessing, deciding, appraising, criticizing, concluding, standardizing, and evaluating.

The implied challenge for training designers is to include training in all the skills that are necessary for moving up from a lower-level objective to a higher-level one. As a manager reviewing the design of courses, you can train yourself to spot the inconsistencies in level of instruction by using Bloom's taxonomy of objectives in the cognitive domain as a guide. Remember that the closer the training comes to the applications of the job, the better the chance of transfer.

## Psychomotor Skills

### Key Reference
Simpson, E. J. *The Classification of Objectives, Psychomotor Domain.* Urbana, IL: University of Illinois, 1966. These are the skills required to operate equipment involving the use of principles, procedures, and muscles. Training for psychomotor skill development, like that for cognitive skill development, requires careful design of training for both low-level and high-level skills.

These are the psychomotor skill levels, from low to high:

1. **Perception.** Perception involves the ability to respond to a sensory stimulus at the very basic level. It means that one's channels of communication are open to the environment through the five senses. Perception means that you are aware of a stimulus that is having some effect on you. Training in using computer systems, for example, requires many lessons in perceiving the various visual, tactile, and auditory stimuli that are created by system builders.

2. **Preparation.** Preparation means that you are ready for action. Preparation comes from verifying that the stimuli you have received are adequate and that all procedures, cues, props, and steps are in place so that you can act. Training customer service reps, for example, involves training in following procedures, using certain forms, and knowing the choices one has in executing an acceptable service response to a customer's inquiry. Training for preparation often includes training in meeting time standards and in placing or locating materials.

3. **Guided Response.** Guided response means that you can respond on command or on cue. It means that with a coach or tutor to prod you, you will respond appropriately. It means that you have prepared yourself for action and that you will take action, given the right cues.

Training unfortunately often stops here. Training for transfer, on the other hand, has to remove the trainee's dependence on the instructor and build in two higher levels of psychomotor objectives.

4. **Pattern.** Patterned response, or patterned behavior, is that kind of habitual, predictable action that is made possible through practice. However, patterned response doesn't just happen because a trainee knows the rules. The motor response (eye-hand coordination, large muscle involvement, etc.) requires training—after the training in guided response—to enable the trainee to perform the required pattern of movements with no instructor, no cues, and with seemingly little effort. Coordination training is often required at this level of objective. Overlearning, or repeated practice beyond mastery level, is often used as a training technique for learning patterned behavior.

5. **Performance.** This is the ability to demonstrate a skill consistently and reliably over time. Performance involves the synthesis of all the preparation information and mastery of all the patterned actions learned in earlier skill development lessons. It means that time pressures have been conquered and that one is in complete control of all of the many skills that have to work together in order to perform without cues or coaching.

## Hierarchy of Human Needs

### Key Reference

Maslow, A. H. *Motivation and Personality.* New York: Harper, 1959. Maslow, a professor at Brandeis University and president of the American Psychological Association, studied motivation and how people act in order to get what they need. He developed a hierarchy of needs that has influenced the way in which organizations relate to people as well as the design of instruction insofar as it captures the designs for trainee interaction during learning exercises. His work often forms the foundation for training in attitude development.

# Models for Individual and Organizational Learning

These needs are listed from the lowest-level, or most basic, need to the highest-level need.

1. **Physiological Needs.** These are bodily needs—for food, drink, sex, and sleep. They need to be satisfied before any other needs can be met.
2. **Safety.** People need to be safe, secure, and protected. Related to this is a need for structure and order.
3. **Need for Love and Belonging.** People need friends, family, and intimacy.
4. **Esteem.** People need to receive the esteem of others, to be seen as important, useful, and competent. Individuals need self-esteem.
5. **Self-Actualization.** People need to become the best that they can be. At this level of motivation, people are spontaneous, natural, self-governed, and self-assured. They work for intrinsic rewards such as pride in workmanship, a desire to grow, or a desire to help and to contribute to the good of the whole.

In training, it is easy to assume that because the students are adults, they will somehow automatically arrive at the self-actualization stage of motivation when they enter your classroom. The wise training manager makes sure that instructors and the design of the course itself include training experiences that address stages 2 (safety) and 4 (esteem). The motivation for safety is especially strong among adults faced with the unknown of a new and important learning situation. Adults fear looking foolish or stupid in front of their peers; they need much reassurance that they are psychologically safe in class. Lack of attention to needs for safety and esteem can sabotage training that is otherwise complete from a content perspective. Adults facing a computer learning system also need safety, belonging, and esteem.

## Stages of Concern About Innovation

### Key Reference
G. E. Hall. *Concerns Based Adoption Model.* Austin, TX: R&D Center for Teacher Education, University of Texas, 1973. Gene Hall and his colleagues at the University of Texas at Austin developed a model of personal concern regarding the adoption of new ideas. His work on innovation and change has appeared in journals for several decades and has special relevance to learning and transfer, as they are defined as change.

He has shown that individuals exhibit concern at one of several levels at the point at which they are faced with change. Instructors can sensitize themselves to a trainee's level of concern and can listen for the verbal and nonverbal clues to an individual's concern about the learning situation. The trick in instructional design and in instruction is to assess that level of concern correctly, and then to respond appropriately. A great deal of worthy change is aborted because an instructor didn't correctly hear a trainee's concern and provided instruction at a totally inappropriate level. Trainees whose personal concerns about the innovation are not met simply turn off during class and may or may not politely sit through the lessons.

These are Gene Hall's seven stages of concern about innovation:

1. **Awareness.** At this stage, the trainee shows no concern at all. The trainee who "got sent" to class might be at this stage. That trainee might say something like, "I have no idea why I'm here!" or "I just joined the company yesterday and don't really know what's going on yet. I was told to show up here."

2. **Information.** At this stage, the trainee simply wants more information. Comments from the trainee seem very focused on the content or on the course as an intellectual exercise. The trainee wants to be in training but as yet sees no personal or organizational benefits. The trainee might say something like, "I want an update of the field" or "I'm just checking out what's new" or "Can you elaborate on items 3, 10, and 25?"

3. **Personal Role.** At this stage, the trainee exhibits concern for his or her personal role in the training. Issues surrounding one's academic background, experience base, or organizational position may come out. The trainee may feel unprepared academically or be concerned that he or she won't be able to perform well in class because he or she comes from another department. The trainee may say something like, "Our school never taught that stuff" or "I'm not real sure about the application to my department" or "Sure, I'll give it a try, but I've never been known for my agility."

4. **Management.** At this stage, the trainee exhibits concern over the procedures and tasks involving use of the newly learned skills. Trainees at this level worry about getting the rules learned, practicing a new task during training so that it becomes efficient and doesn't waste time, or developing some sequence or organization scheme so that the new skill will work. Trainees at this level might say, "Why don't we figure out how to do this faster?," "Check me when I substitute these numbers in the new formula," "Are the manuals ready?," or "Are all the peripheral devices working?"

5. **Consequence.** At this stage, the trainee is concerned about the impact of the new skills on his or her job or personal life. The trainee might ask, "Will I be so smart that I'll put myself out of a job?," "This means that I'll have to change my car pool to get here half an hour earlier, right?," "This is great—this means that I'll advance to the next salary level with this new skill," or "Will I be responsible for training the other members of my quality team?"

# Models for Individual and Organizational Learning

6. **Collaboration.** At this stage of concern, the focus is on coordination and cooperation with others. This stage contrasts with stage 4 (consequence) in that the fear of the risks of personal involvement is eliminated. In collaboration, the focus is on the trainee's initiative in helping and sharing. You'll hear such comments as, "I'll present this at the next department meeting," "I can see the application of this in several of our task forces," "I'm concerned about a potential lack of commitment and time from Rudy's group," or "We need to get to Elaine and Shirley."

7. **Refocusing.** At this stage, the trainee is concerned about making improvements on what was just learned. The trainee has internalized the new learning so well that he or she can modify or refocus it in some useful way to make a positive change. This stage sometimes happens during training but generally comes during the first few weeks of using new skills on the job. To capture these concerns and to build even more transfer training into them, some kind of follow-up encounter is suggested. This concern is likely to be expressed by remarks such as, "I have a better idea," "Look what we tried with this, and see what we got?," "Would you come take a look at our modification?," or "What do you think of this approach?"

Transfer has a better chance of occurring when trainees are at levels 4, 5, 6, or 7 in their concerns. In order to get to these stages, however, lower-level concerns must be satisfied.

## Habits of Successful People

### Key Reference
Covey, Stephen R. *The 7 Habits of Highly Successful People: Powerful Lessons in Personal Change.* New York: Fireside, Simon & Schuster, 1989. Other popular books by Stephen Covey are based on ideas similar to those in this book and include: *The 7 Habits of Highly Effective Families, First Things First,* and *Principle-Centered Leadership.*

Covey's works appeal to workers everywhere who are striving to be more responsible for themselves, to know themselves better, and to be more empowered. Covey's seven habits of highly successful people move from dependence through independence to interdependence. They include:

1. **Be proactive.**
2. **Begin with the end in mind.**
3. **Put first things first.**
4. **Think win/win.**
5. **Seek first to understand . . . then to be understood.**
6. **Synergize,** bringing the parts into the whole and making the whole greater.

7. **"Sharpen the saw,"** meaning having the wisdom to see when one's effort needs to be balanced with sharpened awareness of self in physical, mental, spiritual, and emotional ways.

## Diversity

### Key Reference
Thomas, R. Roosevelt, Jr. *Beyond Race and Gender: Unleashing the Power of Your Total Work Force by Managing Diversity.* New York: AMACOM, 1991.

Roosevelt Thomas's book was one of the first to suggest that diversity in the workplace should be both valued and managed. Many attempts throughout the American workplace in the 1980s had been "affirmative" acts of hiring, placement, and training, unfortunately accompanied by a good deal of turnover and lack of promotion. Efforts to gain a diverse workforce before Thomas's influence were all too often marked by programs to "assimilate" persons of "difference" into what was perceived as the mainstream. Thomas shook up this thinking when he published this book on managing diversity.

Demographics spoke for themselves: more and more people of color, women, and ethnic minorities were entering the workforce and would continue to grow in numbers into the next century. Complementing this trend in worker demographics was the reality that markets were also becoming more diverse. Diversity became a business issue and not simply a civil rights issue.

Thomas has many good prescriptions for action in this book. Throughout, he uses the metaphor of a tree, and especially of the root system of a tree. He suggests examining an organization's root system in order to get started with managing diversity.

These are his suggestions for growing new roots:

1. **Repeatedly articulate the definition of your new roots.**
2. **Create supportive traditions and ceremonies.**
3. **Create appropriate heroes and heroines.**
4. **Create supportive symbols.**
5. **Influence communications networks.**
6. **Recruit new "root guards"**—supportive persons who can protect change efforts.
7. **Reward change agents.**

## Advancement of Women

### Key References
Hewlett, Sylvia Ann. "Executive Women and the Myth of Having It All" in *Harvard Business Review*, April 2002, pp. 66–73.

# Models for Individual and Organizational Learning

United States Bureau of Labor Statistics
United States 2000 Census
Wellington, Sheila and Catalyst. *Be Your Own Mentor*. New York: Random House, 2001.

In spite of years of trying, women still do not advance as far as men, nor do they earn as much money. Federal antidiscrimination legislation, incentives, and some truly heroic and creative corporate programs have made some difference, but not enough. In the last thirty years, the proportion of women ages 25 to 34 who had completed four or more years of college increased two and a half times, surpassing men of the same age cohort. Today, women make up 47 percent of the workforce.

Yet as of spring 2002, only six women were CEOs of *Fortune* 500 companies; a trend has been recently noted that well-educated mothers were choosing not to work, thus jeopardizing the source of high-quality workers; and working mothers (not working fathers) overwhelmingly still have primary responsibility for child care and household chores. Seventy-two percent of mothers with children under eighteen are in the workforce. Yet women still earn only about three quarters of what men earn.

Catalyst, catalystwomen.org, a nonprofit research and advisory organization, works to advance women in business. In year 2002, Catalyst celebrates forty years of being the leading source of information on women in business and leader of dialogue on the issues facing both women and businesses. Training managers need to be aware of the work of Catalyst because it so directly addresses the advancement of women at work. Training managers need to be sure that through training and learning opportunities, women in their workplaces are learning the right things and do, in fact, have equal opportunity to succeed.

These are some of the work-life policies that the authors of the two references cited above suggest; training managers can be instrumental in helping to change policy to make work more equitable for working mothers:

1. Increase paid leave for working parents to six months, to be taken in portions as needed throughout a child's life.
2. Create high-level jobs that allow for reduced hours.
3. Devise processes that encourage employees to return after leave, without hurting their chances of advancement.
4. Extend the Family Medical Leave Act (FMLA), now covering unpaid leave and for companies with more than fifty workers. Revise it to include all companies, regardless of size, and make it paid leave.
5. Provide government tax incentives to companies that provide a variety of parent-friendly policies and programs.
6. Take steps to reduce the effects of the long hours typical of the American work culture. Remove bonus and benefit incentives for working long hours.

A 1998 Catalyst study, *Two Careers, One Marriage,* listed three programs as ones that mothers would look for in a new employer. More than 65 percent of working mothers surveyed wanted:

1. Flexible hours
2. Family leave
3. Cafeteria-style benefits
4. A customized career path
5. A formal flexible work program
6. Home-office/telecommuting
7. Company-supported child care

Wellington's work, *Be Your Own Mentor,* is full of supportive ideas and suggestions based on years of research and experience. Among these are:

1. **Having a winning strategy for getting ahead. This includes:**
   discipline,
   persistence,
   smarts, and
   courage
2. **Perform beyond expectations.**
3. **Be sure you put in as much time as the men do.**
4. **Blow your own horn. Increase your visibility.**
5. **Develop expertise.**
6. **Just do it. Don't wait to be asked.**
7. **Diversify your management experiences within the company.**
8. **Stretch; take risks; snoop around for new opportunities.**
9. **Get paid what you're worth. Ask for it.**
10. **Develop a personal style that makes others comfortable.**
11. **Demonstrate that you are a team player.**
12. **Network: Become part of informal networks and never stop networking.**

## Right Brain, Left Brain

### Key Reference
Springer, S. P., and Deutsch, G. *Left Brain, Right Brain.* San Francisco: W. H. Freeman, 1981. Medical and psychological research in the late 1970s and early 1980s included landmark studies on brain lateralization, or what has come to be known to laymen as "right brain, left brain" differences. The cooperative efforts between psychology and neurology have given trainers and school educators a foundation for developing new teaching methodologies. The development of the concept of learning style and the accelerated learning methodology are two examples commonly found in corporate training programs.

The following lists abbreviate the findings and hypotheses of the various researchers. There seems to be ample evidence that training designed to appeal to both brain hemispheres is training that is more engaging and that can perhaps transfer more readily because it is more thoroughly integrated in one's psyche.

| *Left Hemisphere* | *Right Hemisphere* |
| --- | --- |
| Verbal | Nonverbal, visual-spatial |
| Sequential, temporal | Simultaneous, spatial |
| Digital | Analogic, metaphoric |
| Logical, analytical | Gestalt, synthesizing |
| Rational | Intuitive |
| Western thought | Eastern thought |
| Convergent | Divergent |
| Intellectual | Sensuous |
| Deductive | Imaginative |
| Vertical | Horizontal |
| Discrete | Continuous |
| Concrete | Abstract |
| Realistic | Impulsive |
| Directed | Free |
| Differential | Existential |
| Historical | Timeless |
| Explicit | Tacit |
| Objective | Subjective |

# Psychological Types

## Key References

Bolton, Robert, and Bolton, Dorothy Grover. *People Styles at Work: Making Bad Relationships Good and Good Relationships Better.* New York: AMACOM, 1996.

*Consulting Psychologists Press (CPP) 1997 Catalog: Defining Individuality, Delivering Potential.* Palo Alto, CA: Consulting Psychologists Press, Inc., 1997.

Psychologist Carl Jung in 1921 defined the term "psychological type" and described just four essentially different types of people: thinkers, feelers, intuitors, and sensors. His work was widely accepted and followed, and persists in its relevancy even to the present time. Among the most prolific followers have been Isabel Briggs Myers and Katharine C. Briggs, who developed the Myers-Briggs Type Indicator (MBTI) based on Jung's four types. The many versions of and enhancements to the basic MBTI are published by Consulting Psychologists Press, Inc., of Palo Alto. Assessment instruments of all sorts, administration and scoring materials, and books about the Myers-Briggs are available through CPP.

The essence of the MBTI is one's personal preference for certain actions. Persons taking the MBTI rate themselves according to four scales that mirror Jung's research. The various combinations of these preferences result in sixteen different personality types. A profile is then generated of a person's psychological type, with descriptions of an individual's preferred way of thinking and approaching life. The types are generally abbreviated by a single letter, such as "E" for Extrovert, or "J" for Judging. Many different kinds of reports are possible based on an individual's profile. The MBTI scales are:

1. **Extroversion—Introversion**
2. **Sensing—Intuition**
3. **Thinking—Feeling**
4. **Judging—Perceiving**

The MBTI is widely used in business, and is especially popular with companies who are looking for ways to support teamwork. Other uses include leadership development, outplacement support, counseling for career change, coaching, student advising, and conflict resolution. It is available in Spanish as well as English. The MBTI is the classic work in the field.

With today's sweep of change in the direction of valuing diversity, building empowered employees, and working in teams of all sorts, there have been numerous classification and assessment models of personality and behavior type based on the MBTI and Jungian models. One such new work is the work of the Boltons, referenced above. Their work focuses on the behavioral applications of "typing." They argue that the MBTI and Jung are too inward-focused, and that the business community needs an outward-focused or behavioral-type assessment and action-planning model. They present this model in their book. Their point, after the assessment of type is done, is that in order to create the best working relationships, it is necessary to "get in synch with the style-based behavioral patterns" of those with whom you work. They note that every individual is essentially a minority, behaviorally speaking. If the population is approximately equally divided into four types (which is what behavioral science research from Jung forward says), that means that 75 percent of the population is different from you. Individuals think differently, communicate differently, handle emotions differently, deal with criticism differently, work at a different pace, etc. In teamwork especially, progress and success depend on the interrelationships of many persons who are differ-

# Models for Individual and Organizational Learning

ent from each other along many dimensions. The Boltons advocate learning "style flex" in order to remain true to oneself and be able to work successfully in today's more diverse and empowered workplaces.

The Boltons organize their behavioral types along an "assertiveness/responsiveness" axis; they include these four behavioral types:

1. **Analytical**
2. **Amiable**
3. **Driver**
4. **Expressive**

Their analysis is typically done using a 2 × 2 matrix along the assertiveness/responsiveness axis. Their book is an easy to follow guide for understanding and assessing behavioral style. A very useful and extensive set of appendixes deals with the practicalities of working with various types.

## Memory

### Key Reference

Eysenck, M. W. *A Handbook of Cognitive Psychology.* London: Lawrence Erlbaum, 1984. Particularly in the last decade, two important movements have affected the increase in intensity of studies in human information processing, especially the study of memory. One movement is the search for and development of better expert systems and wider varieties of computer-based training; the other is the increase in the number of older workers. In both cases, a deeper understanding of how memory works is critical to the optimal use of these resources, one a technological resource and the other a human resource.

Researchers seem to agree that there are three basic types of memory: short-term memory, long-term memory, and processing memory that records, searches, accesses, and retrieves. In addition, researchers have attempted to categorize memory in a number of ways, such as memory for specific events and details, memory for semantics or meaning, and memory for doing repetitive tasks.

Training that is designed to improve the various components of memory can assist the process of transfer. Training must be designed to help get information into memory as well as to get information out of memory. The lists below suggest some focus for design aimed at the three basic types of memory:

| *Short-Term Memory* | *Long-Term Memory* |
|---|---|
| Visual/audial scanning | Associations |
| Estimation of length, width | Pattern recognition |
| Perception of speed | Mnemonics |

Spatial orientation  
Chunks of information  
Focus  
Concentration  

Modifications  
Verbal comprehension  
Number facility  
Reasoning  
Originality  

*Processing Memory*

Ordering/organizing

Signaling/alerting

Searching

Monitoring

Regulating

Addressing

Retrieving

Rehearsing/practicing

## Conditions of Learning

### Key Reference

Gagne, R.M. *The Conditions of Learning.* New York: Holt, Rinehart, and Winston, 1977. Robert Gagne, in academic research spanning several decades at Florida State University, has theorized that five basic and different categories of human performance can be established by learning. These are: intellectually interacting with symbols, verbalizing information, cognitive strategizing and managing one's own behavior, executing coordinated movement, and developing attitudes. Each of these categories has a hierarchy of prerequisite skills associated with it, comprising Gagne's representation of the conditions of learning.

The following list suggests the hierarchy of learning conditions in the category of intellectual skills. Each form of learning beyond the basic skill of associations and chains builds on the earlier skill. Good training design heeds Gagne's research and begins at the lowest level, working upward, to satisfy the conditions that encourage learning that will last over time.

1. **Basic Forms: Associations and Chains.** Associations are the elementary kinds of learning that feature perception of and response to a stimulus. Chains are sets of associations.

2. **Discriminations.** Discrimination learning is that which is associated with the distinctive characteristics or features of stimuli. These can be

shapes, colors, sounds, odors, textures—in objects, people, and situations. Discrimination learning depends on having succeeded at the stimulus level.

3. **Concepts.** Learning concepts requires a person to group things into classes and to be able to include any future instance or example of that class appropriately. Learning concepts requires that one has first learned to discriminate correctly among the many possible associations of information.

4. **Rules.** Learning rules involves being able to behave the same way regularly and consistently when faced with a variety of stimulus situations. Rules cannot be learned without first having learned concepts. Trainers often err by trying to teach rules too soon.

5. **Problem Solving.** Learning to solve problems means that a trainee can use rules in an appropriate and sometimes original way. It also means that a trainee has in place a well-functioning, self-governing "process control center" that "runs" the rest of the learning steps. The ultimate goal of problem solving can be achieved only when the other four conditions of learning have been satisfied.

# Self-Study

### Key Reference
Norman, Donald A. *Things That Make Us Smart: Defending Human Attributes in the Age of the Machine.* Reading, MA: Addison-Wesley, 1993.

Donald Norman, cognitive psychologist, is a Fellow at Apple Computer, Inc. He was founder and formerly chair of the Department of Cognitive Science at the University of California, San Diego. He has written many classic works in the field; this particular book is of special importance to today's workers because of its focus on the comparisons between human information processing and computer information processing. With more and more learning done online, alone, using information processing machines and electronic devices, it is important for training managers to refer to cognitivists such as Norman for ideas regarding design and delivery of instruction.

As could be expected, Norman loudly insists that human cognition is not machine cognition, and he implores the reader to resist attempts at such foolish comparisons. Of course, he acknowledges that the human mind is limited in its power and capacities, and that machines can make us smarter.

But he also suggests that our cognition as human beings is characterized by such things as irony, ambiguity, a need for spatial orientation, ability to make intuitive midcourse correction, a preference for anecdotes and play over data, and musical ability, to name a short list. Norman suggests that as we build better and bigger (or smaller) computers and other information machines, we work harder to incorporate the cognitive essence of what makes us human into them—or, at least, to preserve the learning value of each venue and to combine venues only when each truly complements the other.

Norman is easy to read and full of challenges. His work is especially important to training designers who are trying to discover the intellectual "framing" that is the necessary underpinning of self-study. Trainers who become internal performance consultants need to pay attention to thinkers like Norman who build bridges between advances in the study of cognition and the integration of these advances into our network of information processing machines. These are some of the ideas in Norman's research:

1. **Experiential and reflective cognition.** There are two basic kinds of cognition: experiential (data-driven, dependent on long-term memory), and reflective (concept-driven, dependent on ability to reason and make inferences from information in short-term memory).

2. **Cognitive artifacts.** Human beings have the propensity to create cognitive artifacts, external and supplemental aids to learning such as filing cabinets, pocket calculators, whiteboards, flip charts, calendars, and, the ultimate cognitive artifact according to Norman, Post-it Notes. These cognitive artifacts compensate for our lack of ability of various sorts. Technology fits into the definition of cognitive artifact; but we need always to remember that we create it, not the other way around.

3. **Three kinds of learning: accretion, tuning, and restructuring.** These seem to be the most obvious and differentiated kinds of learning. *Accretion* is the accumulation of facts. *Tuning* is the practice of skills between novice and expert states. Both these types of learning are largely experiential or based on memory stores of experience. *Restructuring*, on the other hand, is largely reflective, the difficult part of learning where new conceptual knowledge is acquired and mentally manipulated.

4. **Learning is grounded in social behavior.** Highly successful learners seem to need to get into the heads of their fellow learners, their teachers, their customers, their families, and their friends in order to validate and motivate their own learning. In this regard, learning must be a social activity. Social groups require flexibility, cooperation, collaboration, resilience, and the interactions of diverse actors. Technology, particularly, as a cognitive artifact often has a head-on collision with a social group. It is inflexible, always predictable, and a powerful and singular force with no room for contradictions or ironies. In this sense, technology is antihuman and outside of the social requirements for learning. However, when the individual learner has designed the control of technology and it supports

the learner, great strides can be made toward individual learning—true self-study.

Thinkers such as Donald Norman probe the nature of cognition and give us approaches to learning as individuals that recognize the elements of the learning process that we need to exercise. Norman, particularly, speaks to the learning dilemmas of our information age and clarifies instructional design issues. His work gives a whole new focus to self-study.

# Frames of Mind

## Key Reference

Gardner, H. *Frames of Mind: The Theory of Multiple Intelligence.* New York: Basic Books, 1985. Howard Gardner, a psychologist associated with Boston University School of Medicine and Harvard University, is the latest in a line of thinkers, including L. L. Thurstone and J. P. Guilford, who believe that intelligence cannot be captured by a single IQ score and that individuals have many kinds of intelligence, each of which can be developed to a greater or lesser degree. Gardner's work is different from that of the others in that he synthesizes a very large amount of information from developmental psychology, neurology, psychometrics, exceptionality, and cultural systems.

Gardner has studied and measured what happens in the brain during specific kinds of learning. He has found that learning is not widely diffused throughout the brain but is localized in certain nerve cells and that learning results from altered connections between cells.

Gardner found that individuals have a tendency to behave brilliantly in certain areas while being incapable of performing in other areas. He has investigated the structure of development within each of his "frames of mind" and in this sense has created a taxonomy of intellectual development. His frames are co-equal, rather than forming a hierarchy. He believes that each intelligence has its own organizing processes, reflecting each's structuring principles and preferred avenues of expression.

Gardner's work diverges into hypotheses regarding the impact of culture on the environment for learning, including issues of values, achievement, transfer, and even what is considered a "learning disability." His work is worth reading by trainers because of its implications for understanding the role of corporate culture in the development of training programs.

These are Gardner's six frames of mind:

1. **Linguistic Intelligence.** This includes rhetoric, the ability to use language to convince others; mnemonics, the ability to use language to remember information; explanation, the ability of language to serve pedagogical purposes; and metalinguistics, the ability of language to use itself

to study itself—grammar and syntax, semantics, metaphor, and differences between oral language and written language.

2. **Musical Intelligence.** Musical intelligence involves both understanding the emotional effects of music and comprehending its forms—its meter, rhythm, tones, timbres, pitches, musical contour, phrasing, cadence, scale, and harmony. Gardner notes that while very young children exhibit wide variations in musical intelligence, American schools in general tolerate musical illiteracy. Musical intelligence seems to have a low cultural value in our society.

3. **Logical-Mathematical Intelligence.** Gardner believes that this kind of intelligence derives from one's "confrontation" with the world of things. Developing a sense of quantification, ordering, substituting, sizing, grouping, rearranging, and abstracting is accomplished by concrete interaction with material objects. Hypothesis building and testing, the hallmark of scientific investigation, similarly is structured around the initial definition of objects; it is a different kind of "frame" from Gardner's others.

4. **Spatial Intelligence.** Spatial intelligence involves the ability not only to perceive the physical world accurately but also to transform and modify one's perception. Spatial intelligence means that one can recreate that original correct perception anywhere, any time, under many circumstances, even in situations in which the original stimuli are lacking. Mental imaging plays an important part in the exercise of spatial intelligence.

5. **Bodily-Kinesthetic Intelligence.** The two basic properties of this kind of intelligence are the capacity to use one's small and large muscle systems to work skillfully with objects and the ability to use one's entire body in expressive and/or goal-directed ways.

6. **Personal Intelligence.** Personal intelligences are essentially those that focus inward on one's own feelings and unique bases of behavior and those that focus outward to the feelings and motivations of others. Although corporate life in America has been criticized for undervaluing personal intelligences, considerable attention has been paid to understanding these "frames" by a myriad of courses and programs in management training.

## Emotional Intelligence

### Key Reference
Goleman, Daniel. *Emotional Intelligence: Why It Can Matter More Than IQ.* New York: Bantam Books, 1995.

Daniel Goleman's book is a popular book—a best seller for many months; a favorite selection of book clubs; a book for parents, school teachers, and trainers. It contains just enough theory and scientific underpinnings to make it worthy of notice for instructional designers, training managers, and human resource generalists in the workplace.

Goleman's point of view is that emotional intelligence is what counts "in real life." People in interaction with each other must have the social survival skills of character, self-discipline, altruism, and compassion before any intellectual skills. The word "emotion," he notes, has its root in the Latin word for "move." Goleman points out that, in fact, emotions come first—before thought—in triggering action. He points out, time and again, many examples in which passion overwhelms reason in all kinds of endeavors and relationships. "First feelings; second thoughts" is how he puts it.

What all this has to say about workplace learning is critical in today's overstressed, angry, harassed, and scared workforce. Trusting others, believing in the future, supporting colleagues, and operating in a safe place are all enormously important qualities for success on the job. Individuals need to have faith, hope, devotion, and love in order to act intelligently. The good news seems to be that emotional intelligence can be learned, and that emotional trauma can be lessened through active, intentional learning. Some of the things Goleman suggests as components of emotional intelligence are self-awareness, self-motivation, control of impulses, persistence on task, and having empathy.

Following are his categories of emotion, with characteristics of particular importance to the workplace noted:

1. **Anger:** Fury, outrage, resentment, exasperation, acrimony, irritability, hostility
2. **Sadness:** Sorrow, gloom, self-pity, dejection, loneliness, grief
3. **Fear:** Anxiety, apprehension, misgivings, wariness, edginess, dread, terror
4. **Enjoyment:** Happiness, relief, delight, contentment, satisfaction, pride, amusement
5. **Love:** Acceptance, friendliness, kindness, affinity, trust
6. **Surprise:** Shock, amazement, astonishment, wonder
7. **Disgust:** Contempt, scorn, aversion, revulsion
8. **Shame:** Guilt, embarrassment, humiliation, remorse, regret, contrition

# Bibliography

Anderson, J. R. *Skill Acquisition: Compilation of Weak-Method Problem Solutions.* Washington, D.C.: National Science Foundation (1985), Research Report ED 264 257.

Argyris, Chris. *Knowledge for Action.* San Francisco: Berrett-Koehler, 1993.

ASTD, "Leading the Learning Revolution: A Manifesto," *T+D,* January 2002, p. 7.

ASTD, *State of the Industry Report 2002,* Alexandria, Va.: ASTD, February 2002.

*ASTD's Guide to Learning Organization Assessment Instruments.* Alexandria, Va.: American Society for Training and Development (ASTD), June 1996.

Bader, Gloria E., A. E. Bloom, and R. Y. Chang. *Measuring Team Performance.* Irvine, Calif.: Richard Chang Associates, Inc., Publications Division, 1994.

Banathy, B. H. *Instructional Systems.* Belmont, Calif.: Fearon, 1968.

Barbian, Jeff. "The Road Best Traveled." *Training,* May 2002, pp. 38–42.

Bennis, Warren, Gretchen M. Spreitzer, and Thomas G. Cummings, editors. *The Future of Leadership.* San Francisco: Jossey-Bass, a Wiley Company, 2001.

Berglas, Steven. "The Very Real Dangers of Executive Coaching." *Harvard Business Review,* June 2002, pp. 87–92.

Berner, Robert. "Why P&G's Smile Is So Bright." *Business Week,* August 12, 2002, pp. 58–60.

Blanchard, Ken, J. P. Carlos, and A. Randolph. *Empowerment Takes More Than a Minute.* San Francisco: Berrett-Koehler, 1996.

Bloom, B. S., ed. *Taxonomy of Educational Objectives, Handbook I: Cognitive Domain.* New York: Longman, 1954.

*BNAC Communicator.* Rockville, Md.: Bureau of National Affairs, Fall 1996.

Bolton, Robert, and Dorothy Grover Bolton. *People Styles at Work.* New York: AMACOM, 1996.

Brown, John Seeley, ed. *Seeing Differently.* Boston: a Harvard Business Review Book, 1997.

Brown, M. G., and J. E. Schwarz. "What to Fix When Everything's Broken." *Performance and Instruction,* April 1988, pp. 6–11.

Brown, Patricia Leigh. "Blinded by Science," *The New York Times,* July 14, 2002, p. 3.

Carr, Clay. *Team Leader's Problem Solver.* Englewood Cliffs, N.J.: Prentice Hall, 1996.

Catalyst. *Perspective* newsletters from March 2001 through June 2002, New York, N.Y.

Clutterbuck, David. "Passport: How Teams Learn." *T+D*, March 2002, pp. 67–69.
Covey, Stephen R. *The 7 Habits of Highly Successful People.* New York: Fireside, Simon & Schuster, 1989.
Deming, W. Edwards. *Out of the Crisis.* Cambridge: MIT Press, 1986.
Deterline, W. A., and M. J. Rosenberg. *Workplace Productivity, Performance Technology Success Stories.* Washington, D.C.: International Society for Performance Improvement (ISPI), 1992.
Edwards, Mark R., and Ann J. Ewen. *360 Degree Feedback.* New York: AMACOM, 1996.
Eysenck, M. W. *A Handbook of Cognitive Psychology.* London: Lawrence Erlbaum, 1984.
*Federal Register.* Washington, D.C. August 25, 1978.
Fischel, Corrie I., Esquire. "EEOC Issues Practical Guidance on Employers' Obligations to Prevent Post-September 11th Related Discrimination in the Workplace." *Mosaics*: Alexandria, Va: Society for Human Resource Management (SHRM), July/August 2002, p. 5.
Fishman, Attorney Stephen. *The Copyright Handbook: How to Protect & Use Written Works.* Berkeley, Calif.: Nolo Press, 1997.
Gagne, E. D. *The Cognitive Psychology of School Learning.* Boston: Little Brown & Company, 1985.
Gagne, R. M. *Conditions of Learning.* New York: Holt, Rinehart & Winston, 1977.
Gagne, R. M., and L. J. Briggs. *Principles of Instructional Design.* New York: Holt, Rinehart & Winston, 1979.
Gardner, H. *Frames of Mind: The Theory of Multiple Intelligences.* New York: Basic Books, 1985.
Gelb, Michael J. *Thinking for a Change.* New York: Harmony Books, 1995.
Gery, Gloria J. *Electronic Performance Support Systems (EPSS).* Cambridge, Mass.: Ziff Institute, 1991.
Gilbert, T. F. *Human Competence: Engineering Worthy Performance.* New York: McGraw-Hill, 1978.
Goleman, Daniel. *Emotional Intelligence.* New York: Bantam Books, 1995.
Goleman, Daniel, Richard Boyatzis, and Annie McKee. *Primal Leadership.* Boston: Harvard Business School Press, 2002.
Green, Paul C. *Building Robust Competencies.* San Francisco: Jossey-Bass, 1999.
Green, Robert. "2001 Baldrige Award Winner Profile: Chugach School District," *Quality Digest*, August 2002, pp. 46–47.
Guilford, J. P. *Intelligence, Creativity, and Their Educational Implications.* San Diego: Robert R. Knapp, 1968.
Guilot, Tara L. *Team Building in a Virtual Environment.* INFO-LINE No. 250205. ASTD, 2002.
Hartley, Darin E., M.Ed. *On-Demand Learning.* Amherst, Mass.: HRD Press, 2000.
*Harvard Business Review Special Issue: The Innovative Enterprise.* August 2002.
Hernez-Broome, Gina. "In It for the Long Haul: Coaching Is Key to Continued Development," *Leadership in Action*, vol. 22, number 1, March 2002, pp. 14–16.
Hipple, Jack, David Hardy, Steven A. Wilson, and James Michalski. "Back to the Future: Putting Innovation Efforts on Solid Ground," *Leadership In Action*, vol. 22, number 1, March/April 2002, pp. 8–11.
Honold, Linda. *Developing Employees Who Love to Learn.* Palo Alto, Calif.: Davies-Black Publishing, 2000.
"Industry Report 2001" and "Industry Report 1996," *Training Magazine.* Minneapolis: Lakewood Publications, October 1996.

*Introduction to Performance Technology,* vol. 1. Washington, D.C.: National Society for Performance and Instruction, 1986.

"Issues and Trends Report," *Technical and Skills Training Magazine,* Alexandria, Va.: American Society for Training and Development (ASTD), Fall 1996.

Jonassen, D. H., and N. D. C. Harris. "Analyzing and Selecting Instructional Strategies and Tactics," *Performance Improvement Quarterly* (1990), 3(2), pp. 29–47.

Kaplan, Robert S. and David P. Norton. *The Balanced Scorecard.* Boston: Harvard Business School Press, 1996.

Kelly, H. B. "A Primer on Transfer of Training" in *Training and Development Journal,* November 1982, pp. 102–06.

Kelly, Kevin. *New Rules for the New Economy: 10 Radical Strategies for a Connected World.* New York: Penguin Books, 1999.

Kirby, P. *Cognitive Style, Learning Style, & Transfer Skill Acquisition:* Information Series No. 195. Columbus, Ohio: National Center for Research in Vocational Education, Ohio State University, 1979.

Kirkpatrick, Donald L. *Evaluating Training Programs: The Four Levels.* San Francisco: Berrett-Koehler, 1994.

Knowles, M. *The Adult Learner: A Neglected Species,* 3rd Ed. Houston, Tex.: Gulf Publishing Company, 1989.

Kotter, John P. *Leading Change.* Boston: Harvard Business School Press, 1996.

Kovacs, Diane K. *The Internet Trainer's Guide.* New York: Van Nostrand Reinhold, 1995.

Krathwohl, D. R., B. S. Bloom, and B. B. Masia. *Taxonomy of Educational Objectives: The Classification of Educational Goals. Handbook II: Affective Domain.* New York: Longman, 1964.

LaFasto, Frank and Carl Larson. *When Teams Work Best.* Thousand Oaks, Calif.: Sage Publications, 2002.

Lee, Robert E. *A Copyright Guide for Authors.* Kent Press: Stamford, Conn.: 1995.

Lessig, Lawrence. *The Future of Ideas.* New York: Random House, 2001.

Lindsay, P. H., and D. A. Norman. *Human Information Processing: An Introduction to Psychology.* New York: Academic Press, 1977.

Lovell, R. B. *Adult Learning.* London: Croan Helm, 1980.

Lowe, Janet. *Welch, An American Icon.* New York: John Wiley & Sons, Inc., 2001.

Mager, R. F. and P. Pipe. *Analyzing Performance Problems, or 'You Really Oughta Wanna.'* Belmont, Calif.: Fearon Pitman, 1970.

Maslow, A. H. *Motivation and Personality,* 3rd ed. New York: Harper, 1987.

McCauley, Cynthia D. *Job Challenge Profile: Participant Workbook.* San Francisco: Jossey-Bass/Pfeiffer, 1999.

McLellan, Hilary, ed. *Situated Learning Perspectives.* Englewood Cliffs, N.J.: Educational Technology Publications, 1996.

Mross, Audrey E. "Updating Your FMLA Policy and Procedures," *Legal Report.* Alexandria,, Va.: Society for Human Resource Management (SHRM), July/August 2002, pp. 4–8.

*Myers-Briggs Type Indicator (MBTI),* Palo Alto, Calif.: Consulting Psychologists Press, 1997.

National Society for Performance and Instruction (NSPI). 1126 16th Street NW, Suite 102, Washington, D.C. 20036.

Nilson, C. *Training Program Workbook and Kit.* Englewood Cliffs, N.J.: Prentice Hall, 1989.

Nilson, C. *Training for Non-Trainers: A Do-It-Yourself Guide for Managers.* New York: AMACOM, 1990.

# Bibliography

Nilson, Carolyn. *How to Start a Training Program in Your Growing Business.* New York: AMACOM, 1992.

Nilson, Carolyn. *Trainer's Complete Guide to Management and Supervisory Development.* Englewood Cliffs, N.J.: Prentice Hall, 1992.

Nilson, Carolyn. *Team Games for Trainers.* New York: McGraw-Hill, 1993.

Nilson, Carolyn. *Peer Training.* Englewood Cliffs, N.J.: Prentice Hall, 1994.

Nilson, Carolyn. *Games That Drive Change.* New York: McGraw-Hill, 1995.

Nilson, Carolyn. *Training and Development Yearbook 1996–1997.* Englewood Cliffs, N.J.: Prentice Hall, 1996.

Nilson, Carolyn. *Training and Development Yearbook 1997.* Englewood Cliffs, N.J.: Prentice Hall, 1997.

Nonaka, Ikujior, and Hirotaka Takeuchi. *The Knowledge-Creating Company.* New York: Oxford University Press, 1995.

Norman, Donald A. *Things That Make Us Smart.* Reading, Mass.: Addison-Wesley, 1993.

O'Neill, Mary Beth. *Executive Coaching with Backbone and Heart.* San Francisco: Jossey-Bass Inc. Publishers, 2000.

Puterbaugh, G., M. Rosenberg, and R. Sofman. "Performance Support Tools: A Step Beyond Training," *Performance & Instruction*, November/December 1989, pp. 1–5.

Rayner, Steven B. *Team Traps.* New York: John Wiley & Sons, 1996.

Redding, R. C. "Metacognitive Instruction: Trainers Teaching Thinking Skills," *Performance Improvement Quarterly* (1990), 3 (1).

Resnick, L. B., ed. *The Nature of Intelligence.* Hillsdale, N.J.: Lawrence Erlbaum, 1976.

Robbins, Harvey and Michael Finley. *Why Teams Don't Work.* Princeton, N.J.: Peterson's/Pacesetter Books, 1995.

Robinson, Dana Gaines, and James C. Robinson. *Performance Consulting.* San Francisco: Berrett-Koehler, 1995.

Rosenberg, Marc J. *e-Learning.* New York: McGraw-Hill, 2001.

Ross, Sherwood. "Firms Augment Training with Online Courses," *Yahoo! News*, Technology-Reuters, May 4, 2002, pp. 1–2.

Rossett, A. *Training Needs Assessment.* Englewood Cliffs, N.J.: Educational Technology Publications, 1987.

Rothwell, William J. *ASTD Models for Human Performance Improvement.* Alexandria, Va.: American Society for Training and Development (ASTD), 1996.

Rothwell, W. J., and H. C. Kazanas. "Training: Key to Strategic Management." *Performance Improvement Quarterly* (1990), 3 (1).

Rothwell, William J. *Beyond Training and Development.* New York: AMACOM, 1996.

Rummler, Geary A., and Alan P. Brache. *Improving Performance*, 2nd ed., San Francisco: Jossey-Bass, 1995.

Ryan, Kathleen D., and Daniel K. Oestreich. *Driving Fear Out of the Workplace.* San Francisco: Jossey-Bass, 1991.

Senge, Peter M. *The Fifth Discipline.* New York: Doubleday Currency, 1990.

Senge, Peter M. et al. *The Fifth Discipline Fieldbook.* New York: Doubleday Currency, 1995.

Seymour, Dale and Ed Beardslee. *Critical Thinking Activities.* Palo Alto, Calif.: Dale Seymour Publications, 1990.

Shank, Patti. "Humble Opinion: No More Yawns," *OnlineLearning*, May 2002, pp. 22–23.

Simpson, E. J. *The Classification of Objectives, Psychomotor Domain.* Urbana, Ill.: University of Illinois, 1966.

# Bibliography

Sloman, Martyn. *The E-Learning Revolution.* New York: AMACOM, 2002.

Spitzer, D. *Improving Individual Performance.* Englewood Cliffs, N.J.: Educational Technology Publications, 1986.

Springer, S. P., and G. Deutsch. *Left Brain, Right Brain.* San Francisco: W. H. Freeman, 1981.

Stamatis, D. H. "Guidelines for Six Sigma Design Reviews—Part One," *Quality Digest,* April 2002, pp. 27–31.

Starr, Paul. "The Great Telecom Implosion," *The American Prospect,* September 9, 2002, pp. 20–24.

Stepich, D. A., and T. J. Newby. "Teaching Psychomotor Skills," *Performance and Instruction* (April 1990), vol. 29, no. 4.

Sternberg, R. J., ed. *Advances in the Psychology of Human Intelligence,* Vol. 1. Hillsdale, N.J.: Lawrence Erlbaum, 1982.

Stufflebeam, D. L., and A. J. Shinkfield, *Systematic Evaluation.* Boston: Kluwer-Nijhoff, 1985.

Thomas, R. Roosevelt, Jr. *Beyond Race and Gender.* New York: AMACOM, 1991.

Thomas, R. Roosevelt, Jr. *Redefining Diversity.* New York: AMACOM, 1996.

Thorndike, R. L., and E. P. Hagen. *Measurement and Evaluation in Psychology and Education.* New York: John Wiley & Sons, 1977.

Thurstone, L. L. *The Vectors of the Mind.* Chicago: University of Chicago Press, 1955.

Tobin, Daniel R. *All Learning Is Self-Directed.* Alexandria, Va.: ASTD, 2000.

Tornow, Walter W., Manuel London, and CCL Associates. *Maximizing the Value of 360-Degree Feedback.* San Francisco: Jossey-Bass Inc. Publishers, 1998.

Tracey, W. R. *Designing Training and Development Systems.* New York: AMACOM, 1984.

*Training America: Learning to Work for the 21st Century.* Alexandria, Va.: American Society for Training and Development (ASTD), 1989.

Tuma, D. T., and F. Reif. *Problem Solving and Education: Issues in Research and Teaching.* Hillsdale, N.J.: Lawrence Erlbaum, 1980.

Turner, Kirk W. and Christopher S. Trutchley, PHR. "Employment Law and Practices Training: No Longer the Exception—It's the Rule," *Legal Report.* Alexandria, Va.: Society for Human Resource Management (SHRM), July/August 2002, pp. 1–4.

U.S. Department of Commerce. *1997 Malcolm Baldrige National Quality Award Criteria for Performance Excellence.* Gaithersburg, Md.: National Institute of Standards and Technology, 1997 and 2001.

U.S. Department of Commerce. *Are We Making Progress?: An Assessment Tool.* National Institute of Standards and Technology, Technology Administration, 2001.

U.S. Department of Labor, Employment and Training Administration. *Dictionary of Occupational Titles,* 4th edition and supplements of 1982 and 1986. Washington, D.C.: U.S. Government Printing Office.

Vaidhyanathan, Siva. *Copyrights and Copywrongs: The Rise of Intellectual Property and How It Threatens Creativity.* New York: New York University Press, 2001.

Van Merrienboer, Jeroen J.G. *Training Complex Cognitive Skills.* Englewood Cliffs, N.J.: Educational Technology Publications, 1997.

Wallace, Guy W. *T&D Systems: Learning by Design versus Learning by Chance.* Naperville, Ill.: CADDI Press, 2001.

Wellington, Sheila and Catalyst. *Be Your Own Mentor.* New York: Random House, 2001.

Wellins, Richard S. *Empowered Teams.* San Francisco: Jossey-Bass, 1991.

Wells, Melanie. "D-Day for E-Bay," *Forbes*, July 22, 2002, pp. 68–70.
Welsch, Edward. "SCORM: Clarity or Calamity?" *OnlineLearning*, Summer 2002, pp. 14–18.
Wenger, Etienne, Richard McDermott, and William M. Snyder. *Cultivating Communities of Practice*. Boston: Harvard Business School Press, 2002.
Whittington, Larry. "Ten Tips for Moving to ISO 9001:2000," *Quality Digest*, April 2002, pp. 49–51.
Witherspoon, Robert and Randall P. White. *Four Essential Ways That Coaching Can Help Executives*. Greensboro, N.C.: Center for Creative Leadership, 1997.
Worth, Robert F. and Anemona Hartocollis. "Johnny Can Read, but Well Enough to Vote?" *The New York Times*, June 30, 2002, p. 21.
Zemke, R., and J. Gunkler, "Techniques for Transforming Training into Performance," *Training*, April 1985, pp. 48–63.
Zuboff, Shoshana. *In the Age of the Smart Machine*. New York: Basic Books, 1988.

# Index

accounting, 82, 158
action/reflection learning (form), 19
active processes (for moving beyond data), 198
active voice, 296
ADA (Americans with Disabilities Act), 49
ADL initiative, *see* Advanced Distributed Learning initiative
adult learning, 191, 250, 340–341
Advanced Distributed Learning (ADL) initiative, 29, 389
affirmative action, 49, 400
African Americans, 150
age (of training programs), 86
AICC (Aviation Industry Computer-Based Training Committee), 29
Allied Signal, 388
American Society for Training and Development (ASTD), 4, 5; benchmarking forum of, 25; and e-learning costs, 42; human performance improvement process of, 81; implementation/delivery publications from, 312; and innovation, 155; and learners on their own, 208; and learning organizations, 24–25; mentoring studies by, 150; and performance levels of training, 380; performance technology checklist from, 175–176; team training ideas/resources from, 110, 129, 130; telephone number for, 51; and training profession, 185
Americans with Disabilities Act (ADA), 49
analysis, 395
application, 394
Argyris, Chris, 385, 386
Asian Americans, 150
assessment, *see* evaluation; needs assessment; self-assessment
ASTD, *see* American Society for Training and Development
*ASTD Models for Human Performance Improvement* (Rothwell), 175
authoring system software, 267

authorization to begin evaluation, 362
authors, 265
Aviation Industry Computer-Based Training Committee (AICC), 29
awareness, 398

balanced scorecard, 387–388
*The Balanced Scorecard* (Kaplan and Norton), 387
Barbian, Jeff, 149, 150
behavioral feedback, 118–119
behavior (level 3), 348
benchmarking, 25, 348–349
benefits, employee, 157
Berglas, Steven, 150–151
best practices, 25, 132
*Beyond Race and Gender* (Thomas), 24, 400
*Be Your Own Mentor* (Wellington), 401, 402
bibliography, 413–419
big picture, 393
blended training, 27–28, 39
Bloom, B. S., 394
*BNAC Communicator*, 188
bodily-kinesthetic intelligence, 410
"boilerplate," 86
bold typeface, 298
Bolton, Dorothy Grover, 403–405
Bolton, Robert, 403–405
Brache, Alan P., 390
brain lateralization, 306–307, 402–403
breadth of courses, 343
Briggs, Katharine C., 404
Brown, John Seely, 391
budgets, 56, 71
building community, 392
Bureau of National Affairs Reports, 188
Bush, George W., 48
business factors analysis, 79
business needs, 390
business plans, 55, 68–70, 79
business strategy, 6
*Business Week*, 156

cameras, 301
"capture the flag" form, 126
career development, 159–161

catalog design, 264
catalog entry format, 286
Catalyst, 132, 150, 401, 402
cause analysis, 310, 311
CBT, *see* computer-based training
CD-ROMs, guidelines for words on, 301
"cell phone tooth," 156
change; in business, 5–6; changing view of, 1–2; organizational, 1, 309–310; workforce, 2
change management, 184, 306
Chugach School District, 187–188
Cisco Systems, 44
Civil Rights Act of 1964, 47
Civil Rights Act of 1991, 48
*The Classification of Objectives, Psychomotor Domain* (Simpson), 395
classroom trainee manuals, 290–291
classroom training, 329, 335, 337, 339
closed questions, 234
coaches, 135
coaching and mentoring, 26, 131–153; advantages of, 133; budget and staff for, 151–153; cautions about, 133, 137, 150–151; checklists for, 134–139; and cross-training, 133, 145; diversity training through, 132; facilitation and support services for, 132–133, 138; feedback from, 139; forms for, 140–148; individual learning plan for, 148; needs assessment form for, 146–147; psychotherapy vs., 150–151; reasons for, 141, 149–150; skills for, 143–144; of skills/relationships/best practices, 132; studies on, 149–150
cognitive psychology, 23–24
cognitive skills, 304–305, 394–395
collaboration, 28, 208, 399
Collins, Allan, 391
communication, 158, 209
communities of practice, 392–393
community, building, 392
competencies, author, 265
comprehension, 394

# Index

computer-based training (CBT), 270–271, 322–323, 336
computer-generated evaluation reports, 383
computer-generated word guidelines, 300–301
*Concerns Based Adoption Model* (Hall), 397–399
conditions of learning, 307–308, 406–407
*The Conditions of Learning* (Gagne), 406
Conference Board (New York City), 48
conferences, 43, 331
consequence, 398
consultants, 2, 90, 98–100
*Consulting Psychologists Press*, 403
contacts, 218, 232, 273
content, 28–29, 193, 344
continuous enabling, 260
contracts, 90, 99–100
contrast, screen, 300–301
copyright law, 104–106
core competencies, 133
corporate culture, 159–160, 177
corporate goals, 158
corporate universities, 5
cost assignment, three-phase, 81–82
cost-benefit analysis, 226–227, 237
cost centers, 45
costs; and benefits of hiring outsiders, 93; of design and development, 86; of e-learning, 42
course elements, 266
course evaluations, 357, 358, 374–376
course registration forms, 75, 76
courseware, content vs., 29
Covey, Stephen R., 399
creativity, 183
criterion-reference performance, 382–383
critical paths (form), e-learning, 38
critical thinking, 209
cross-functional teams, 108
crossing organizational boundaries, 212
cross-training, 133, 145
*Cultivating Communities of Practice* (Wenger, McDermott, and Snyder), 392
cultural practices, 47
curriculum chart, 72
customer contact sheet, 273
customers' needs, designing and writing for, 241, 247

DCOV (Define, Characterize, Optimize, Verify), 388
"D-Day for E-Bay" (Wells), 209
defensiveness, 386
Define, Characterize, Optimize, Verify (DCOV), 388
delivery, training; budget and staff for, 343–345; checklists for, 316–331; for classroom training, 276–277, 329, 335, 337; with computer-based/interactive video, 322–323, 336; and conference planning, 331; for distance training, 330; with Electronic Performance Support Systems, 324; forms for, 332–339; via the Internet, 325; and master schedule form, 333; model of, 341–342; obtaining feedback about, 315; one-to-one, 328, 334; presentation primer for, 342–343; selecting mode of, 314–315; via self-study, 338; and setting up intranet delivery, 326–327; in training department, 7–8
DeLorenzo, Richard, 187
Deming, W. Edwards, 129
departmental self-study problem analysis chart, 366–367
depth of content coverage, 344
design, training, 7, 391; for adult learners, 250; and brain lateralization, 306–307; and catalog design, 264; and change management, 306; checklists for, 245, 247–260; and cognitive skills, 304–305; components of, 274, 276–277; and continuous enabling, 260; and creating objectives, 275; customer contact sheet for, 273; for customers' needs, 241; for customer training, 247; for different learning styles, 242, 254–255; and dissemination, 244; and feedback follow-up form, 284; and focus on results, 259; and follow-up questionnaire, 283; forms for, 272–284; and fostering learning to learn, 252–253; and hierarchy of skills, 242–243; and the learning organization, 308–309; and learning styles, 306–307; of learning taxonomies, 256; learning to learn methodology in, 242; and memory, 307; and motivation/human needs, 305–306; and multiple intelligences, 308; and organizational change, 309–310; and overcoming transfer constraints, 251; and packaging, 243; and performance technology, 310–311; of post-training support, 243; problem analysis worksheet for, 279–280; and problem solving, 304; and psychomotor skills, 305; and readiness to learn, 307–308; and setting expectations, 248–249; setting expectations for, 242; staffing for, 243–244; and survival skills hierarchy, 282; and taxonomies, 242–243; and timeline for organizational support, 281; training opportunity profile for, 278; for types of transferable skills, 257–258; and writing, *see* writing
Deutsch, G., 402
developing practice, 392
diet, 47
directness, 296
disabilities legislation, 49
discrepancies, 212, 221
dissemination of training, 244
distance delivery mode, 314, 330
distributed teams, 110
diversity, 8, 24, 132, 400
DMAIC, 388
documentation, evaluation, 352
domain, defining, 392
double-loop learning, 386
drawings, 299
dress code, 47

drivers of change, 219–220
drug testing, 50
Duguid, Paul, 391
during or after issue (of evaluation), 347
"duty of accommodation," 47

E-Bay, 209
education; accountability legislation for, 48; employer-provided assistance for, 50; quality award in, 187–188
*Educational Technology*, 391
EEOC, *see* Equal Employment Opportunity Commission
e-learning, 27–45; in blended training, 27–28, 39; budget and staff for, 43–44; checklist for successful transition from classroom to, 32; checklists for, 31–36; collaboration for, 28; content of, 28–29; criticisms of, 30, 42–43; development standards form for, 41; forms for, 37–41; growing pains of, 29–30, 33; LCMS checklist for, 35; learning objects characteristics checklist for, 34; planning critical paths and milestones form for, 38; readiness checklist for, 36; researching costs of, 42; team assignment development with, 40; trends in, 29
Electronic Performance Support Systems (EPSS), 324
emotional intelligence, 410–411
*Emotional Intelligence* (Goleman), 410–411
employability skills, 170–171
employee benefits, 157
employees; changes in makeup of, 2; retention of, 149; skill observation evaluation form for, 378; training opportunity profile for, 278
employer-provided education assistance, 50, 413–419
empowered listening, 20
empowerment, 161, 166–169
enabling, continuous, 260
enabling-performance resources, 205
"engineering worthy performance," 185
English as a Second Language (ESL), 5
EPSS (Electronic Performance Support Systems), 324
Equal Employment Opportunity Commission (EEOC), 47, 49, 87
equipment deployment form, 77
Ernst & Young, 44
ESL (English as a Second Language), 5
esteem, 397
ethics, 46, 66, 347
*Evaluating Training Programs* (Kirkpatrick), 379
evaluation(s), 346–384, 395; accuracy of, 346–347; authorization to begin, 362; benchmarking for, 348–349; budget and staff for, 383–384; checklists for, 349–360; from coach/mentor, 139; course, 357, 358, 374–376; departmental self-study problem analysis chart for, 366–367; documentation of,

352; ethics of, 347; field test, 345, 356, 372–373; formative, 359; forms for, 361–378; instructors' course, 358, 376; Kirkpatrick's 4 Levels of, 379–380; by leadership, 8; models of, 348; during or after issue of, 347; overall program, 350; PC-generated, 383; practicality of, 347; program by objectives report of, 365; project monitoring form for, 364; skill observation form for, 378; standards for, 363, 379; of team learning, 354; terminology for, 381–383; of tests, 360, 377; 360 Degree, 347–348; trainees' course, 357, 374–375; of training materials, 355; training materials criteria for, 370–371; training project, 351; of training staff, 353; training staff form for, 368–369; usefulness of, 347; of vendor training, 319
evaluators, selection of, 381
executive coaching, 131, 150–151
"Executive Women and the Myth of Having It All" (Hewlett), 400
expectations, 242, 248–249, 325
experience, 208
Eysenck, M. W., 405

"face time," 110
facilities layout, 78
fair use policy, 106
Family and Medical Leave Act (FMLA), 48–49
Federal minimum wage, 49
feedback, 394; behavioral, 118–119; classroom training form for, 337; from coach/mentor, 139; on delivery, 315; follow-up, 284; from instructors, 345; to outside vendors, 87; self-study form for, 338
field testing (of courses), 345, 356, 372–373
"fifth discipline," 309
*The Fifth Discipline* (Senge), 24–25, 386
figures, 299
films, guidelines for words on, 301
flexibility, 6, 154–155, 209
FMLA, *see* Family and Medical Leave Act
follow-up, 283, 284
formative evaluation checklist, 359
frames of mind, 308, 409–410
*Frames of Mind* (Gardner), 409

Gagne, R. M., 406
Galvin, Tammy, on human capital, 5
Gardner, H., 409–410
Gelb, Michael J., 24
gender-neutral language, 296
General Electric, 388
Gilbert, Thomas, 185, 391
goals, 126, 158, 160, 391
Goleman, Daniel, 410–411
government jobs programs, 50
grammar, 296–297
group delivery mode, 314
group discussion guide for self-assessment, 231
growing pains, 33
guided response, 396
"Guidelines for Six Sigma Design Reviews—Part One" (Stamatis), 388
*Guide to Learning Organization Assessment Instruments* (ASTD), 25
Guilford, J. P., 409

habits of successful people, 399–400
Hall, G. E., 397
*A Handbook of Cognitive Psychology* (Eysenck), 405
hazards, workplace, 50
headings, 298
Hernez-Brooms, Gina, 149
Hewlett, Sylvia Ann, 400
hierarchy of human needs, 306, 396–397
hierarchy of skills, 242–243, 256, 282
hiring, 57, 58
Honeywell, 388
HRD plan, 48
*Human Competence* (Gilbert), 391
human needs, 305–306
*Human Resource Magazine*, 129
Human Resources Development (HRD) plan, 48

IBM, 44
IEEE (Institute of Electrical and Electronics Engineers), 29
implementation, training; and instructor's job design, 312–313; in training department, 7–8; training the trainer for, 313–314
*Improving Performance* (Rummler and Brache), 390
IMS (Information Management Society), 29
incentives, 46
individual delivery mode, 314
individual learning designs, 199
individual learning plan, 148, 202
*Info-Line*, 110
information, 398
Information Management Society (IMS), 29
"In It for the Long Haul" (Hernez-Brooms), 149
innovation, 154–189; budget and staff for, 188–189; and career development, 159–161; characteristic/behaviors form for, 183; checklists for, 162–177; in education, 187–188; employability skills checklist for, 170–171; and empowerment, 161; empowerment checklists for, 166–169; and flexibility, 154–155; forms for, 178–184; journal form for, 181; learning process of, 155–156; and linkage, 156–159; needs assessment form for, 179; online who's who skills directory form for, 180; on-the-job training ideas for, 172–174; organizational indicators of, 177; performance technology checklist for, 175–176; process quality assessment form for, 182; stages of concern about, 397–399; trainer/performance consultant form for, 184; trustbusters checklist for, 163–165
Institute for Research on Learning (IRL), 110, 208
Institute of Electrical and Electronics Engineers (IEEE), 29

instructional designers, rational for hiring, 57
instructional media, 320
Instructional System Design (ISD), 80–82, 190–192, 199, 310–311
instructor manuals, 269, 295
instructors; course evaluation by, 358, 376; job design for, 312–313; performance review for classroom, 339; personal presentation primer for, 342–343
intellectual property, 96, 103–105
intelligences, multiple, 308
interactive videodisc (IVD), 270–271, 322–323
interactivity, e-learning, 42–43
Internet; authoring systems found on, 44; checklist for training via, 325; involvement in planning of training via, 345; learning tools on, 192–193
intervention selection, 310, 311
interviews, 26, 44, 234
*In the Age of the Smart Machine* (Zuboff), 23
intranet delivery, 326–327, 345
investigation methodology, 222
IRL, *see* Institute for Research on Learning
ISD, *see* Instructional System Design
ISO 9001:2000, 388–389
IVD, *see* interactive videodisc

Japan, 129
job aids, 321
job analysis, 223, 235
job description form, 74
job design, instructor's, 312–313
job responsibility, task list by, 236
journal, 181
Jung, Carl, 403–404
just-in-time learning, 208

Kaplan, Robert S., 387, 388
key contact chart, 232
Kirkpatrick, Donald, 348, 379–380
Kirkpatrick's 4 Levels of evaluation, 348, 379–380
knowledge, 394
*The Knowledge-Creating Company* (Nonaka and Takeuchi), 24
*Knowledge for Action* (Argyris), 385
Kotter, John P., 310

labels, 299
language, 124, 296–297
Latinas, 150
LCMS (learning content management system), 35
leadership, 1–26, 413–419; ASTD's benchmarking forum for, 25; budget and staff for, 25–26; and change, 1–2; checklists for, 10–16; and cognitive psychology, 23–24; and design/writing of training, 7; evaluation by, 8; forms for, 17–22; and implementation/delivery of training, 7–8; and longevity of training, 8–9; and management assumptions, 2–3; and operation, 4–6; questions for, 2, 13–14; systems orientation for, 3–4; and systems thinking, 24–25; training needs assessment by, 6–7; and value of diversity, 24

learner objective (form), 288
learning; conditions of, 406–407; level 2 evaluation of, 348; from mistakes, 129; team, 387
"learning as an act of membership," 208
learning content management system (LCMS), 35
learning objects, 34
learning on their own; active processes for, 198; benefits of, 200; enabling-performance resources for, 205; how to use information for, 197; individual learning designs for, 199; individual learning plan for, 202; learning to learn skills for, 195; needs assessment self-evaluation for, 203–204; opportunities for, 206; self-assessment tool for, 196; 360 Degree feedback for, 207; *see also* supporting learners
learning organizations, 15–17, 24–25, 308–309
learning styles, 242, 254–255, 306–307
learning to learn methodology, 195, 242, 252–253
left brain, 306–307, 402–403
*Left Brain, Right Brain* (Springer and Deutsch), 402
*Legal Report*, 48
legislation, 5, 47–51
Lessig, Lawrence, 155
lesson plans, 289
levels of performance, 348, 379–380
lie detector testing, 50
linguistic intelligence, 409–410
linkage, 127, 156–159
listening, empowered, 20
literacy, 5
logical-mathematical intelligence, 410
longevity, training, 8–9
love and belonging, need for, 397
Lowe, Janet, 388
loyalty, 149

Mager, Robert, 185
make-or-buy decision, 46, 86
Malcolm Baldrige National Quality Award, 129–130, 186–188
Malcolm Baldrige Quality Award Foundation, 196
management, 2–3, 87, 391, 398
Managers' Mentors, 150
manuals, 268, 269, 290–291, 295
margins, 299
marketing, 158
Marsick, Victoria, 24–25
Martineau, Jennifer W., 208
Maslow, A. H., 396
master schedule, 333
mastery, personal, 386
materials, training, 344, 355, 370–371
MBTI (Myers-Briggs Type Indicator), 404
McDermott, Richard, 392
McLellan, Hilary, 391
measurement, 109–110, 382–383
media, 270–271, 300–301, 320
medical organizations, 157
memory, 307, 405–406
mental models, 386

mentoring, 131, 136, 139, 142
milestones (form), e-learning, 38
minimum wage, 49
minorities, 132, 150
mistakes, learning from, 129, 386
MIT Sloan School of Management, 155
modules, 299
monitoring, 364, 394
*Mosaics*, 48
motivation, 114–115, 159–160, 305–306, 340–341
*Motivation and Personality* (Maslow), 396
Motorola, 44, 388
multiple intelligences, 308
musical intelligence, 410
music industry, 105
Myers, Isabel Briggs, 404
Myers-Briggs Type Indicator (MBTI), 404

National Institute of Standards and Technology (NIST), 188, 189
national origin, 49
National Quality Award, *see* Malcolm Baldrige National Quality Award
needs, hierarchy of human, 306, 396–397
needs assessment, 211–240; budget and staff for, 239–240; checklists for, 214–228; coaching/mentoring form for, 146–147; company-wide contacts for, 218; cost-benefit analysis for, 226–227, 237; crossing organizational boundaries in, 212; defining results of, 225; discrepancies in, 212; drivers of change checklist for, 219–220; form for personal learning, 18; forms for, 229–237; guide to closed and open questions for, 234; innovation form for, 179; investigation methodology guidelines for, 222; job analysis checklist for, 223; key contact chart for, 232; by leadership, 6–7; methodology selection for, 212–213; people-data-things job analysis for, 235; performance discrepancies checklist for, 221; performance discrepancy form for, 233; self-assessment readiness check for, 217; self-evaluation for, 203–204; and success guidelines, 215–216; task analysis checklist for, 224; task list by job responsibility for, 236; time crunch problem with, 238–239; training proposal rationale for, 228
networking, 132
new product development, 155
*New York Times*, 156
NIST, *see* National Institute of Standards and Technology
No Child Left Behind Act, 48
"No More Yawns" (Shank), 192
Nonaka, Ikujior, 24
Norman, Donald, 23, 388, 407–409
norm-reference performance, 382
Norton, David P., 387
notebook format, 102
nurturing, 243

objectives, 275, 288
observation, 208
Occupational Safety and Health Act (OSHA), 50
"off the shelf" courses, 86
one-to-one instruction, 328, 334
online skills bank form, 22
online who's who skills directory form, 180
on-the-job training, 172–174
open questions, 234
operation, training, 45–84; budget and staff for, 82–83; business factors analysis for, 79; checklists for, 52–66; as cost center vs. profit center, 45; ethics in, 46; forms for, 67–78; and Instructional System Design, 80; and leadership, 4–6; legislation regarding, 47–51; make-or-buy decision for, 46; and performance technology, 80–81; quality of management in, 46; and Task By Objective Accounting, 82; technology in, 47; three-phase cost assignment for, 81–82; and training business plan, 79
opportunities for learning on their own, 206
organizational assessment, 182
organizational boundaries, 212
organizational change, 309–310
organizational linkages, 156–159
organizational support timeline, 281
organization chart, 73
organization development, 260
OSHA (Occupational Safety and Health Act), 50
outsourcing, 85–107; budget and staff for, 106–107; checklists for, 89–96; and copyright law, 105–106; cost benefits of, 93; and fair use policy, 106; forms for, 97–103; identifying factors leading to, 85–86; and intellectual property, 104–105; management of, 87; paperwork for, 86–87; percentage of, 4; reasons for, 92; relationship with vendor of, 87–88, 104; *see also* vendors
overprotectiveness, 386

packaging, 243
paperwork for hiring vendors, 86–87
parallel structure, 297
part-time workers, 2
patterned behavior, 396
"paying attention," 208–209
people-data-things job analysis, 235
*People Styles at Work* (Bolton and Bolton), 403
"percentage of total words," 106
perception, 395
performance, 348, 396
performance consultants, 184
*Performance Consulting* (Robinson and Robinson), 390
performance discrepancies, 221, 233
"performance engineering," 185
performance evaluations, 120–121, 157, 339
"performance gaps," 185

performance needs, 390
performance technology, 310–311, 390–391; checklist for, 175–176; government influence on standards of, 186–187; overview of, 80–81
personal goals, 160
personal intelligence, 410
personality type, 123
personal learning needs and wants form, 18
personal mastery, 386
Personal Responsibility and Work Opportunity Reconciliation Act, 50
personal role, 398
personal skill development, 116–117
P&G (Procter and Gamble), 156
physiological needs, 397
"plan—do—check—act," 388, 389
planning, 393; conference, 331; cross-training, 145; e-learning critical paths and milestones, 38
PMT (program module teams), 388
policy development guidelines, 261
policy statement, 285
polygraph testing, 50
post-training support, 243
practice, developing, 392
prayer breaks, 47
preparation, 396
presentation primer, 342–343
problem analysis chart, 366–367
problem analysis worksheet, 279–280
problem definition, 393
problem solving, 21, 304, 393–394
*Problem Solving and Education* (Tuma and Reif), 393
process improvement, 125
process quality, 182, 188
process thinking words checklist, 12
Procter and Gamble (P&G), 156
profit centers, 45
program by objectives evaluation report, 365
program evaluation checklist, 350
program module teams (PMT), 388
project management, 94
project monitoring form, 364
project notebook format, 102
project status report form, 101
promotion; of coaching/mentoring programs, 132; with public relations articles, 287; of training programs, 263
proposals, vendor, 262
proprietary information, 86
psychological testing, 50
psychological types, 403–405
psychology, blended training and, 28
psychomotor skills, 305, 395–396
psychotherapy, 150–151
"public good," 105
public relations articles, 287
punctuation, 297–298

QSA (quality system assessment), 388
quality; guidelines for building in, 53–54; of management, 46; of training materials, 344; of training staff, 344

quality assurance department linkages, 158–159
*Quality Digest*, 187
quality system assessment (QSA), 388
questionnaires, 234, 283

race, 49
Rayner, Steven, 128
reaction (level 1), 348
readiness to learn, 307–308
reading, 208
"reasonable accommodation," 49
"recognized hazards," 50
*Redefining Diversity* (Thomas), 24
refocusing, 399
Reif, F., 393
Reinventing Schools Coalition, 187
relationships; coaching and mentoring of, 132; design considerations for Internet, 192–193; with outside vendors, 87–88, 104
relevance (of training programs), 86
religion, 49
religious beliefs, 47
Request for Proposal (RFP), 86–87
research, online learning, 30
resolution, screen, 300
resources, enabling-performance, 205
results (level 4), 348
Reusable Learning Objects (RLO), 389
rewards, team training, 114–115
RFP, *see* Request for Proposal
right brain, 306–307
right brain, left brain, 402–403
RLO (Reusable Learning Objects), 389
"The Road Best Traveled" (Barbian), 149, 150
Robinson, Dana Gaines, 390
Robinson, James C., 390
Rothwell, William J., 175
Rummler, Geary A., 390

safety, 50, 397
sales linkages, 158
sans serif typefaces, 300, 301
scalability, 28
scales, measurement, 382
scheduling, training, 62–63, 333
schools, accountability of, 48
"school-to-work" programs, 50
SCORM, 29, 389–390
"SCORM" (Welsch), 389
screen-projected writing guidelines, 300
self-actualization, 397
self-assessment, 182; checklist for, 196; group discussion guide for, 231; readiness check for, 217; skills inventory for, 230
self-directed learners, 191–192, 197
self-evaluation, needs assessment, 203–204
self-study, 292–294, 338, 407–409
Senge, Peter, 24–25, 309, 386
September 11, 2001 terrorist attacks, 1, 47–48
serif typefaces, 300
*The 7 Habits of Highly Successful People* (Covey), 399
"70–40" rule, 51
sex, 49
sexual harassment, 47, 48

Shank, Patti, on e-learning courses, 192
share vision, 386
SHRM, *see* Society for Human Resource Management
Simpson, E. J., 395
situated learning, 391–392
*Situated Learning Perspectives* (McLellan), 391
six-sigma—quality, 388
skill bank online form, 22
skill development, team training, 116–117
skill observation form, 378
skills; categorizing types of transferable, 257–258; for coaching, 143–144; coaching and mentoring of, 132; employability, 170–171; hierarchy of, 242–243, 256, 282; maintenance of, 160–161; self-assessment inventory of, 230
slides, guidelines for words on, 301
Snyder, William M., 392
social activities, 157
Society for Human Resource Management (SHRM), 5, 47–48, 51
software, instructional design, 267
solution options, 393
spatial intelligence, 410
"SpinBrush," 156
Springer, S. P., 402
staff/staffing; and course author competencies, 265; of design and writing, 243–244; design checklist for, 59; of e-learning training, 28; evaluation form for, 368–369; evaluation of, 353; quality of, 344
Stamatis, D. H., 388
standards, 393; for design and writing, 244; for evaluation, 379; form for e-learning development, 41; for intranet use, 345; need for training, 5; for training program evaluation, 363
statistics, 381–382
status report form, 101
Sterling Engineering, 209
strategies checklist, 11
subproblems, 393
support, timeline for organizational, 281
supporting learners, 190–210; budget and staff for, 209–210; checklists for, 194–200; forms for, 201–207; with Internet tools, 192–193; with ISD, 191–192; and paying attention, 208–209; in small groups, 209; and taking charge, 190–191; *see also* learning on their own
support networks, 127
support services, coaching and mentoring, 132–133, 138
survival skills hierarchy, 282
synthesis, 395
systems orientation, 3–4
systems thinking, 24–25, 385–387

tables, 299
Takeuchi, Hirotaka, 24
task analysis checklist, 224
Task By Objective Accounting, 82
task list by job responsibility, 236
taxonomies, 242–243, 256
*Taxonomy of Educational Objectives* (Bloom), 394

# Index

Taylor, Frederick, 129
team delivery mode, 314
team learning, 354, 387
team training, 108–130; behavioral feedback for, 118–119; budget and staff for, 129–130; checklists for, 111–121; and defining work of teams, 109–110; distributed and virtual, 110; facilitating "the whole" vs. "the parts" in, 128; form for e-learning development for, 40; forms for, 122–127; individual learning factors within, 112–113; and learning from mistakes, 129; motivation and rewards for, 114–115; new designs for, 109; performance checklist for, 120–121; personal skill development to facilitate, 116–117; structural challenges of, 108–109
*Team Traps* (Rayner), 128
technology decisions, 47
"Ten Tips for Moving to ISO 9001:2000" (Whittington), 388
test evaluation, 360, 377
testing, field, 345, 356, 372–373
*Things That Make Us Smart* (Norman), 23, 407
*Thinking for a Change* (Gelb), 24
Thomas, R. Roosevelt, Jr., 24, 400
360 Degree Evaluation, 207, 347–348
three-phase cost assignment, 81–82
Thurstone, L. L., 409
time crunch problem, 238–239
timeline, organizational support, 281
timing, evaluation, 347
Title VII, 47–48
tools, 393
"tragedy of the commons," 155
trainee manuals, 268, 290–291
trainee ownership, 393
trainees, course evaluation by, 357, 374–375
trainee workbooks, 292–294
trainers; innovation form for, 184; training of, 313–314, 317–318
training; and adult motivation for learning, 340–341; assessing needs for, 6–7; as business strategy, 6; changes in field of, 185–186; delivery of, *see* delivery, training; design of, *see* design, training; evaluation of, 8; evaluation of vendor, 319; follow-up questionnaire to, 283; gaps in workplace, 188; guaranteeing longevity of, 8–9; implementation and delivery of, 7–8, 312–314; job aids vs., 321; media quality checklist for, 320; money spent on, 4–5; on-the-job, 172–174; operation of, *see* operation, training; percentage of employees receiving, 5; problem analysis worksheet for, 279–280; promotion of, 263; of trainer, 313–314, 317–318; trends in, 208; writing for, *see* writing
training business plan, 79
*Training Complex Cognitive Skills* (van Merrienboer), 24
training department, 3–4, 4–6
*Training & Development*, 129
training equipment checklist, 61
training facilities checklist, 61
training files, setting up, 60
Training Industry Reports, 5
*Training* magazine, 4, 5, 129, 149, 185, 324, 380
training manager, 36
training needs, 390
training opportunity profile, employee's, 278
training organization chart, 73
training policy, 285
training project evaluation, 351
training proposal, 228
training specialists, rationale for hiring, 58
transferable skills, 257–258
transition, checklist for classroom to e-learning, 32
transparencies, guidelines for words on, 301
"triggers," *see* drivers of change
trust, 163–165
Tuma, D. T., 393
*Two Careers, One Marriage* (Catalyst), 402
typeface, 300

University of Chicago, 155
U.S. Congress, 48
U.S. Department of Commerce, 186, 188
U.S. Department of Defense, 29, 389
U.S. Department of Labor, 5, 49, 50
U.S. Supreme Court, 48

value-added outsider proposals, 91
values, corporate, 159–160
van Merrienboer, Jeroen J. G., 24
vendors; analysis of, 98; characteristics for e-learning, 94; contracts with, 90, 99–100; e-learning, 44; evaluation of training by, 319; proposals from, 91, 262; relationships with, 87–88, 104
"The Very Real Dangers of Executive Coaching," 150
veterans, 49
videotapes, guidelines for words on, 301
video training, 270–271

Vietnam era veterans, 49
virtual teams, 110
visibility, 64–65, 132
vision, shared, 386

"The Way I See It" journal, 181
Weber, Max, 129
Weintraub, Robert S., 208
*Welch* (Lowe), 388
welfare reform, 50–51
Wellington, Sheila, 132, 401, 402
Wells, Melanie, on E-Bay, 209
Welsch, Edward, 389
Wenger, Etienne, 392
White House Office of Science and Technology, 29
Whittington, Larry, 388
who's who skills directory form, 180
women, 2, 132, 136, 150, 400–402
workbooks, trainee, 292–294
work environment need, 390
"workfare," 50
workplace hazards, 50
writing, 7; and analysis of vendor proposals, 262; authoring system software for, 267; budget and staff for, 302–304; of catalog, 264; and catalog entry format, 286; for CD-ROMs, 301; checklists for, 245–246, 261–271; of classroom training manuals, 290–291; of computer-based/interactive video training, 270–271; and computer-generated words, 300–301; and course author competencies, 265; and course elements, 266; and dissemination of materials, 244; for films, 301; forms for, 272, 285–295; grammar and usage for, 296–297; headings for, 298; of instructor manuals, 269, 295; labels for, 299; and learner objectives, 288; and lesson plans, 289; margins for, 299; policy development guidelines for, 261; of policy statement, 285; for promotion of training, 263; of public relations articles, 287; punctuation for, 297–298; screen-projected guidelines for, 300; of self-study trainee workbooks, 292–294; for slides, 301; staffing for, 243–244; standards for, 244; of trainee manual, 268; for transparencies, 301; typeface for, 300; for videotapes, 301

*Yahoo! News*, 5

Zuboff, Shoshana, 23

# About the Author

**Carolyn Nilson** is a recognized expert in all aspects of training. Corporate training positions have included work on the technical staff at AT&T Bell Laboratories, where she was part of the "Advanced Programs, Standards, Audits, and Inspection Group" of the Systems Training Center. She implemented and promoted quality standards in training design, delivery, and evaluation throughout AT&T. In addition, she taught the Bell Labs' train-the-trainer course and helped produce an instructional video archive of systems training courses. Dr. Nilson also served as Manager of Simulation Training at Combustion Engineering (CE) for Asea Brown Boveri, where she managed the training operation, including the creation of high-level computer-based training for clients internationally. At CE, she was on a corporation-wide training design team using expert system technologies to create an electronic performance support system (EPSS) in learner evaluation. Dr. Nilson held the executive position as Director of Training for a management consulting firm with a broad-based *Fortune* 500 clientele in the New York City area, where she was responsible for budgets and consultant staff supervision as well as for training analysis, design, development, implementation, and evaluation on client projects. Corporations she has served include: AT&T, Chemical Bank, Chevron, Nabisco, Martin-Marietta, Dun & Bradstreet, National Westminster Bank, and others. She has been an advisor to the American Management Association/AMACOM, Hungry Minds, and The MASIE Center, and a faculty member for Padgett-Thompson Seminars throughout the United States, The Center for the Study of Work Teams in Dallas, and USAID's Management Development Initiative in Cairo, Egypt.

Dr. Nilson has also been a consultant to government organizations in the areas of training design, delivery, evaluation, and management. These include: The World Bank, The U.S. Department of Labor, The U.S. Department of Education, The National Institute of Education, The U.S. Armed Services Training Institute, and The United States Agency for International Development (USAID). She has been a speaker at conferences of ASTD, ISPI, and the American Management Association. Her work has been featured in *TRAINING Magazine, Training & Development (T + D), HR Magazine, Successful Meetings, Entrepreneur,* and *Fortune.* She is the author of numerous training papers, speeches, articles, manuals, and books; her writings are selling worldwide to a diverse customer base. Four of her books appeared in amazon.com's list of "50 Best-Selling Training Books," including the second edition (1998) of this book. She is a Schwartz Business Books 1995 "Celebrity Author" (Milwaukee, Wisconsin), and was on the 1996 "This Year's Best Sellers" of Newbridge Book Clubs (Delran, New Jersey). Her books have also been chosen by Macmillan's Executive Program Book Club, The Training Professionals Book Club, and the *Business Week* Book Club.

Her books include:

> *Training & Development Yearbook,* Prentice Hall (seven annual editions: 1996, 1997, 1998, 1999, 2000, 2001, 2002)
> *How to Start a Training Program,* ASTD, 1999, 2002
> *The Performance Consulting Toolbook,* McGraw-Hill, 1999
> *How to Manage Training,* AMACOM, 1991, 1998
> *Complete Games Trainers Play,* Vol. 2, with Scannell and Newstrom, McGraw-Hill, 1998
> *More Team Games for Trainers,* McGraw-Hill, 1997
> *Games That Drive Change,* McGraw-Hill, 1995
> *Peer Training: Improved Performance One by One,* Prentice Hall, 1994
> *Team Games for Trainers,* McGraw-Hill, 1993
> *How to Start a Training Program in Your Growing Business,* AMACOM, 1992
> *Trainer's Complete Guide to Management and Supervisory Development,* Prentice Hall, 1992
> *Training for Non-Trainers,* AMACOM, 1990; Spanish edition 1994, 1999
> *Training Program Workbook and Kit,* Prentice Hall, 1989

An active member of the American Society for Training and Development, she received her doctorate from Rutgers University with a specialty in measurement and evaluation in vocational and technical education.